AN URBAN EXPLORATION ADVENTURE

THE LAST BROADCAST ™

ANDRÉ **SIRANGELO**   GABRIEL **IUMAZARK**

Published by
ARCHAIA

FOLLOW THE MA
UNCOVER THE TRU

THE LAST BROADCAST, June 2015. Published by Archaia, a division of Boom Entertainment, Inc. The Last Broadcast is ™ & © 2015 André Sirangelo and Gabriel Iumazark. Originally published in single magazine form as THE LAST BROADCAST No. 1-7. ™ & © 2014 André Sirangelo and Gabriel Iumazark. All rights reserved. Archaia™ and the Archaia logo are trademarks of Boom Entertainment, Inc., registered in various countries and categories. All characters, events, and institutions depicted herein are fictional. Any similarity between any of the names, characters, persons, events, and/or institutions in this publication to actual names, characters, and persons, whether living or dead, events, and/or institutions is unintended and purely coincidental. BOOM! Studios does not read or accept unsolicited submissions of ideas, stories, or artwork.

BOOM! Studios, 5670 Wilshire Boulevard, Suite 450, Los Angeles, CA 90036-5679. Printed in China. First Printing.

ISBN: 978-1-60886-693-9
eISBN: 978-1-61398-364-5

ARCHAIA™

ALWAYS TRESPASS

1 SOCIETY FOR PSYCHIC INVESTIGATION
est. { X1 }

7 Don't turn your *back* on the mystery, you need only discover the passphrase.
{X1} 0 {X2} 2 1 {X3} {X4}
_____

6 Signal detected at radio frequency 67.18mHz
-..../ ..../ -../ ..../
..../ ..../ -../
..../ ../ ../ .-../
..../ ---../

2 1 is T. 2 is K. E is 3. 9 is A.
{ X4 } mHz = radio frequency

Pulgas Water Temple: Built to celebrate the completion of the Bay Area Hetch Hetchy Project in 1934. Later rebuilt in 1938, the structure is located over the aqueduct's terminus. The ring of columns is inscribed with *Isaiah { X3 }:20*.

5 **Blaise de Vigenére**
French diplomat and cryptographer.
Born April 5, 1523.
Died February 19, 15{ X2 }.

4 "{ X1 } only pictures.
Leave only footprints."
—0ack0one UrbEx Motto

3

YOU ARE ON THE RIGHT PATH

Find the passphrase. Look for the seven skulls. Turn the seven wheels. Always trespass. See the cipher. The passphrase is the key. Unlock the truth.

Urban Exploration (URBEX, UE): *noun,* exploration of man-made structures; commonly abandoned ruins or unseen components of man-made environments. May involve the act of trespassing. Commonly referred to as: Infiltration, Draining, Building Hacking.

AN URBAN EXPLORATION ADVENTURE
THE LAST BROADCAST™
CREATED BY ANDRÉ SIRANGELO & GABRIEL IUMAZARK

WRITTEN BY
ANDRÉ **SIRANGELO**

ILLUSTRATED BY
GABRIEL **IUMAZARK**

LETTERER
DERON **BENNETT**

COVER BY
GABRIEL **IUMAZARK**

DESIGNERS
MICHELLE **ANKLEY** & SCOTT **NEWMAN**

ASSOCIATE EDITOR
WHITNEY **LEOPARD**

EDITOR
REBECCA **TAYLOR**

KEEP EXPLORING. Access: *noun,* the access point to a site. **Crane:** *verb,* to scale construction cranes to reach a viewpoint. **Tag:** *noun,* a graffitied mark left as a personal signature. **Breach:** *noun,* site in a city an average person would not know existed. **Live:** *adj,* describing a site that is not abandoned. **Lift Surf:** *verb,* to ride on the roof of an elevator. **Splore:** *noun,* short for *explore,* referring to a specific excursion. e.g. *Backbone will begin a splore tomorrow.*

Crack the code. Secrets will be revealed.
Enter **thelastbroadcast.tumblr.com** for Darknet access.

1 6 3 5 2 7 4

CHAPTER 1: NOTES FROM THE UNDERGROUND

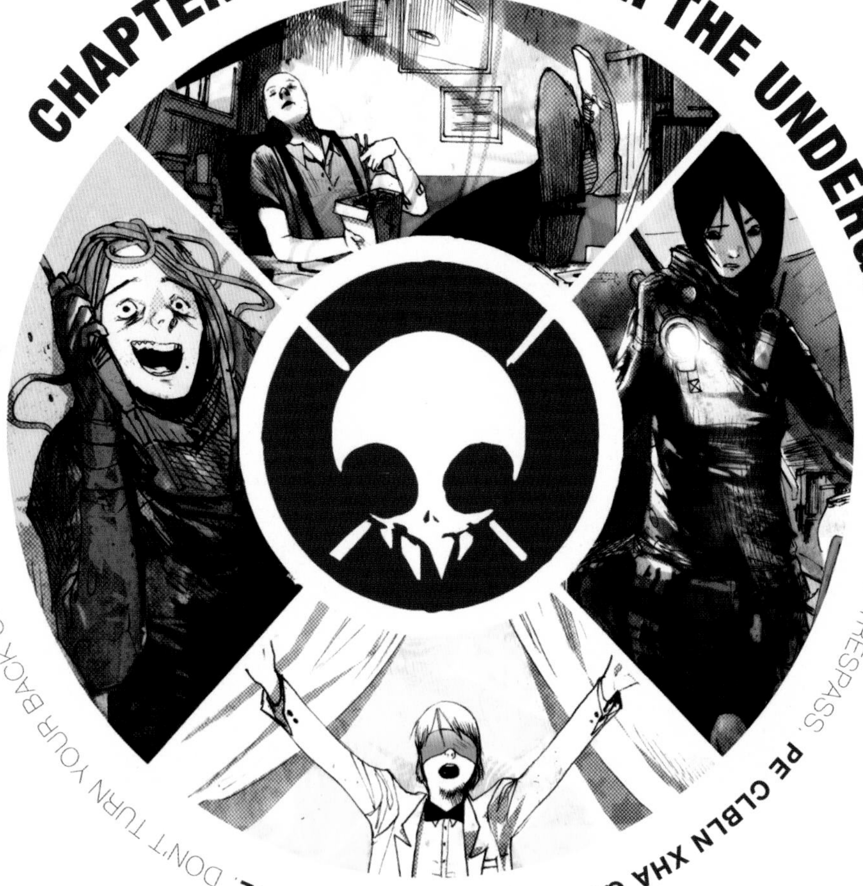

ALWAYS TRESPASS. PE CLBLN XHA GGILC YRYQ FXRVHYEVQHL. DON'T TURN YOUR BACK ON THE MYSTERY.

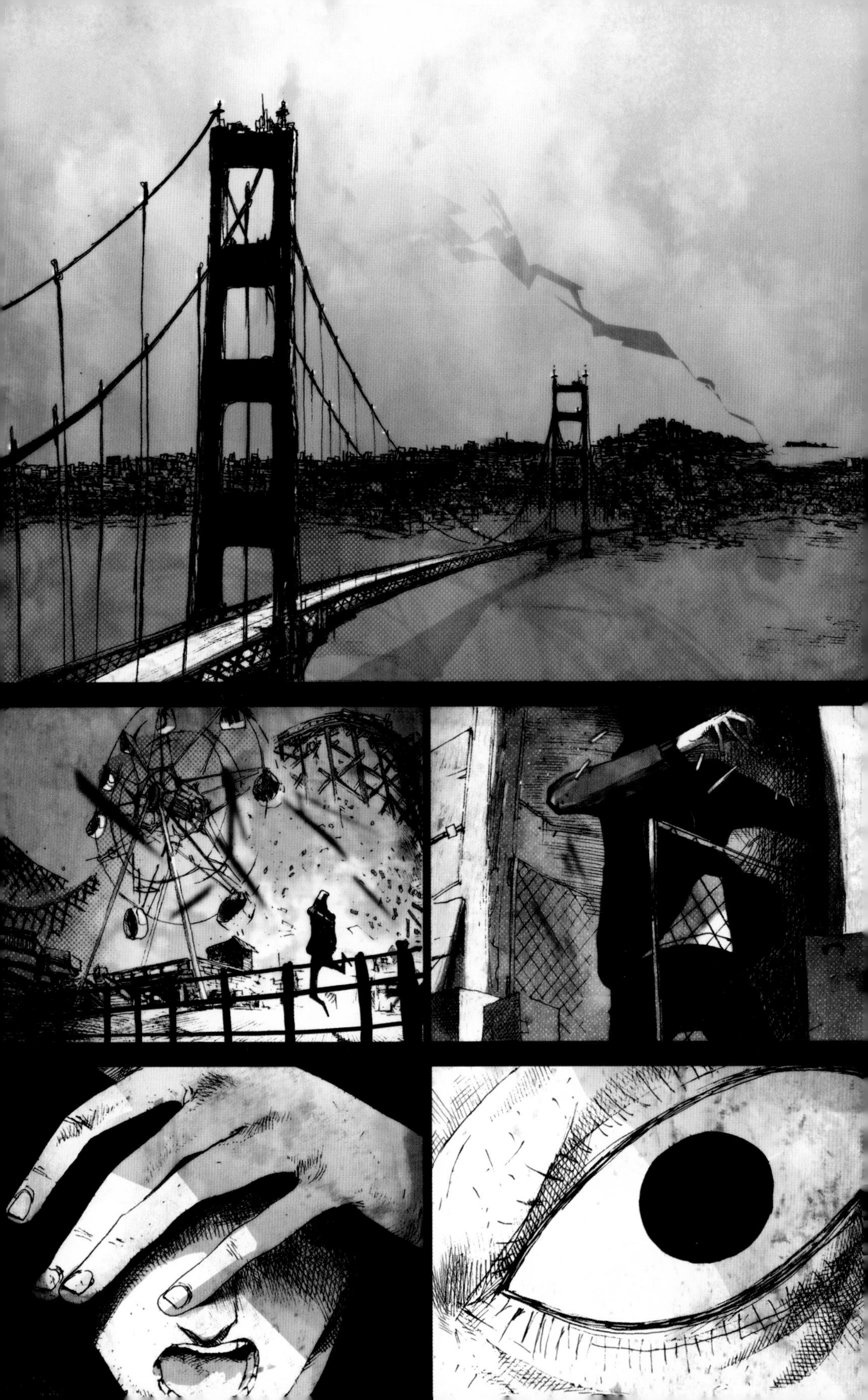

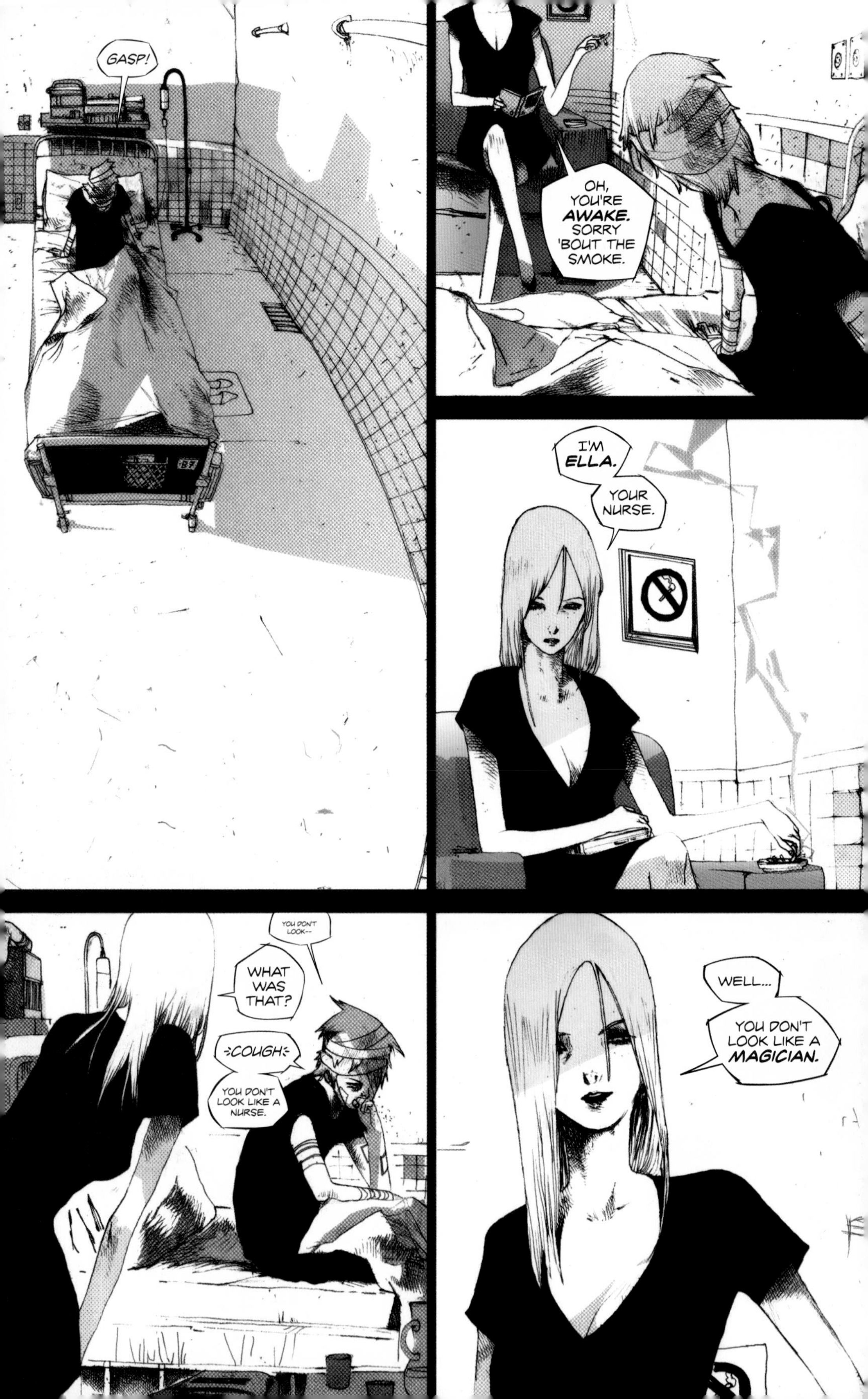
GASP!
OH, YOU'RE AWAKE. SORRY 'BOUT THE SMOKE.
I'M ELLA.
YOUR NURSE.
YOU DON'T LOOK--
WHAT WAS THAT?
COUGH
YOU DON'T LOOK LIKE A NURSE.
WELL...
YOU DON'T LOOK LIKE A MAGICIAN.

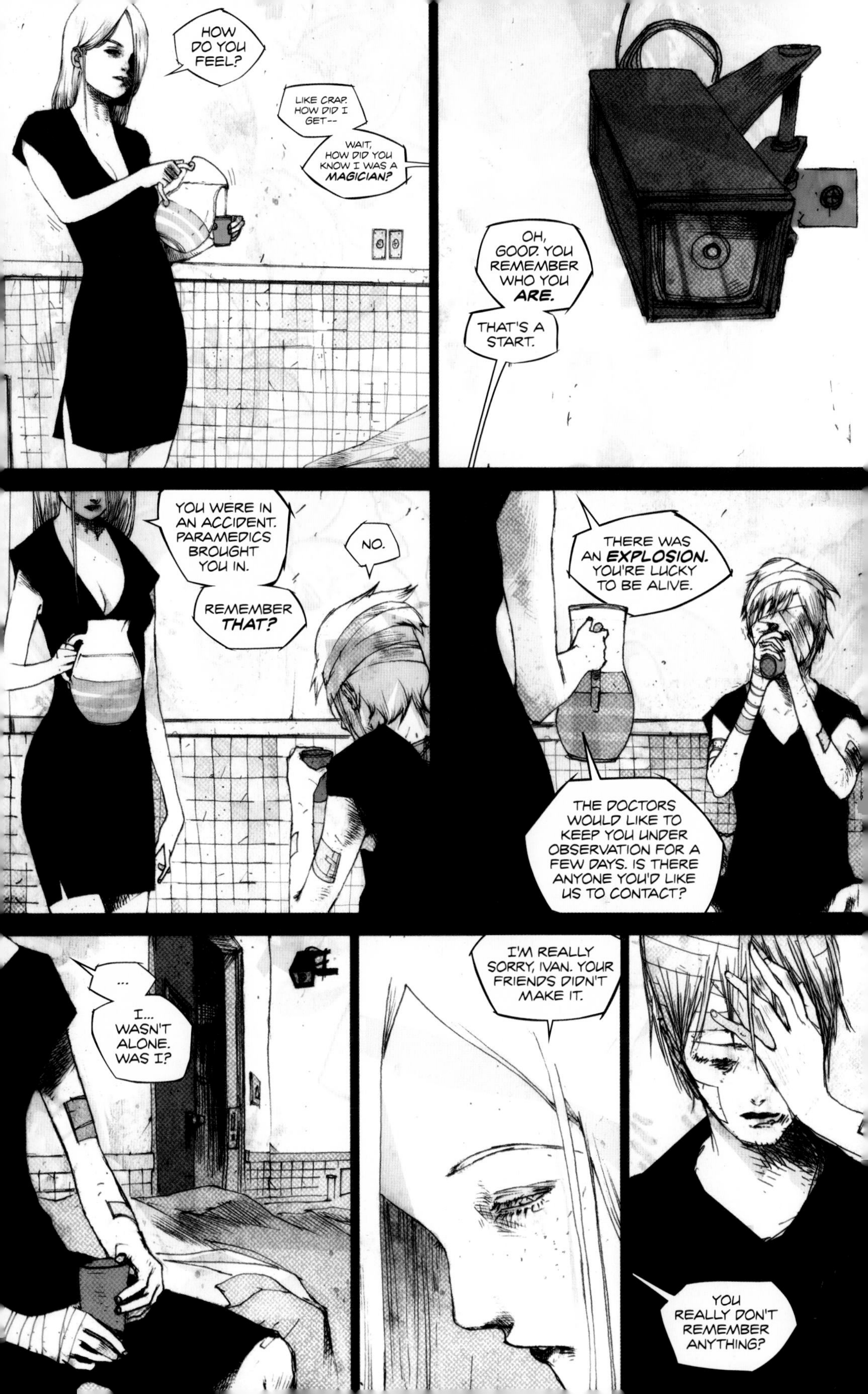
HOW DO YOU FEEL?
LIKE CRAP. HOW DID I GET--
WAIT, HOW DID YOU KNOW I WAS A *MAGICIAN?*
OH, GOOD. YOU REMEMBER WHO YOU *ARE.*
THAT'S A START.
YOU WERE IN AN ACCIDENT. PARAMEDICS BROUGHT YOU IN.
REMEMBER *THAT?*
NO.
THERE WAS AN *EXPLOSION.* YOU'RE LUCKY TO BE ALIVE.
THE DOCTORS WOULD LIKE TO KEEP YOU UNDER OBSERVATION FOR A FEW DAYS. IS THERE ANYONE YOU'D LIKE US TO CONTACT?
...
I... WASN'T ALONE. WAS I?
I'M REALLY SORRY, IVAN. YOUR FRIENDS DIDN'T MAKE IT.
YOU REALLY DON'T REMEMBER ANYTHING?

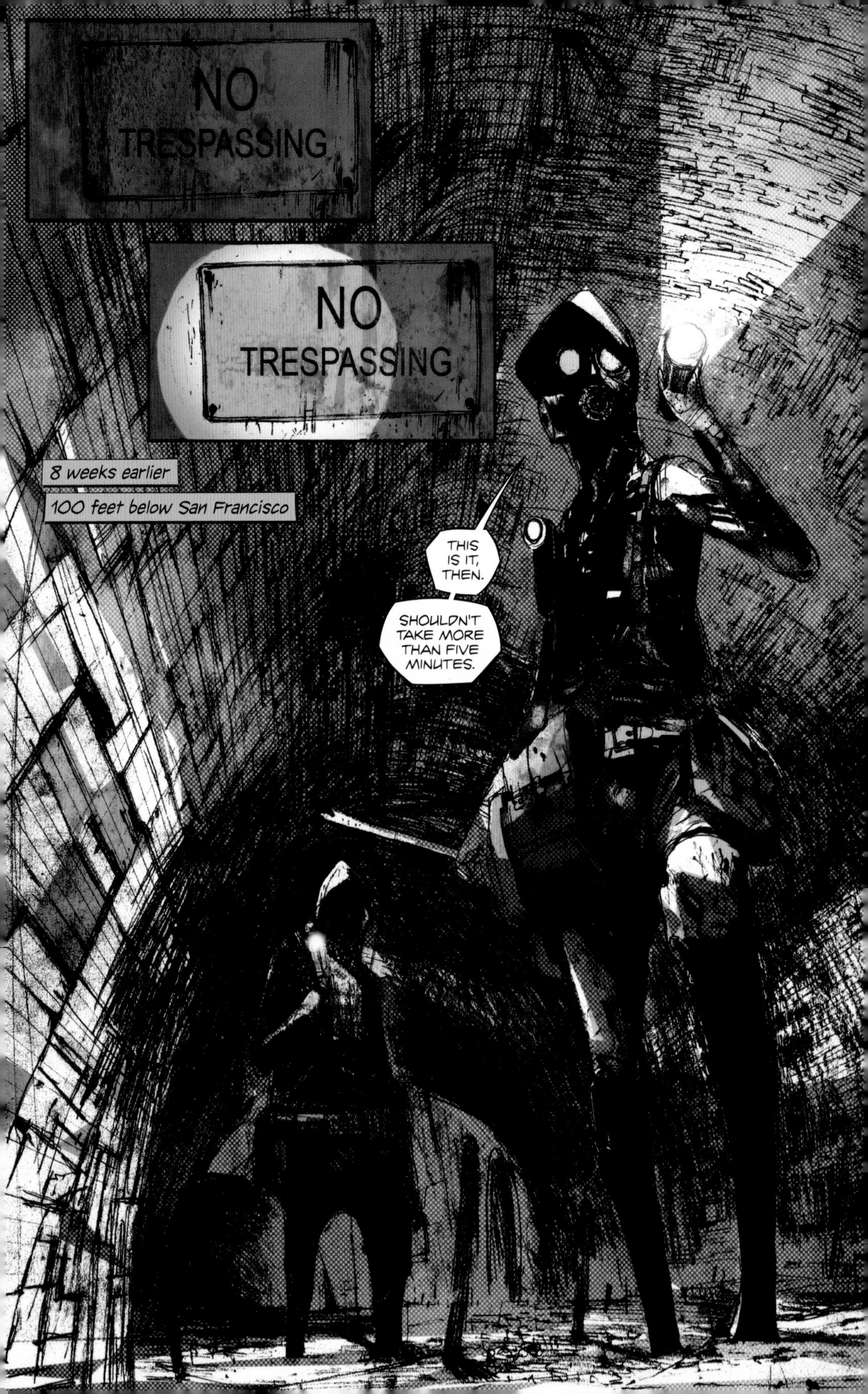
NO
TRESPASSING
NO
TRESPASSING
8 weeks earlier
100 feet below San Francisco
THIS IS IT, THEN.
SHOULDN'T TAKE MORE THAN FIVE MINUTES.

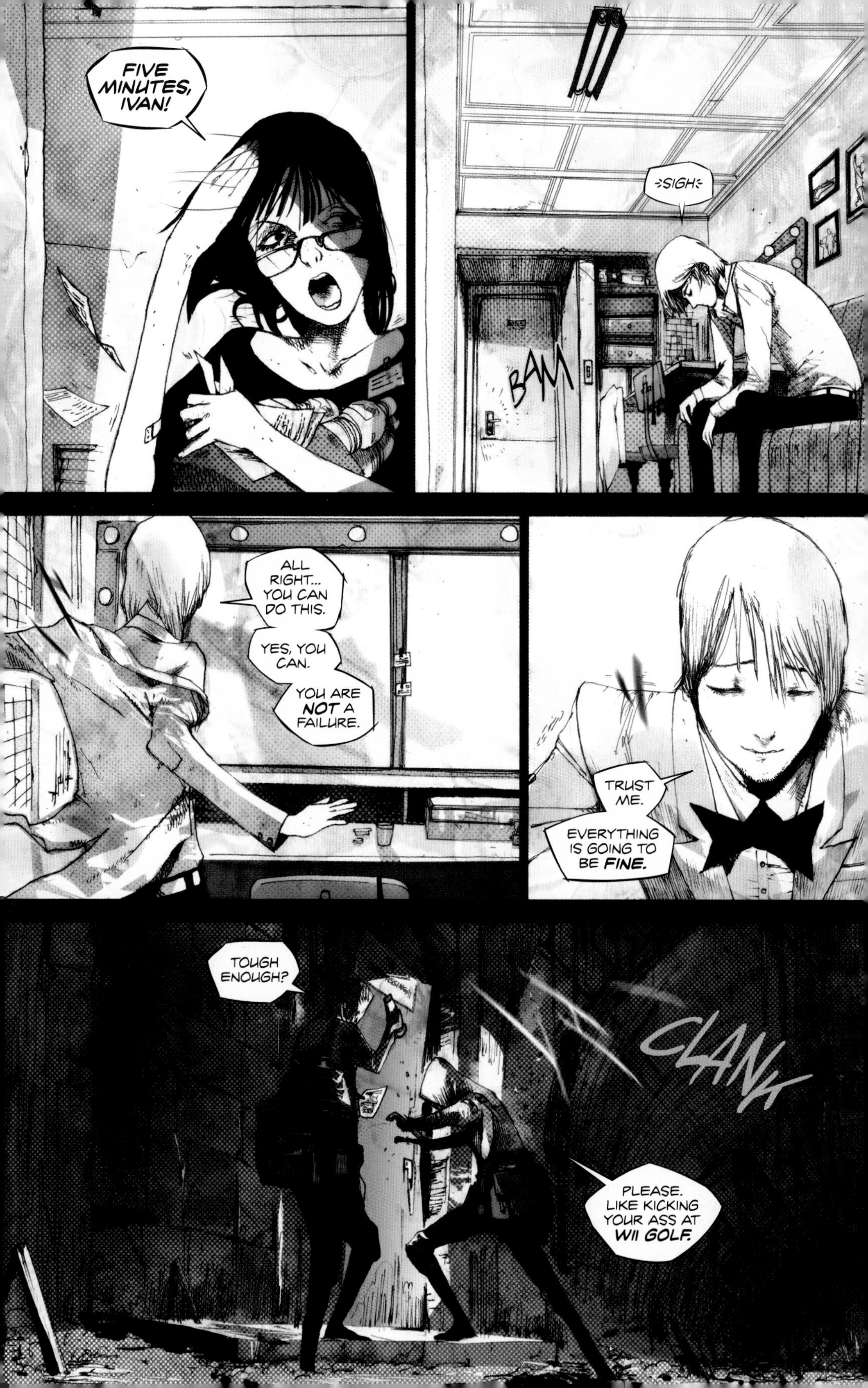
FIVE MINUTES, IVAN!
BAM
-SIGH-
ALL RIGHT... YOU CAN DO THIS.
YES, YOU CAN.
YOU ARE **NOT** A FAILURE.
TRUST ME.
EVERYTHING IS GOING TO BE **FINE.**
TOUGH ENOUGH?
CLANK
PLEASE. LIKE KICKING YOUR ASS AT **WII GOLF.**

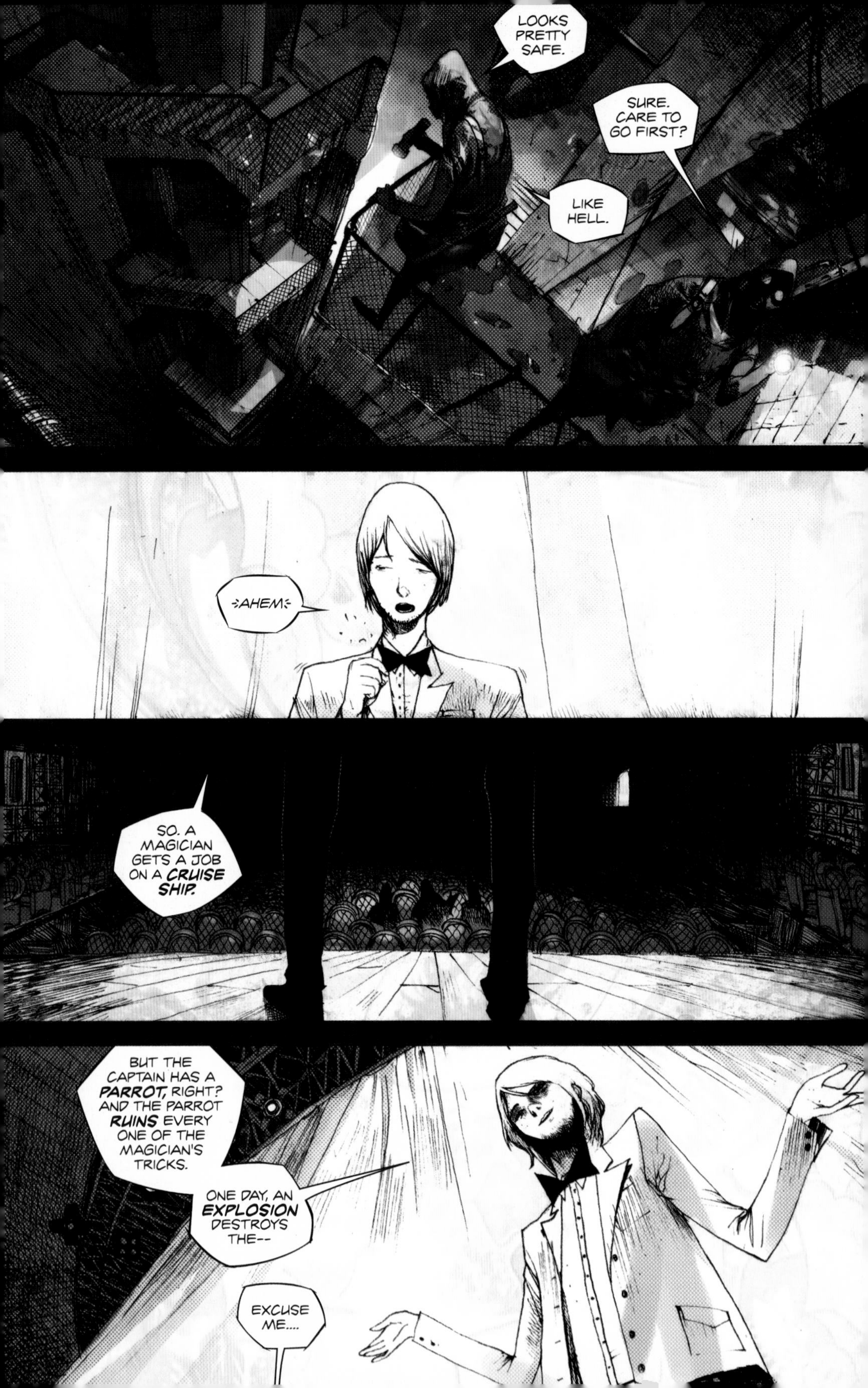
LOOKS PRETTY SAFE.
SURE. CARE TO GO FIRST?
LIKE HELL.
AHEM
SO. A MAGICIAN GETS A JOB ON A CRUISE SHIP.
BUT THE CAPTAIN HAS A PARROT, RIGHT? AND THE PARROT RUINS EVERY ONE OF THE MAGICIAN'S TRICKS.
ONE DAY, AN EXPLOSION DESTROYS THE--
EXCUSE ME....

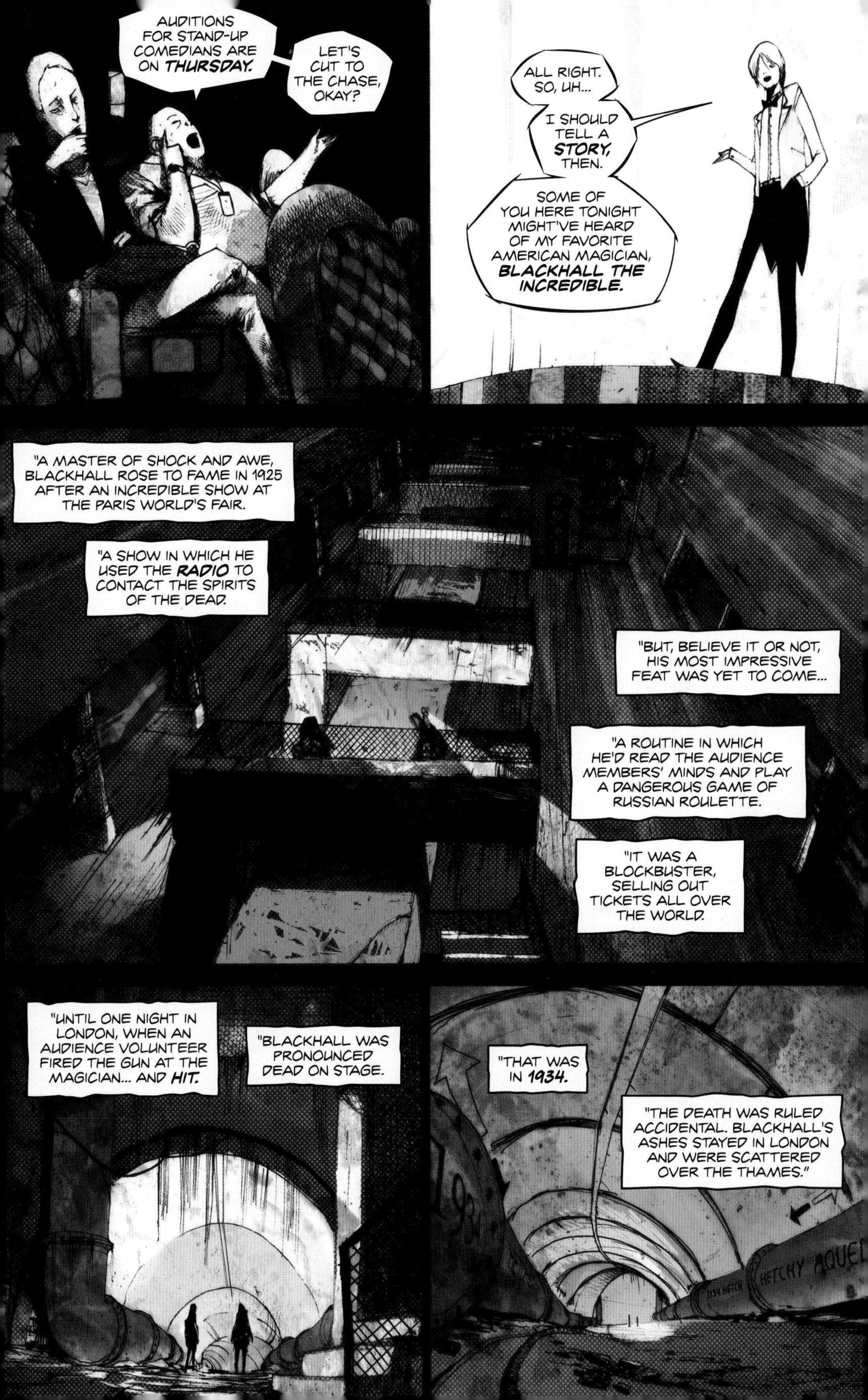

AUDITIONS FOR STAND-UP COMEDIANS ARE ON **THURSDAY.**
LET'S CUT TO THE CHASE, OKAY?
ALL RIGHT. SO, UH...
I SHOULD TELL A **STORY,** THEN.
SOME OF YOU HERE TONIGHT MIGHT'VE HEARD OF MY FAVORITE AMERICAN MAGICIAN, **BLACKHALL THE INCREDIBLE.**
"A MASTER OF SHOCK AND AWE, BLACKHALL ROSE TO FAME IN 1925 AFTER AN INCREDIBLE SHOW AT THE PARIS WORLD'S FAIR.
"A SHOW IN WHICH HE USED THE **RADIO** TO CONTACT THE SPIRITS OF THE DEAD.
"BUT, BELIEVE IT OR NOT, HIS MOST IMPRESSIVE FEAT WAS YET TO COME...
"A ROUTINE IN WHICH HE'D READ THE AUDIENCE MEMBERS' MINDS AND PLAY A DANGEROUS GAME OF RUSSIAN ROULETTE.
"IT WAS A BLOCKBUSTER, SELLING OUT TICKETS ALL OVER THE WORLD.
"UNTIL ONE NIGHT IN LONDON, WHEN AN AUDIENCE VOLUNTEER FIRED THE GUN AT THE MAGICIAN... AND **HIT.**
"BLACKHALL WAS PRONOUNCED DEAD ON STAGE.
"THAT WAS IN **1934.**
"THE DEATH WAS RULED ACCIDENTAL. BLACKHALL'S ASHES STAYED IN LONDON AND WERE SCATTERED OVER THE THAMES."
HETCHY AQUE

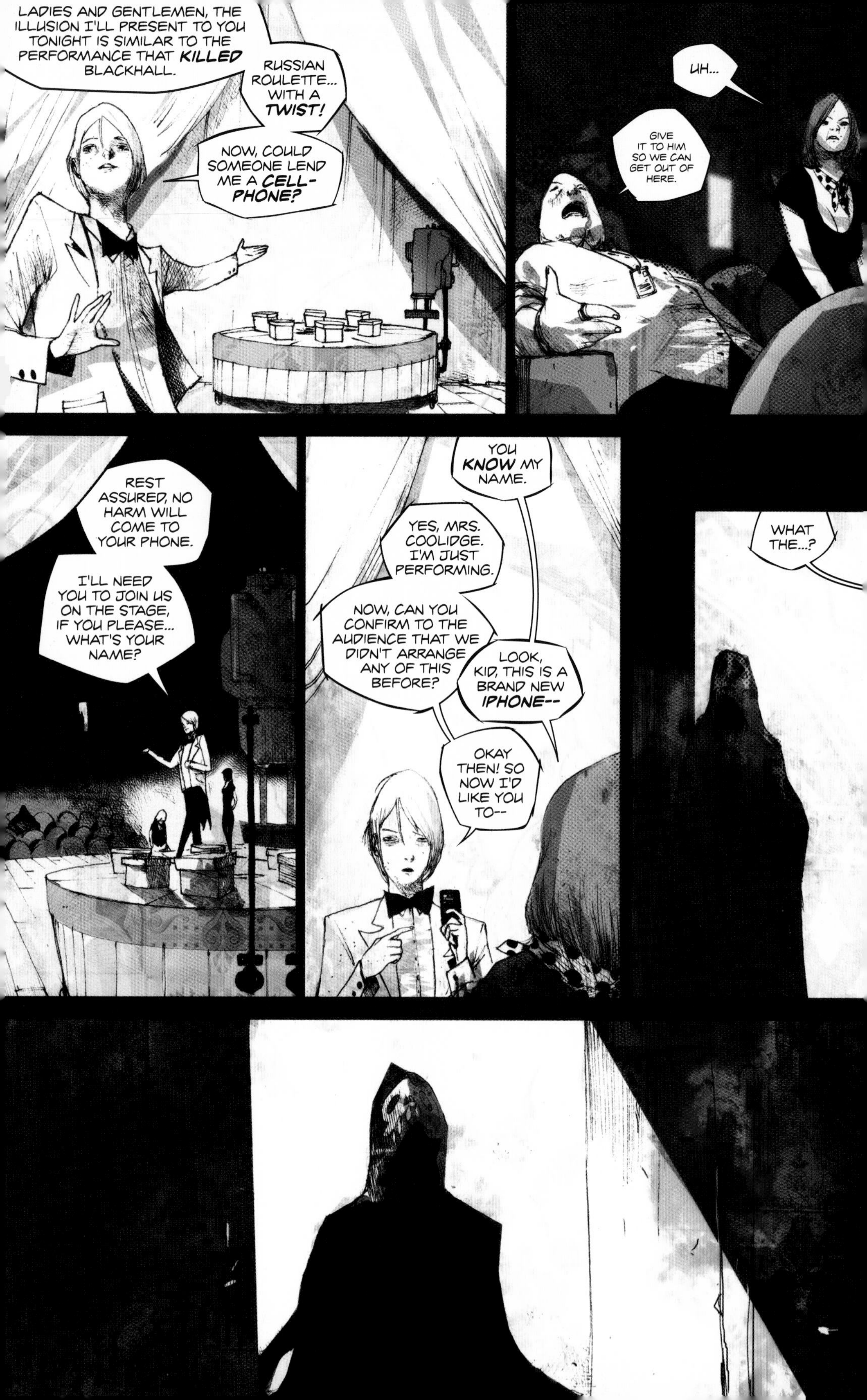
LADIES AND GENTLEMEN, THE ILLUSION I'LL PRESENT TO YOU TONIGHT IS SIMILAR TO THE PERFORMANCE THAT KILLED BLACKHALL.
RUSSIAN ROULETTE... WITH A TWIST!
NOW, COULD SOMEONE LEND ME A CELL-PHONE?
UH...
GIVE IT TO HIM SO WE CAN GET OUT OF HERE.
REST ASSURED, NO HARM WILL COME TO YOUR PHONE.
I'LL NEED YOU TO JOIN US ON THE STAGE, IF YOU PLEASE... WHAT'S YOUR NAME?
YOU KNOW MY NAME.
YES, MRS. COOLIDGE. I'M JUST PERFORMING.
NOW, CAN YOU CONFIRM TO THE AUDIENCE THAT WE DIDN'T ARRANGE ANY OF THIS BEFORE?
LOOK, KID, THIS IS A BRAND NEW IPHONE--
OKAY THEN! SO NOW I'D LIKE YOU TO--
WHAT THE...?

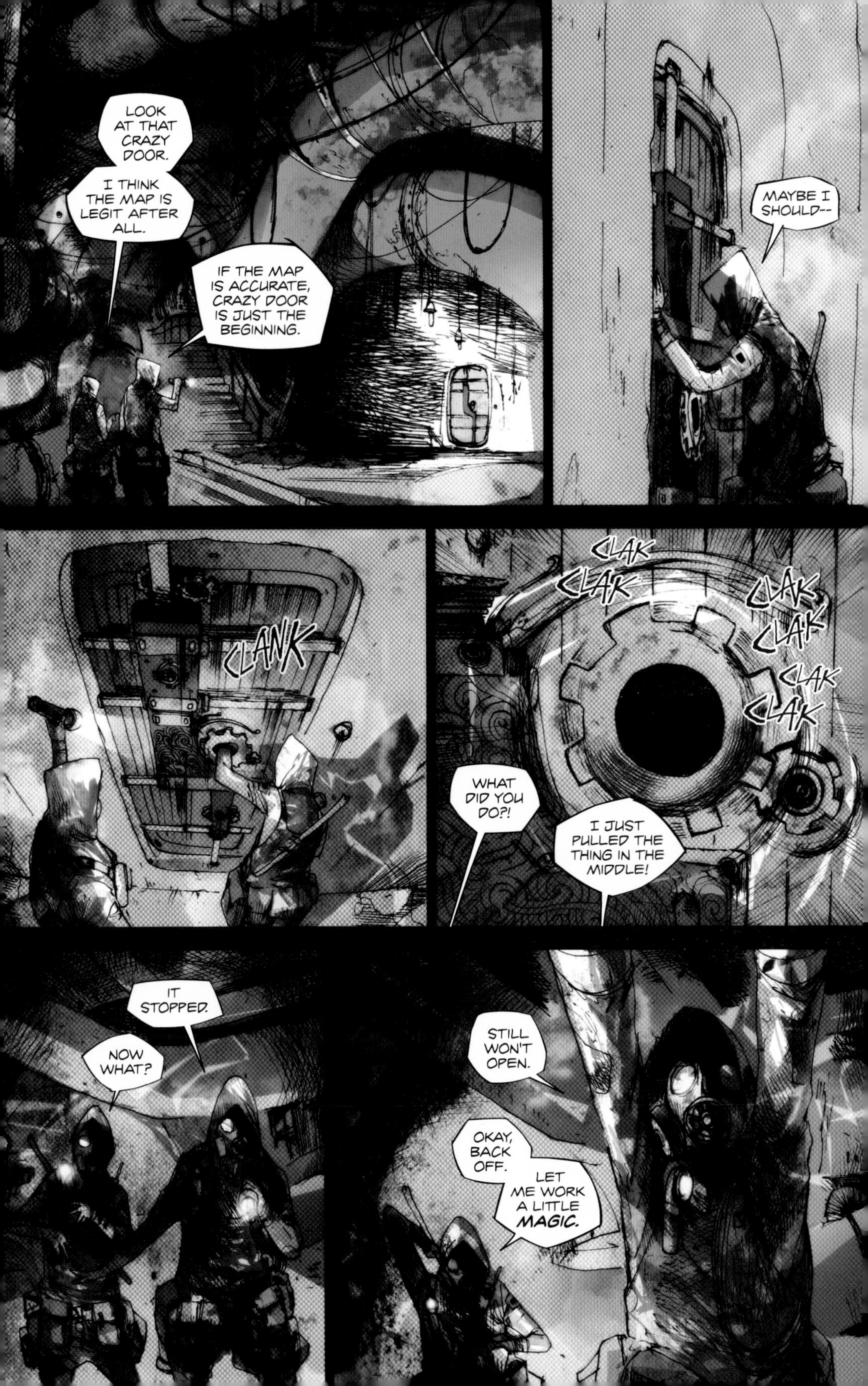
LOOK AT THAT CRAZY DOOR.
I THINK THE MAP IS LEGIT AFTER ALL.
IF THE MAP IS ACCURATE, CRAZY DOOR IS JUST THE BEGINNING.
MAYBE I SHOULD--
CLANK
CLAK CLAK
CLAK CLAK
CLAK CLAK
WHAT DID YOU DO?!
I JUST PULLED THE THING IN THE MIDDLE!
IT STOPPED.
NOW WHAT?
STILL WON'T OPEN.
OKAY, BACK OFF.
LET ME WORK A LITTLE MAGIC.

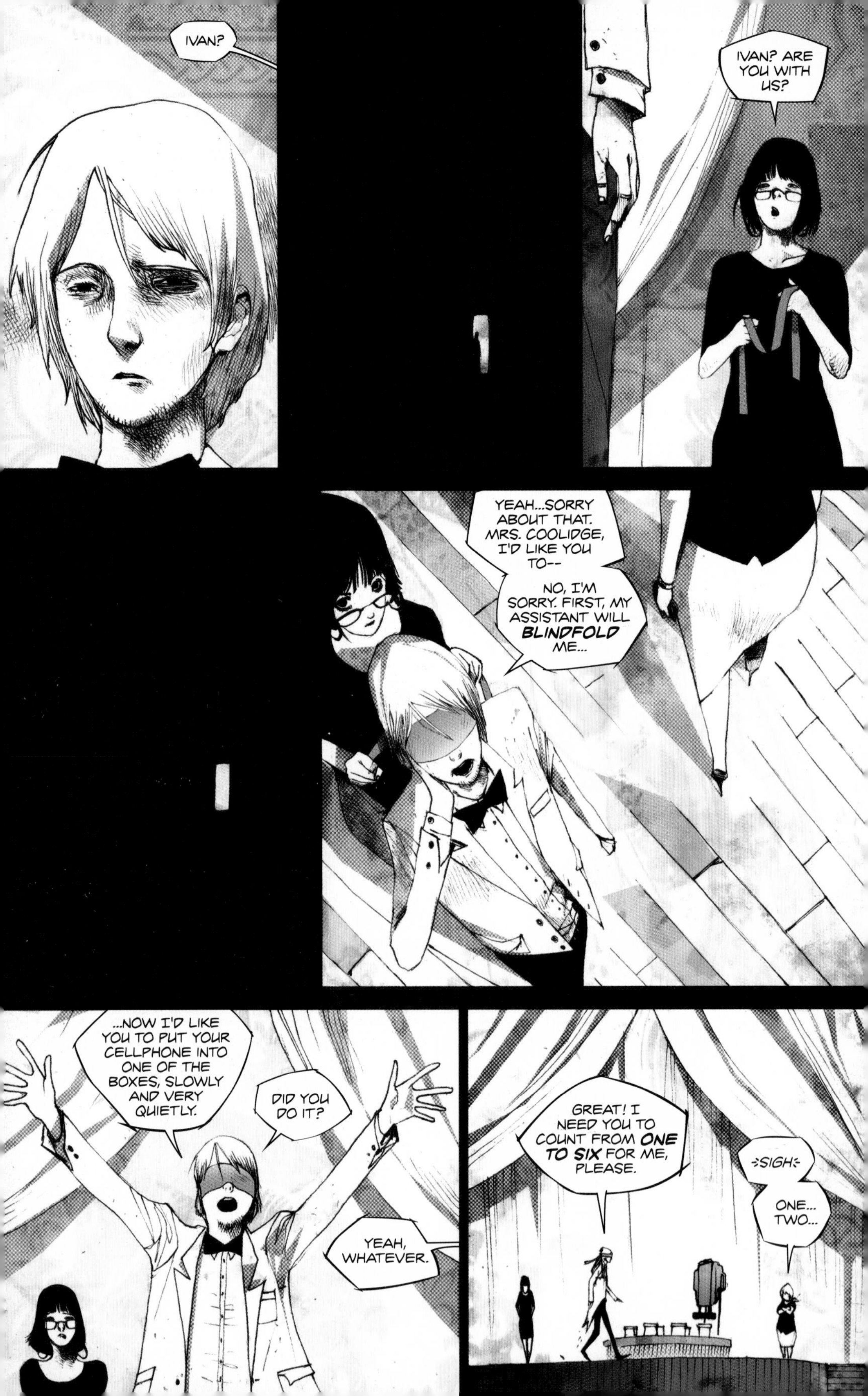
IVAN?
IVAN? ARE YOU WITH US?
YEAH...SORRY ABOUT THAT. MRS. COOLIDGE, I'D LIKE YOU TO--
NO, I'M SORRY. FIRST, MY ASSISTANT WILL **BLINDFOLD** ME...
...NOW I'D LIKE YOU TO PUT YOUR CELLPHONE INTO ONE OF THE BOXES, SLOWLY AND VERY QUIETLY.
DID YOU DO IT?
YEAH, WHATEVER.
GREAT! I NEED YOU TO COUNT FROM **ONE TO SIX** FOR ME, PLEASE.
-SIGH-
ONE... TWO...

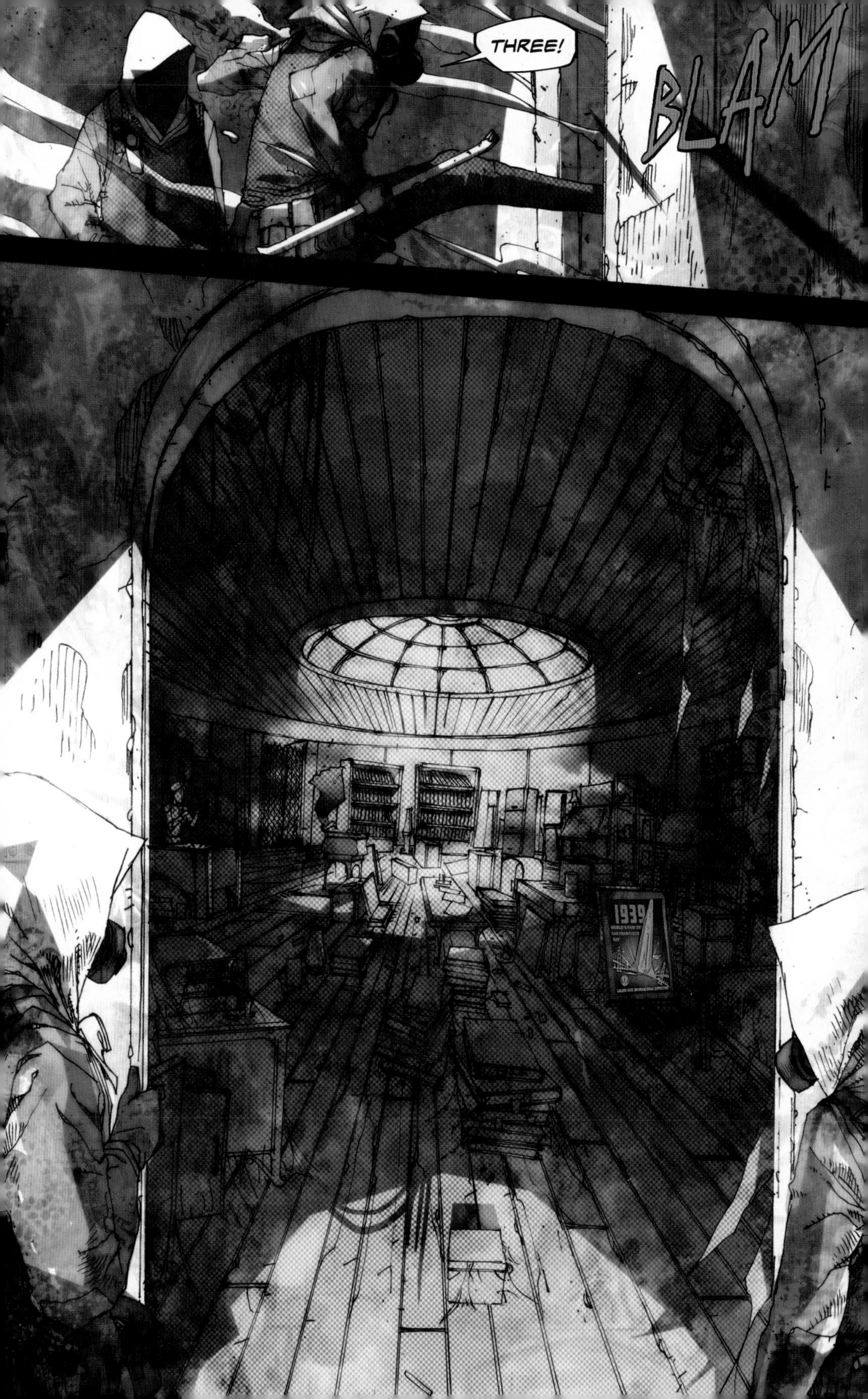
THREE!
BLAM
1939

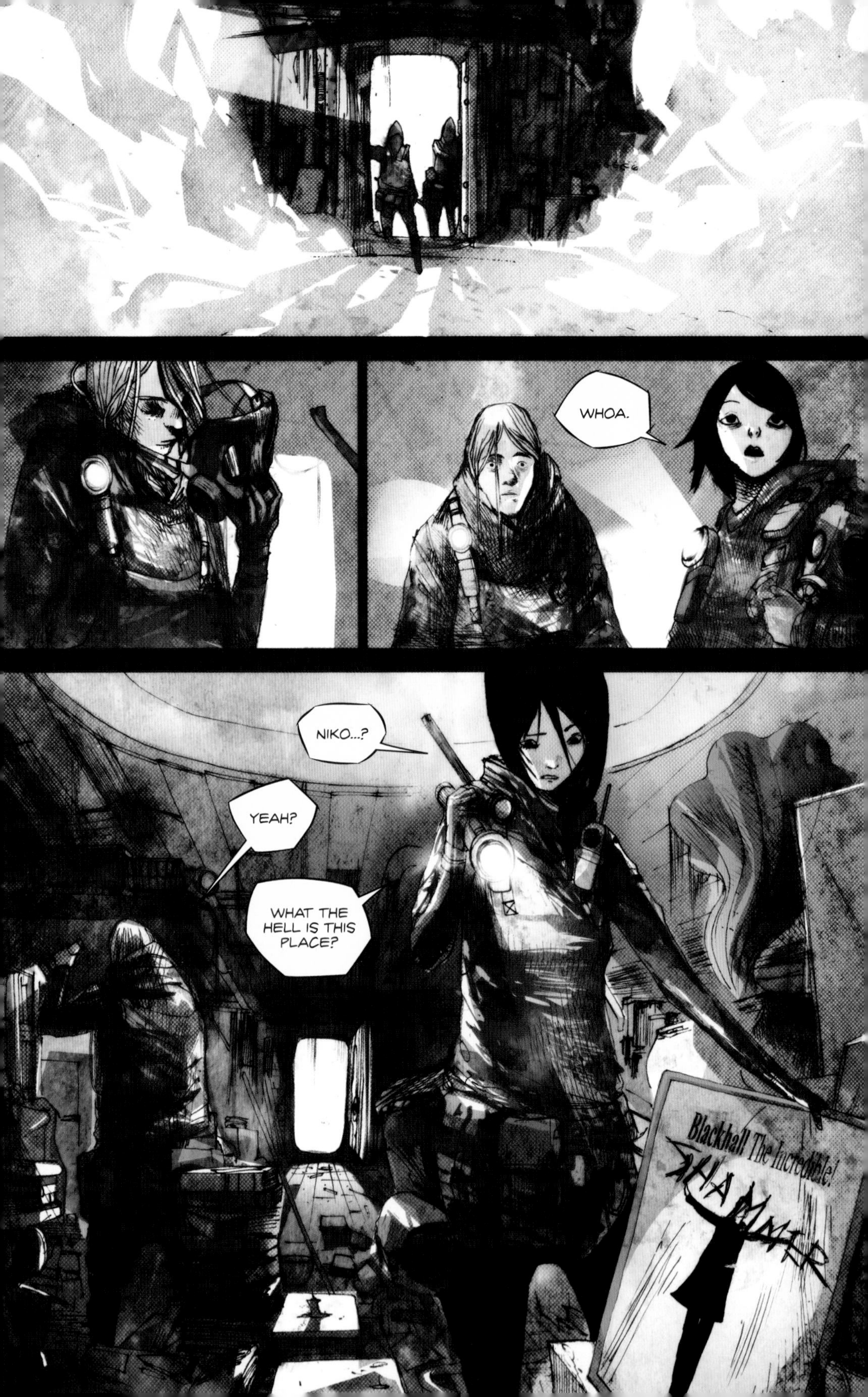
WHOA.
NIKO...?
YEAH?
WHAT THE HELL IS THIS PLACE?
Blackhall! The Incredible!
HAMMER

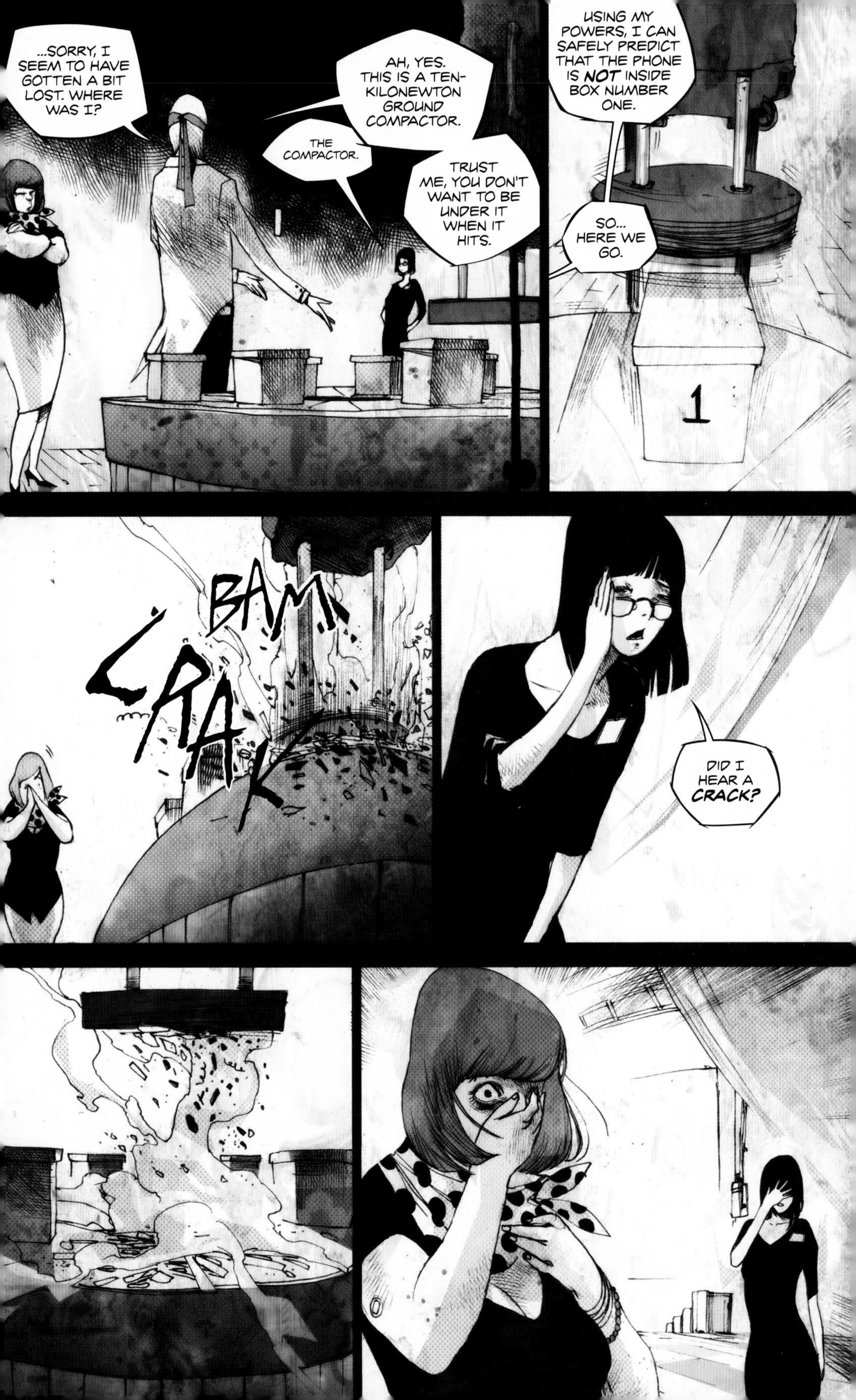
...SORRY, I SEEM TO HAVE GOTTEN A BIT LOST. WHERE WAS I?
THE COMPACTOR.
AH, YES. THIS IS A TEN-KILONEWTON GROUND COMPACTOR.
TRUST ME, YOU DON'T WANT TO BE UNDER IT WHEN IT HITS.
USING MY POWERS, I CAN SAFELY PREDICT THAT THE PHONE IS **NOT** INSIDE BOX NUMBER ONE.
SO... HERE WE GO.
1
BAM
CRAK
DID I HEAR A ***CRACK?***

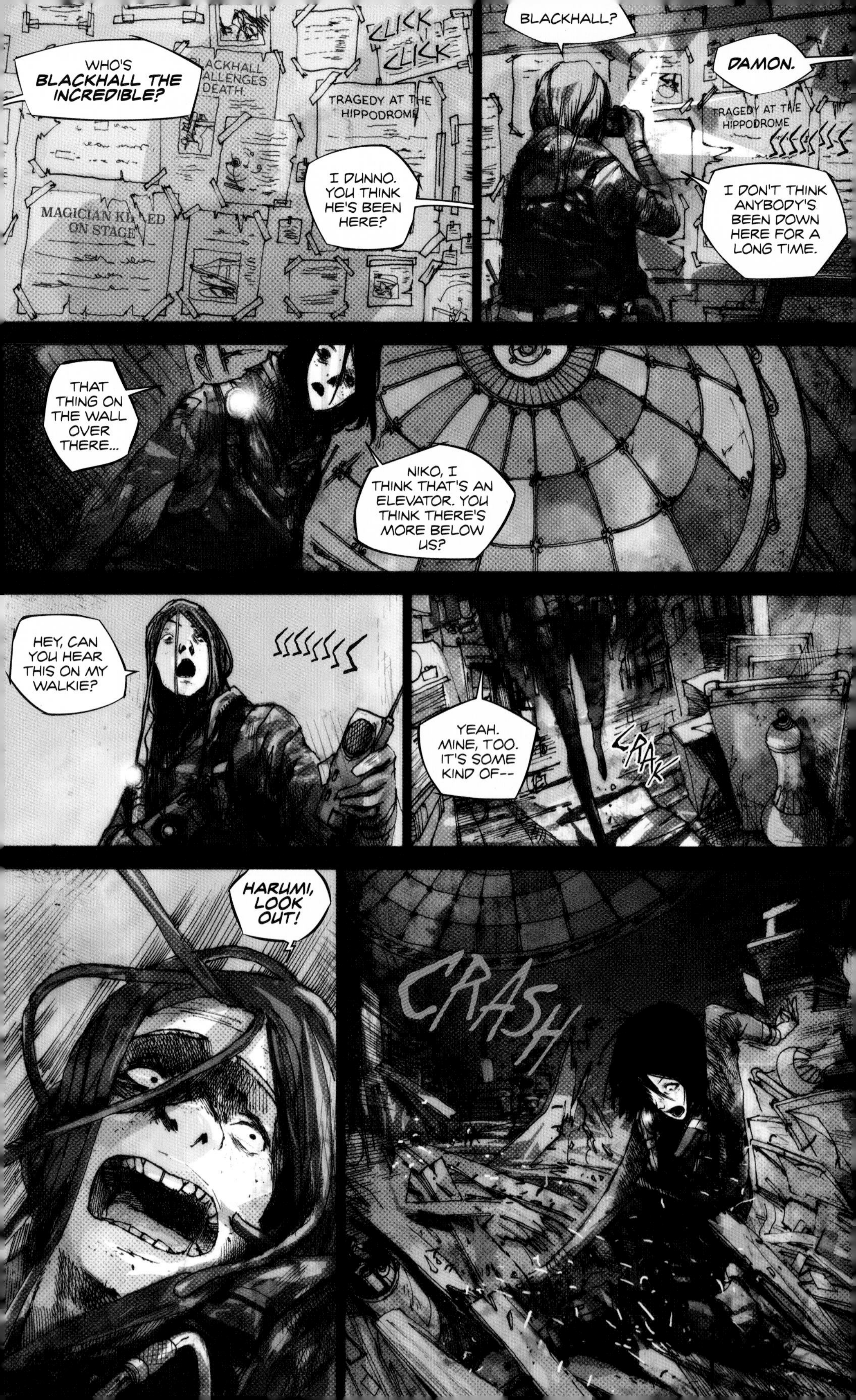
WHO'S BLACKHALL THE INCREDIBLE?
BLACKHALL CHALLENGES DEATH.
CLICK CLICK
TRAGEDY AT THE HIPPODROME
MAGICIAN KILLED ON STAGE
I DUNNO. YOU THINK HE'S BEEN HERE?
BLACKHALL?
DAMON.
TRAGEDY AT THE HIPPODROME
SSSSSSSS
I DON'T THINK ANYBODY'S BEEN DOWN HERE FOR A LONG TIME.
THAT THING ON THE WALL OVER THERE...
NIKO, I THINK THAT'S AN ELEVATOR. YOU THINK THERE'S MORE BELOW US?
HEY, CAN YOU HEAR THIS ON MY WALKIE?
SSSSSSSS
YEAH. MINE, TOO. IT'S SOME KIND OF--
CRAK
HARUMI, LOOK OUT!
CRASH

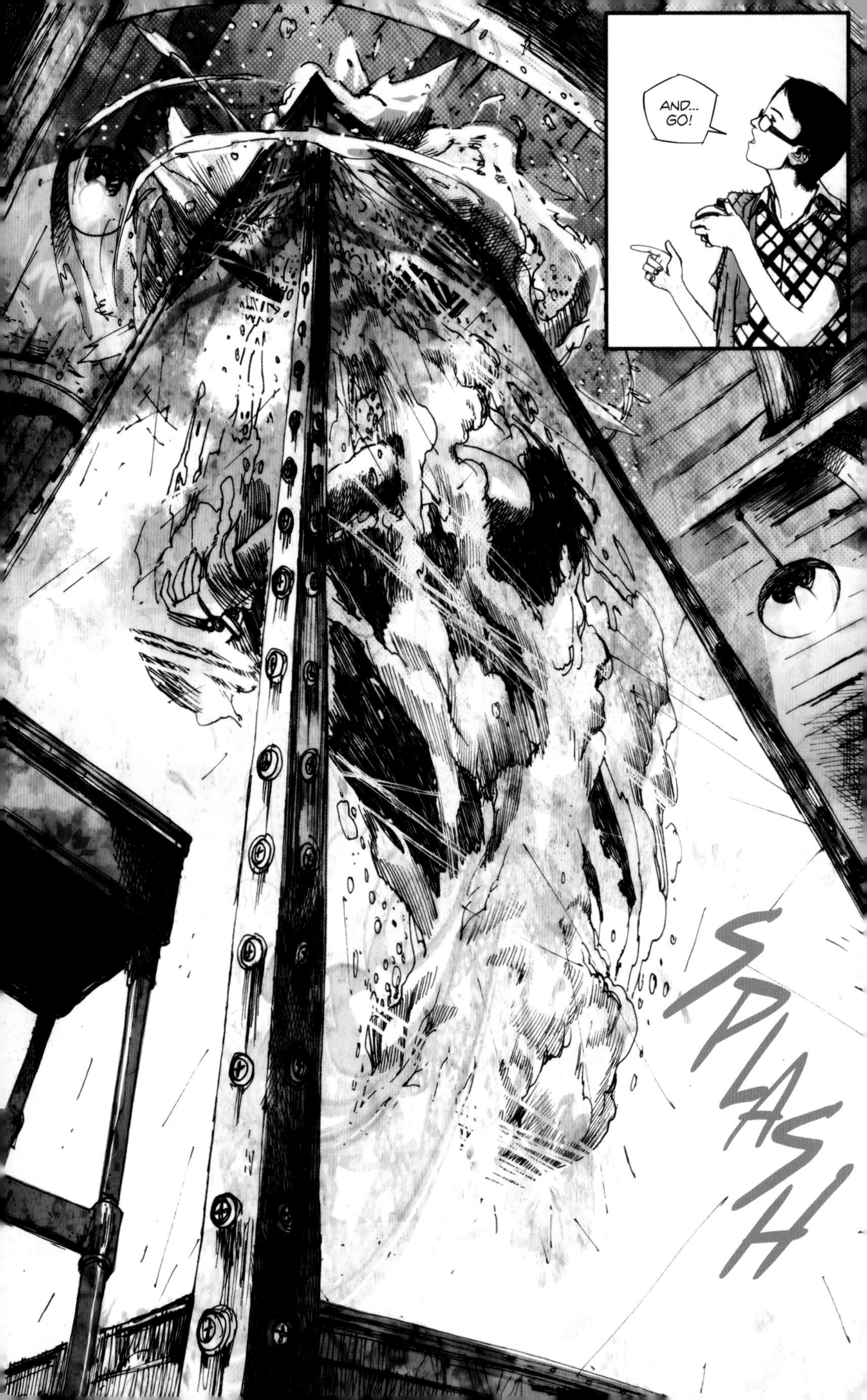
AND... GO!
SPLASH

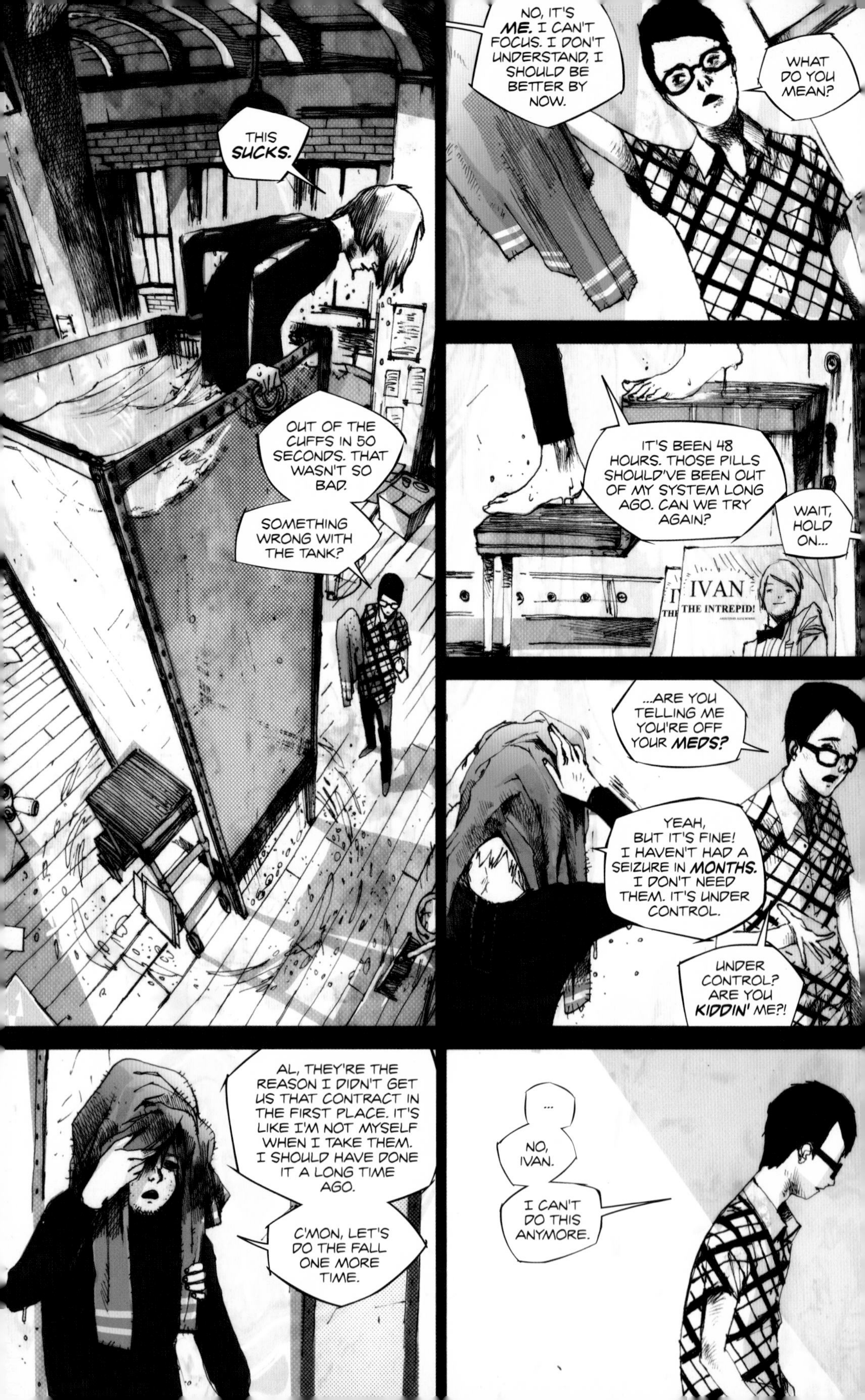
THIS SUCKS.
OUT OF THE CUFFS IN 50 SECONDS. THAT WASN'T SO BAD.
SOMETHING WRONG WITH THE TANK?
NO, IT'S ME. I CAN'T FOCUS. I DON'T UNDERSTAND, I SHOULD BE BETTER BY NOW.
WHAT DO YOU MEAN?
IT'S BEEN 48 HOURS. THOSE PILLS SHOULD'VE BEEN OUT OF MY SYSTEM LONG AGO. CAN WE TRY AGAIN?
WAIT, HOLD ON...
IVAN THE INTREPID!
...ARE YOU TELLING ME YOU'RE OFF YOUR MEDS?
YEAH, BUT IT'S FINE! I HAVEN'T HAD A SEIZURE IN MONTHS. I DON'T NEED THEM. IT'S UNDER CONTROL.
UNDER CONTROL? ARE YOU KIDDIN' ME?!
AL, THEY'RE THE REASON I DIDN'T GET US THAT CONTRACT IN THE FIRST PLACE. IT'S LIKE I'M NOT MYSELF WHEN I TAKE THEM. I SHOULD HAVE DONE IT A LONG TIME AGO.
C'MON, LET'S DO THE FALL ONE MORE TIME.
...
NO, IVAN.
I CAN'T DO THIS ANYMORE.

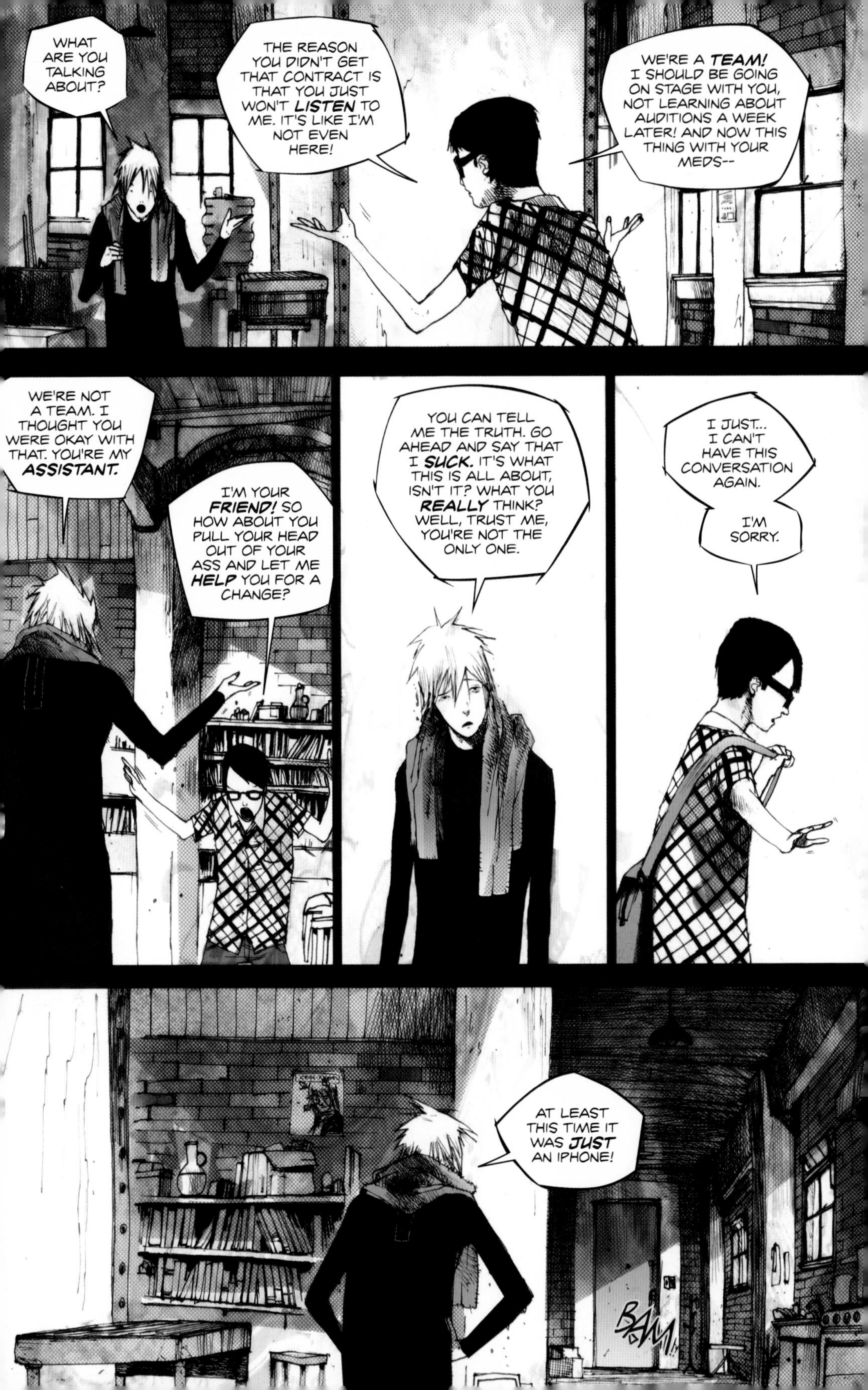
WHAT ARE YOU TALKING ABOUT?
THE REASON YOU DIDN'T GET THAT CONTRACT IS THAT YOU JUST WON'T LISTEN TO ME. IT'S LIKE I'M NOT EVEN HERE!
WE'RE A TEAM! I SHOULD BE GOING ON STAGE WITH YOU, NOT LEARNING ABOUT AUDITIONS A WEEK LATER! AND NOW THIS THING WITH YOUR MEDS--
WE'RE NOT A TEAM. I THOUGHT YOU WERE OKAY WITH THAT. YOU'RE MY ASSISTANT.
I'M YOUR FRIEND! SO HOW ABOUT YOU PULL YOUR HEAD OUT OF YOUR ASS AND LET ME HELP YOU FOR A CHANGE?
YOU CAN TELL ME THE TRUTH. GO AHEAD AND SAY THAT I SUCK. IT'S WHAT THIS IS ALL ABOUT, ISN'T IT? WHAT YOU REALLY THINK? WELL, TRUST ME, YOU'RE NOT THE ONLY ONE.
I JUST... I CAN'T HAVE THIS CONVERSATION AGAIN.
I'M SORRY.
AT LEAST THIS TIME IT WAS JUST AN IPHONE!

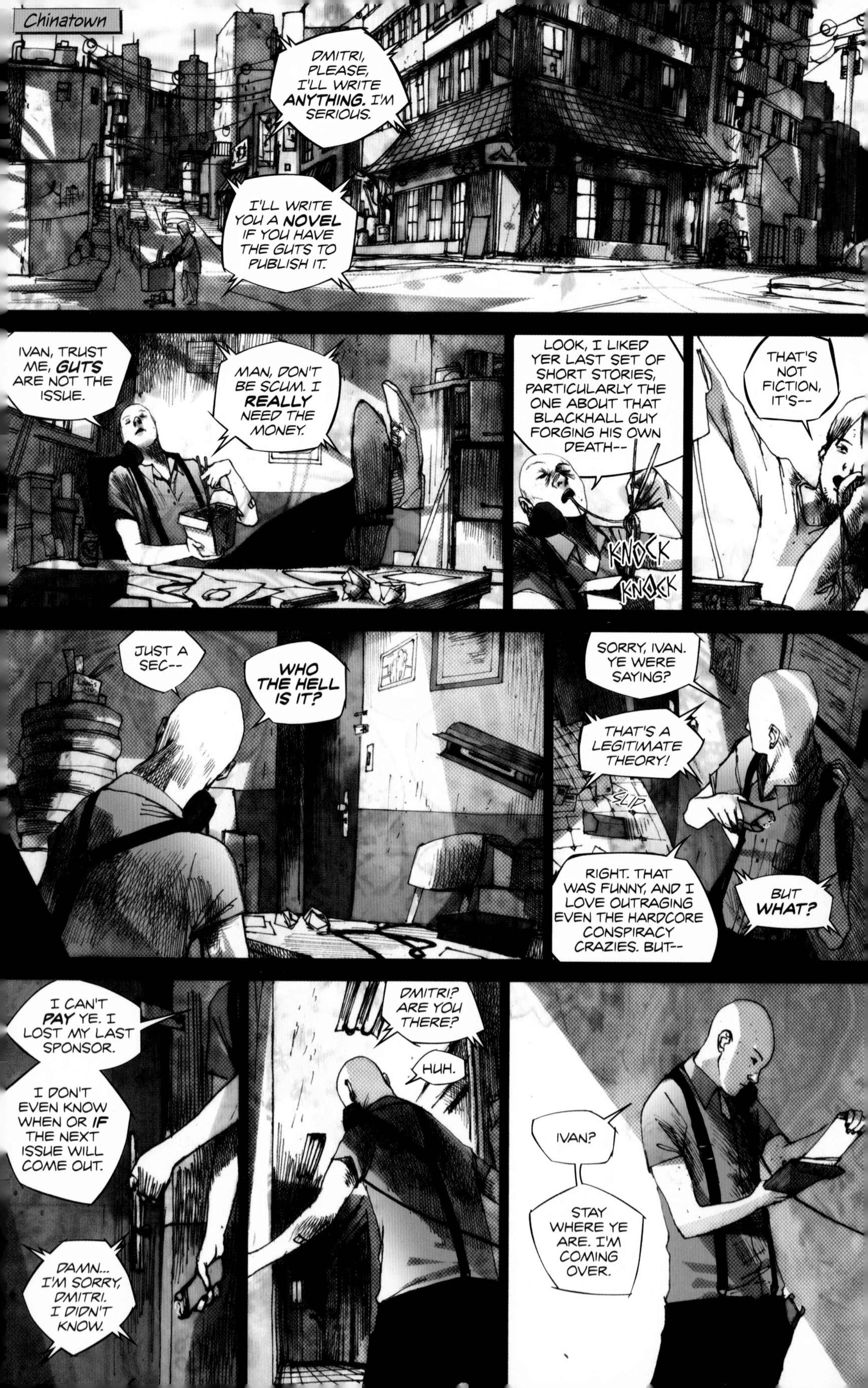
Chinatown
DMITRI, PLEASE, I'LL WRITE ANYTHING. I'M SERIOUS.
I'LL WRITE YOU A NOVEL IF YOU HAVE THE GUTS TO PUBLISH IT.
IVAN, TRUST ME, GUTS ARE NOT THE ISSUE.
MAN, DON'T BE SCUM. I REALLY NEED THE MONEY.
LOOK, I LIKED YER LAST SET OF SHORT STORIES, PARTICULARLY THE ONE ABOUT THAT BLACKHALL GUY FORGING HIS OWN DEATH--
KNOCK
KNOCK
THAT'S NOT FICTION, IT'S--
JUST A SEC--
WHO THE HELL IS IT?
SORRY, IVAN. YE WERE SAYING?
THAT'S A LEGITIMATE THEORY!
SLIP
RIGHT. THAT WAS FUNNY, AND I LOVE OUTRAGING EVEN THE HARDCORE CONSPIRACY CRAZIES. BUT--
BUT WHAT?
I CAN'T PAY YE. I LOST MY LAST SPONSOR.
I DON'T EVEN KNOW WHEN OR IF THE NEXT ISSUE WILL COME OUT.
DAMN... I'M SORRY, DMITRI. I DIDN'T KNOW.
DMITRI? ARE YOU THERE?
HUH.
IVAN?
STAY WHERE YE ARE. I'M COMING OVER.

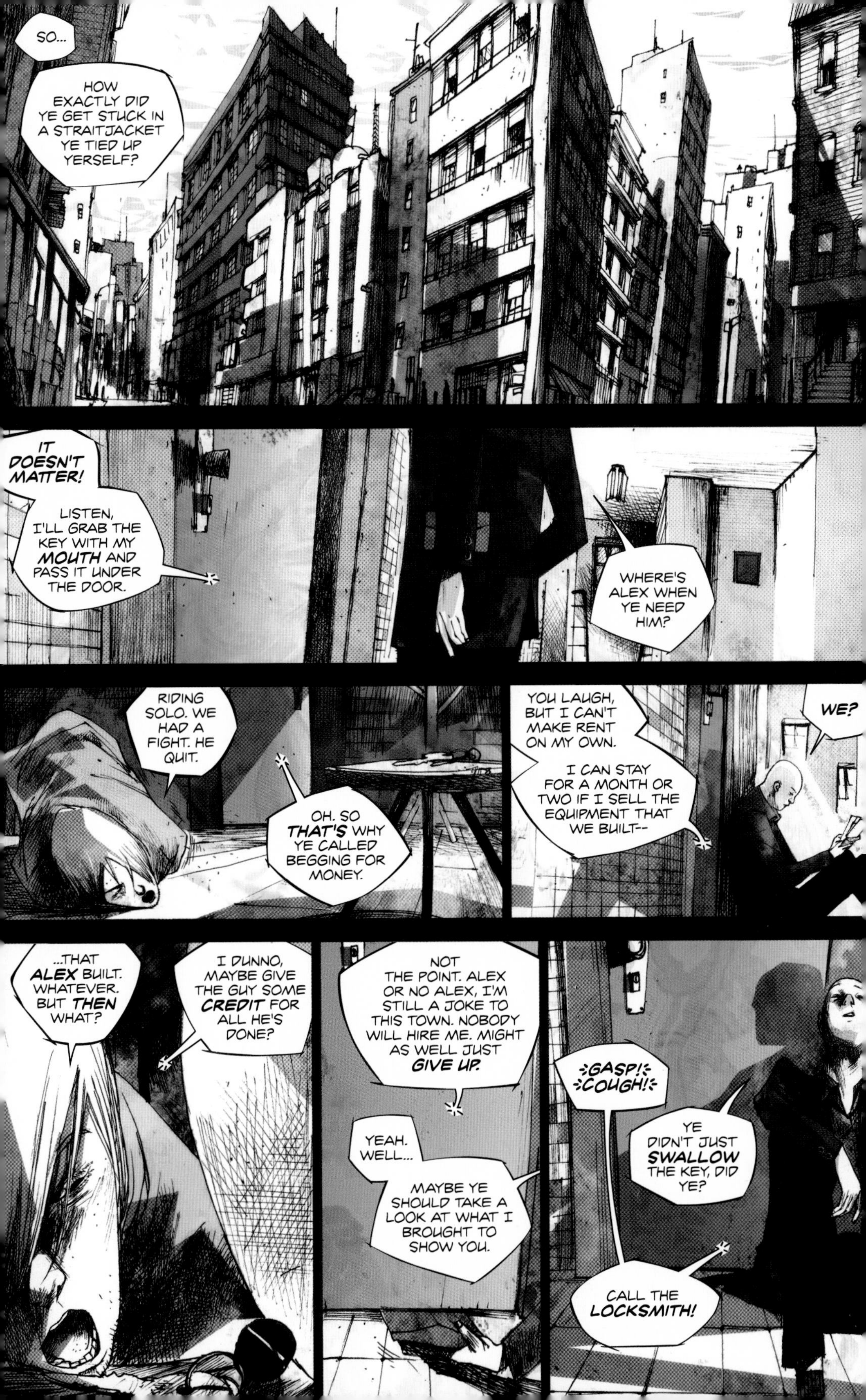
SO...
HOW EXACTLY DID YE GET STUCK IN A STRAITJACKET YE TIED UP YERSELF?
IT DOESN'T MATTER!
LISTEN, I'LL GRAB THE KEY WITH MY MOUTH AND PASS IT UNDER THE DOOR.
WHERE'S ALEX WHEN YE NEED HIM?
RIDING SOLO. WE HAD A FIGHT. HE QUIT.
OH. SO THAT'S WHY YE CALLED BEGGING FOR MONEY.
YOU LAUGH, BUT I CAN'T MAKE RENT ON MY OWN.
I CAN STAY FOR A MONTH OR TWO IF I SELL THE EQUIPMENT THAT WE BUILT--
WE?
...THAT ALEX BUILT. WHATEVER. BUT THEN WHAT?
I DUNNO, MAYBE GIVE THE GUY SOME CREDIT FOR ALL HE'S DONE?
NOT THE POINT. ALEX OR NO ALEX, I'M STILL A JOKE TO THIS TOWN. NOBODY WILL HIRE ME. MIGHT AS WELL JUST GIVE UP.
YEAH. WELL...
MAYBE YE SHOULD TAKE A LOOK AT WHAT I BROUGHT TO SHOW YOU.
GASP! COUGH!
YE DIDN'T JUST SWALLOW THE KEY, DID YE?
CALL THE LOCKSMITH!

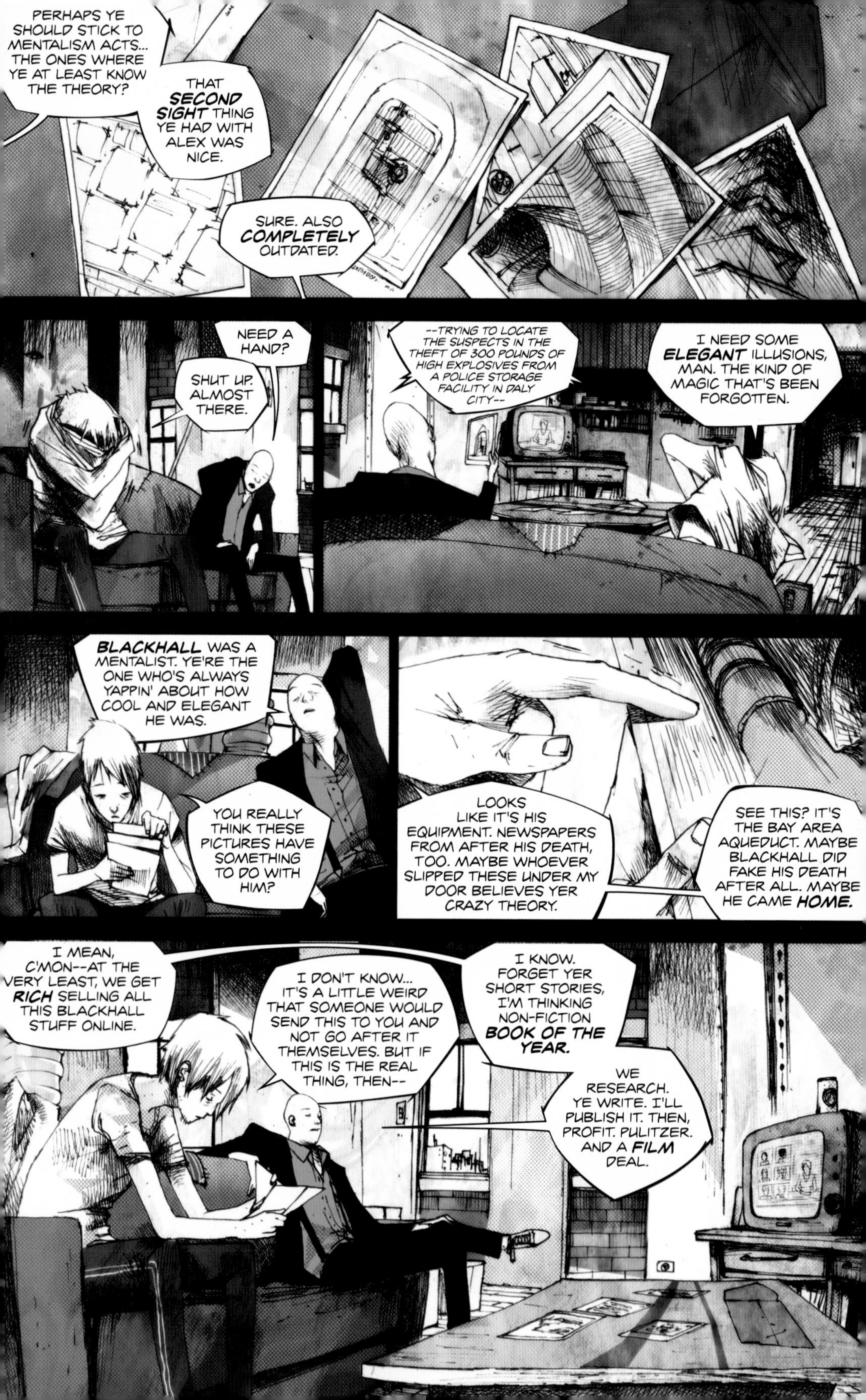

PERHAPS YE SHOULD STICK TO MENTALISM ACTS... THE ONES WHERE YE AT LEAST KNOW THE THEORY?
THAT SECOND SIGHT THING YE HAD WITH ALEX WAS NICE.
SURE. ALSO COMPLETELY OUTDATED.
NEED A HAND?
SHUT UP. ALMOST THERE.
--TRYING TO LOCATE THE SUSPECTS IN THE THEFT OF 300 POUNDS OF HIGH EXPLOSIVES FROM A POLICE STORAGE FACILITY IN DALY CITY--
I NEED SOME ELEGANT ILLUSIONS, MAN. THE KIND OF MAGIC THAT'S BEEN FORGOTTEN.
BLACKHALL WAS A MENTALIST. YE'RE THE ONE WHO'S ALWAYS YAPPIN' ABOUT HOW COOL AND ELEGANT HE WAS.
YOU REALLY THINK THESE PICTURES HAVE SOMETHING TO DO WITH HIM?
LOOKS LIKE IT'S HIS EQUIPMENT. NEWSPAPERS FROM AFTER HIS DEATH, TOO. MAYBE WHOEVER SLIPPED THESE UNDER MY DOOR BELIEVES YER CRAZY THEORY.
SEE THIS? IT'S THE BAY AREA AQUEDUCT. MAYBE BLACKHALL DID FAKE HIS DEATH AFTER ALL. MAYBE HE CAME HOME.
I MEAN, C'MON--AT THE VERY LEAST, WE GET RICH SELLING ALL THIS BLACKHALL STUFF ONLINE.
I DON'T KNOW... IT'S A LITTLE WEIRD THAT SOMEONE WOULD SEND THIS TO YOU AND NOT GO AFTER IT THEMSELVES. BUT IF THIS IS THE REAL THING, THEN--
I KNOW. FORGET YER SHORT STORIES, I'M THINKING NON-FICTION BOOK OF THE YEAR.
WE RESEARCH. YE WRITE. I'LL PUBLISH IT. THEN, PROFIT. PULITZER. AND A FILM DEAL.

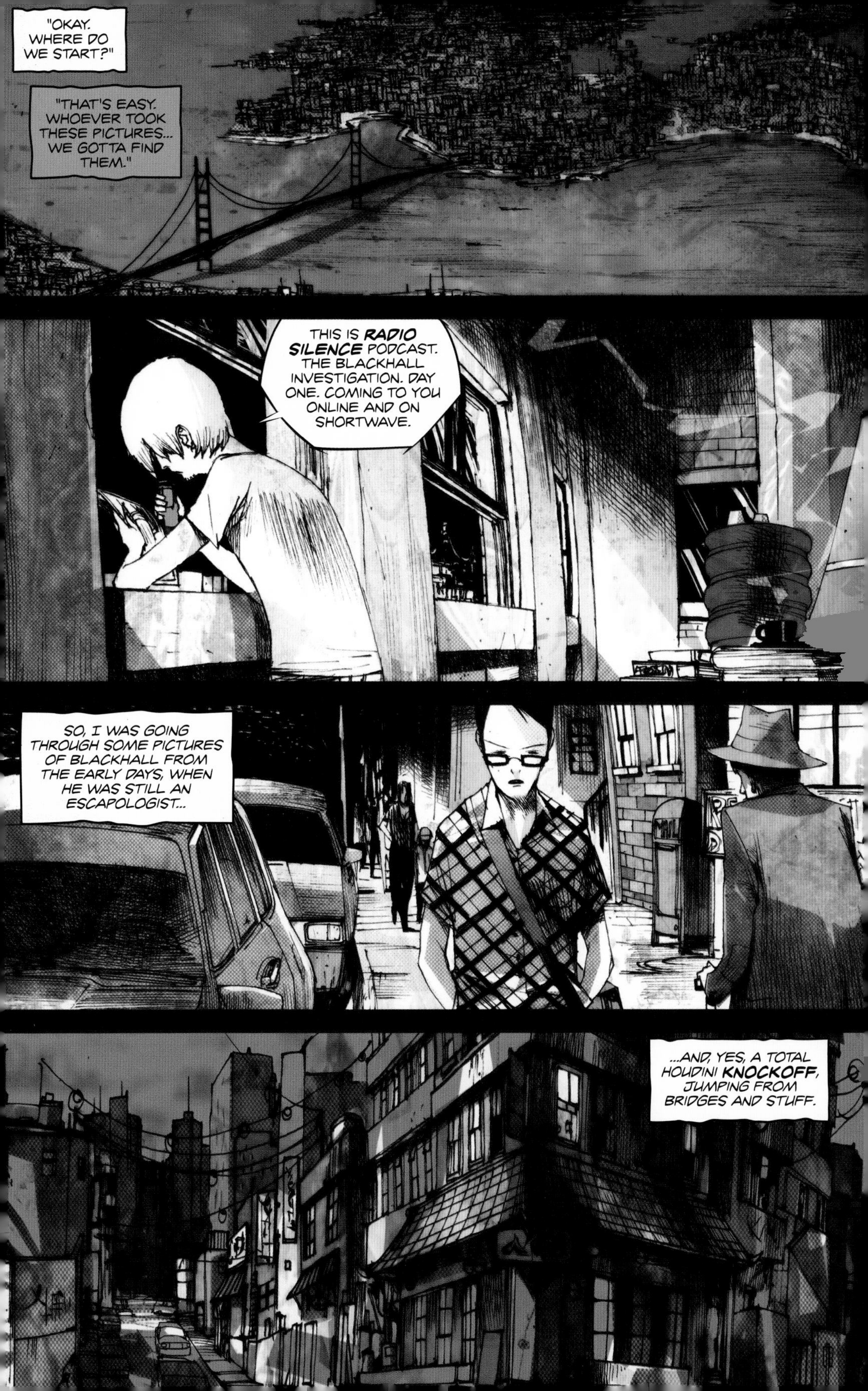
"OKAY. WHERE DO WE START?"
"THAT'S EASY. WHOEVER TOOK THESE PICTURES... WE GOTTA FIND THEM."
THIS IS RADIO SILENCE PODCAST. THE BLACKHALL INVESTIGATION. DAY ONE. COMING TO YOU ONLINE AND ON SHORTWAVE.
SO, I WAS GOING THROUGH SOME PICTURES OF BLACKHALL FROM THE EARLY DAYS, WHEN HE WAS STILL AN ESCAPOLOGIST...
...AND, YES, A TOTAL HOUDINI KNOCKOFF, JUMPING FROM BRIDGES AND STUFF.

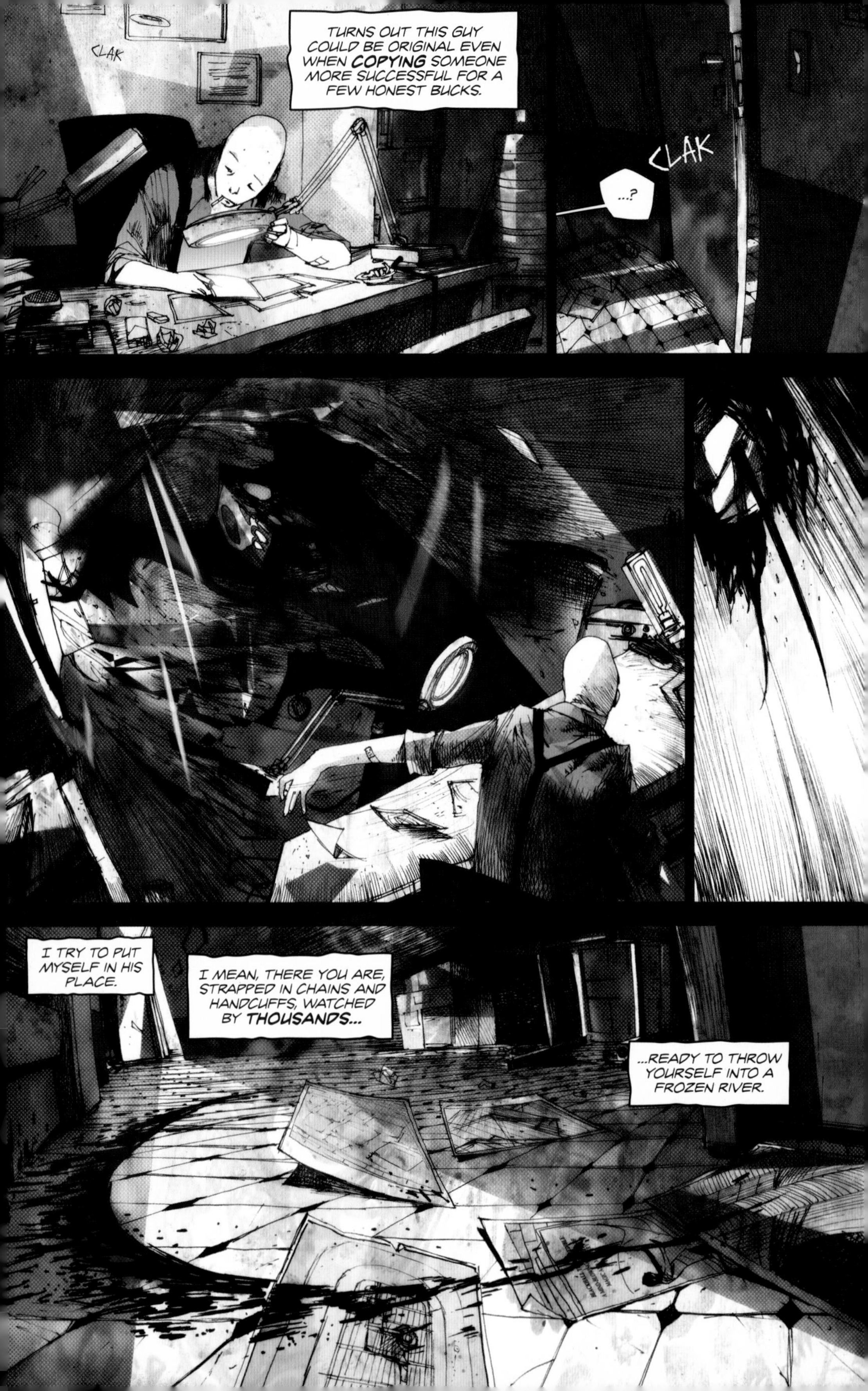
CLAK
TURNS OUT THIS GUY COULD BE ORIGINAL EVEN WHEN COPYING SOMEONE MORE SUCCESSFUL FOR A FEW HONEST BUCKS.
CLAK
...?
I TRY TO PUT MYSELF IN HIS PLACE.
I MEAN, THERE YOU ARE, STRAPPED IN CHAINS AND HANDCUFFS, WATCHED BY THOUSANDS...
...READY TO THROW YOURSELF INTO A FROZEN RIVER.

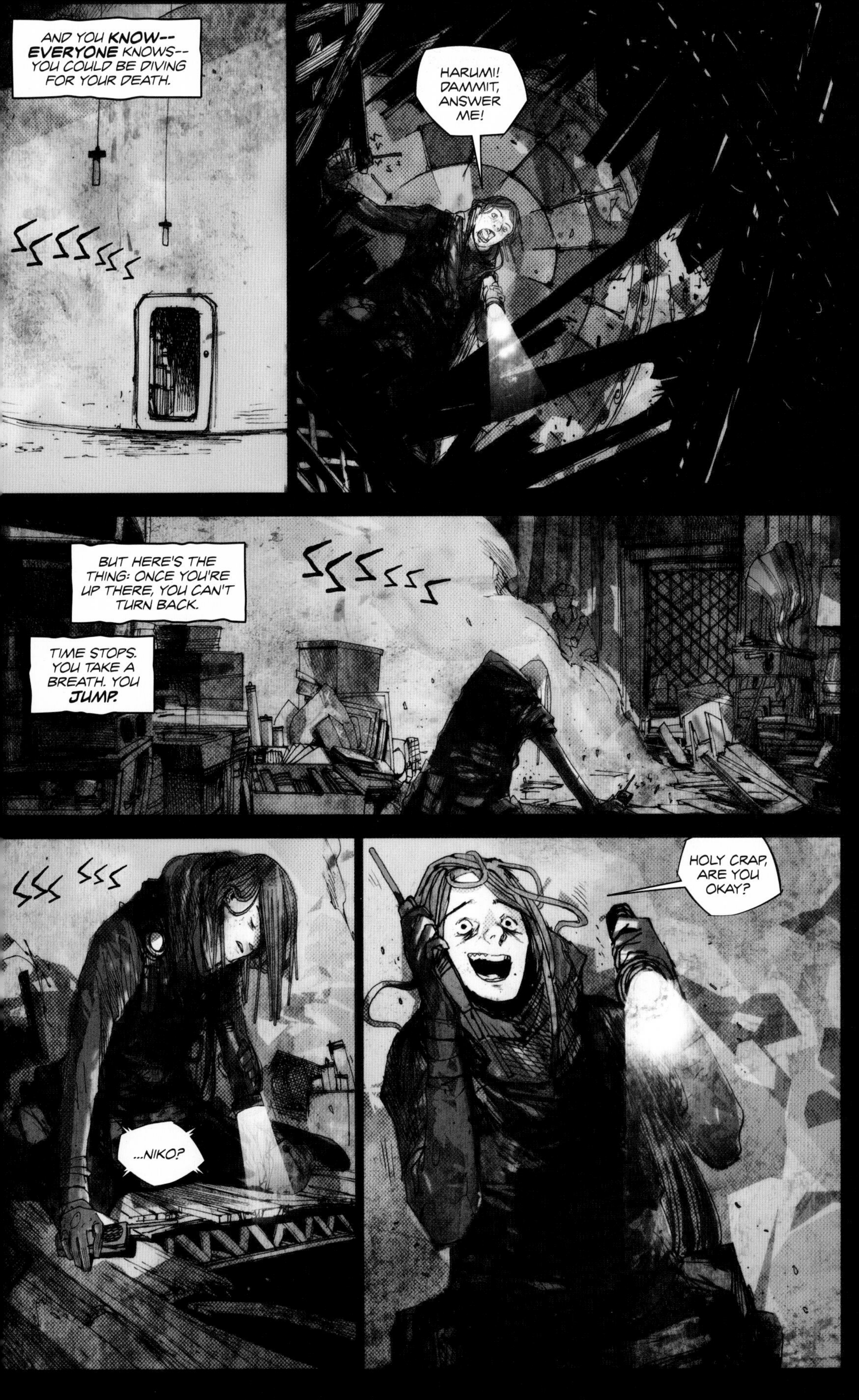
AND YOU KNOW-- EVERYONE KNOWS-- YOU COULD BE DIVING FOR YOUR DEATH.
SSSSSSS
HARUMI! DAMMIT, ANSWER ME!
BUT HERE'S THE THING: ONCE YOU'RE UP THERE, YOU CAN'T TURN BACK.
TIME STOPS. YOU TAKE A BREATH. YOU JUMP.
SSSSSS
SSS SSS
...NIKO?
HOLY CRAP, ARE YOU OKAY?

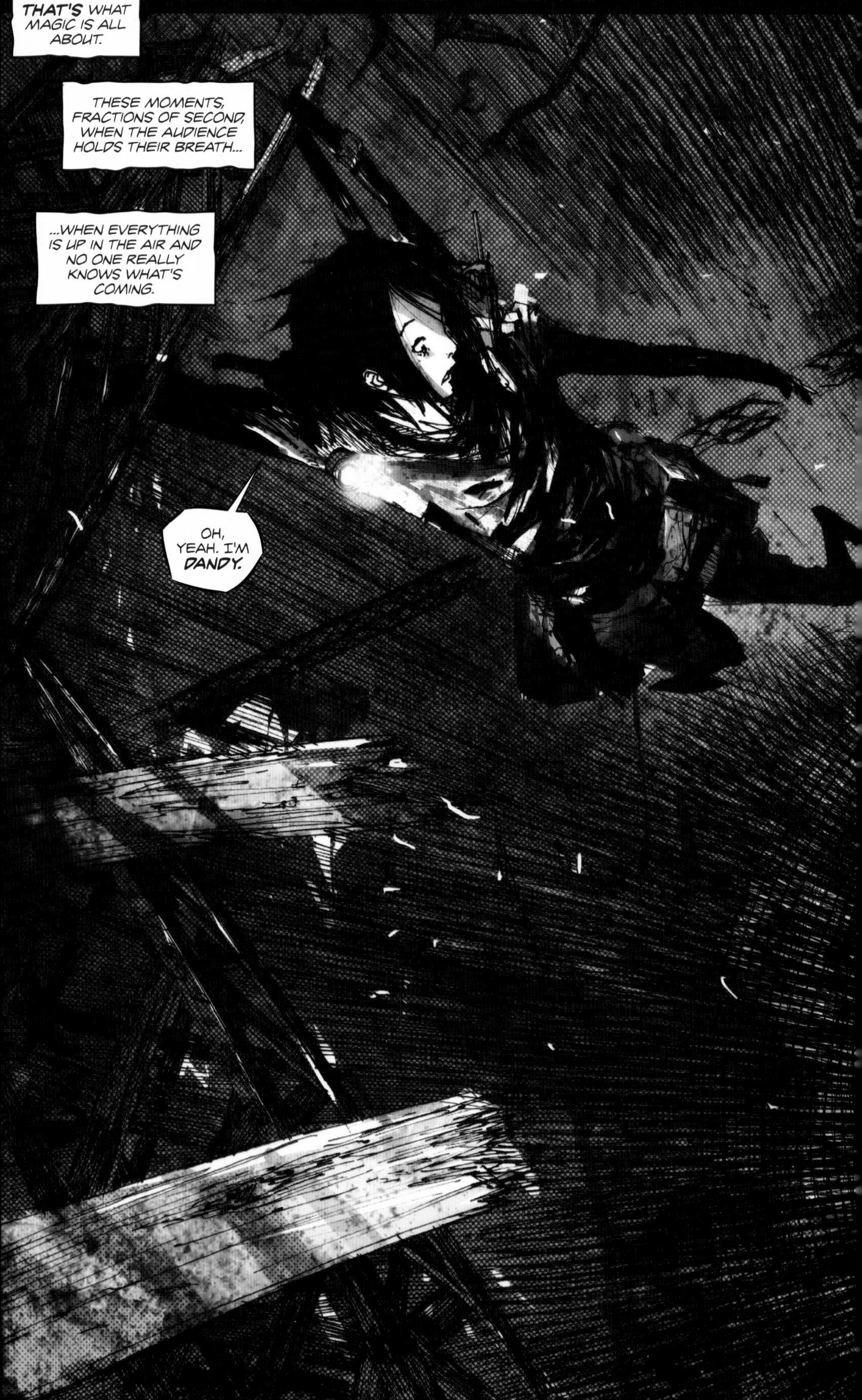
THAT'S WHAT MAGIC IS ALL ABOUT.
THESE MOMENTS, FRACTIONS OF SECOND, WHEN THE AUDIENCE HOLDS THEIR BREATH...
...WHEN EVERYTHING IS UP IN THE AIR AND NO ONE REALLY KNOWS WHAT'S COMING.
OH, YEAH. I'M DANDY.

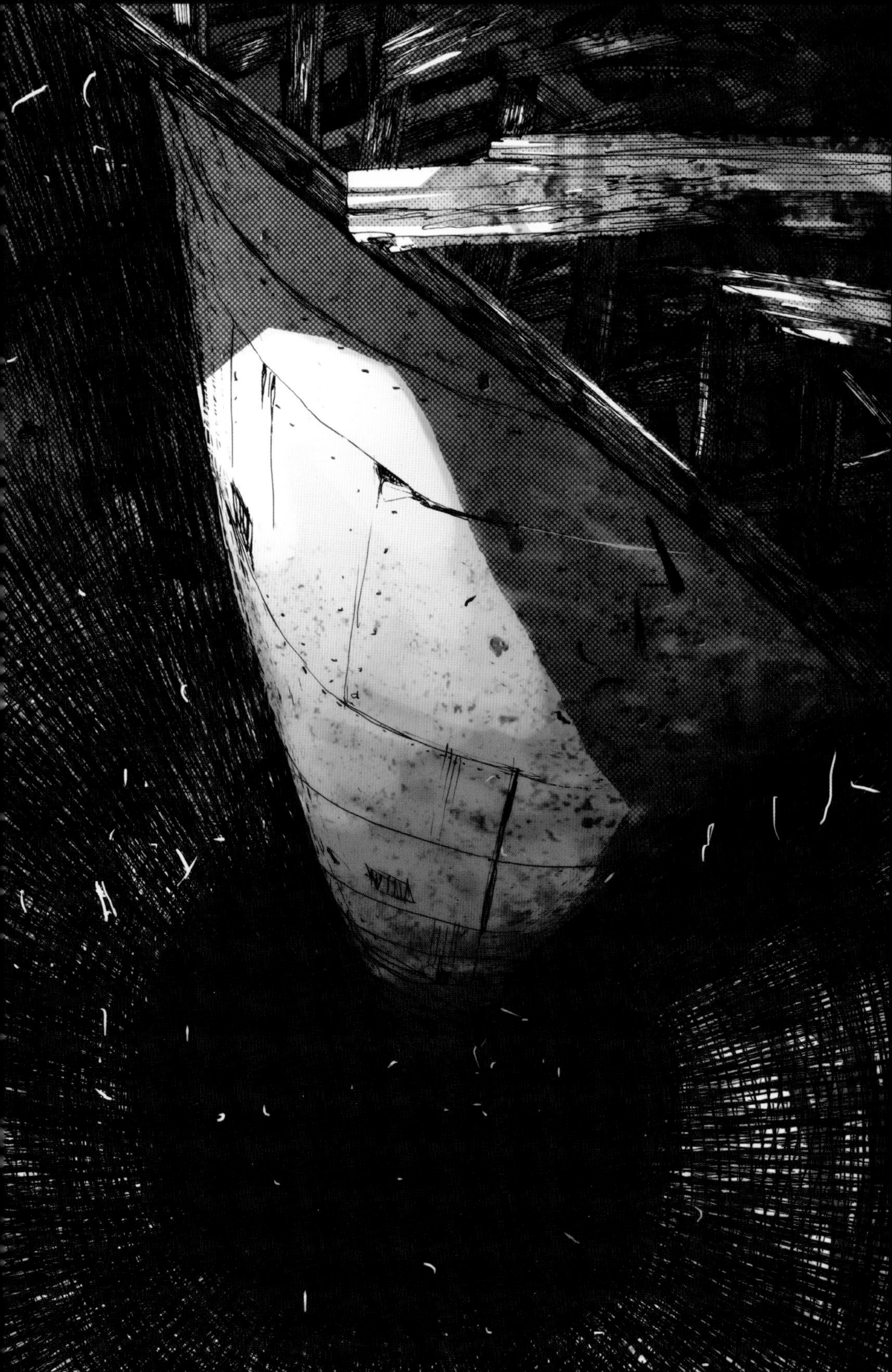

ISSUE ONE COVER

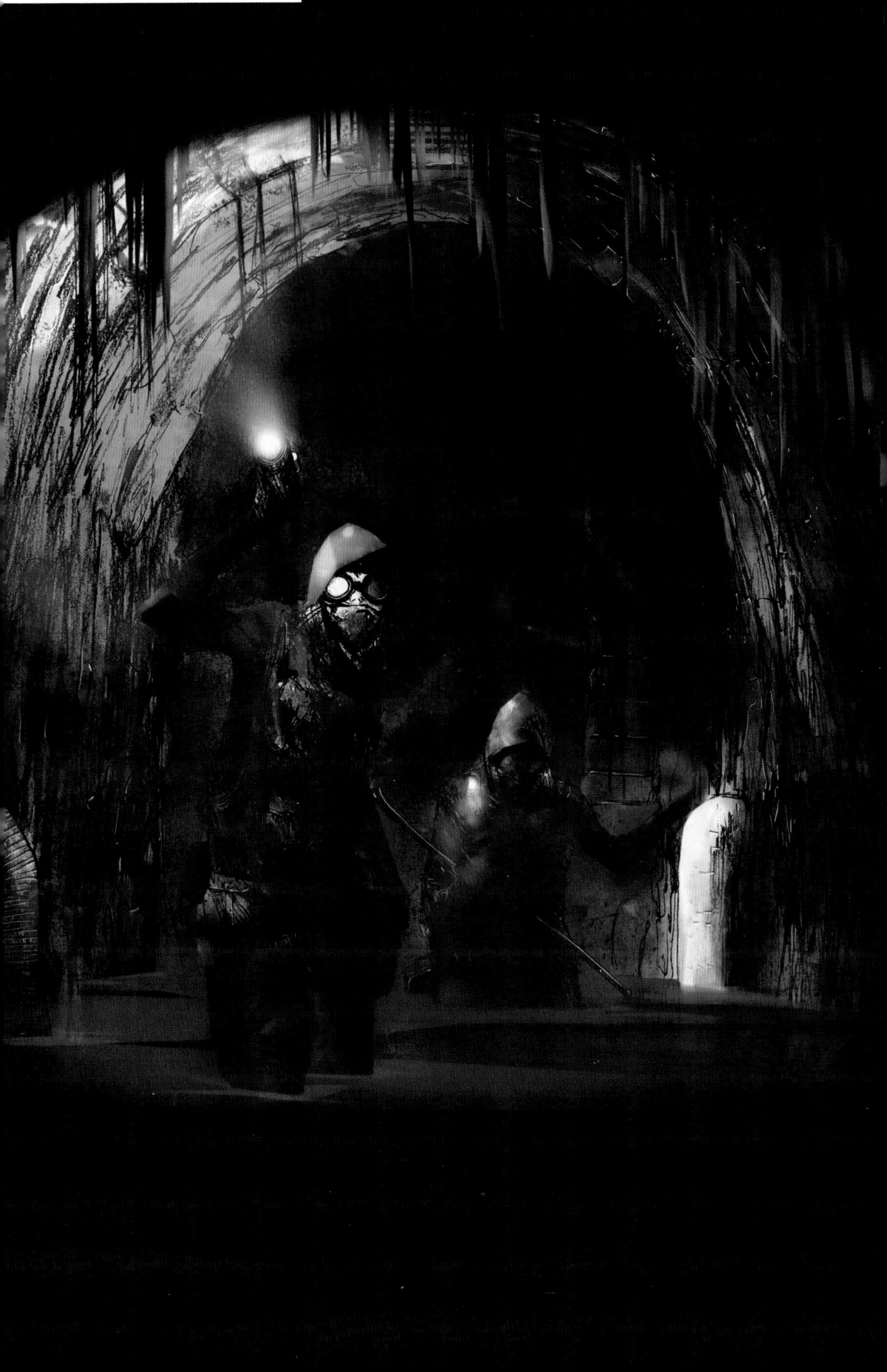

CHAPTER 2: THE TOURIST

ALWAYS TRESPASS. TNN XIE GXW VJ CTE MNR OBQLQBBUK. DON'T TURN YOUR BACK ON THE MYSTERY.

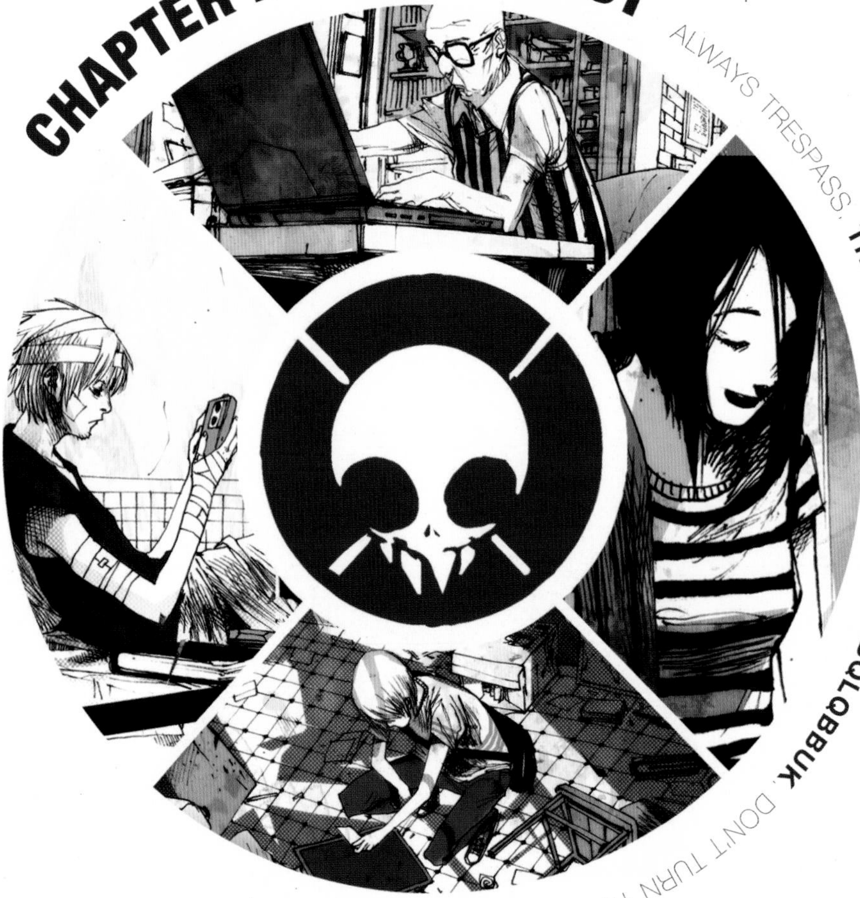

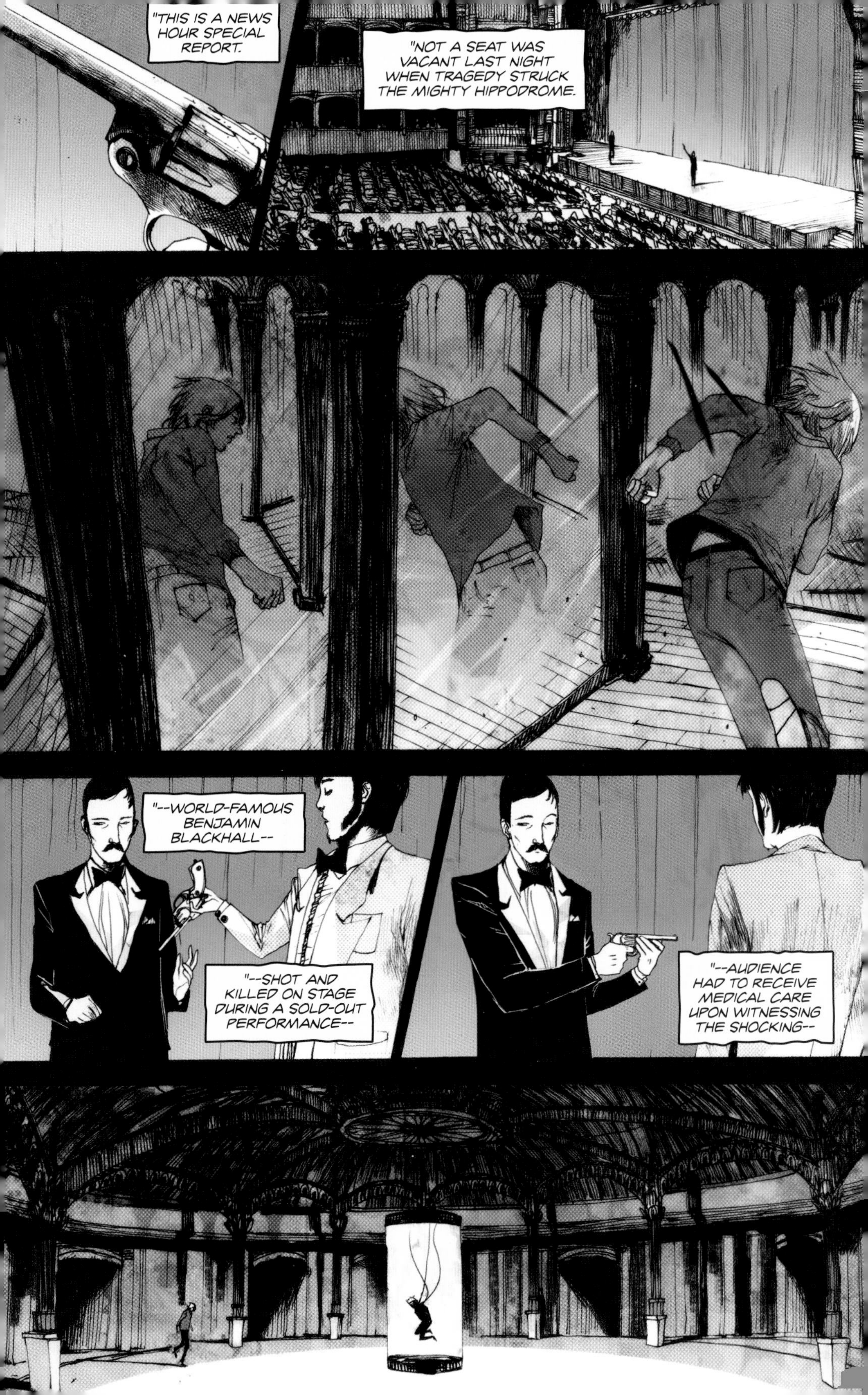
"THIS IS A NEWS HOUR SPECIAL REPORT.
"NOT A SEAT WAS VACANT LAST NIGHT WHEN TRAGEDY STRUCK THE MIGHTY HIPPODROME.
"--WORLD-FAMOUS BENJAMIN BLACKHALL--
"--SHOT AND KILLED ON STAGE DURING A SOLD-OUT PERFORMANCE--
"--AUDIENCE HAD TO RECEIVE MEDICAL CARE UPON WITNESSING THE SHOCKING--

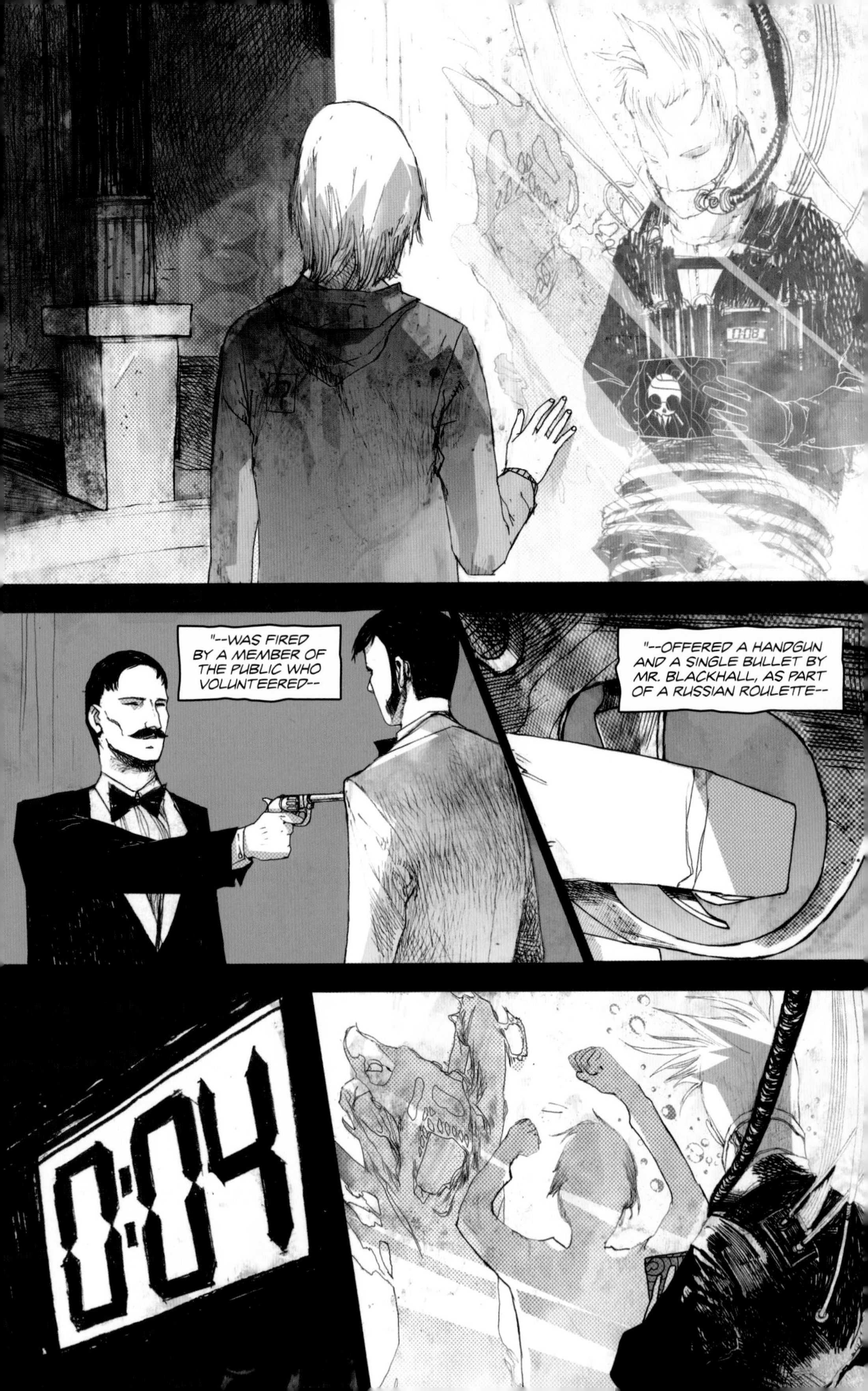
"--WAS FIRED BY A MEMBER OF THE PUBLIC WHO VOLUNTEERED--
"--OFFERED A HANDGUN AND A SINGLE BULLET BY MR. BLACKHALL, AS PART OF A RUSSIAN ROULETTE--
0:08
0:04

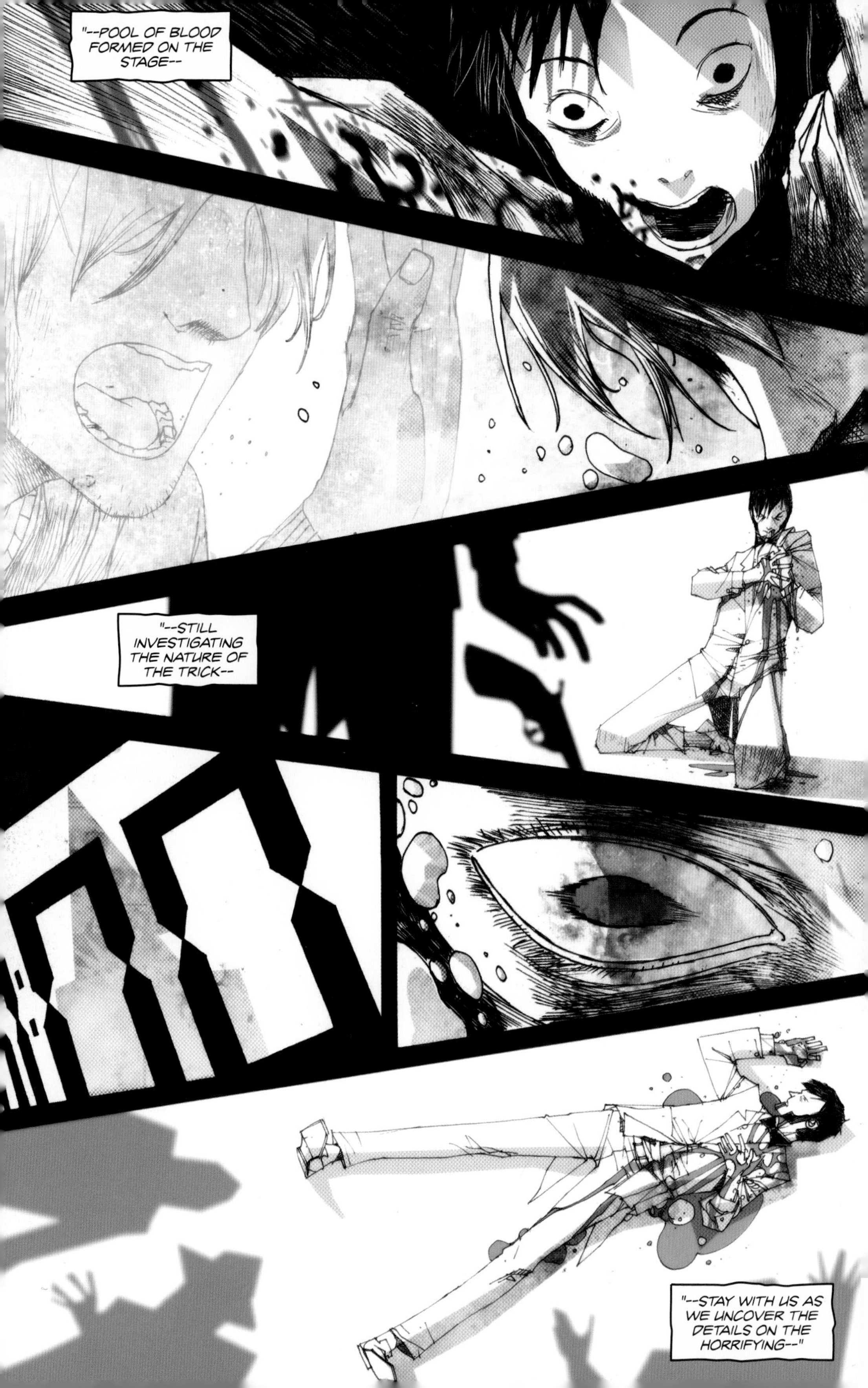
"--POOL OF BLOOD FORMED ON THE STAGE--
"--STILL INVESTIGATING THE NATURE OF THE TRICK--
"--STAY WITH US AS WE UNCOVER THE DETAILS ON THE HORRIFYING--"

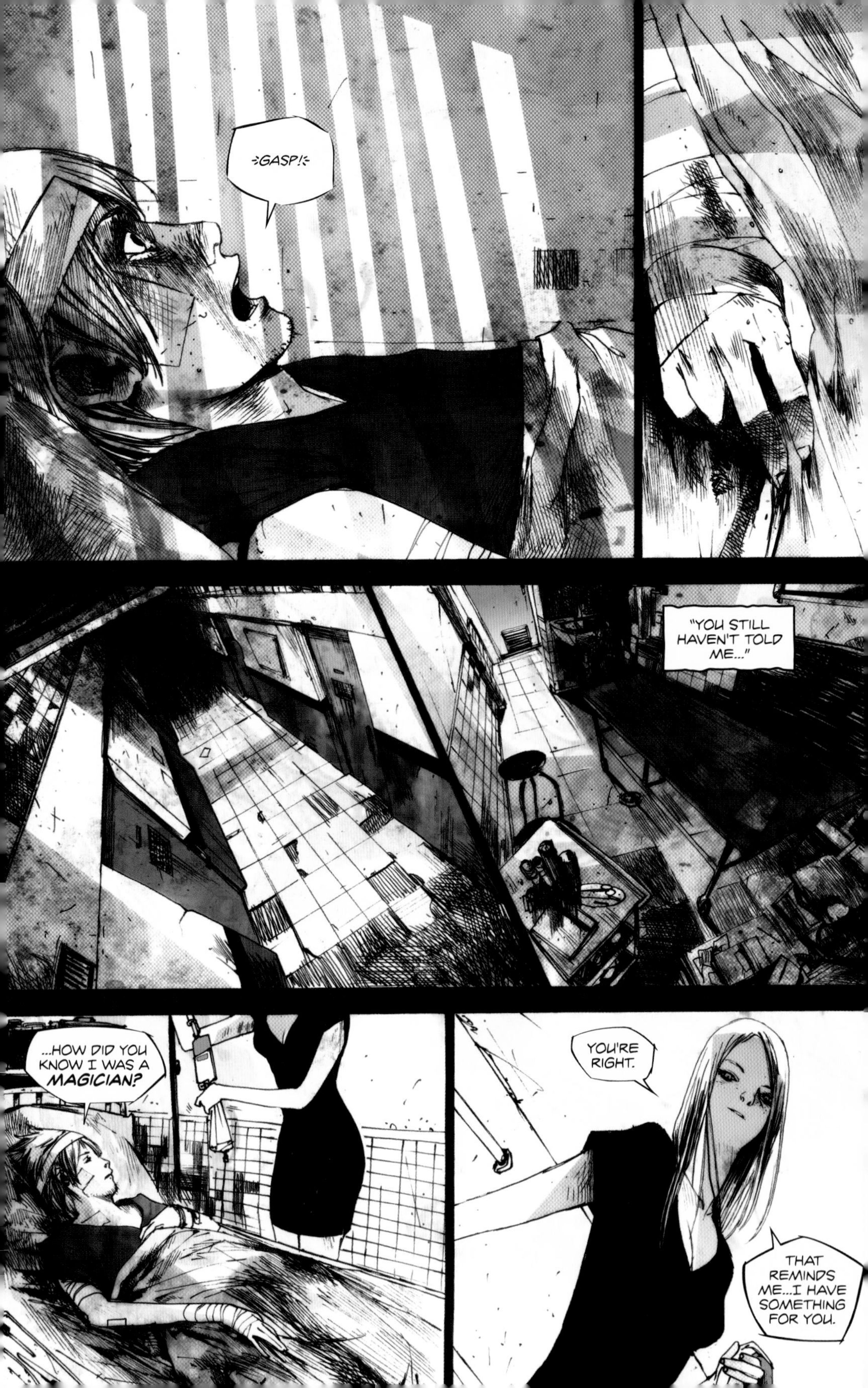
GASP!
"YOU STILL HAVEN'T TOLD ME..."
...HOW DID YOU KNOW I WAS A MAGICIAN?
YOU'RE RIGHT.
THAT REMINDS ME...I HAVE SOMETHING FOR YOU.

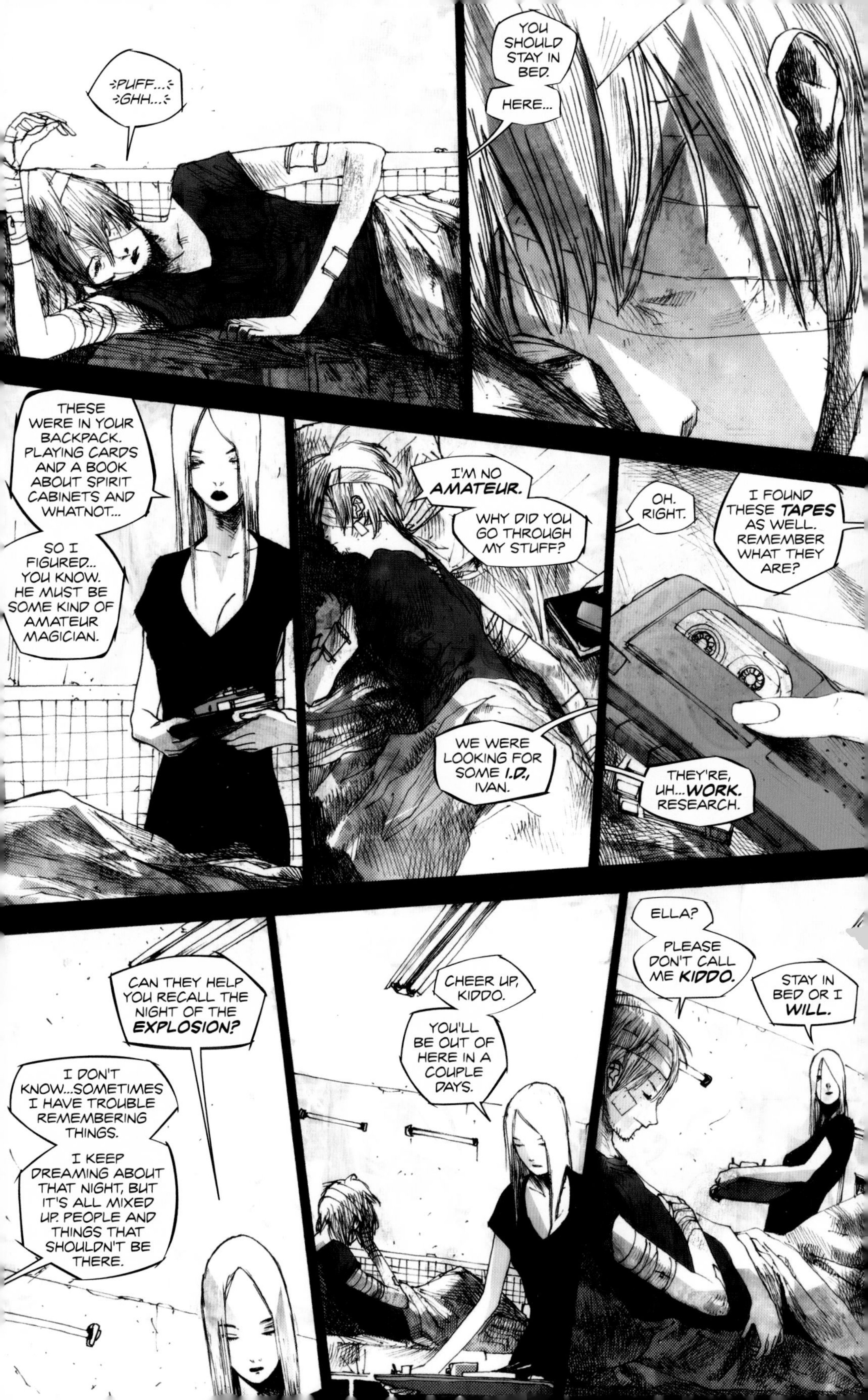
PUFF... GHH...
YOU SHOULD STAY IN BED.
HERE...
THESE WERE IN YOUR BACKPACK. PLAYING CARDS AND A BOOK ABOUT SPIRIT CABINETS AND WHATNOT...
SO I FIGURED... YOU KNOW. HE MUST BE SOME KIND OF AMATEUR MAGICIAN.
I'M NO **AMATEUR.**
WHY DID YOU GO THROUGH MY STUFF?
WE WERE LOOKING FOR SOME **I.D.,** IVAN.
OH. RIGHT.
I FOUND THESE **TAPES** AS WELL. REMEMBER WHAT THEY ARE?
THEY'RE, UH...**WORK.** RESEARCH.
CAN THEY HELP YOU RECALL THE NIGHT OF THE **EXPLOSION?**
I DON'T KNOW...SOMETIMES I HAVE TROUBLE REMEMBERING THINGS.
I KEEP DREAMING ABOUT THAT NIGHT, BUT IT'S ALL MIXED UP. PEOPLE AND THINGS THAT SHOULDN'T BE THERE.
CHEER UP, KIDDO.
YOU'LL BE OUT OF HERE IN A COUPLE DAYS.
ELLA?
PLEASE DON'T CALL ME **KIDDO.**
STAY IN BED OR I **WILL.**

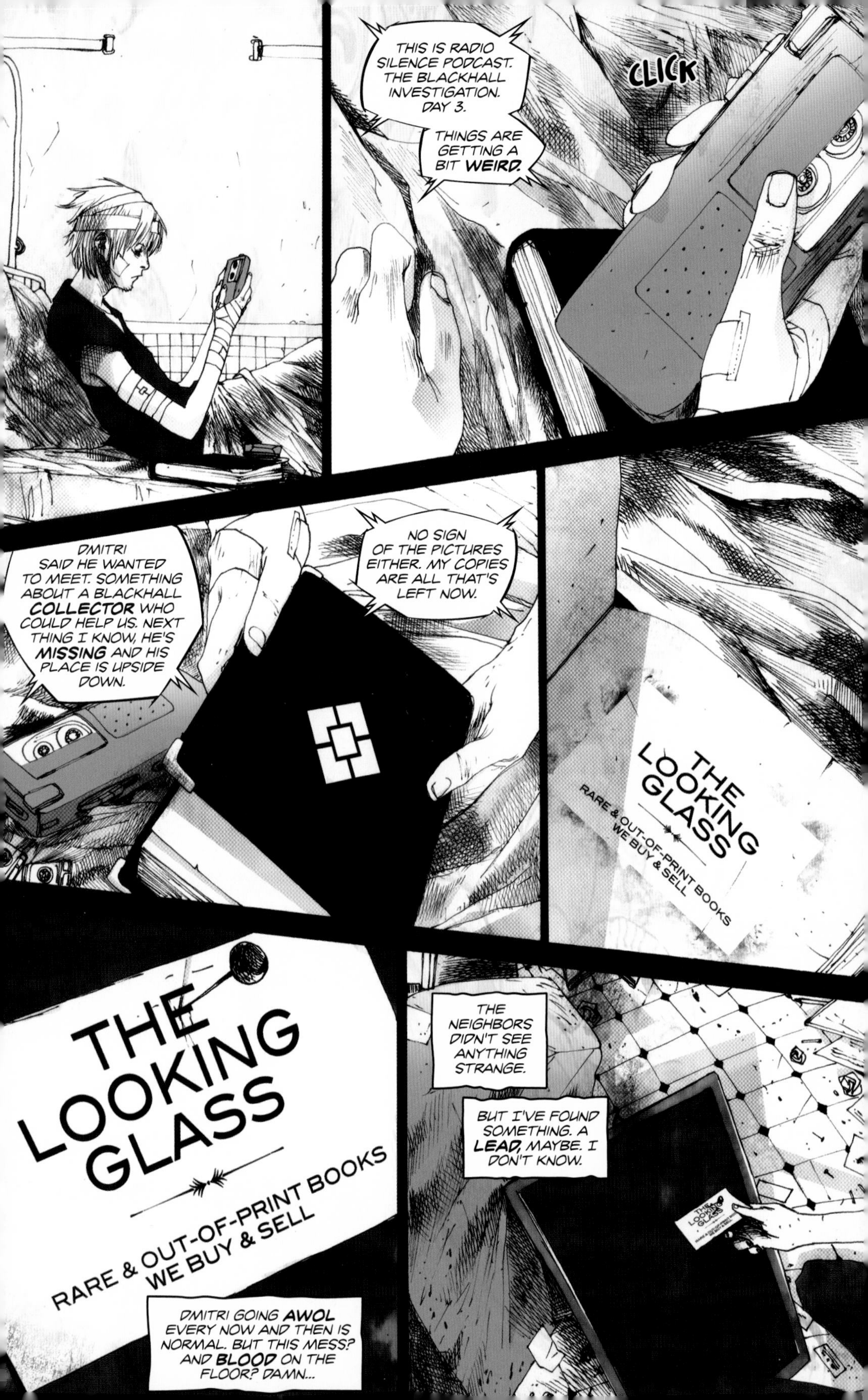

THIS IS RADIO SILENCE PODCAST. THE BLACKHALL INVESTIGATION. DAY 3.
THINGS ARE GETTING A BIT WEIRD.
CLICK
DMITRI SAID HE WANTED TO MEET. SOMETHING ABOUT A BLACKHALL COLLECTOR WHO COULD HELP US. NEXT THING I KNOW, HE'S MISSING AND HIS PLACE IS UPSIDE DOWN.
NO SIGN OF THE PICTURES EITHER. MY COPIES ARE ALL THAT'S LEFT NOW.
THE LOOKING GLASS
RARE & OUT-OF-PRINT BOOKS
WE BUY & SELL
THE LOOKING GLASS
RARE & OUT-OF-PRINT BOOKS
WE BUY & SELL
DMITRI GOING AWOL EVERY NOW AND THEN IS NORMAL. BUT THIS MESS? AND BLOOD ON THE FLOOR? DAMN...
THE NEIGHBORS DIDN'T SEE ANYTHING STRANGE.
BUT I'VE FOUND SOMETHING. A LEAD, MAYBE. I DON'T KNOW.

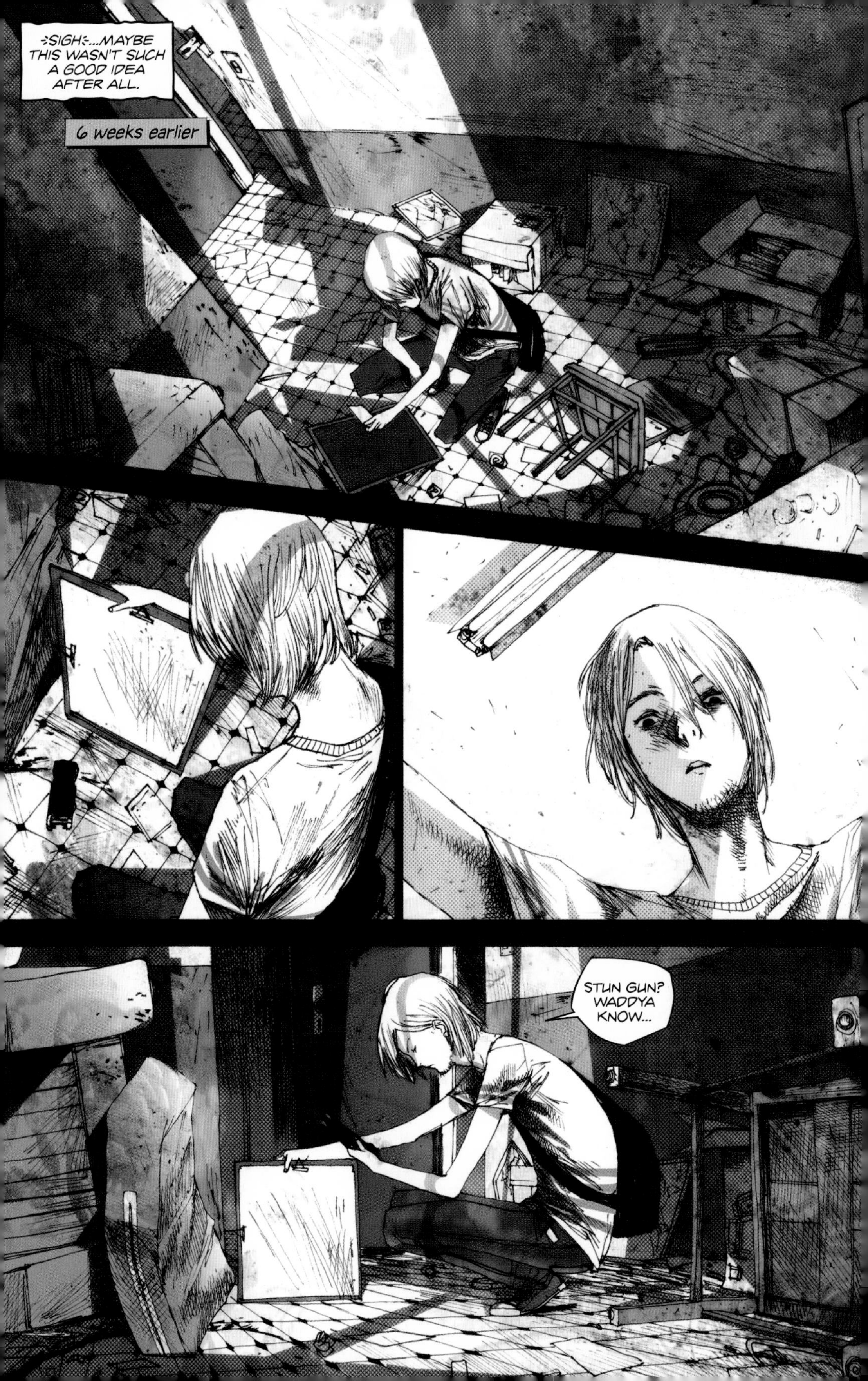

⊰SIGH⊱...MAYBE THIS WASN'T SUCH A GOOD IDEA AFTER ALL.
6 weeks earlier
STUN GUN? WADDYA KNOW...

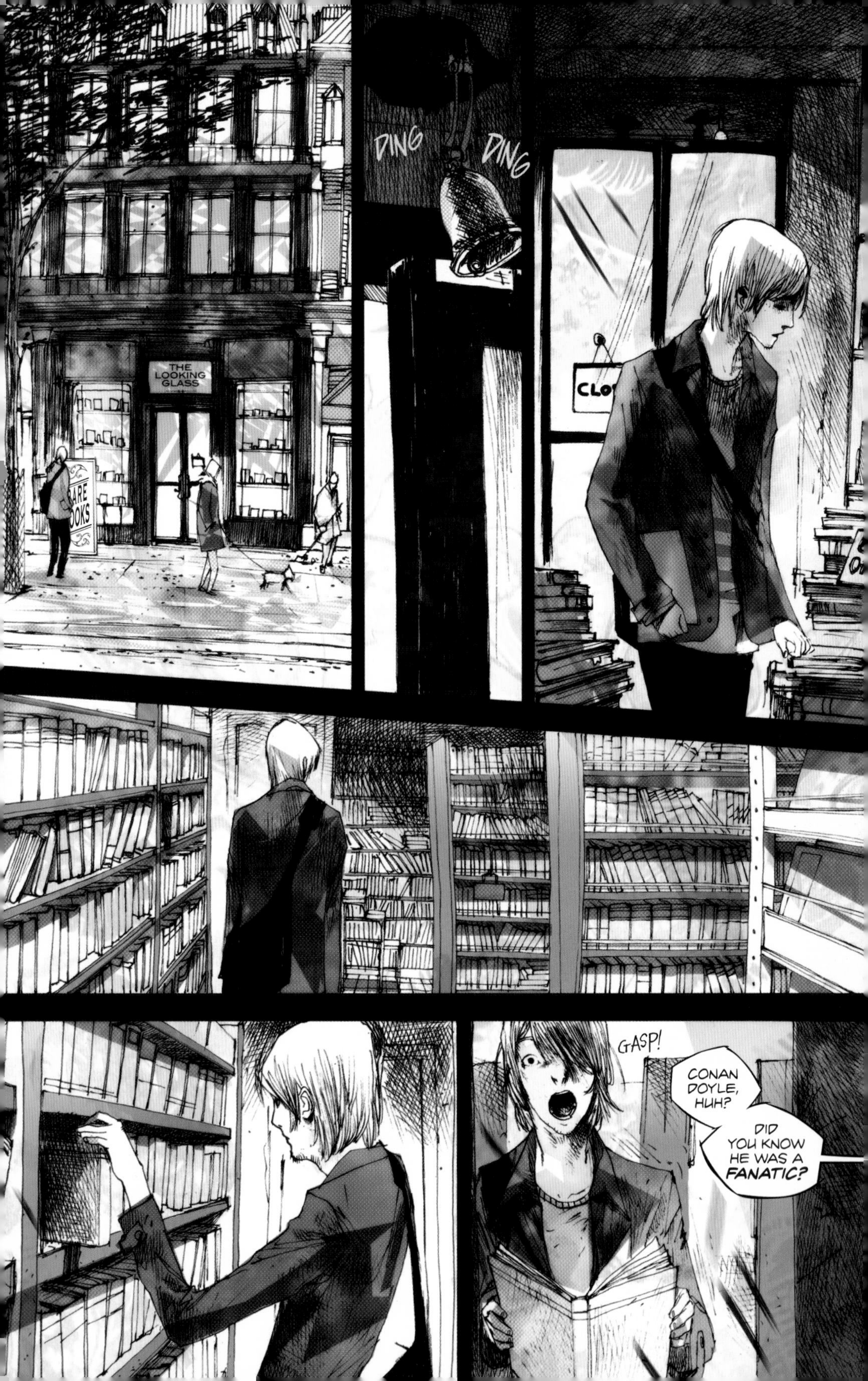
THE LOOKING GLASS
RARE BOOKS
DING
DING
GASP!
CONAN DOYLE, HUH?
DID YOU KNOW HE WAS A **FANATIC?**

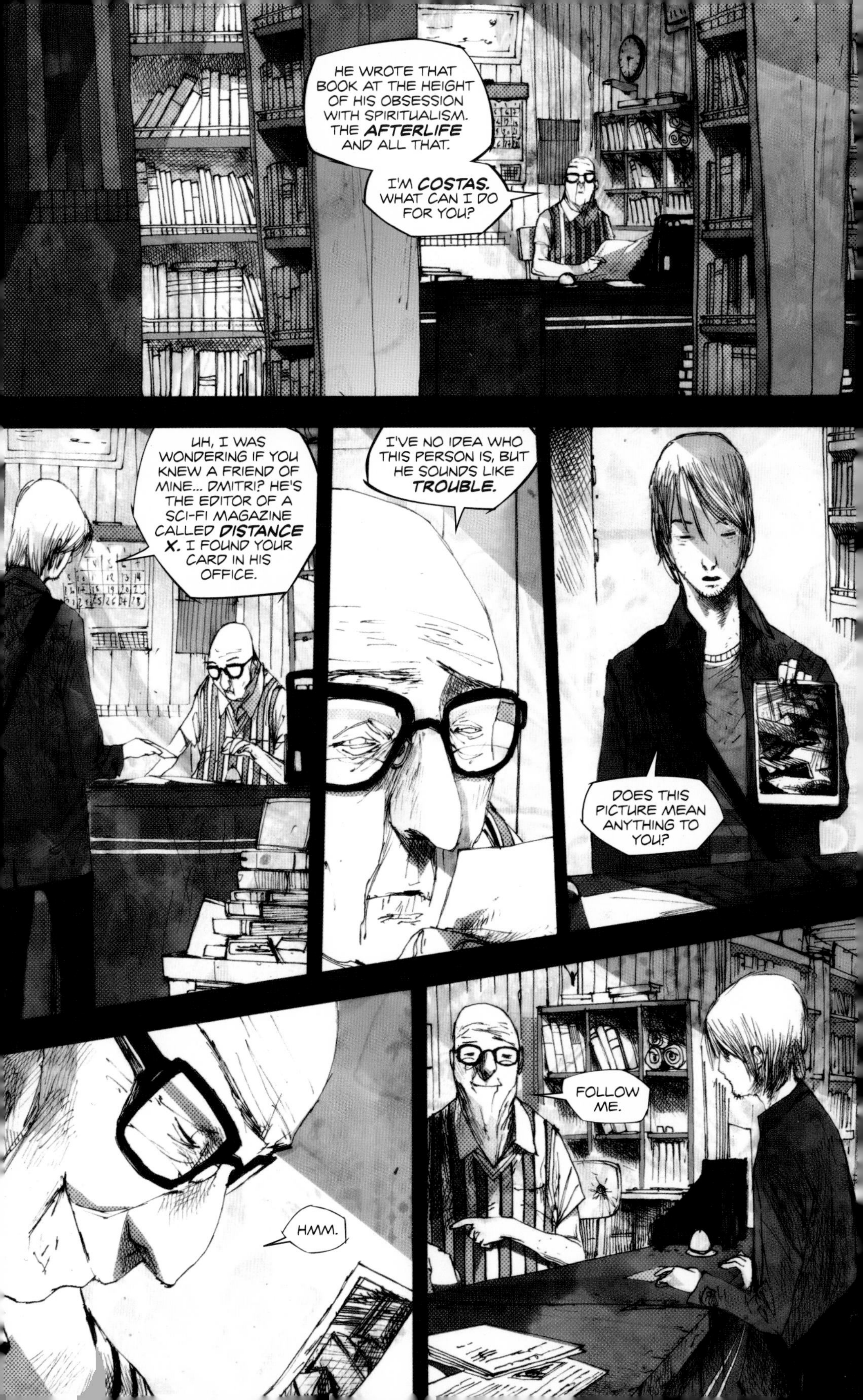
HE WROTE THAT BOOK AT THE HEIGHT OF HIS OBSESSION WITH SPIRITUALISM. THE AFTERLIFE AND ALL THAT.
I'M COSTAS. WHAT CAN I DO FOR YOU?
UH, I WAS WONDERING IF YOU KNEW A FRIEND OF MINE... DMITRI? HE'S THE EDITOR OF A SCI-FI MAGAZINE CALLED DISTANCE X. I FOUND YOUR CARD IN HIS OFFICE.
I'VE NO IDEA WHO THIS PERSON IS, BUT HE SOUNDS LIKE TROUBLE.
DOES THIS PICTURE MEAN ANYTHING TO YOU?
HMM.
FOLLOW ME.

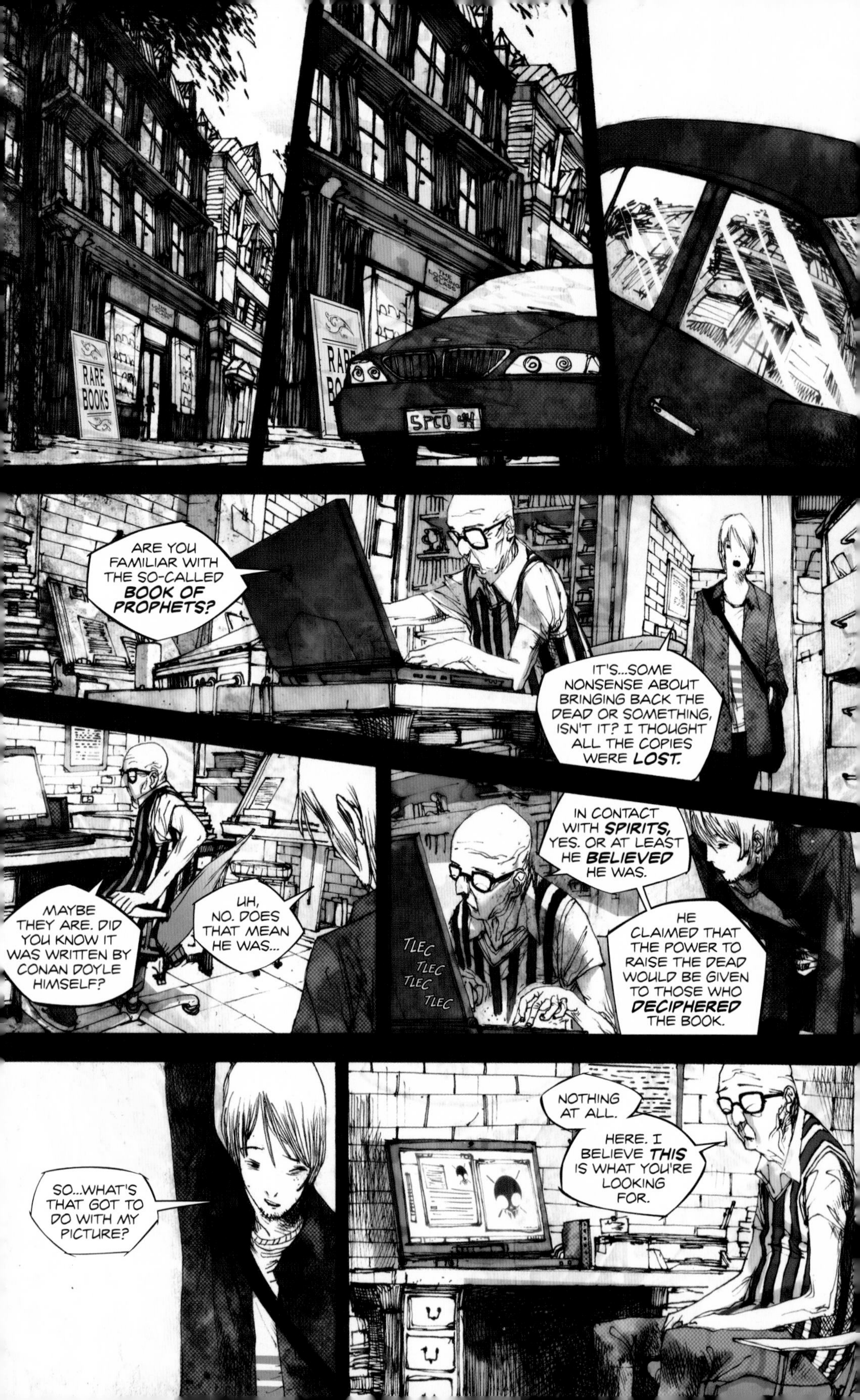
THE LOOKING GLASS
RARE BOOKS
SPCO 44
ARE YOU FAMILIAR WITH THE SO-CALLED BOOK OF PROPHETS?
IT'S...SOME NONSENSE ABOUT BRINGING BACK THE DEAD OR SOMETHING, ISN'T IT? I THOUGHT ALL THE COPIES WERE LOST.
MAYBE THEY ARE. DID YOU KNOW IT WAS WRITTEN BY CONAN DOYLE HIMSELF?
UH, NO. DOES THAT MEAN HE WAS...
IN CONTACT WITH SPIRITS, YES. OR AT LEAST HE BELIEVED HE WAS.
HE CLAIMED THAT THE POWER TO RAISE THE DEAD WOULD BE GIVEN TO THOSE WHO DECIPHERED THE BOOK.
TLEC TLEC TLEC TLEC
SO...WHAT'S THAT GOT TO DO WITH MY PICTURE?
NOTHING AT ALL.
HERE. I BELIEVE THIS IS WHAT YOU'RE LOOKING FOR.

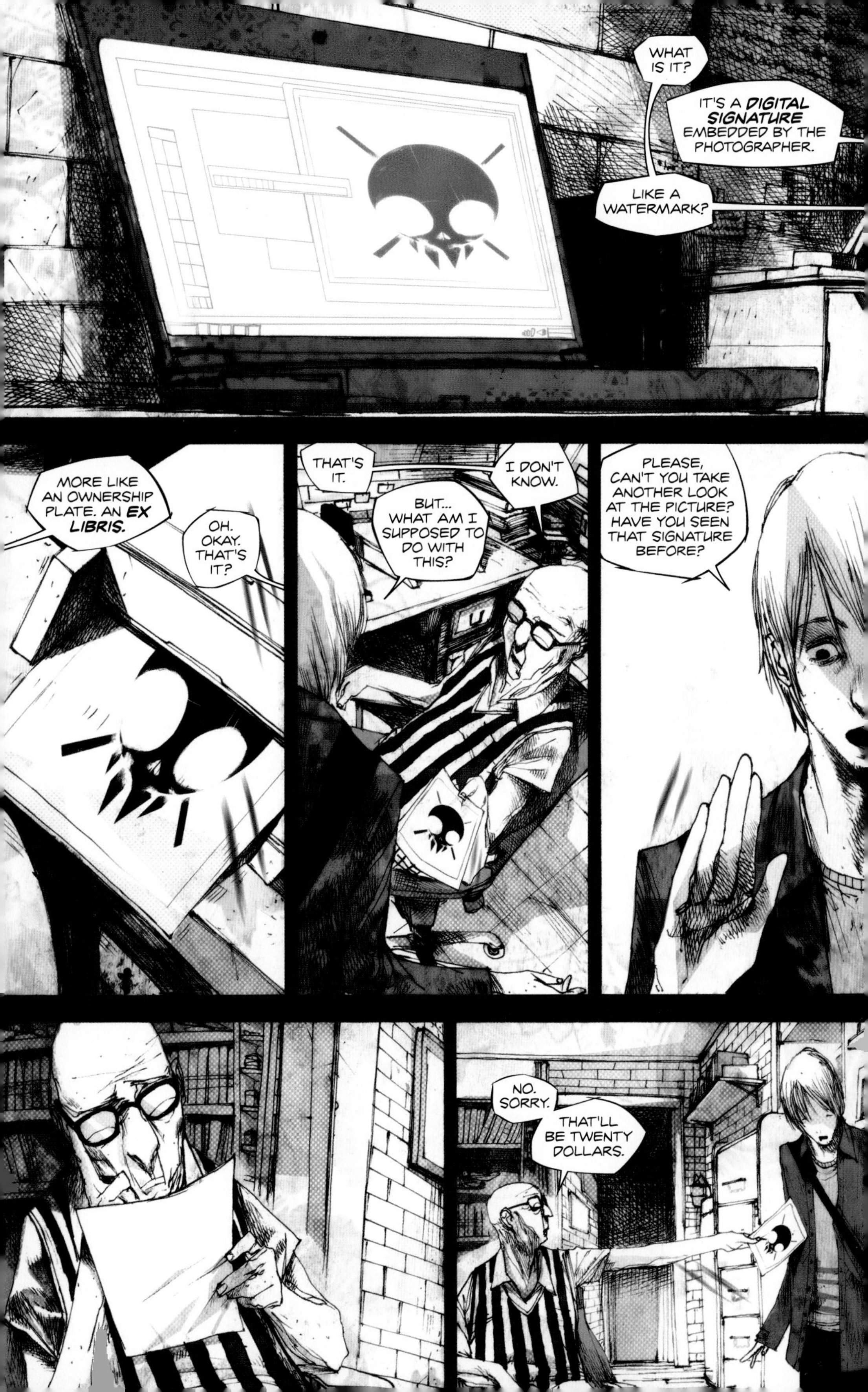
WHAT IS IT?
IT'S A **DIGITAL SIGNATURE** EMBEDDED BY THE PHOTOGRAPHER.
LIKE A WATERMARK?
MORE LIKE AN OWNERSHIP PLATE. AN ***EX LIBRIS.***
OH. OKAY. THAT'S IT?
THAT'S IT.
BUT... WHAT AM I SUPPOSED TO DO WITH THIS?
I DON'T KNOW.
PLEASE, CAN'T YOU TAKE ANOTHER LOOK AT THE PICTURE? HAVE YOU SEEN THAT SIGNATURE BEFORE?
NO. SORRY.
THAT'LL BE TWENTY DOLLARS.

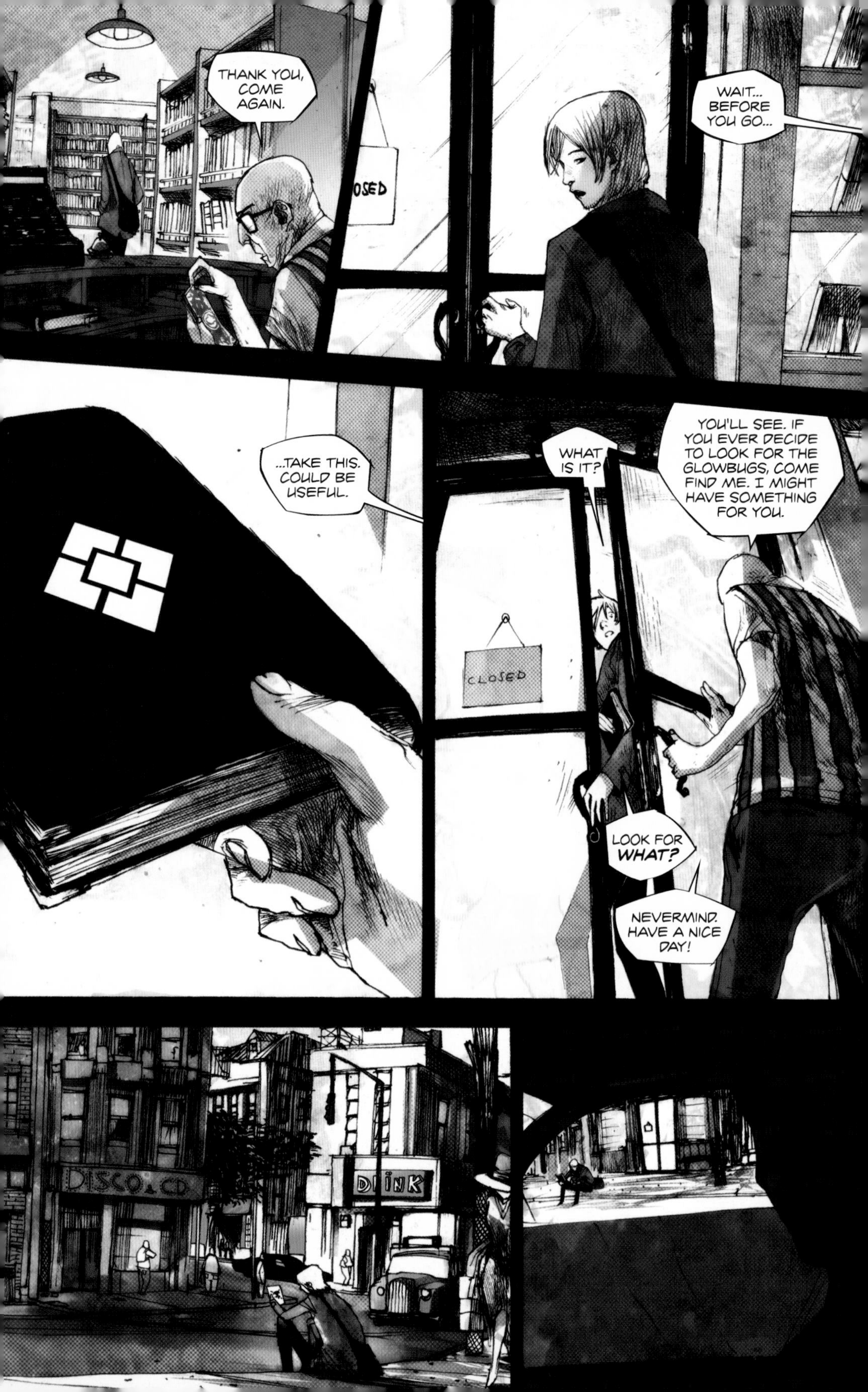
THANK YOU, COME AGAIN.
OSED
WAIT... BEFORE YOU GO...
...TAKE THIS. COULD BE USEFUL.
WHAT IS IT?
YOU'LL SEE. IF YOU EVER DECIDE TO LOOK FOR THE GLOWBUGS, COME FIND ME. I MIGHT HAVE SOMETHING FOR YOU.
CLOSED
LOOK FOR WHAT?
NEVERMIND. HAVE A NICE DAY!
DISCO CD
DRINK

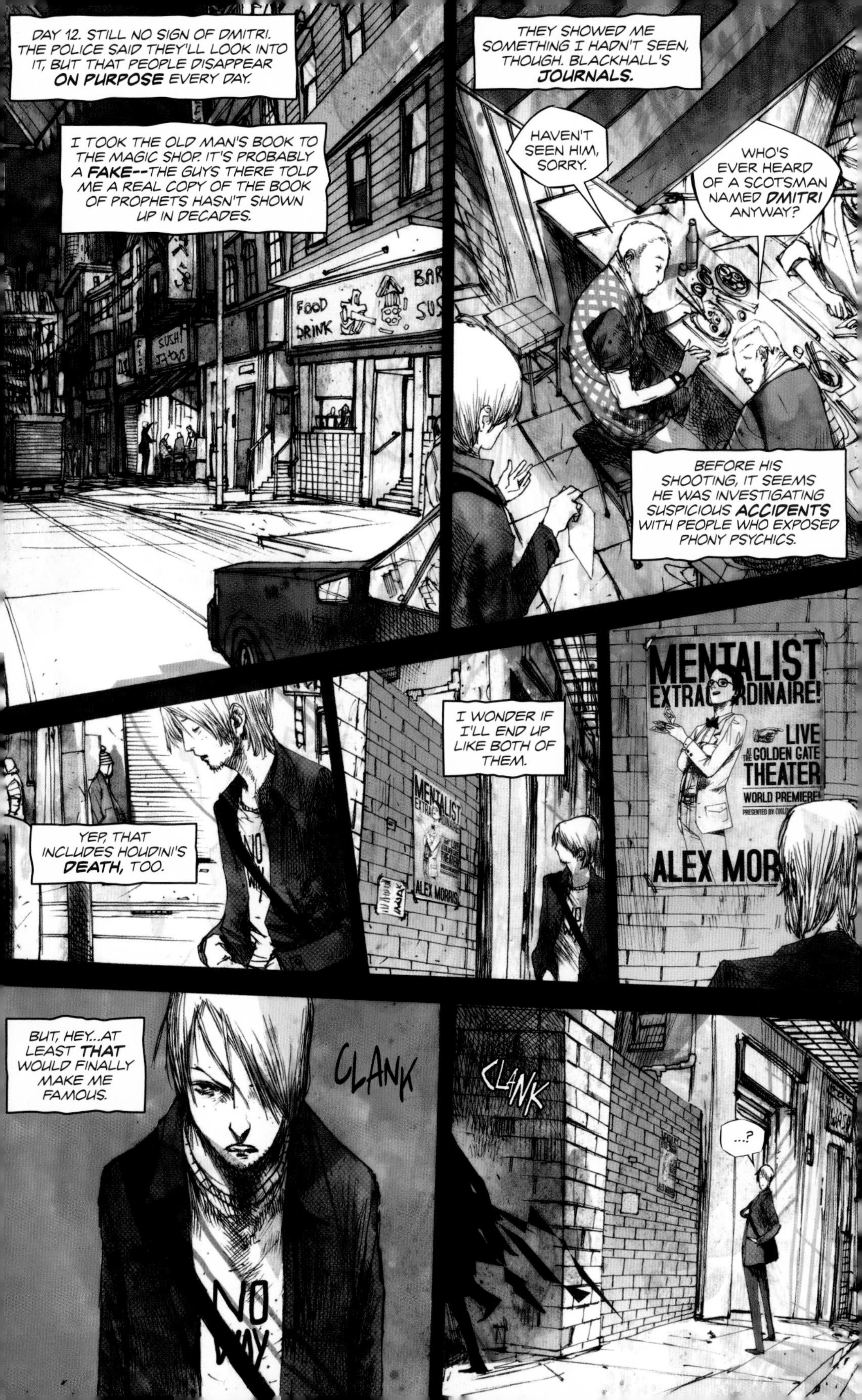
DAY 12. STILL NO SIGN OF DMITRI. THE POLICE SAID THEY'LL LOOK INTO IT, BUT THAT PEOPLE DISAPPEAR ON PURPOSE EVERY DAY.
I TOOK THE OLD MAN'S BOOK TO THE MAGIC SHOP. IT'S PROBABLY A FAKE--THE GUYS THERE TOLD ME A REAL COPY OF THE BOOK OF PROPHETS HASN'T SHOWN UP IN DECADES.
FOOD DRINK
SUSHI
THEY SHOWED ME SOMETHING I HADN'T SEEN, THOUGH. BLACKHALL'S JOURNALS.
HAVEN'T SEEN HIM, SORRY.
WHO'S EVER HEARD OF A SCOTSMAN NAMED DMITRI ANYWAY?
BEFORE HIS SHOOTING, IT SEEMS HE WAS INVESTIGATING SUSPICIOUS ACCIDENTS WITH PEOPLE WHO EXPOSED PHONY PSYCHICS.
YEP, THAT INCLUDES HOUDINI'S DEATH, TOO.
I WONDER IF I'LL END UP LIKE BOTH OF THEM.
MENTALIST EXTRAORDINAIRE!
LIVE AT THE GOLDEN GATE THEATER
WORLD PREMIERE!
ALEX MORRIS
ALEX MOR
BUT, HEY...AT LEAST THAT WOULD FINALLY MAKE ME FAMOUS.
CLANK
NO WAY
CLANK
...?

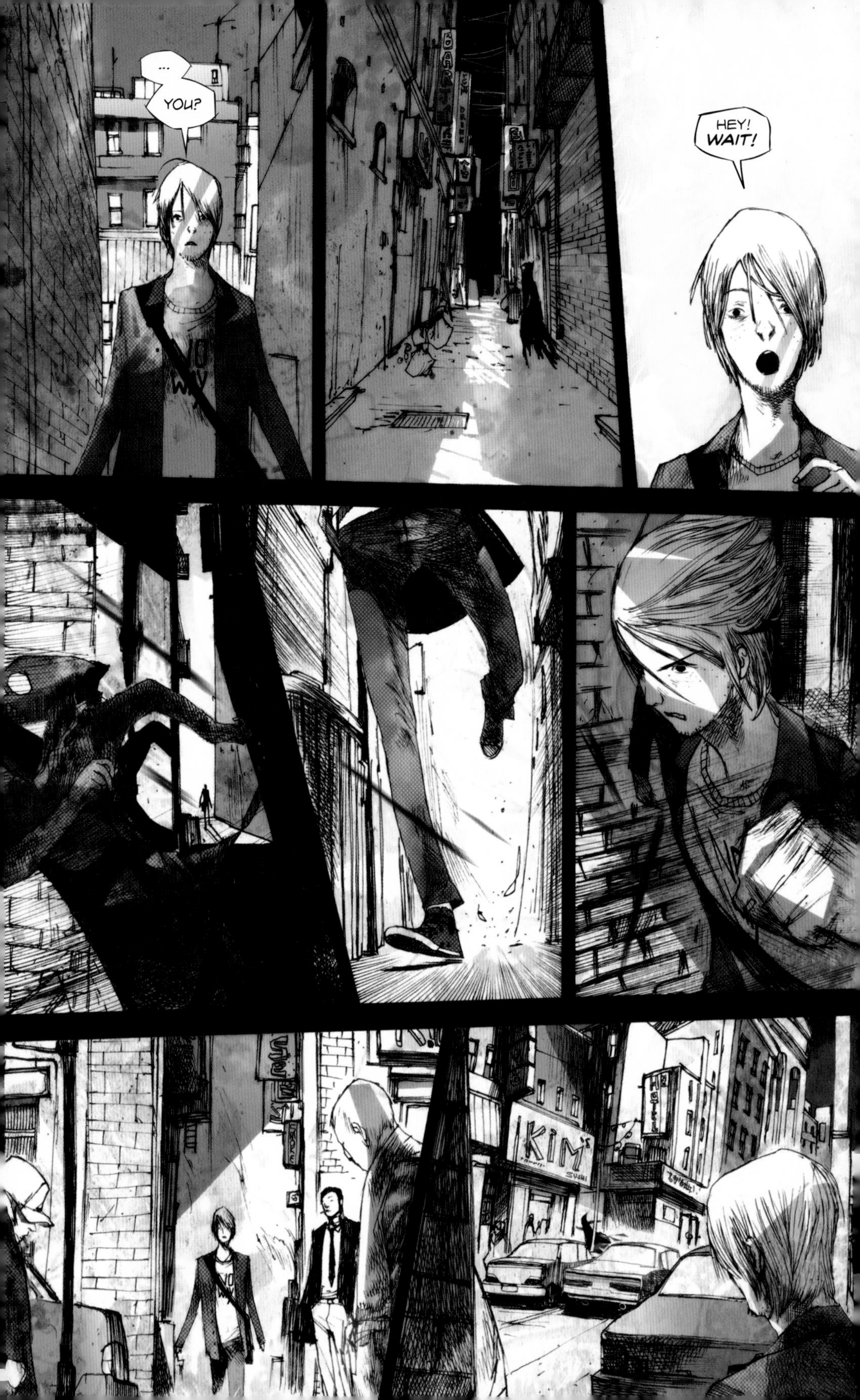
...
YOU?
HEY! WAIT!
KIM'S
SUSHI

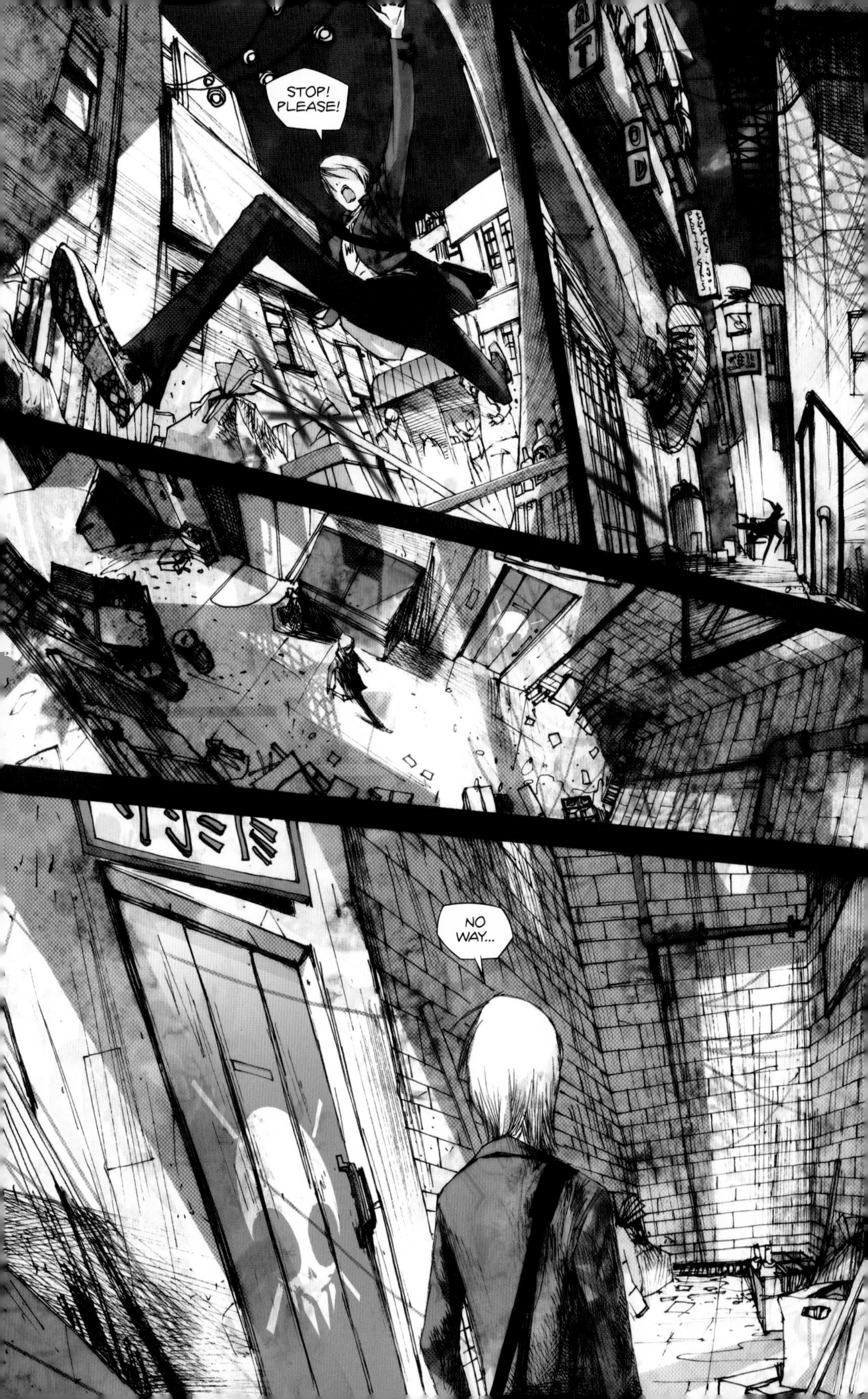
STOP! PLEASE!
NO WAY...

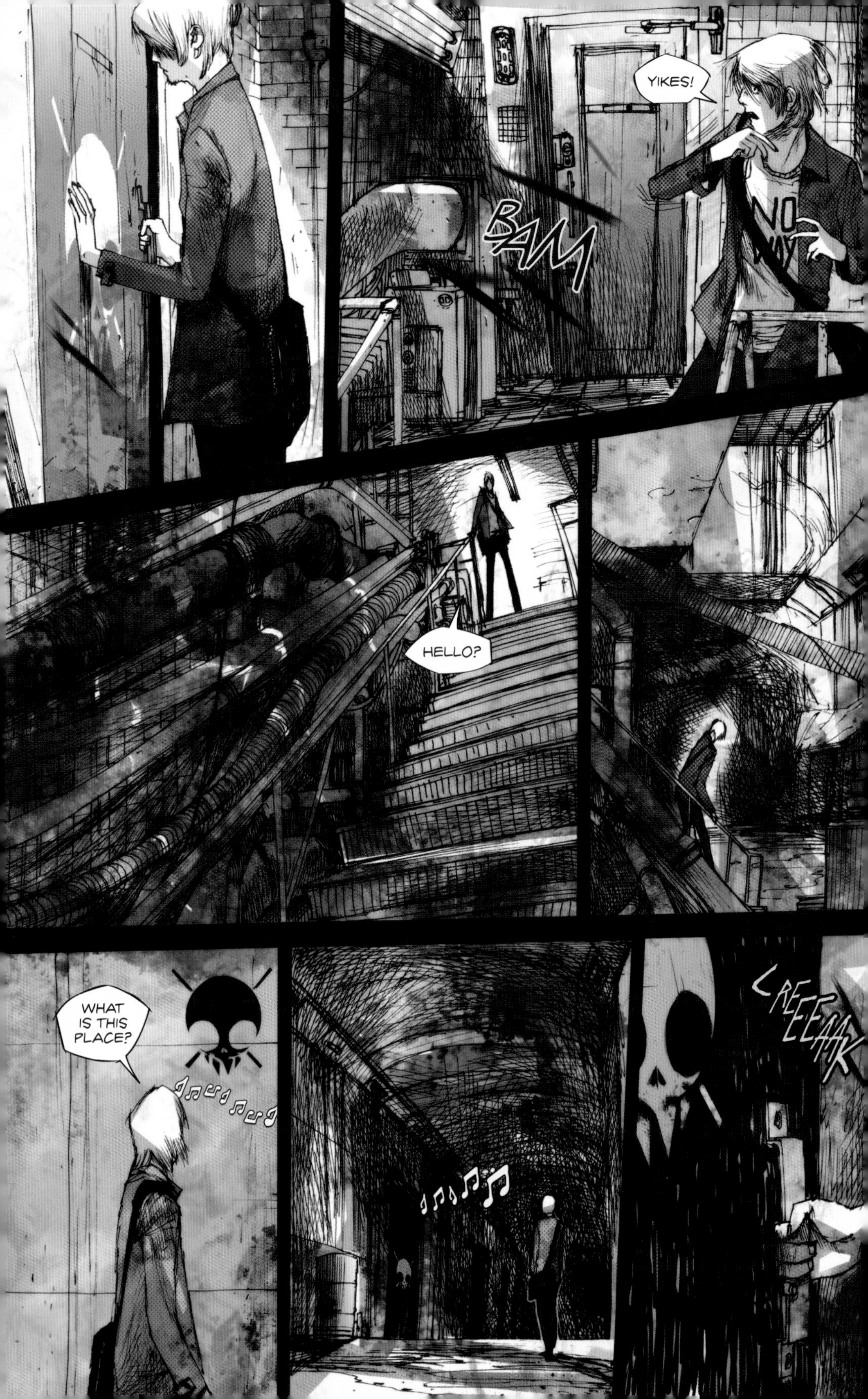
BAM
YIKES!
NO WAY
HELLO?
WHAT IS THIS PLACE?
CREEEAAK

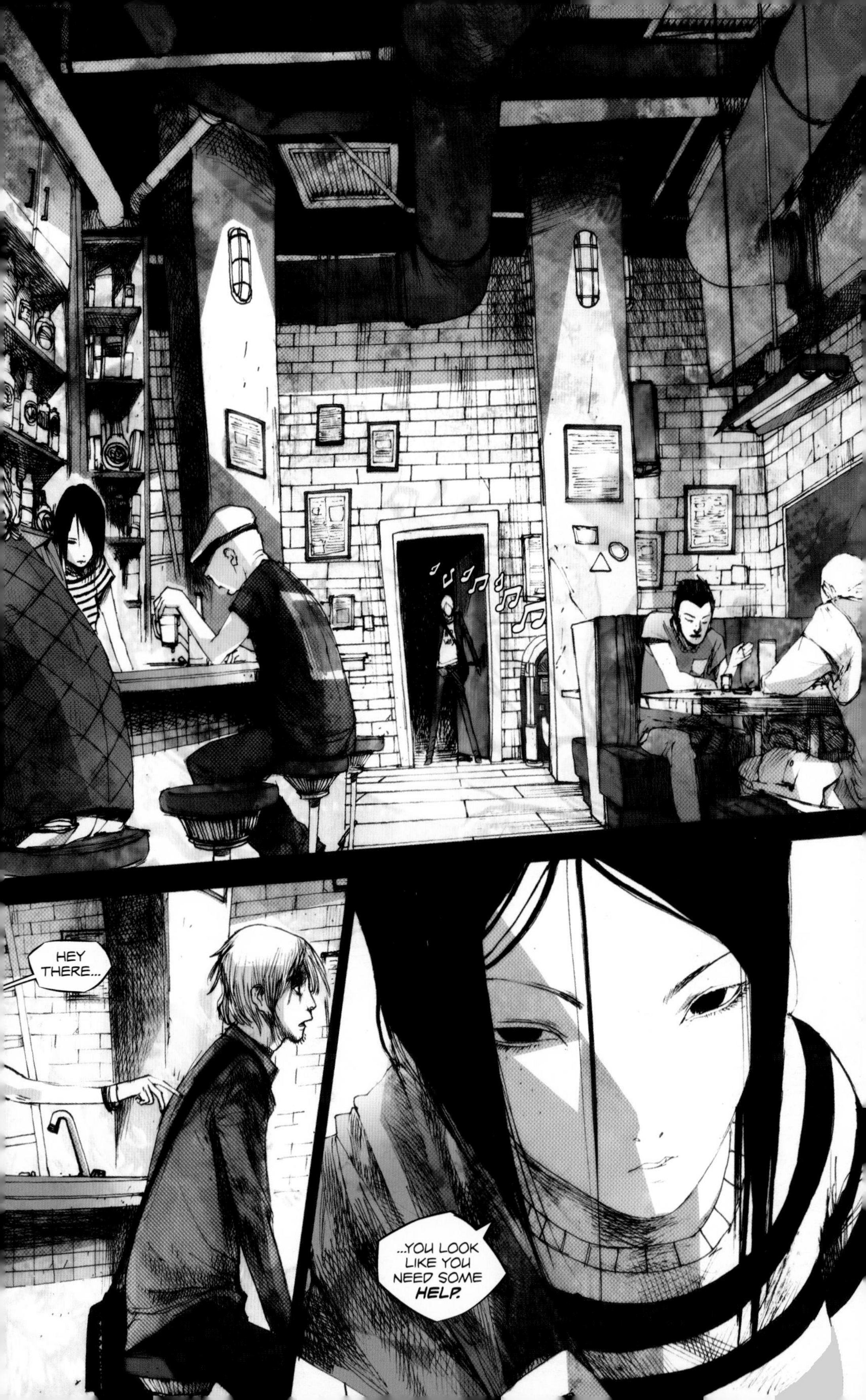
HEY THERE...
...YOU LOOK LIKE YOU NEED SOME HELP.

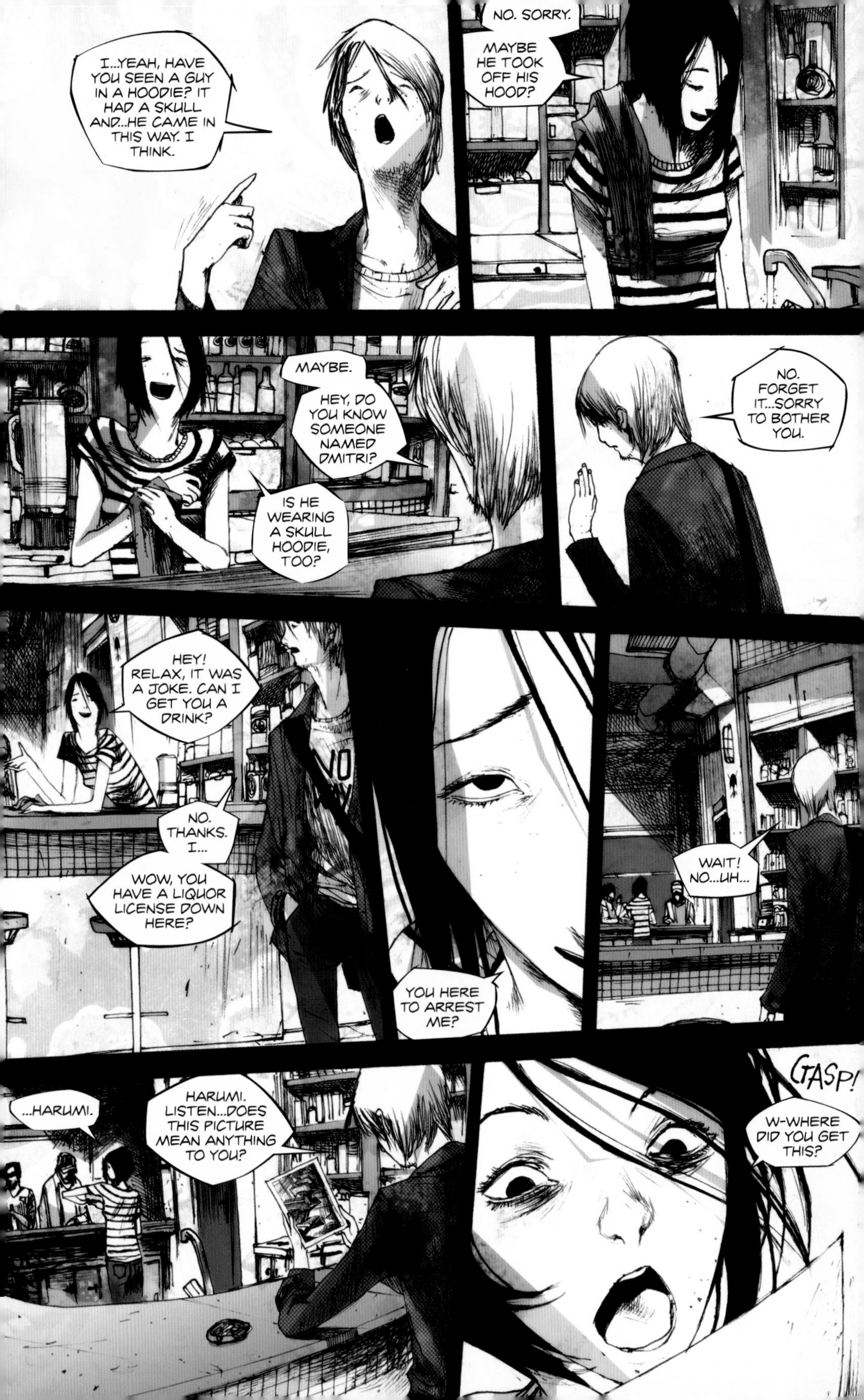
I...YEAH, HAVE YOU SEEN A GUY IN A HOODIE? IT HAD A SKULL AND...HE CAME IN THIS WAY. I THINK.
NO. SORRY.
MAYBE HE TOOK OFF HIS HOOD?
MAYBE.
HEY, DO YOU KNOW SOMEONE NAMED DMITRI?
IS HE WEARING A SKULL HOODIE, TOO?
NO. FORGET IT...SORRY TO BOTHER YOU.
HEY! RELAX, IT WAS A JOKE. CAN I GET YOU A DRINK?
NO. THANKS. I...
WOW, YOU HAVE A LIQUOR LICENSE DOWN HERE?
YOU HERE TO ARREST ME?
WAIT! NO...UH...
...HARUMI.
HARUMI. LISTEN...DOES THIS PICTURE MEAN ANYTHING TO YOU?
GASP!
W-WHERE DID YOU GET THIS?

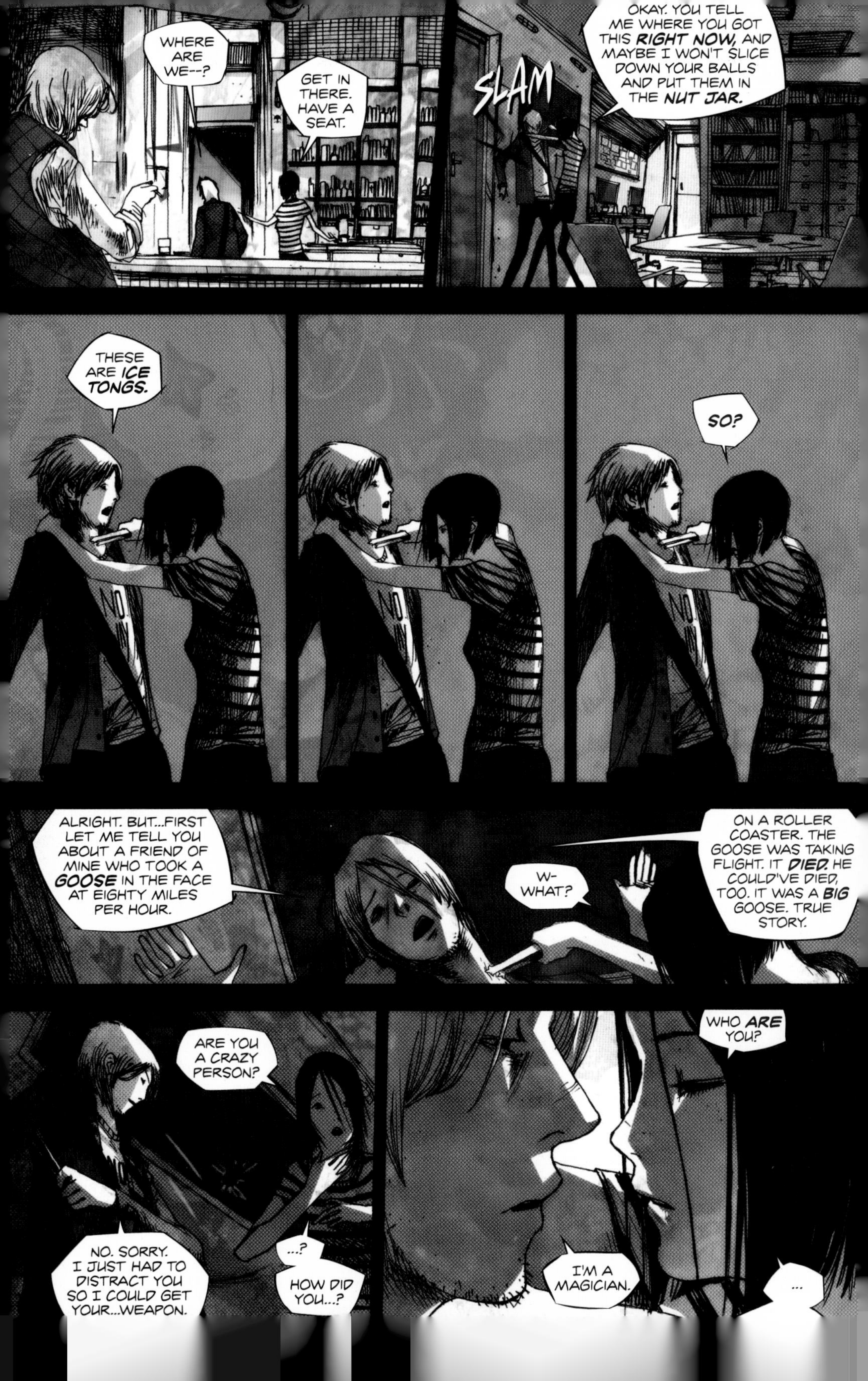
WHERE ARE WE--?
GET IN THERE. HAVE A SEAT.
SLAM
OKAY. YOU TELL ME WHERE YOU GOT THIS RIGHT NOW, AND MAYBE I WON'T SLICE DOWN YOUR BALLS AND PUT THEM IN THE NUT JAR.
THESE ARE ICE TONGS.
SO?
ALRIGHT. BUT...FIRST LET ME TELL YOU ABOUT A FRIEND OF MINE WHO TOOK A GOOSE IN THE FACE AT EIGHTY MILES PER HOUR.
W- WHAT?
ON A ROLLER COASTER. THE GOOSE WAS TAKING FLIGHT. IT DIED. HE COULD'VE DIED, TOO. IT WAS A BIG GOOSE. TRUE STORY.
ARE YOU A CRAZY PERSON?
NO. SORRY. I JUST HAD TO DISTRACT YOU SO I COULD GET YOUR...WEAPON.
...?
HOW DID YOU...?
WHO ARE YOU?
I'M A MAGICIAN.
...

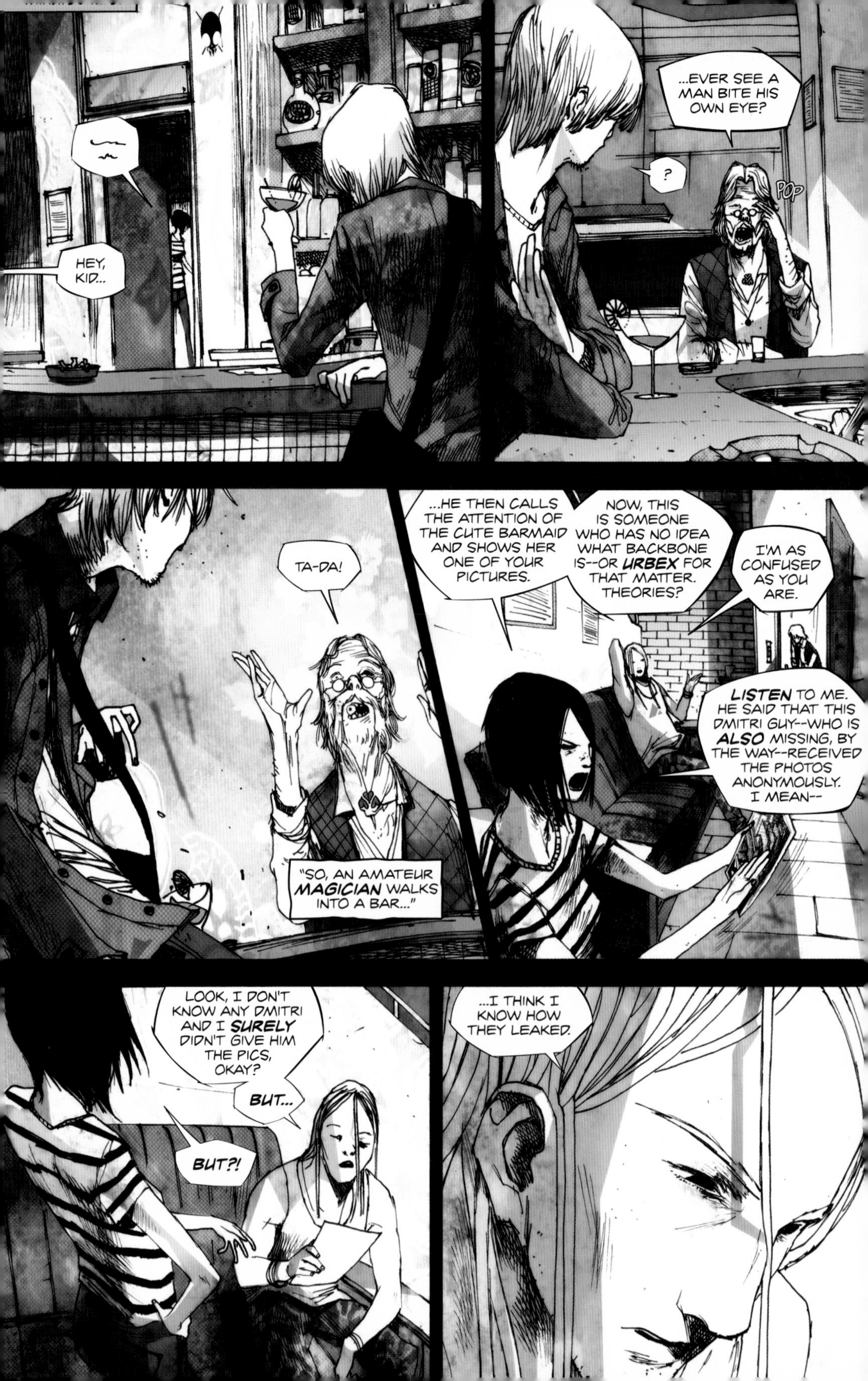

HEY, KID...
...EVER SEE A MAN BITE HIS OWN EYE?
?
POP
TA-DA!
"SO, AN AMATEUR MAGICIAN WALKS INTO A BAR..."
...HE THEN CALLS THE ATTENTION OF THE CUTE BARMAID AND SHOWS HER ONE OF YOUR PICTURES.
NOW, THIS IS SOMEONE WHO HAS NO IDEA WHAT BACKBONE IS--OR URBEX FOR THAT MATTER. THEORIES?
I'M AS CONFUSED AS YOU ARE.
LISTEN TO ME. HE SAID THAT THIS DMITRI GUY--WHO IS ALSO MISSING, BY THE WAY--RECEIVED THE PHOTOS ANONYMOUSLY. I MEAN--
LOOK, I DON'T KNOW ANY DMITRI AND I SURELY DIDN'T GIVE HIM THE PICS, OKAY?
BUT...
BUT?!
...I THINK I KNOW HOW THEY LEAKED.

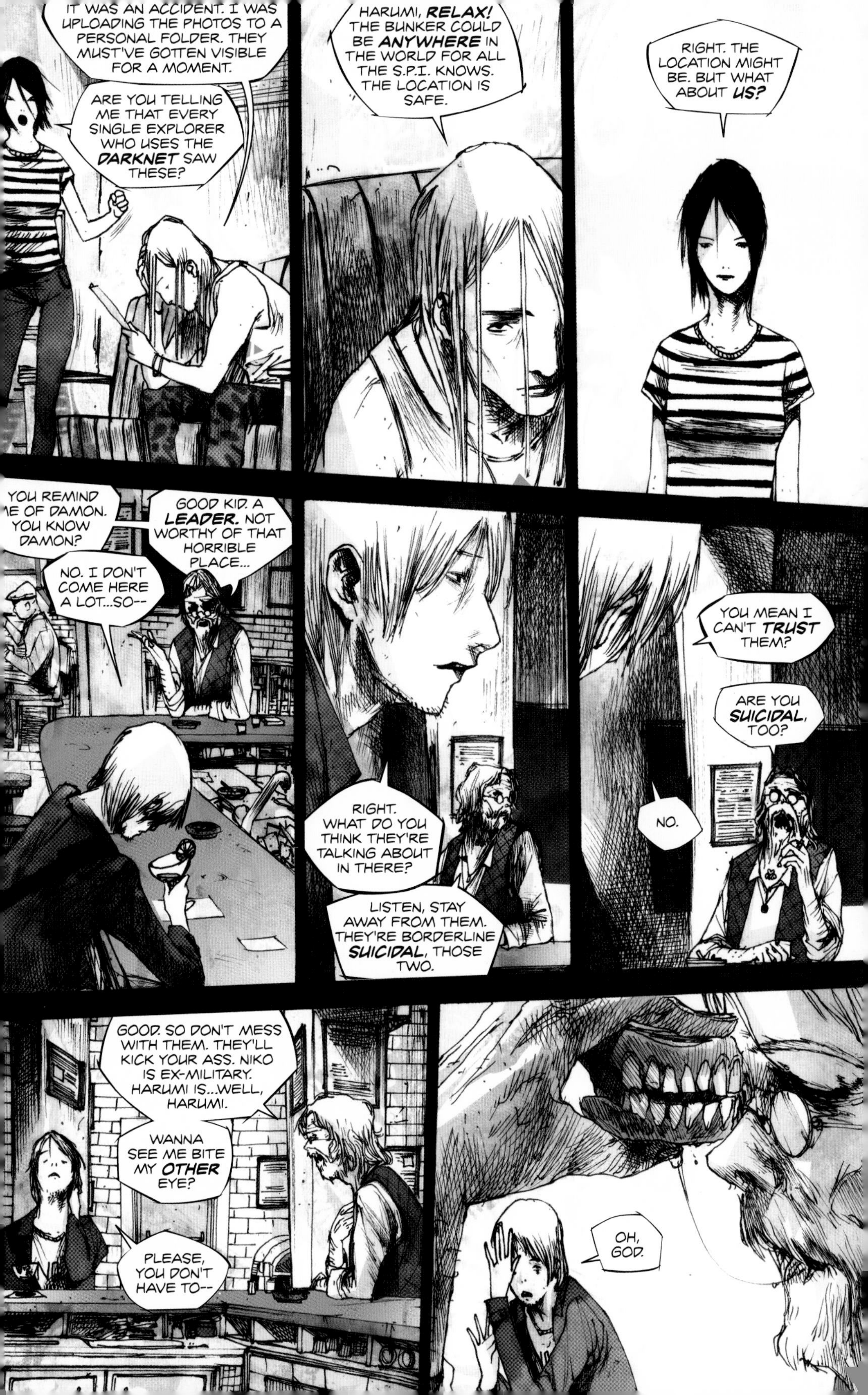
IT WAS AN ACCIDENT. I WAS UPLOADING THE PHOTOS TO A PERSONAL FOLDER. THEY MUST'VE GOTTEN VISIBLE FOR A MOMENT.
ARE YOU TELLING ME THAT EVERY SINGLE EXPLORER WHO USES THE DARKNET SAW THESE?
HARUMI, RELAX! THE BUNKER COULD BE ANYWHERE IN THE WORLD FOR ALL THE S.P.I. KNOWS. THE LOCATION IS SAFE.
RIGHT. THE LOCATION MIGHT BE. BUT WHAT ABOUT US?
YOU REMIND ME OF DAMON. YOU KNOW DAMON?
GOOD KID. A LEADER. NOT WORTHY OF THAT HORRIBLE PLACE...
NO. I DON'T COME HERE A LOT...SO--
RIGHT. WHAT DO YOU THINK THEY'RE TALKING ABOUT IN THERE?
LISTEN, STAY AWAY FROM THEM. THEY'RE BORDERLINE SUICIDAL, THOSE TWO.
YOU MEAN I CAN'T TRUST THEM?
ARE YOU SUICIDAL, TOO?
NO.
GOOD. SO DON'T MESS WITH THEM. THEY'LL KICK YOUR ASS. NIKO IS EX-MILITARY. HARUMI IS...WELL, HARUMI.
WANNA SEE ME BITE MY OTHER EYE?
PLEASE, YOU DON'T HAVE TO--
OH, GOD.

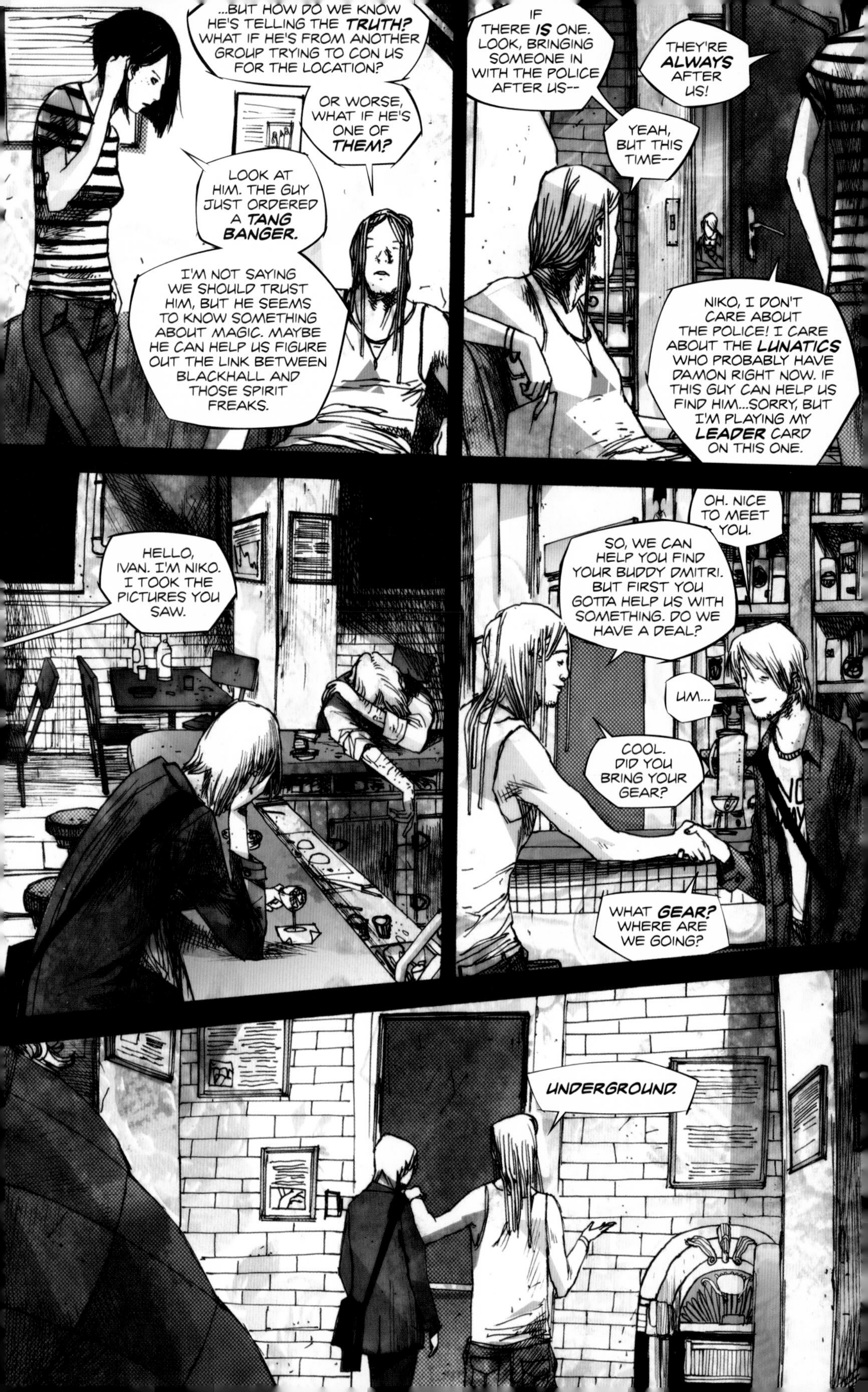
...BUT HOW DO WE KNOW HE'S TELLING THE TRUTH? WHAT IF HE'S FROM ANOTHER GROUP TRYING TO CON US FOR THE LOCATION?
OR WORSE, WHAT IF HE'S ONE OF THEM?
LOOK AT HIM. THE GUY JUST ORDERED A TANG BANGER.
I'M NOT SAYING WE SHOULD TRUST HIM, BUT HE SEEMS TO KNOW SOMETHING ABOUT MAGIC. MAYBE HE CAN HELP US FIGURE OUT THE LINK BETWEEN BLACKHALL AND THOSE SPIRIT FREAKS.
IF THERE IS ONE. LOOK, BRINGING SOMEONE IN WITH THE POLICE AFTER US--
THEY'RE ALWAYS AFTER US!
YEAH, BUT THIS TIME--
NIKO, I DON'T CARE ABOUT THE POLICE! I CARE ABOUT THE LUNATICS WHO PROBABLY HAVE DAMON RIGHT NOW. IF THIS GUY CAN HELP US FIND HIM...SORRY, BUT I'M PLAYING MY LEADER CARD ON THIS ONE.
HELLO, IVAN. I'M NIKO. I TOOK THE PICTURES YOU SAW.
OH. NICE TO MEET YOU.
SO, WE CAN HELP YOU FIND YOUR BUDDY DMITRI. BUT FIRST YOU GOTTA HELP US WITH SOMETHING. DO WE HAVE A DEAL?
UM...
COOL. DID YOU BRING YOUR GEAR?
WHAT GEAR? WHERE ARE WE GOING?
UNDERGROUND.

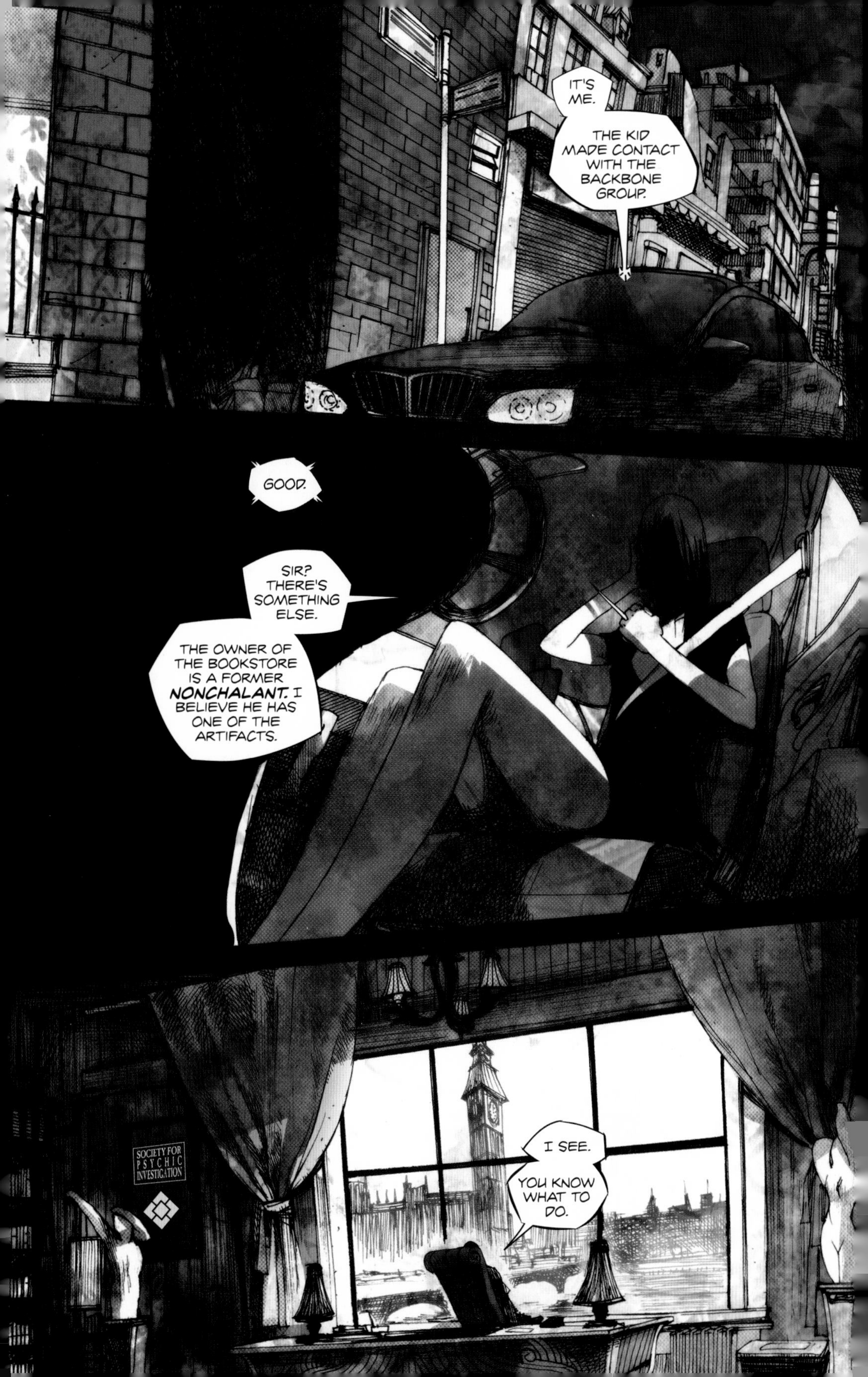

IT'S ME.
THE KID MADE CONTACT WITH THE BACKBONE GROUP.
GOOD.
SIR? THERE'S SOMETHING ELSE.
THE OWNER OF THE BOOKSTORE IS A FORMER NONCHALANT. I BELIEVE HE HAS ONE OF THE ARTIFACTS.
SOCIETY FOR PSYCHIC INVESTIGATION
I SEE.
YOU KNOW WHAT TO DO.

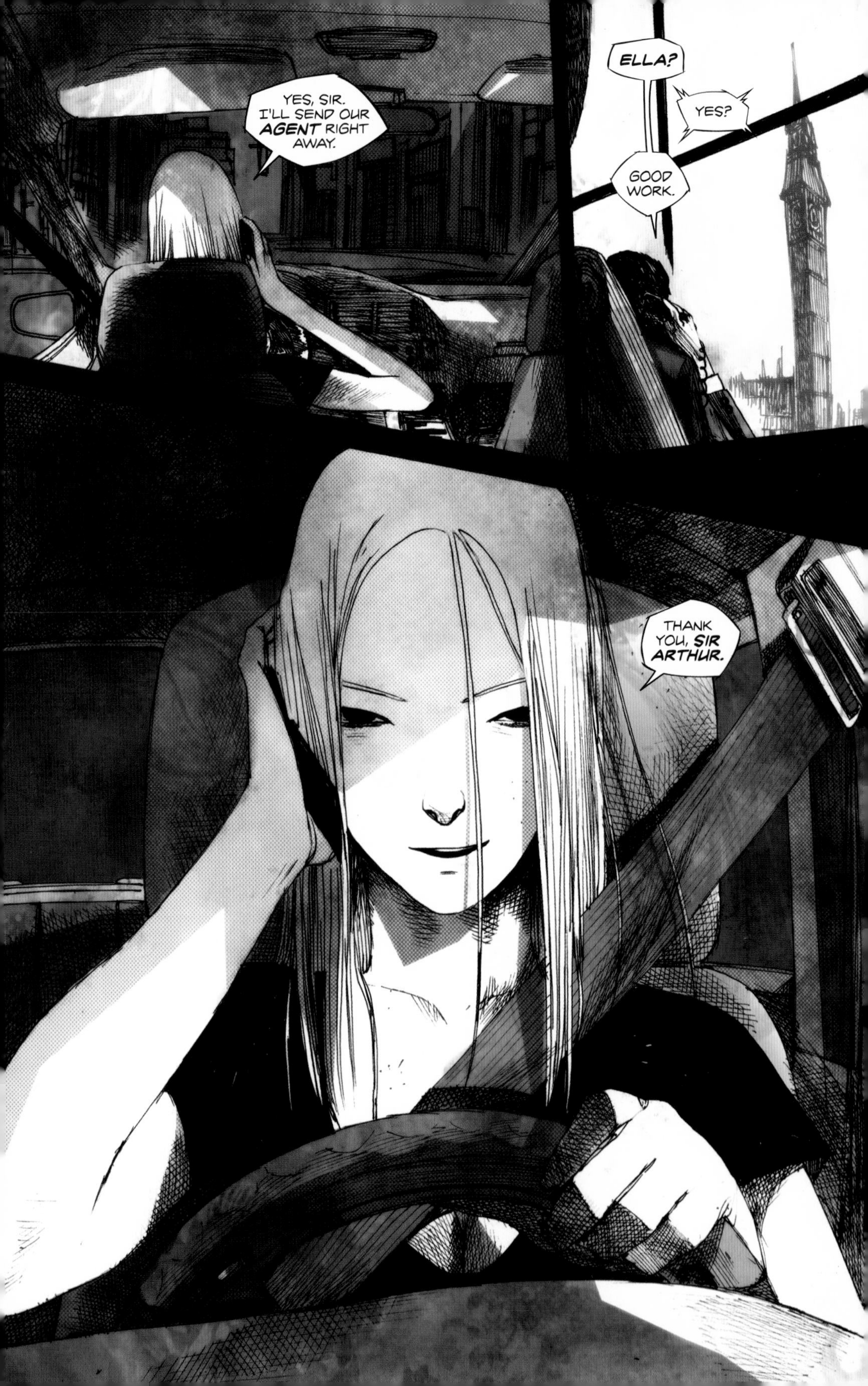
YES, SIR. I'LL SEND OUR AGENT RIGHT AWAY.
ELLA?
YES?
GOOD WORK.
THANK YOU, SIR ARTHUR.

ISSUE TWO COVER

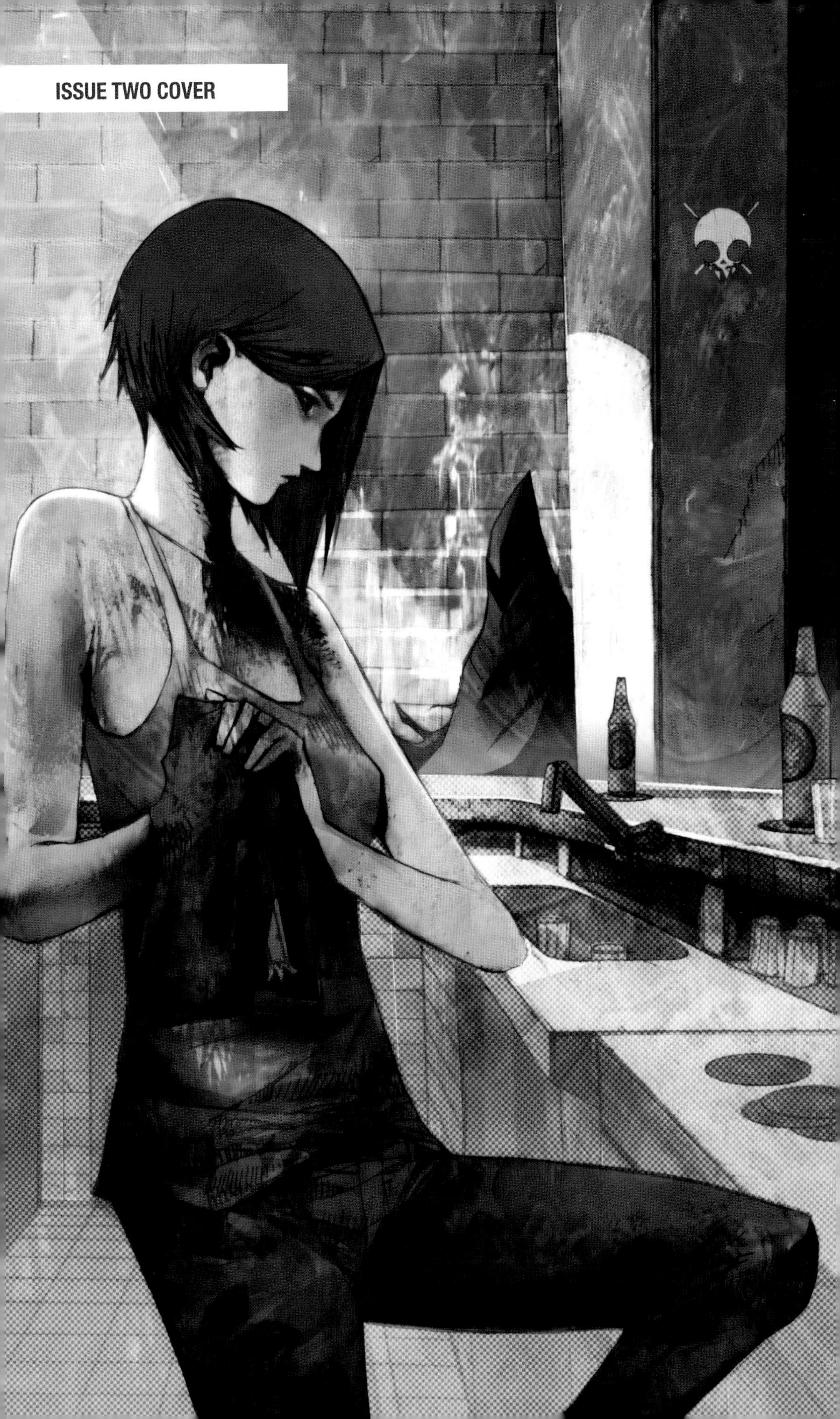

CHAPTER 3: SECOND SIGHT

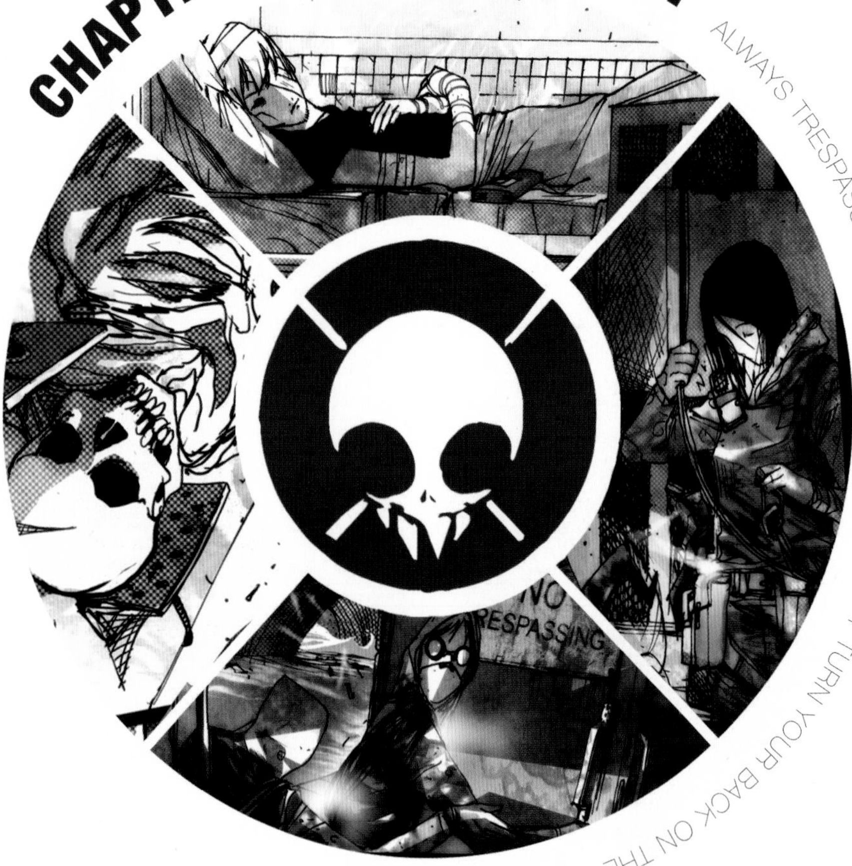
NO
RESPASSING

ALWAYS TRESPASS. **PIVP CE VY TYVKDX**. DON'T TURN YOUR BACK ON THE MYSTERY.

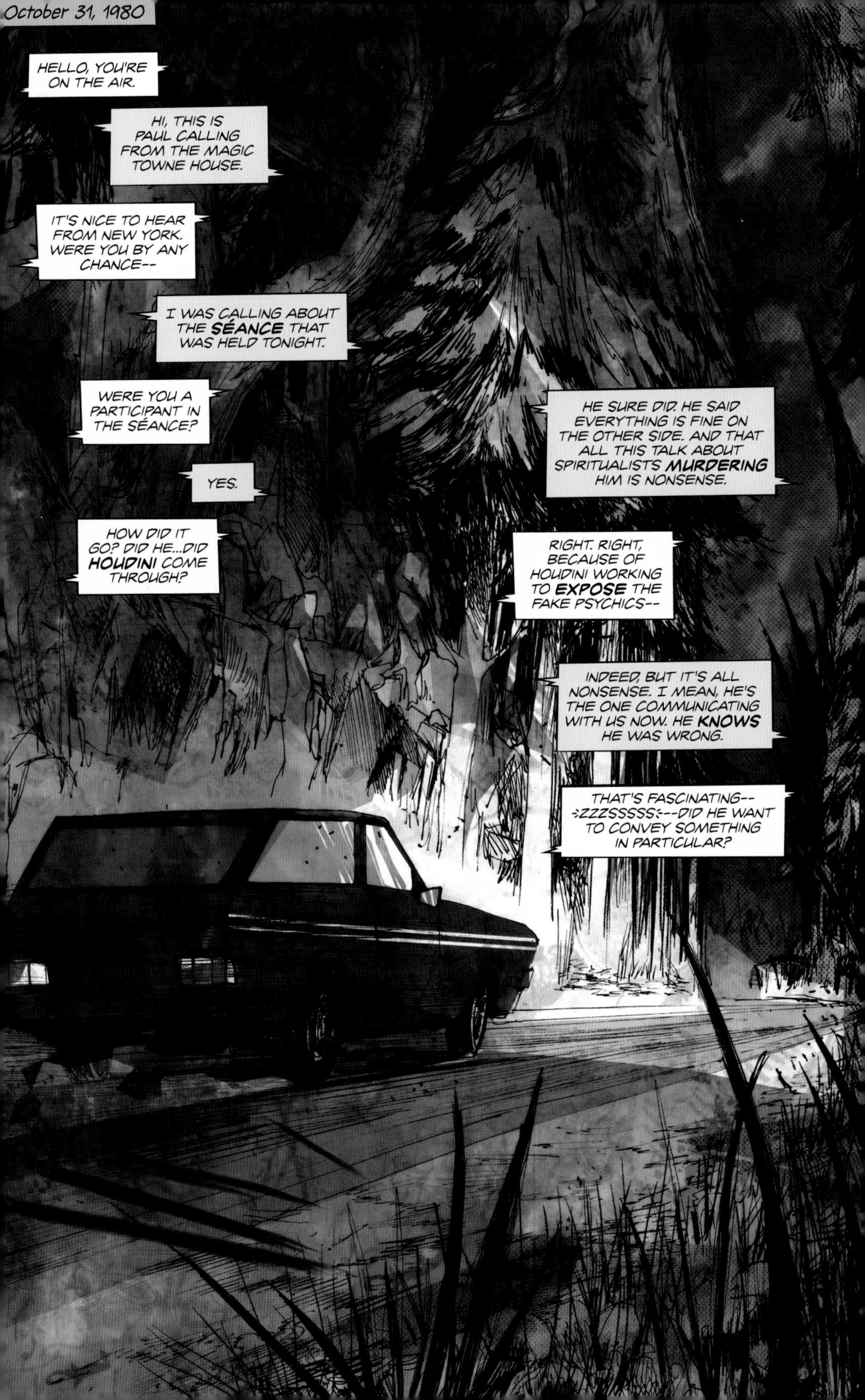
October 31, 1980
HELLO, YOU'RE ON THE AIR.
HI, THIS IS PAUL CALLING FROM THE MAGIC TOWNE HOUSE.
IT'S NICE TO HEAR FROM NEW YORK. WERE YOU BY ANY CHANCE--
I WAS CALLING ABOUT THE **SÉANCE** THAT WAS HELD TONIGHT.
WERE YOU A PARTICIPANT IN THE SÉANCE?
YES.
HOW DID IT GO? DID HE...DID **HOUDINI** COME THROUGH?
HE SURE DID. HE SAID EVERYTHING IS FINE ON THE OTHER SIDE. AND THAT ALL THIS TALK ABOUT SPIRITUALISTS **MURDERING** HIM IS NONSENSE.
RIGHT. RIGHT, BECAUSE OF HOUDINI WORKING TO **EXPOSE** THE FAKE PSYCHICS--
INDEED, BUT IT'S ALL NONSENSE. I MEAN, HE'S THE ONE COMMUNICATING WITH US NOW. HE **KNOWS** HE WAS WRONG.
THAT'S FASCINATING-- ⇒ZZZSSSSS⇐--DID HE WANT TO CONVEY SOMETHING IN PARTICULAR?

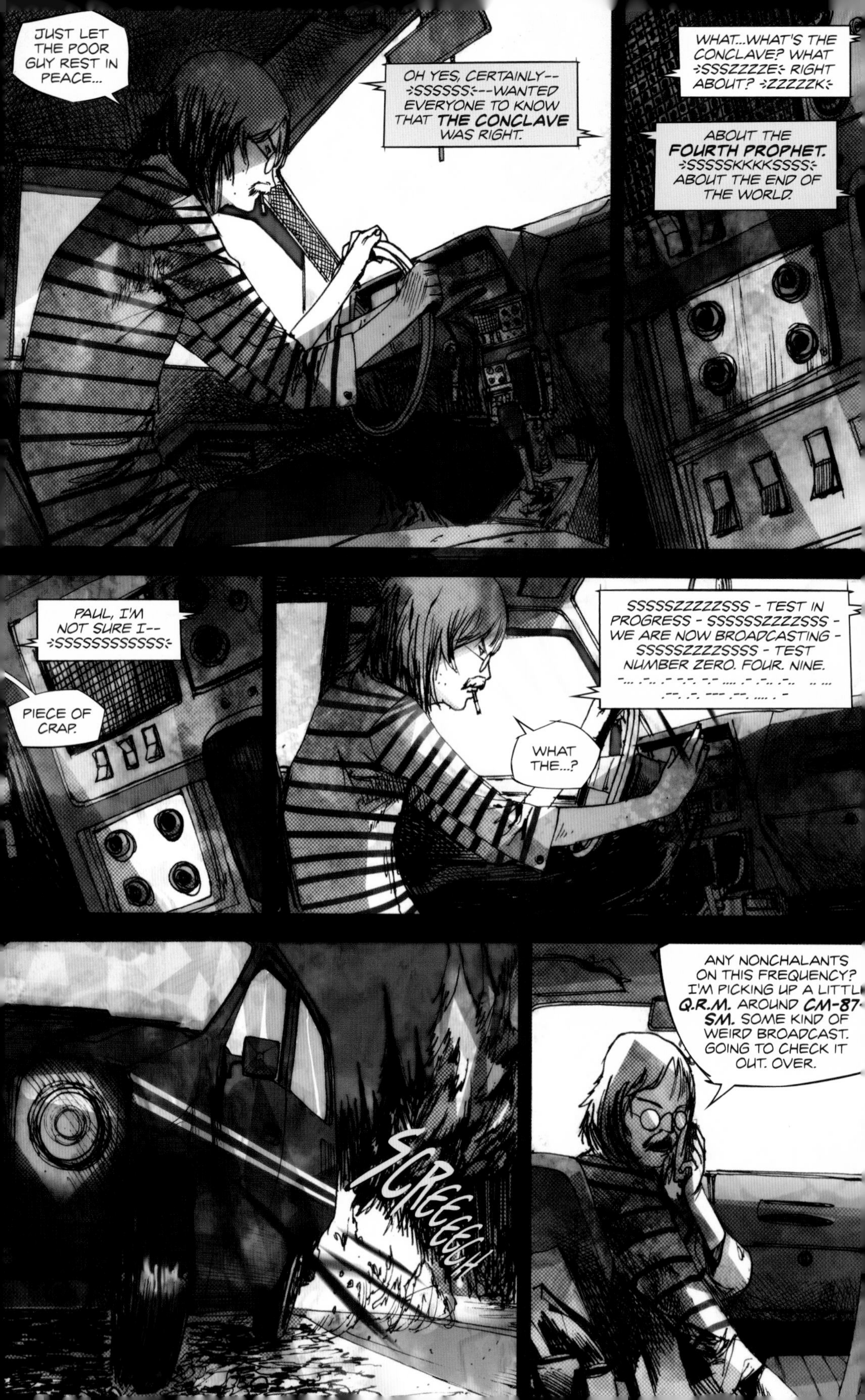

JUST LET THE POOR GUY REST IN PEACE...
OH YES, CERTAINLY-- -SSSSSS- --WANTED EVERYONE TO KNOW THAT THE CONCLAVE WAS RIGHT.
WHAT...WHAT'S THE CONCLAVE? WHAT -SSSZZZZE- RIGHT ABOUT? -ZZZZZK-
ABOUT THE FOURTH PROPHET. -SSSSSKKKKSSSS- ABOUT THE END OF THE WORLD.
PAUL, I'M NOT SURE I-- -SSSSSSSSSSSSS-
PIECE OF CRAP.
SSSSSZZZZZSSS - TEST IN PROGRESS - SSSSSSZZZZSSS - WE ARE NOW BROADCASTING - SSSSSZZZZSSSS - TEST NUMBER ZERO. FOUR. NINE.
-... .-.. .- -.-. -.- .... .- .-.. .-.. .. ...
.--. .-. --- .--. .... . -
WHAT THE...?
SCREEEECH
ANY NONCHALANTS ON THIS FREQUENCY? I'M PICKING UP A LITTL Q.R.M. AROUND CM-87-SM. SOME KIND OF WEIRD BROADCAST. GOING TO CHECK IT OUT. OVER.

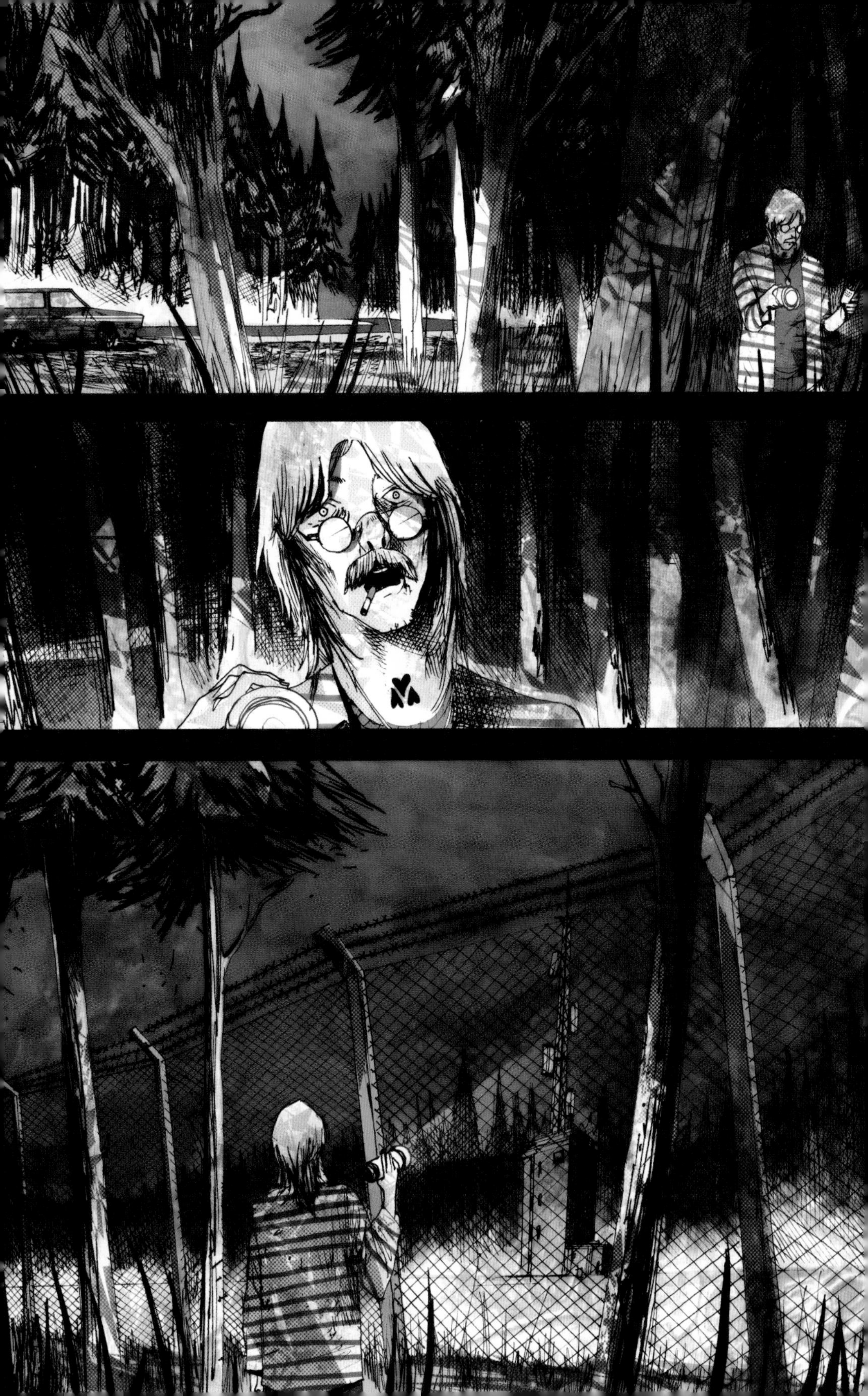

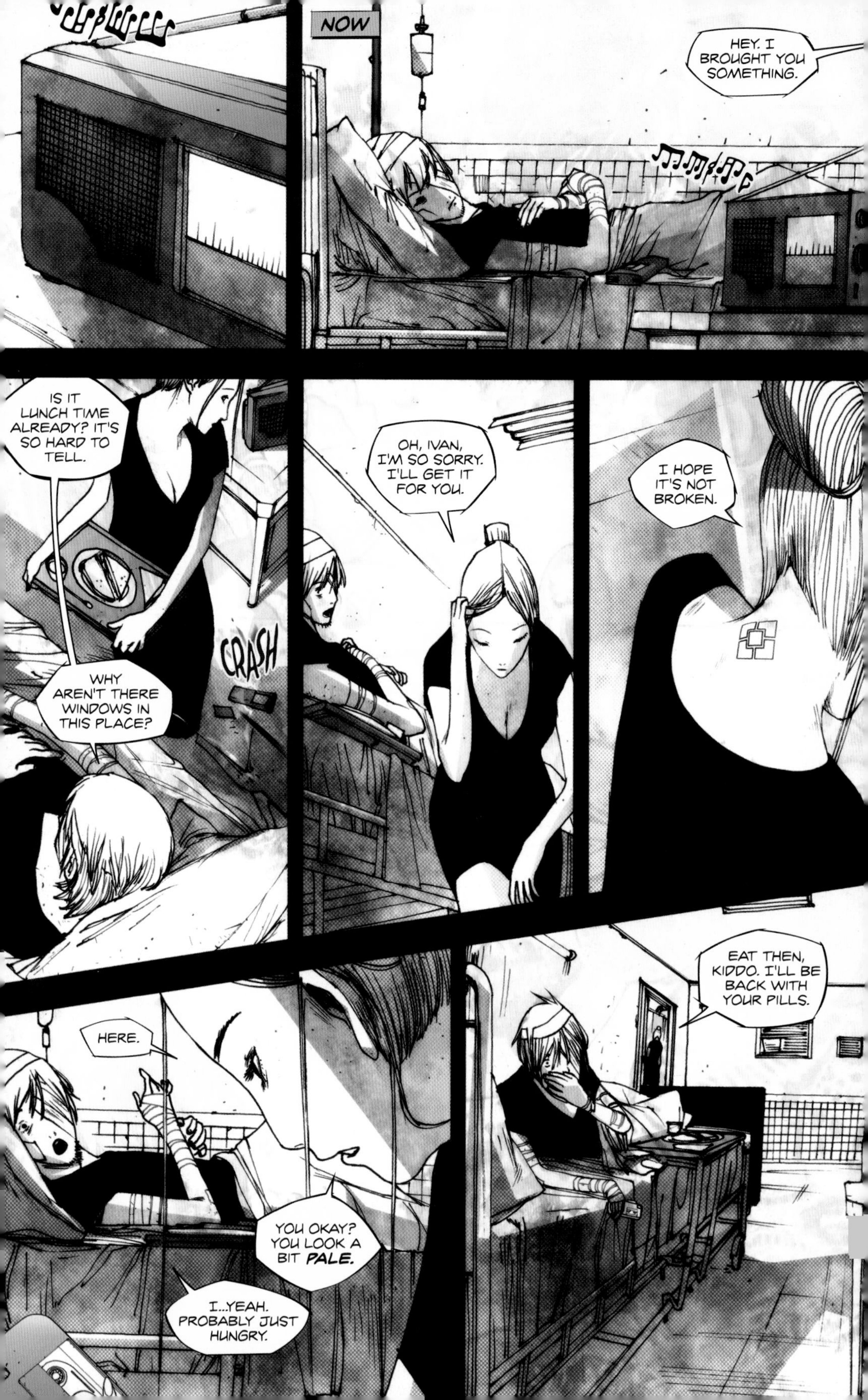
NOW
HEY. I BROUGHT YOU SOMETHING.
IS IT LUNCH TIME ALREADY? IT'S SO HARD TO TELL.
WHY AREN'T THERE WINDOWS IN THIS PLACE?
CRASH
OH, IVAN, I'M SO SORRY. I'LL GET IT FOR YOU.
I HOPE IT'S NOT BROKEN.
HERE.
YOU OKAY? YOU LOOK A BIT **PALE.**
I...YEAH. PROBABLY JUST HUNGRY.
EAT THEN, KIDDO. I'LL BE BACK WITH YOUR PILLS.

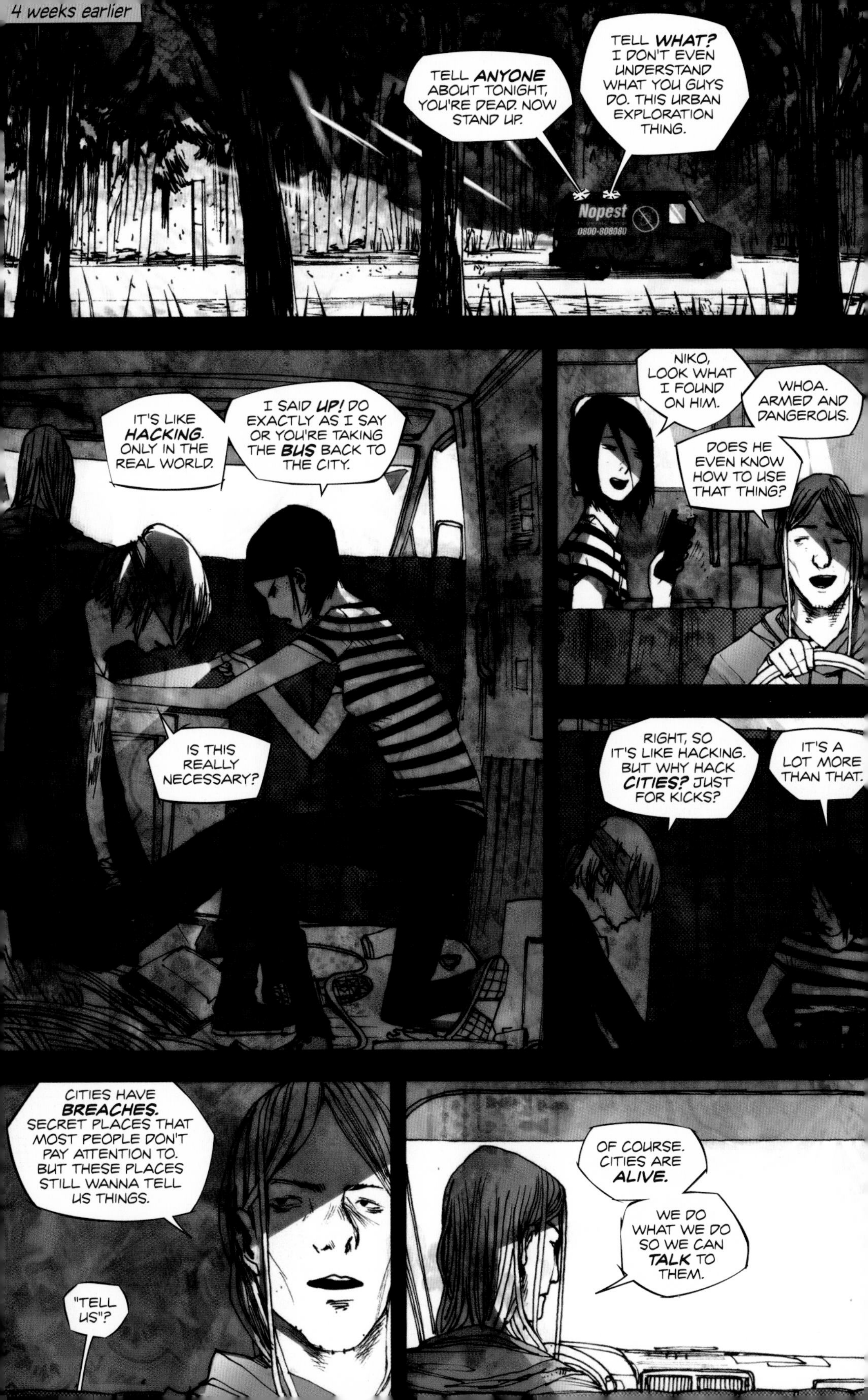
4 weeks earlier
TELL ANYONE ABOUT TONIGHT, YOU'RE DEAD. NOW STAND UP.
TELL WHAT? I DON'T EVEN UNDERSTAND WHAT YOU GUYS DO. THIS URBAN EXPLORATION THING.
Nopest
0800-808080
IT'S LIKE HACKING. ONLY IN THE REAL WORLD.
I SAID UP! DO EXACTLY AS I SAY OR YOU'RE TAKING THE BUS BACK TO THE CITY.
IS THIS REALLY NECESSARY?
NIKO, LOOK WHAT I FOUND ON HIM.
WHOA. ARMED AND DANGEROUS.
DOES HE EVEN KNOW HOW TO USE THAT THING?
RIGHT, SO IT'S LIKE HACKING. BUT WHY HACK CITIES? JUST FOR KICKS?
IT'S A LOT MORE THAN THAT.
CITIES HAVE BREACHES. SECRET PLACES THAT MOST PEOPLE DON'T PAY ATTENTION TO. BUT THESE PLACES STILL WANNA TELL US THINGS.
"TELL US"?
OF COURSE. CITIES ARE ALIVE.
WE DO WHAT WE DO SO WE CAN TALK TO THEM.

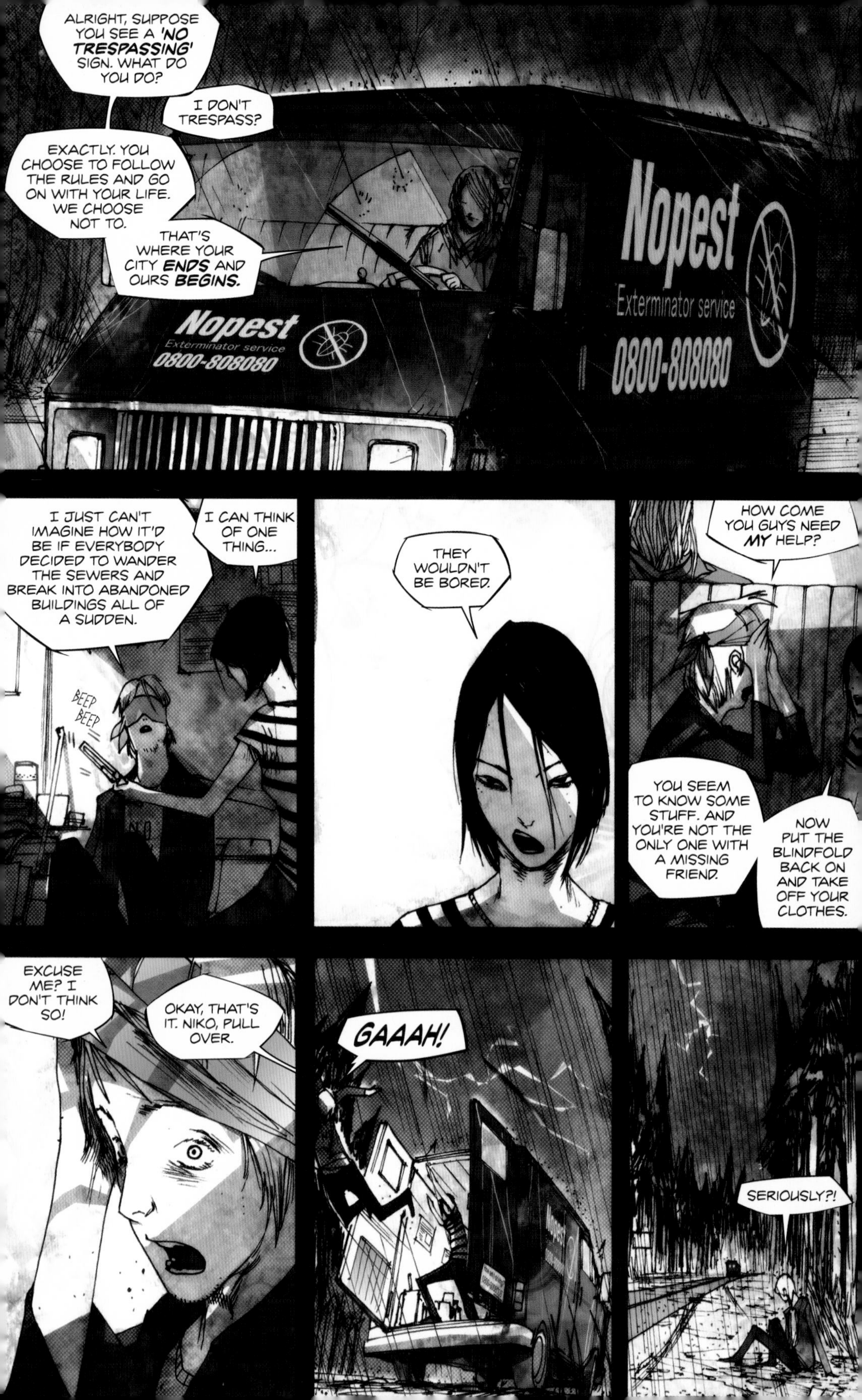
ALRIGHT, SUPPOSE YOU SEE A 'NO TRESPASSING' SIGN. WHAT DO YOU DO?
I DON'T TRESPASS?
EXACTLY. YOU CHOOSE TO FOLLOW THE RULES AND GO ON WITH YOUR LIFE. WE CHOOSE NOT TO.
THAT'S WHERE YOUR CITY ENDS AND OURS BEGINS.
Nopest
Exterminator service
0800-808080
Nopest
Exterminator service
0800-808080
I JUST CAN'T IMAGINE HOW IT'D BE IF EVERYBODY DECIDED TO WANDER THE SEWERS AND BREAK INTO ABANDONED BUILDINGS ALL OF A SUDDEN.
I CAN THINK OF ONE THING...
BEEP BEEP
THEY WOULDN'T BE BORED.
HOW COME YOU GUYS NEED MY HELP?
YOU SEEM TO KNOW SOME STUFF. AND YOU'RE NOT THE ONLY ONE WITH A MISSING FRIEND.
NOW PUT THE BLINDFOLD BACK ON AND TAKE OFF YOUR CLOTHES.
EXCUSE ME? I DON'T THINK SO!
OKAY, THAT'S IT. NIKO, PULL OVER.
GAAAH!
SERIOUSLY?!

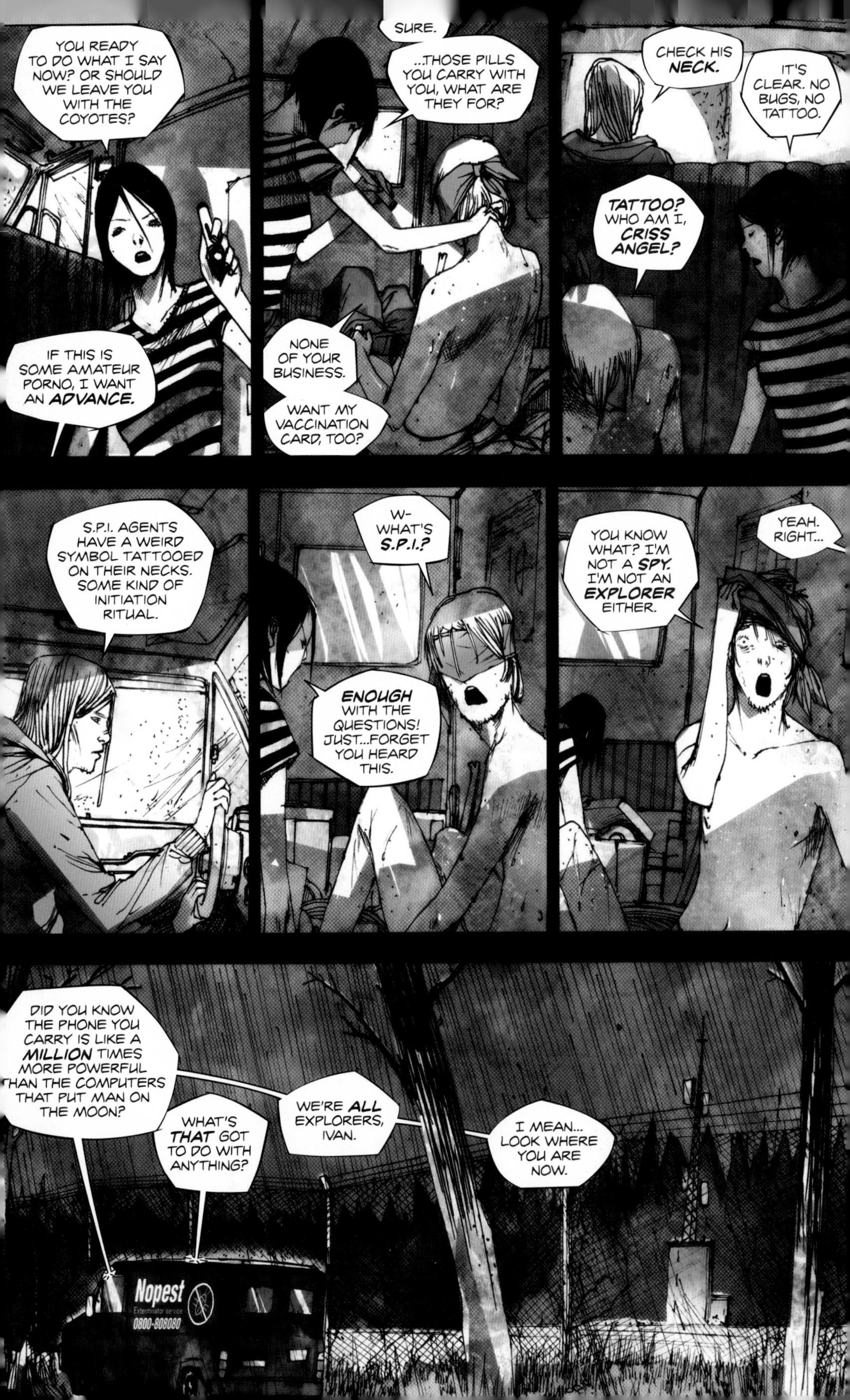
YOU READY TO DO WHAT I SAY NOW? OR SHOULD WE LEAVE YOU WITH THE COYOTES?
IF THIS IS SOME AMATEUR PORNO, I WANT AN ADVANCE.
SURE.
...THOSE PILLS YOU CARRY WITH YOU, WHAT ARE THEY FOR?
NONE OF YOUR BUSINESS.
WANT MY VACCINATION CARD, TOO?
CHECK HIS NECK.
IT'S CLEAR. NO BUGS, NO TATTOO.
TATTOO? WHO AM I, CRISS ANGEL?
S.P.I. AGENTS HAVE A WEIRD SYMBOL TATTOOED ON THEIR NECKS. SOME KIND OF INITIATION RITUAL.
W- WHAT'S S.P.I.?
ENOUGH WITH THE QUESTIONS! JUST...FORGET YOU HEARD THIS.
YOU KNOW WHAT? I'M NOT A SPY. I'M NOT AN EXPLORER EITHER.
YEAH. RIGHT...
DID YOU KNOW THE PHONE YOU CARRY IS LIKE A MILLION TIMES MORE POWERFUL THAN THE COMPUTERS THAT PUT MAN ON THE MOON?
WHAT'S THAT GOT TO DO WITH ANYTHING?
WE'RE ALL EXPLORERS, IVAN.
I MEAN... LOOK WHERE YOU ARE NOW.
Nopest
Exterminator service
0800-808080

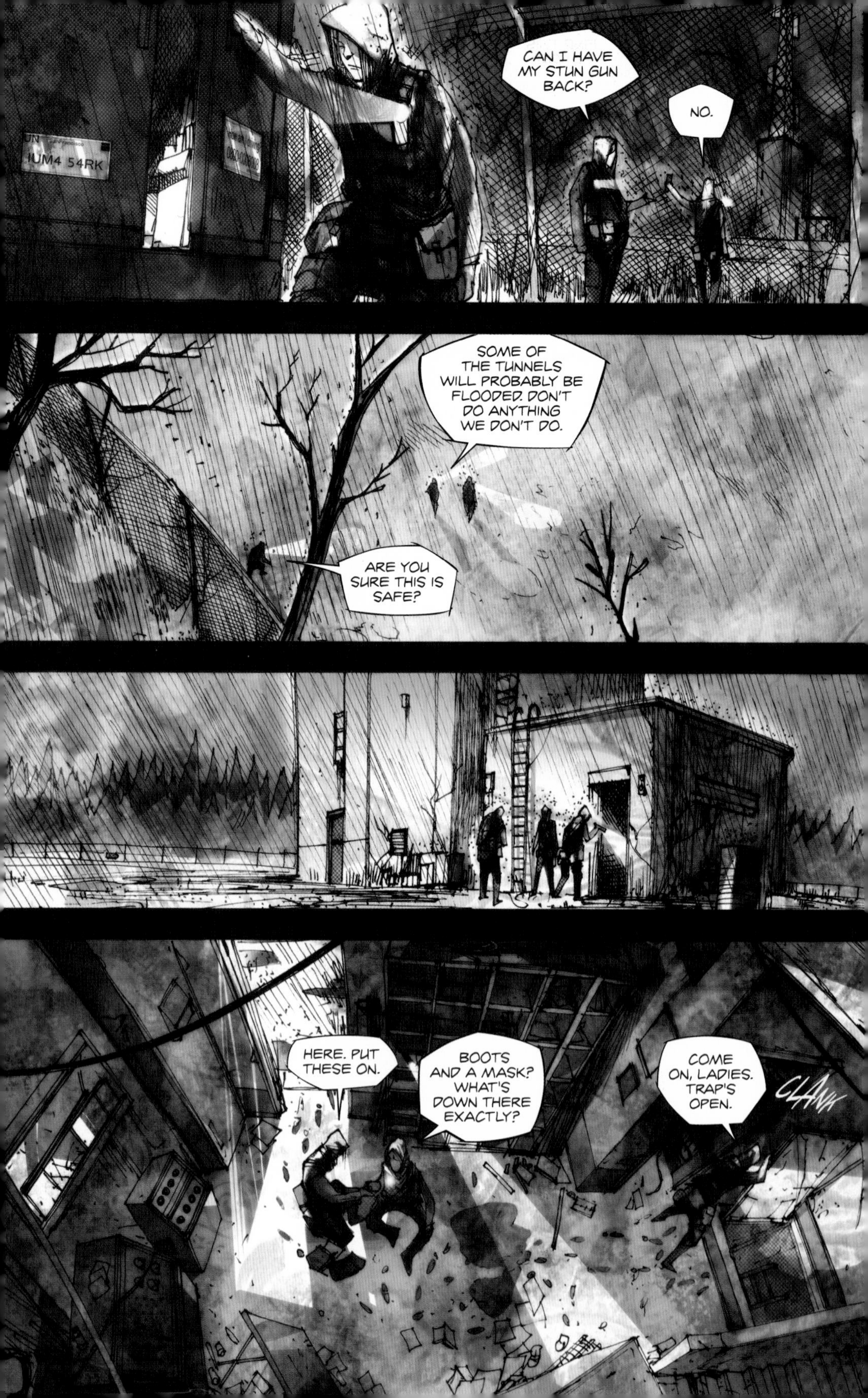
UN
IUM4 54RK
CAN I HAVE MY STUN GUN BACK?
NO.
SOME OF THE TUNNELS WILL PROBABLY BE FLOODED. DON'T DO ANYTHING WE DON'T DO.
ARE YOU SURE THIS IS SAFE?
HERE. PUT THESE ON.
BOOTS AND A MASK? WHAT'S DOWN THERE EXACTLY?
COME ON, LADIES. TRAP'S OPEN.
CLANK

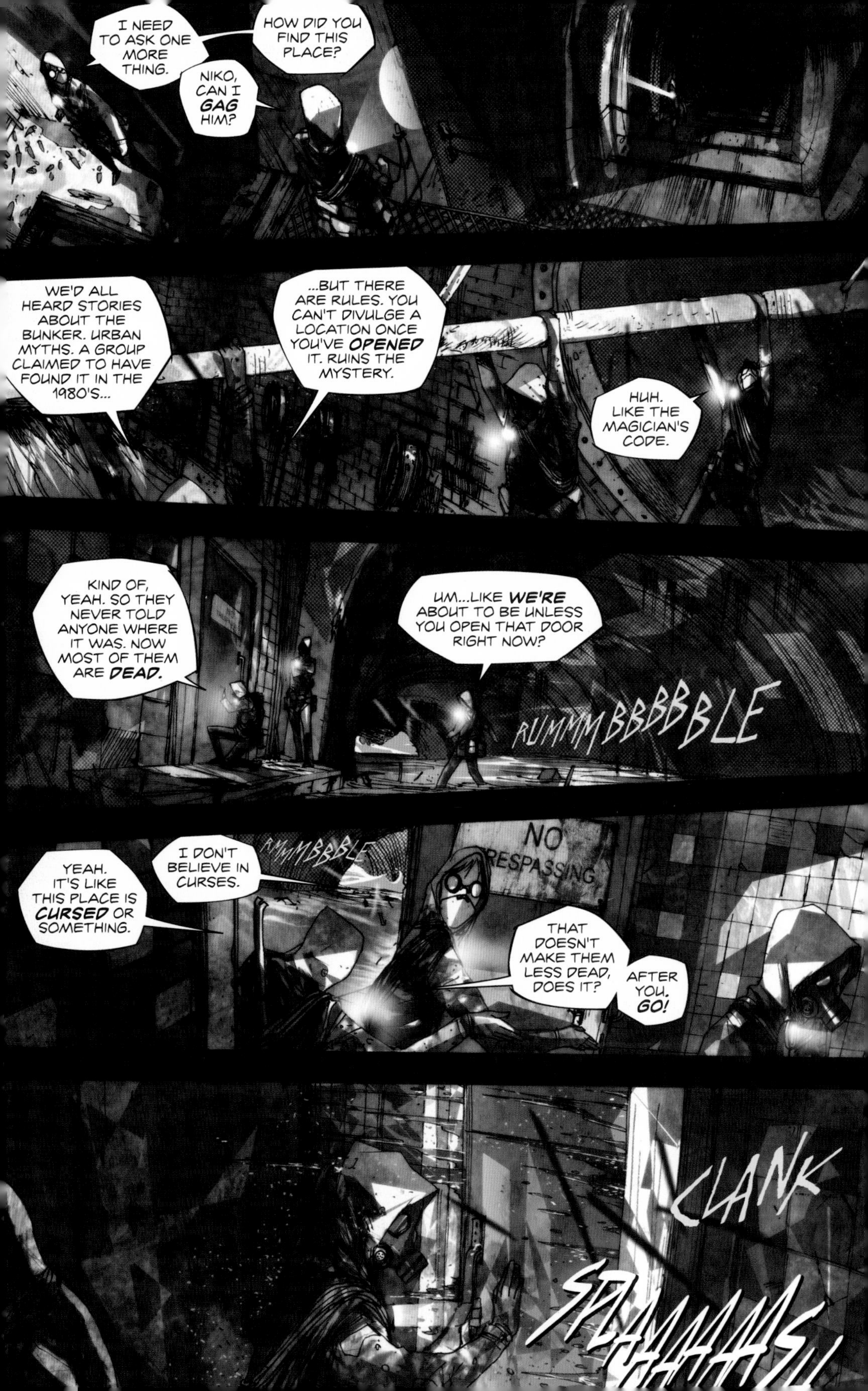
I NEED TO ASK ONE MORE THING.
HOW DID YOU FIND THIS PLACE?
NIKO, CAN I GAG HIM?
WE'D ALL HEARD STORIES ABOUT THE BUNKER. URBAN MYTHS. A GROUP CLAIMED TO HAVE FOUND IT IN THE 1980'S...
...BUT THERE ARE RULES. YOU CAN'T DIVULGE A LOCATION ONCE YOU'VE OPENED IT. RUINS THE MYSTERY.
HUH. LIKE THE MAGICIAN'S CODE.
KIND OF, YEAH. SO THEY NEVER TOLD ANYONE WHERE IT WAS. NOW MOST OF THEM ARE DEAD.
UM...LIKE WE'RE ABOUT TO BE UNLESS YOU OPEN THAT DOOR RIGHT NOW?
RUMMMBBBBBLE
RMMMBBBLE
YEAH. IT'S LIKE THIS PLACE IS CURSED OR SOMETHING.
I DON'T BELIEVE IN CURSES.
NO TRESPASSING
THAT DOESN'T MAKE THEM LESS DEAD, DOES IT?
AFTER YOU. GO!
CLANK
SPLAAAASH

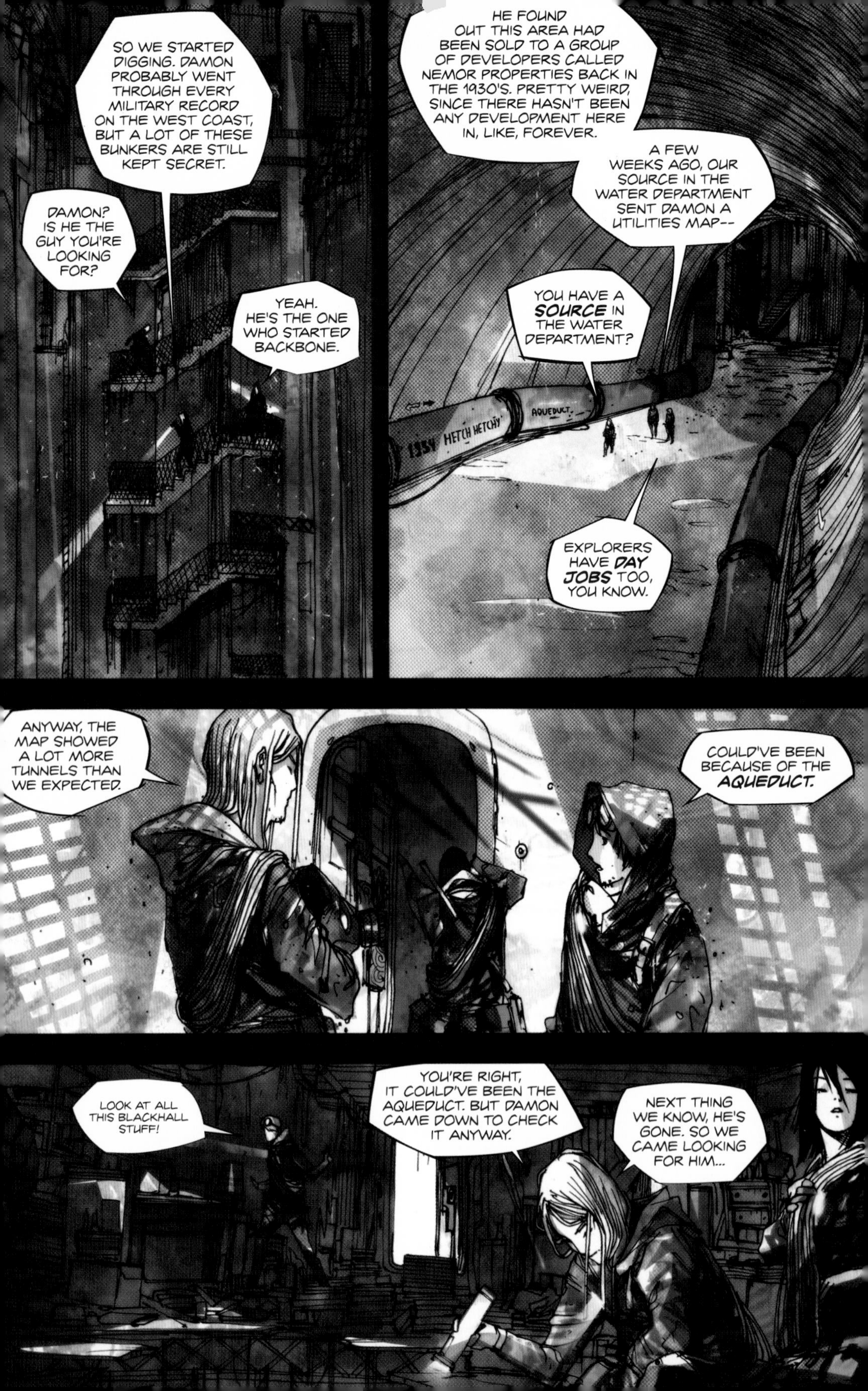
SO WE STARTED DIGGING. DAMON PROBABLY WENT THROUGH EVERY MILITARY RECORD ON THE WEST COAST, BUT A LOT OF THESE BUNKERS ARE STILL KEPT SECRET.
DAMON? IS HE THE GUY YOU'RE LOOKING FOR?
YEAH. HE'S THE ONE WHO STARTED BACKBONE.
HE FOUND OUT THIS AREA HAD BEEN SOLD TO A GROUP OF DEVELOPERS CALLED NEMOR PROPERTIES BACK IN THE 1930'S. PRETTY WEIRD, SINCE THERE HASN'T BEEN ANY DEVELOPMENT HERE IN, LIKE, FOREVER.
A FEW WEEKS AGO, OUR SOURCE IN THE WATER DEPARTMENT SENT DAMON A UTILITIES MAP--
YOU HAVE A SOURCE IN THE WATER DEPARTMENT?
AQUEDUCT
1934 HETCH HETCHY
EXPLORERS HAVE DAY JOBS TOO, YOU KNOW.
ANYWAY, THE MAP SHOWED A LOT MORE TUNNELS THAN WE EXPECTED.
COULD'VE BEEN BECAUSE OF THE AQUEDUCT.
LOOK AT ALL THIS BLACKHALL STUFF!
YOU'RE RIGHT, IT COULD'VE BEEN THE AQUEDUCT. BUT DAMON CAME DOWN TO CHECK IT ANYWAY.
NEXT THING WE KNOW, HE'S GONE. SO WE CAME LOOKING FOR HIM...

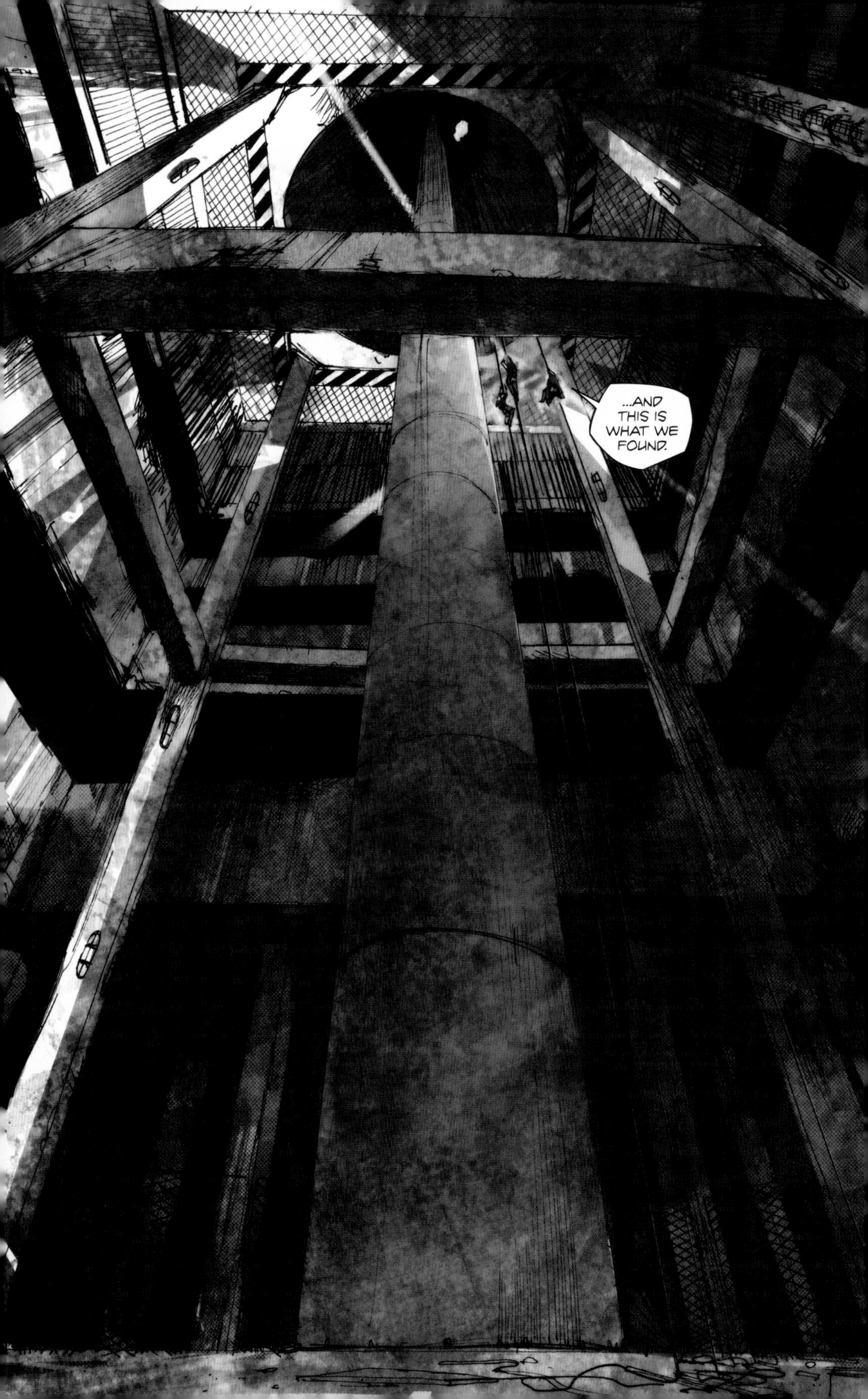
...AND THIS IS WHAT WE FOUND.

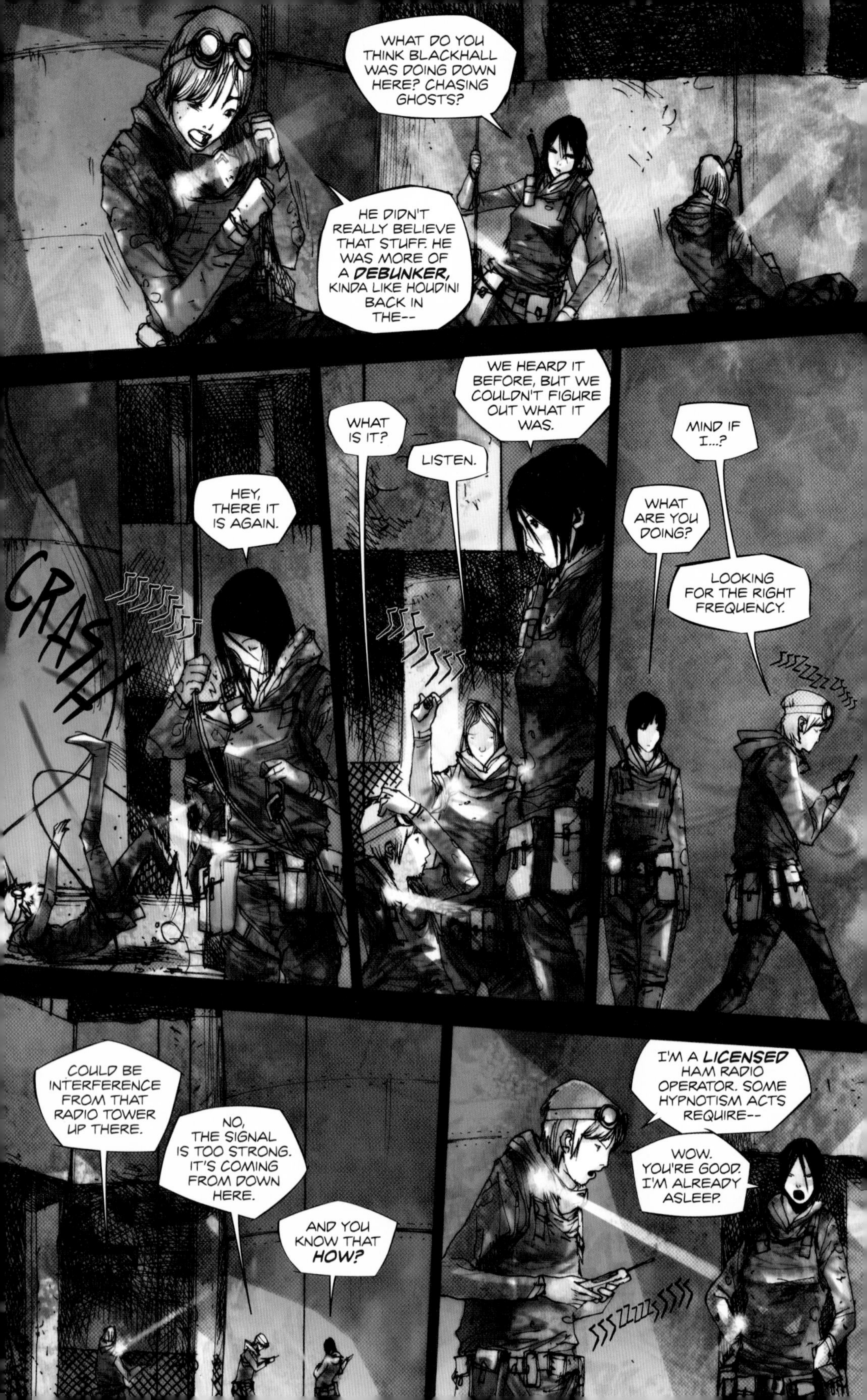
WHAT DO YOU THINK BLACKHALL WAS DOING DOWN HERE? CHASING GHOSTS?
HE DIDN'T REALLY BELIEVE THAT STUFF. HE WAS MORE OF A **DEBUNKER,** KINDA LIKE HOUDINI BACK IN THE--
CRASH
HEY, THERE IT IS AGAIN.
WHAT IS IT?
LISTEN.
WE HEARD IT BEFORE, BUT WE COULDN'T FIGURE OUT WHAT IT WAS.
MIND IF I...?
WHAT ARE YOU DOING?
LOOKING FOR THE RIGHT FREQUENCY.
COULD BE INTERFERENCE FROM THAT RADIO TOWER UP THERE.
NO, THE SIGNAL IS TOO STRONG. IT'S COMING FROM DOWN HERE.
AND YOU KNOW THAT **HOW?**
I'M A **LICENSED** HAM RADIO OPERATOR. SOME HYPNOTISM ACTS REQUIRE--
WOW. YOU'RE GOOD. I'M ALREADY ASLEEP.

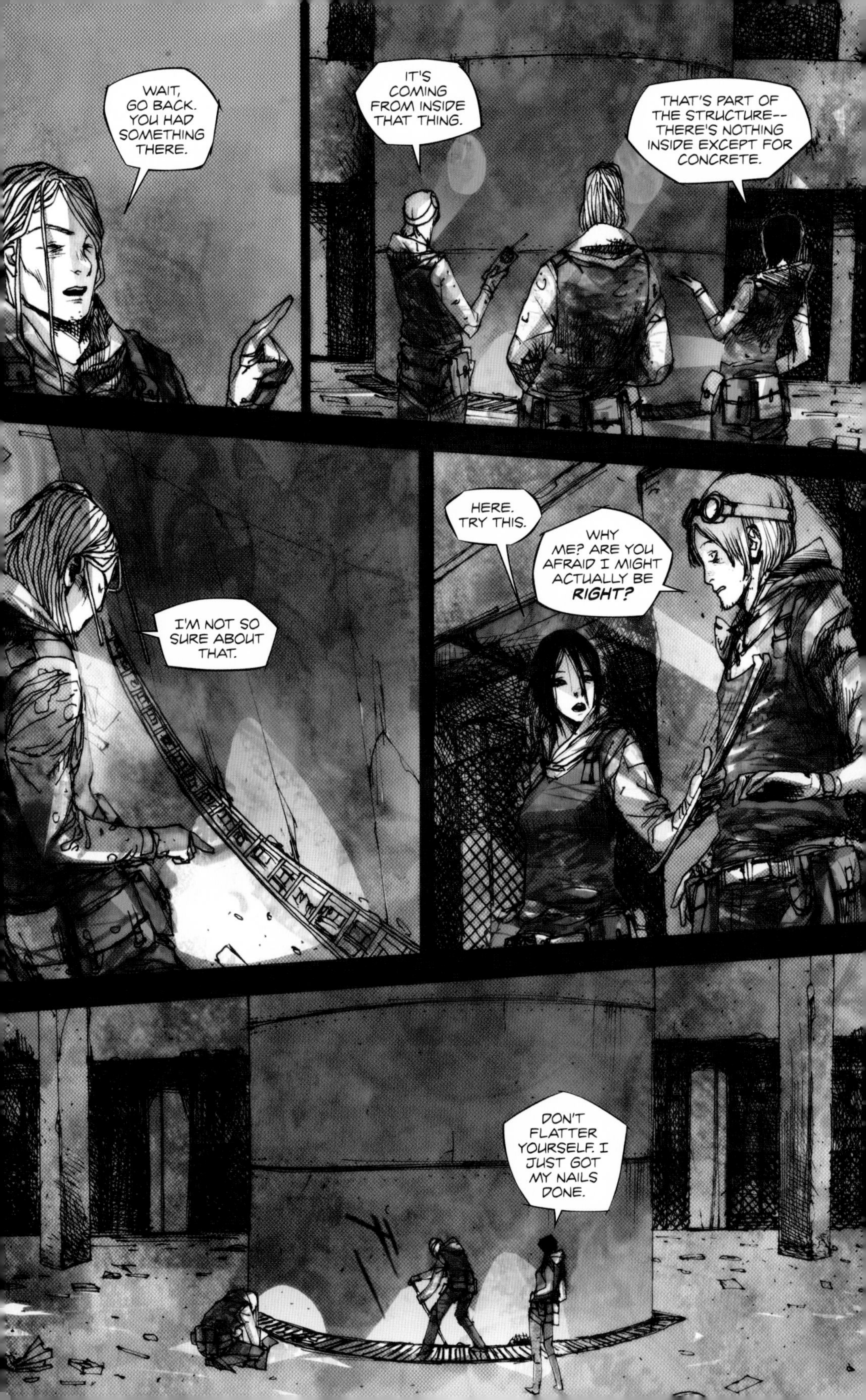
WAIT, GO BACK. YOU HAD SOMETHING THERE.
IT'S COMING FROM INSIDE THAT THING.
THAT'S PART OF THE STRUCTURE-- THERE'S NOTHING INSIDE EXCEPT FOR CONCRETE.
I'M NOT SO SURE ABOUT THAT.
HERE. TRY THIS.
WHY ME? ARE YOU AFRAID I MIGHT ACTUALLY BE **RIGHT?**
DON'T FLATTER YOURSELF. I JUST GOT MY NAILS DONE.

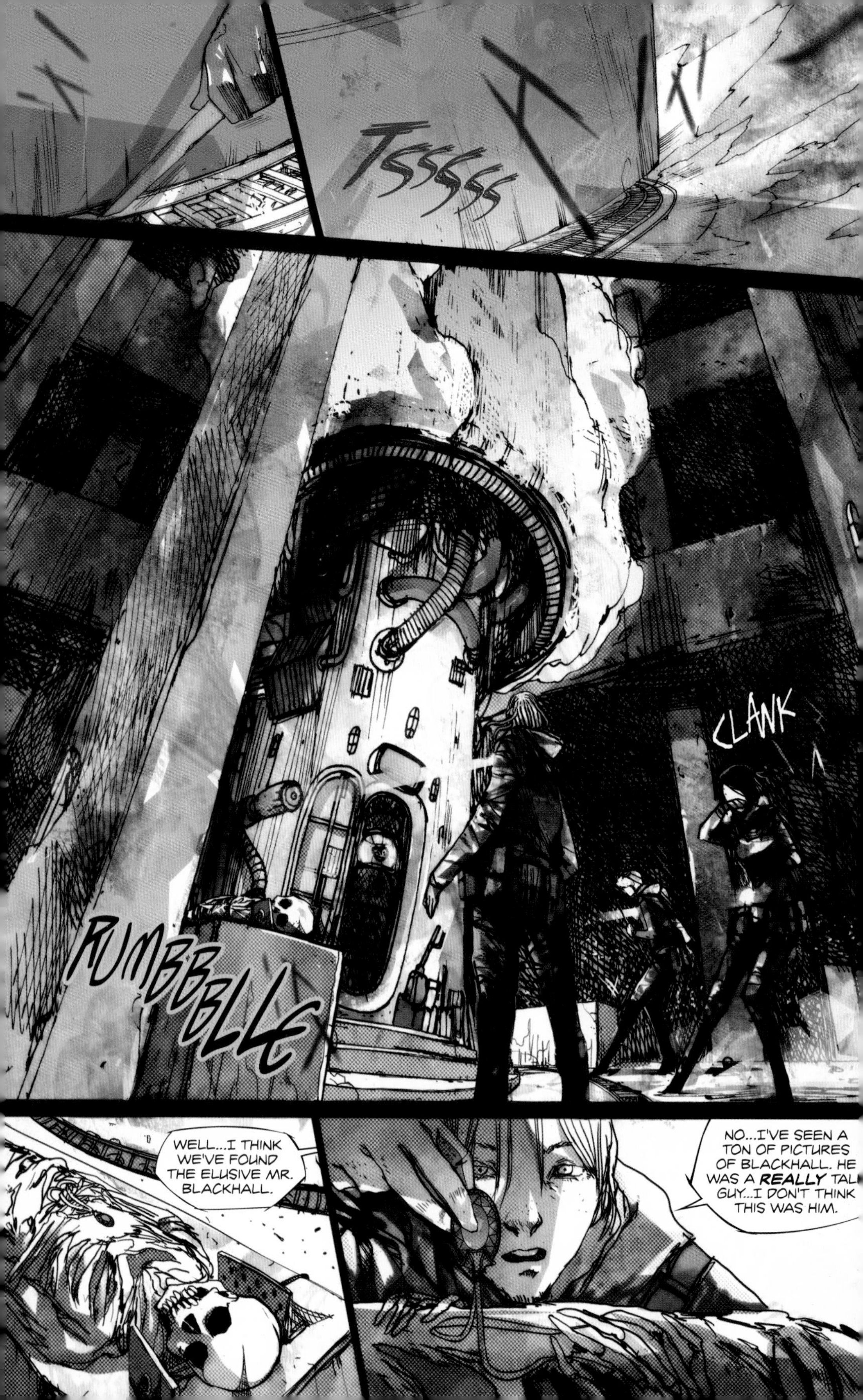
TSSSSS
CLANK
RUMBBBLLE
WELL...I THINK WE'VE FOUND THE ELUSIVE MR. BLACKHALL.
NO...I'VE SEEN A TON OF PICTURES OF BLACKHALL. HE WAS A **REALLY** TALL GUY...I DON'T THINK THIS WAS HIM.

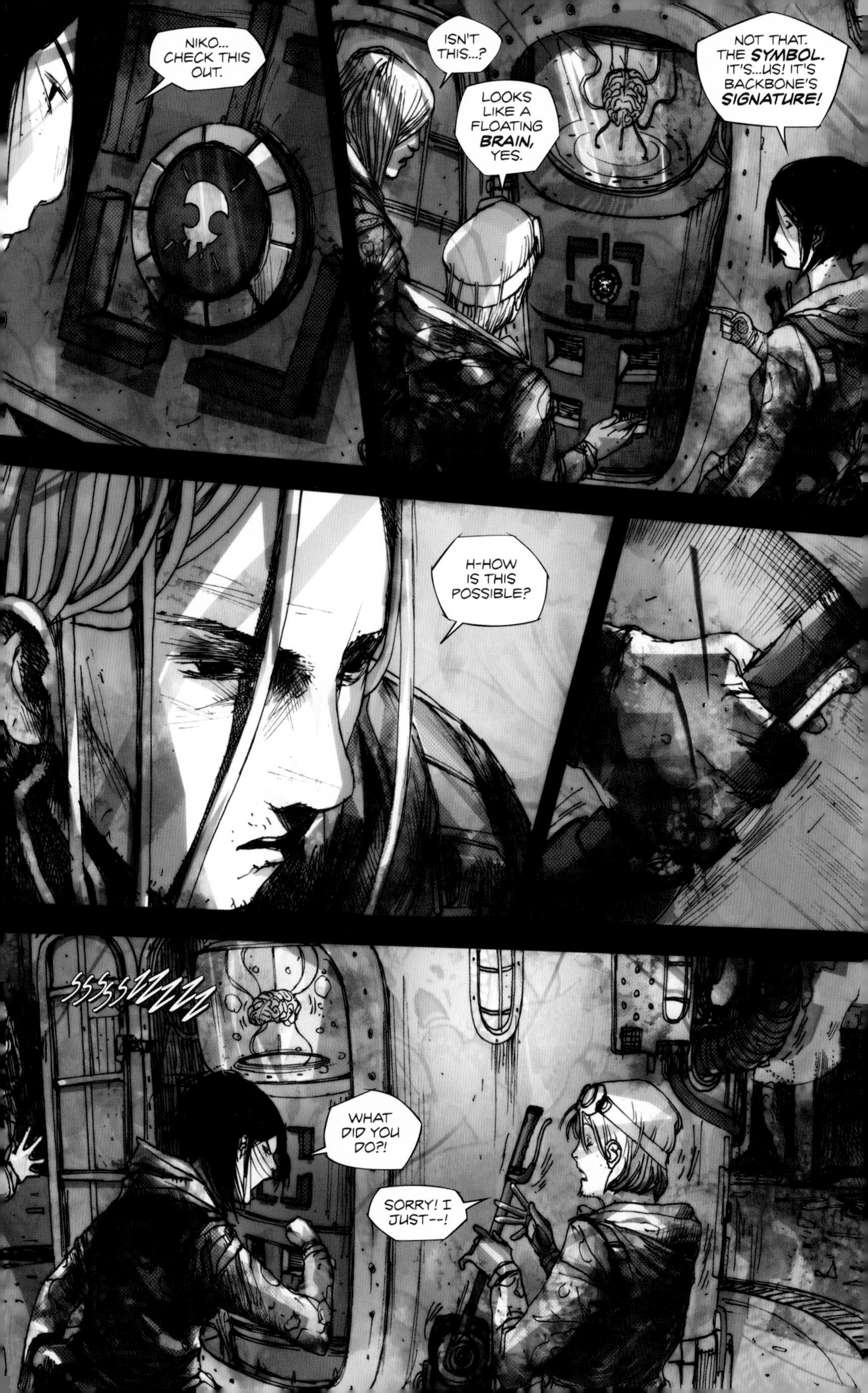
NIKO... CHECK THIS OUT.
ISN'T THIS...?
LOOKS LIKE A FLOATING **BRAIN,** YES.
NOT THAT. THE **SYMBOL.** IT'S...US! IT'S BACKBONE'S **SIGNATURE!**
H-HOW IS THIS POSSIBLE?
SSSSSZZZZZZ
WHAT DID YOU DO?!
SORRY! I JUST--!

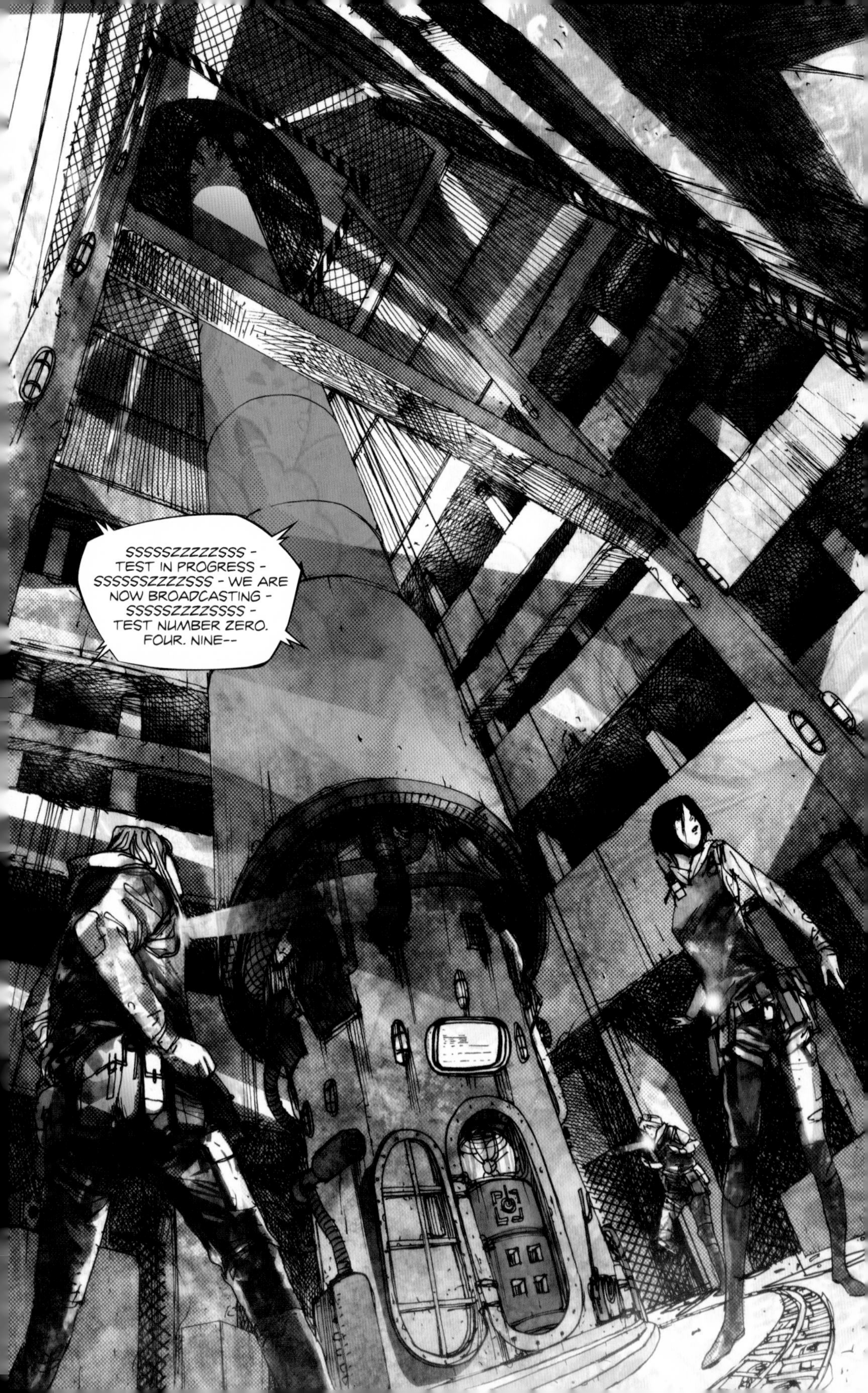
SSSSSZZZZZSSS - TEST IN PROGRESS - SSSSSSZZZZSSS - WE ARE NOW BROADCASTING - SSSSSZZZZSSSS - TEST NUMBER ZERO. FOUR. NINE--

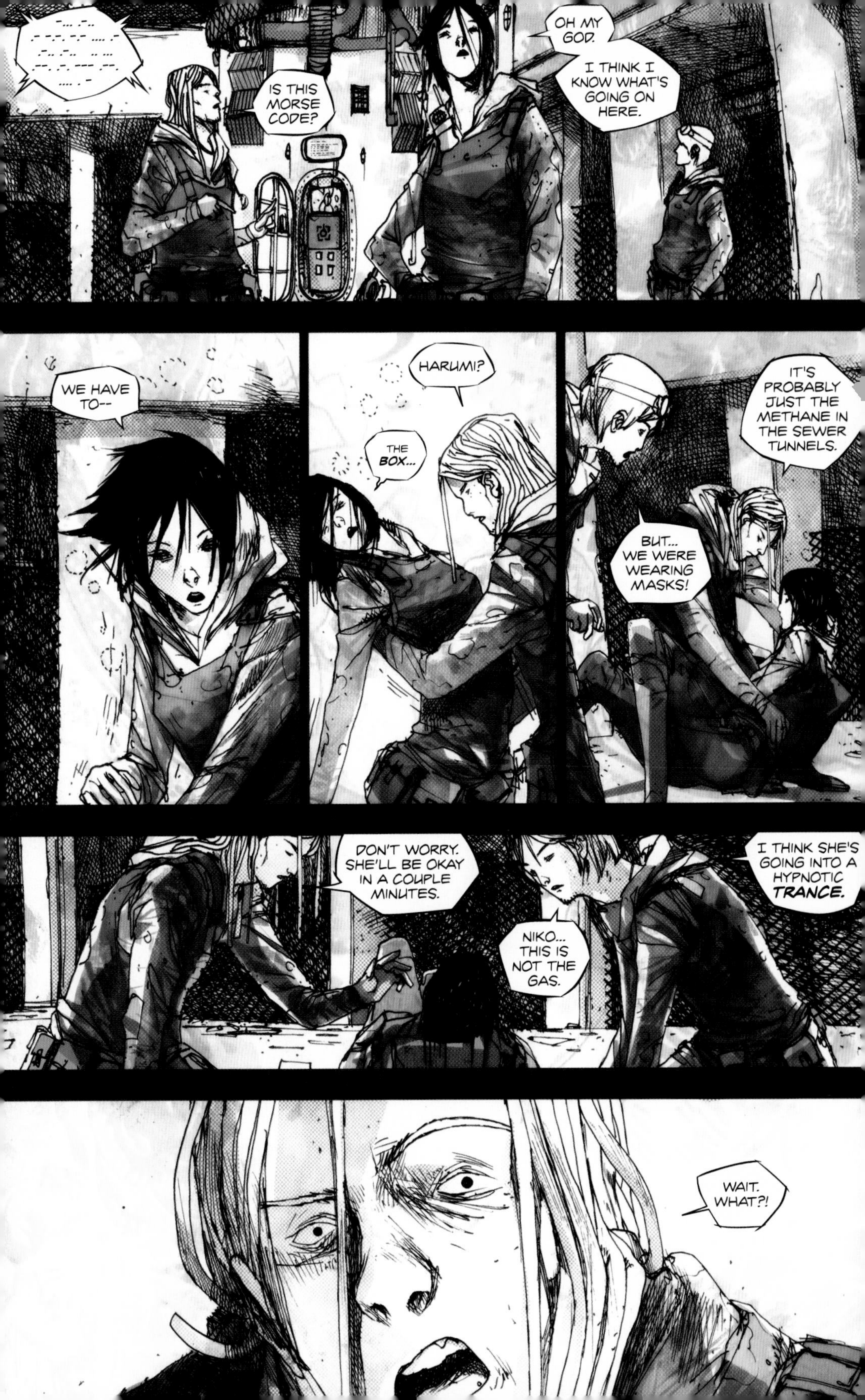
IS THIS MORSE CODE?
OH MY GOD.
I THINK I KNOW WHAT'S GOING ON HERE.
WE HAVE TO--
HARUMI?
THE BOX...
IT'S PROBABLY JUST THE METHANE IN THE SEWER TUNNELS.
BUT... WE WERE WEARING MASKS!
DON'T WORRY. SHE'LL BE OKAY IN A COUPLE MINUTES.
I THINK SHE'S GOING INTO A HYPNOTIC TRANCE.
NIKO... THIS IS NOT THE GAS.
WAIT. WHAT?!

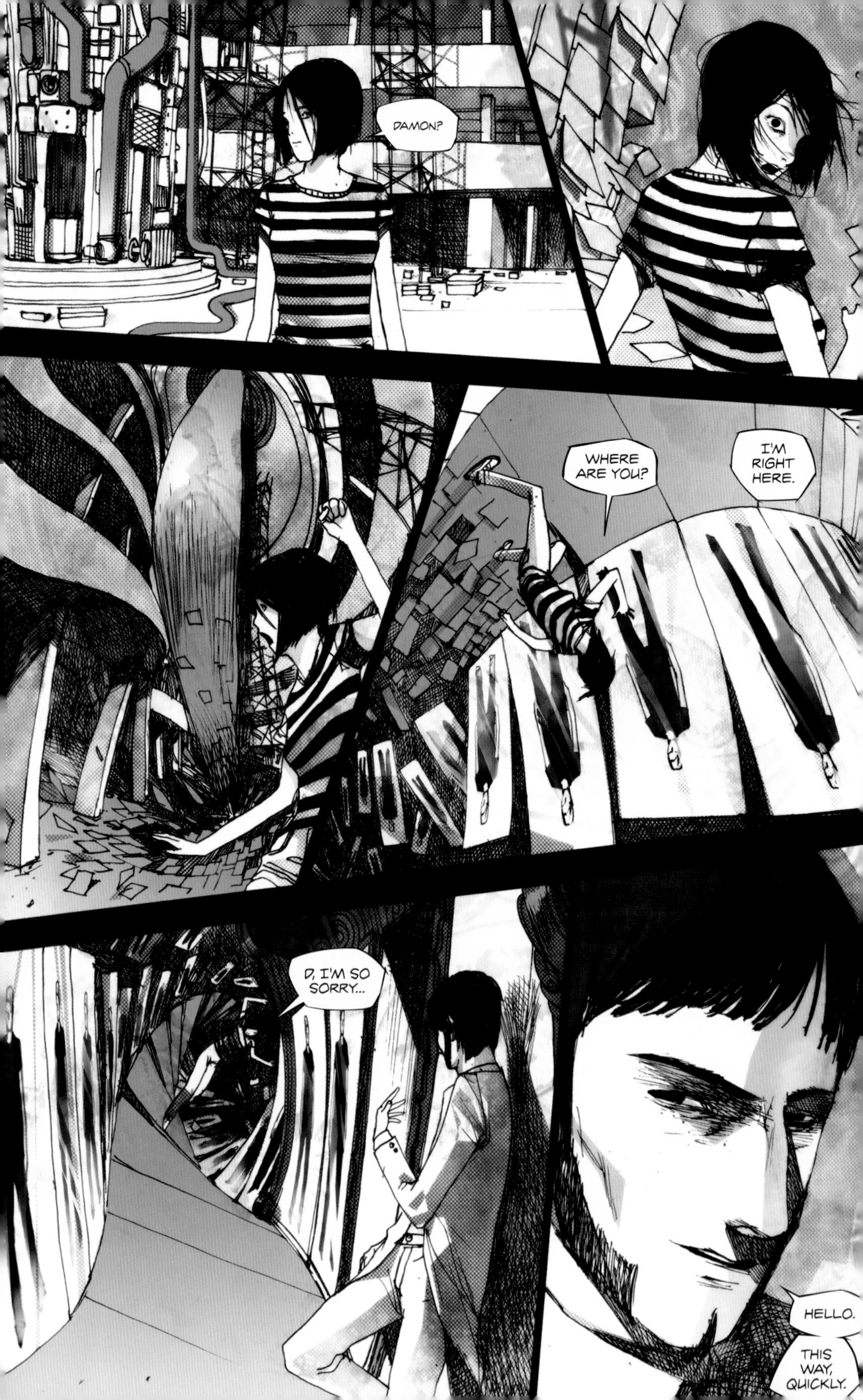
DAMON?
WHERE ARE YOU?
I'M RIGHT HERE.
D, I'M SO SORRY...
HELLO.
THIS WAY, QUICKLY.

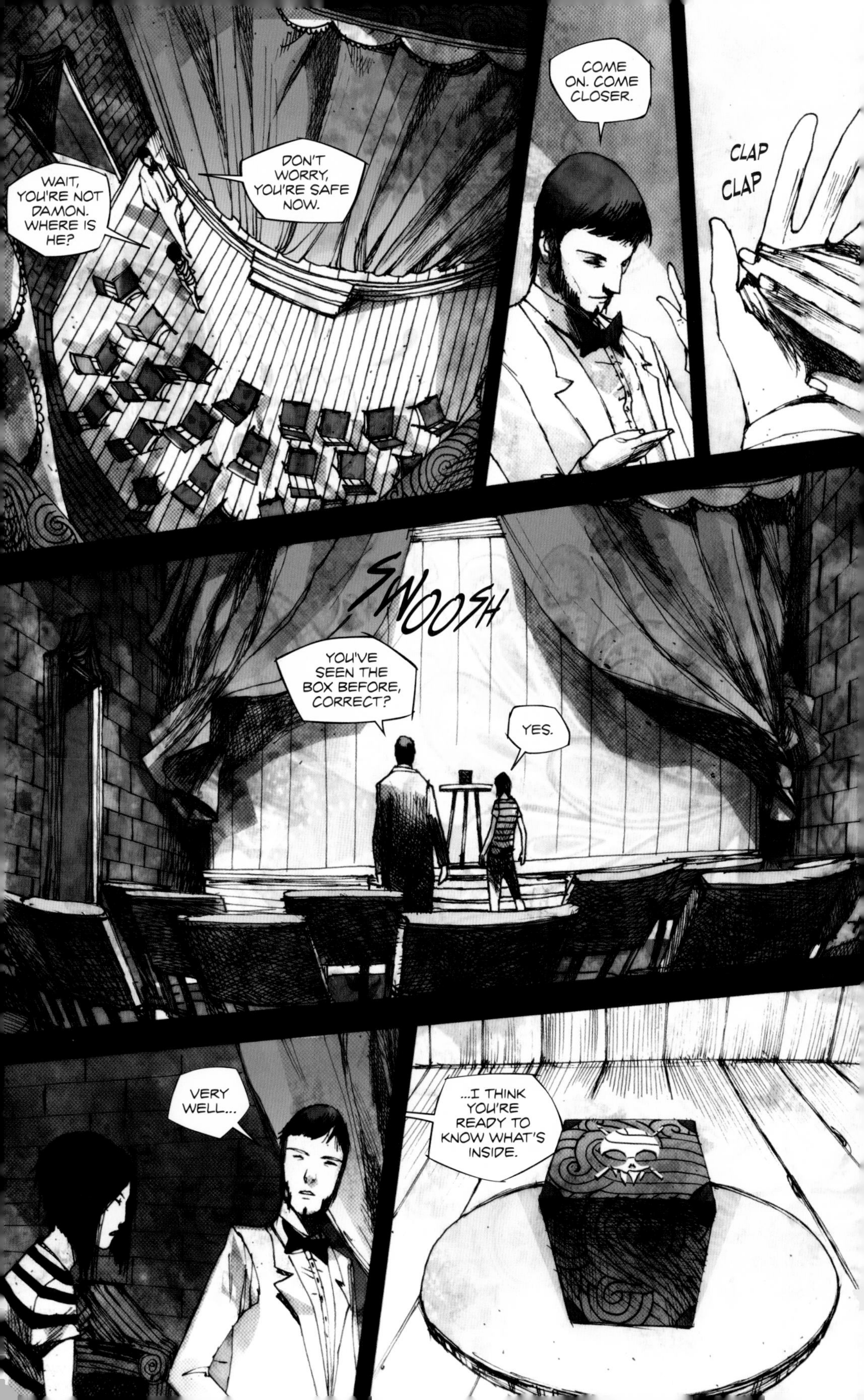
WAIT, YOU'RE NOT DAMON. WHERE IS HE?
DON'T WORRY, YOU'RE SAFE NOW.
COME ON. COME CLOSER.
CLAP
CLAP
SWOOSH
YOU'VE SEEN THE BOX BEFORE, CORRECT?
YES.
VERY WELL...
...I THINK YOU'RE READY TO KNOW WHAT'S INSIDE.

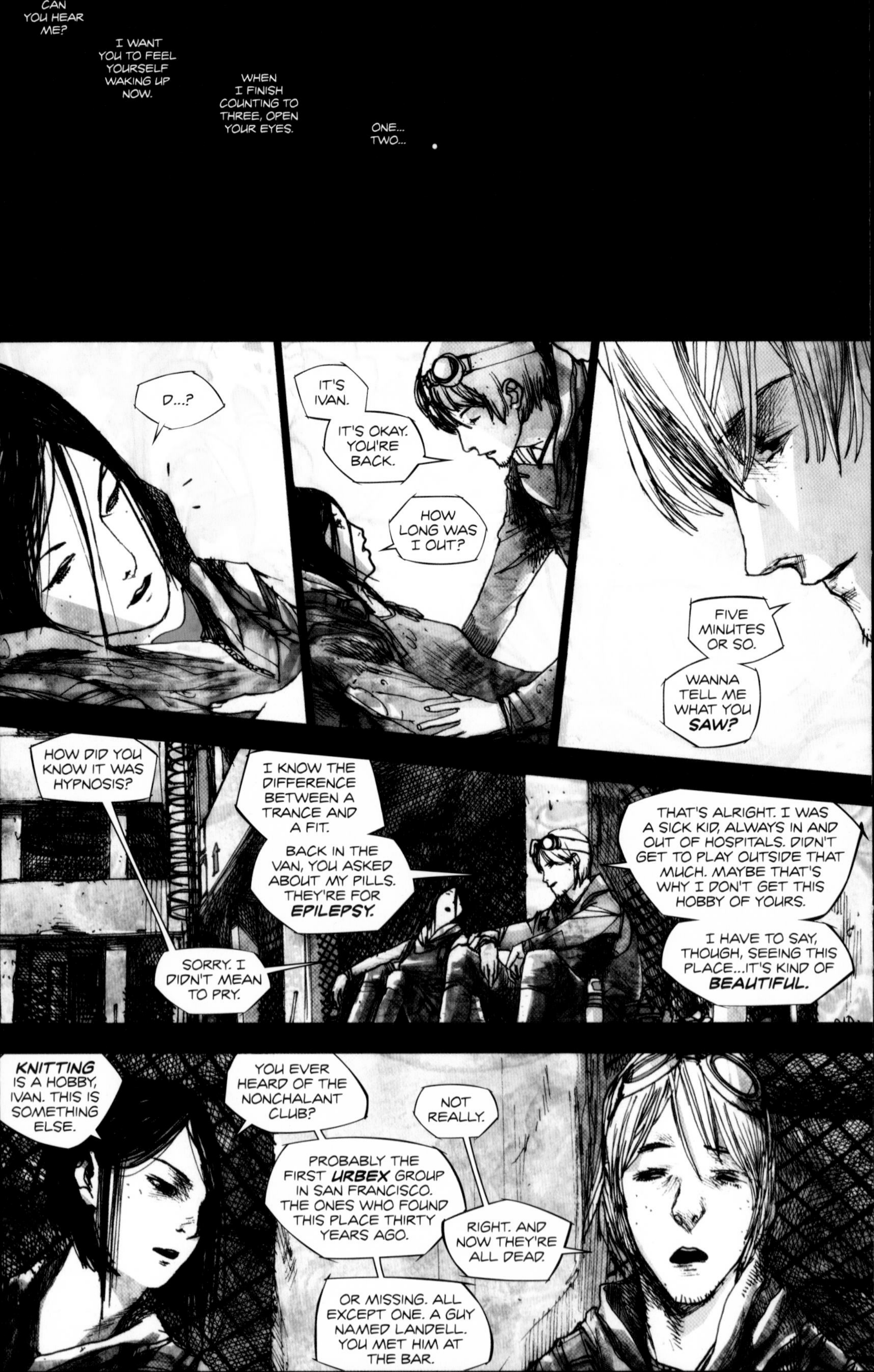

CAN YOU HEAR ME?
I WANT YOU TO FEEL YOURSELF WAKING UP NOW.
WHEN I FINISH COUNTING TO THREE, OPEN YOUR EYES.
ONE... TWO...
D...?
IT'S IVAN.
IT'S OKAY. YOU'RE BACK.
HOW LONG WAS I OUT?
FIVE MINUTES OR SO.
WANNA TELL ME WHAT YOU SAW?
HOW DID YOU KNOW IT WAS HYPNOSIS?
I KNOW THE DIFFERENCE BETWEEN A TRANCE AND A FIT.
BACK IN THE VAN, YOU ASKED ABOUT MY PILLS. THEY'RE FOR EPILEPSY.
SORRY. I DIDN'T MEAN TO PRY.
THAT'S ALRIGHT. I WAS A SICK KID, ALWAYS IN AND OUT OF HOSPITALS. DIDN'T GET TO PLAY OUTSIDE THAT MUCH. MAYBE THAT'S WHY I DON'T GET THIS HOBBY OF YOURS.
I HAVE TO SAY, THOUGH, SEEING THIS PLACE...IT'S KIND OF BEAUTIFUL.
KNITTING IS A HOBBY, IVAN. THIS IS SOMETHING ELSE.
YOU EVER HEARD OF THE NONCHALANT CLUB?
NOT REALLY.
PROBABLY THE FIRST URBEX GROUP IN SAN FRANCISCO. THE ONES WHO FOUND THIS PLACE THIRTY YEARS AGO.
RIGHT. AND NOW THEY'RE ALL DEAD.
OR MISSING. ALL EXCEPT ONE. A GUY NAMED LANDELL. YOU MET HIM AT THE BAR.

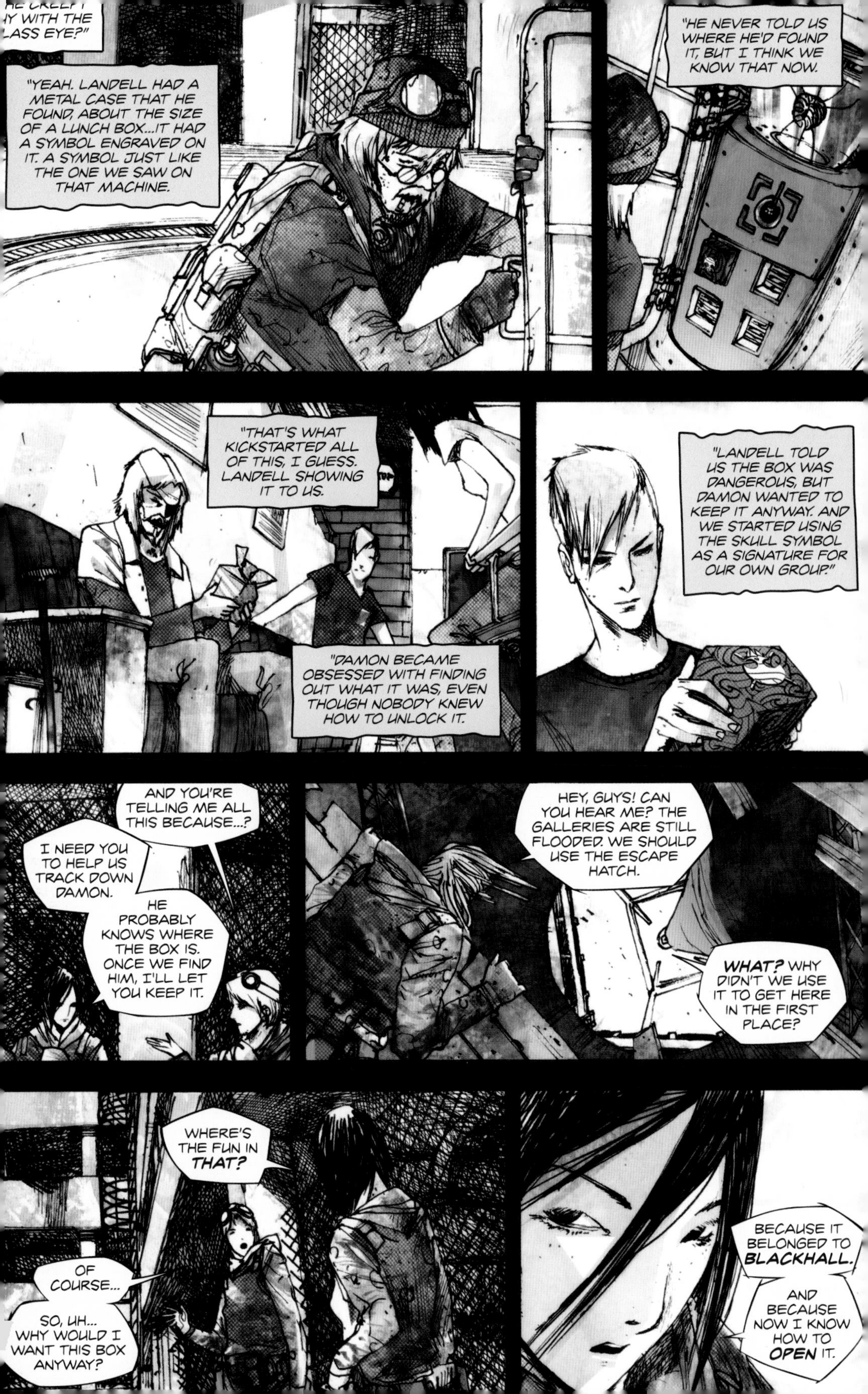

"YEAH. LANDELL HAD A METAL CASE THAT HE FOUND, ABOUT THE SIZE OF A LUNCH BOX...IT HAD A SYMBOL ENGRAVED ON IT. A SYMBOL JUST LIKE THE ONE WE SAW ON THAT MACHINE.
"HE NEVER TOLD US WHERE HE'D FOUND IT, BUT I THINK WE KNOW THAT NOW.
"THAT'S WHAT KICKSTARTED ALL OF THIS, I GUESS. LANDELL SHOWING IT TO US.
"DAMON BECAME OBSESSED WITH FINDING OUT WHAT IT WAS, EVEN THOUGH NOBODY KNEW HOW TO UNLOCK IT.
"LANDELL TOLD US THE BOX WAS DANGEROUS, BUT DAMON WANTED TO KEEP IT ANYWAY. AND WE STARTED USING THE SKULL SYMBOL AS A SIGNATURE FOR OUR OWN GROUP."
AND YOU'RE TELLING ME ALL THIS BECAUSE...?
I NEED YOU TO HELP US TRACK DOWN DAMON.
HE PROBABLY KNOWS WHERE THE BOX IS. ONCE WE FIND HIM, I'LL LET YOU KEEP IT.
HEY, GUYS! CAN YOU HEAR ME? THE GALLERIES ARE STILL FLOODED. WE SHOULD USE THE ESCAPE HATCH.
WHAT? WHY DIDN'T WE USE IT TO GET HERE IN THE FIRST PLACE?
WHERE'S THE FUN IN THAT?
OF COURSE...
SO, UH... WHY WOULD I WANT THIS BOX ANYWAY?
BECAUSE IT BELONGED TO BLACKHALL.
AND BECAUSE NOW I KNOW HOW TO OPEN IT.

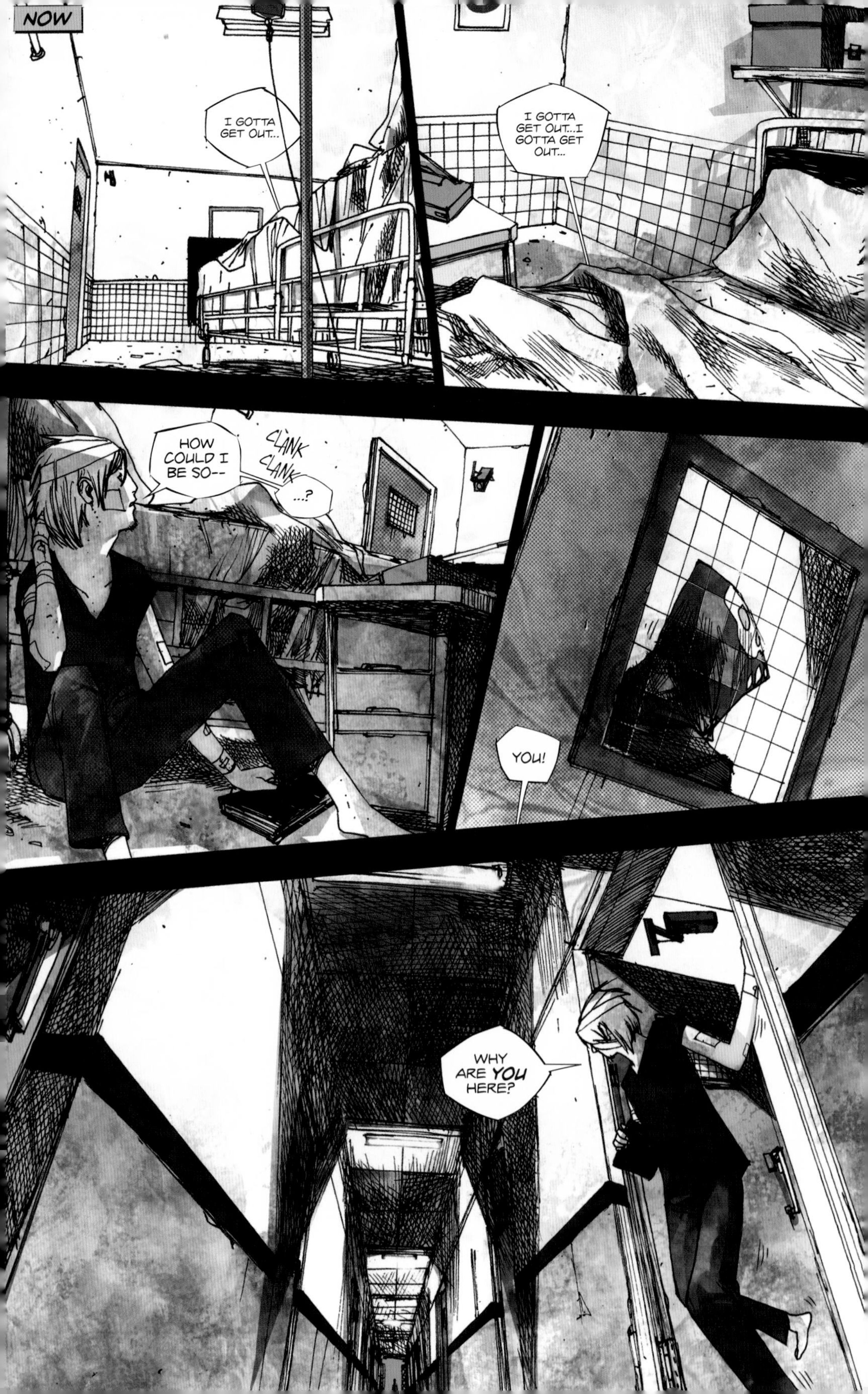
NOW
I GOTTA GET OUT...
I GOTTA GET OUT...I GOTTA GET OUT...
HOW COULD I BE SO--
CLANK CLANK
...?
YOU!
WHY ARE YOU HERE?

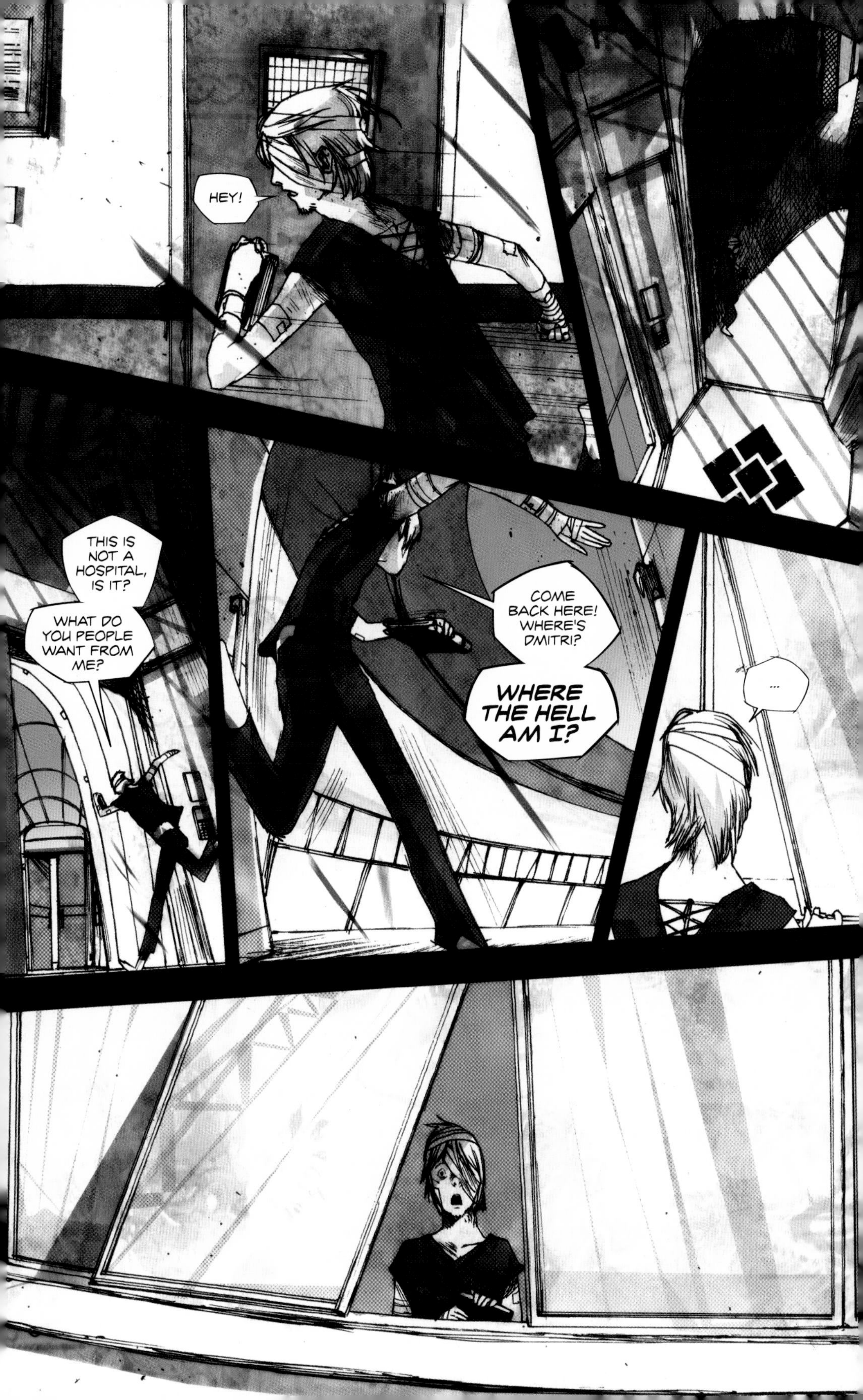
HEY!
THIS IS NOT A HOSPITAL, IS IT?
WHAT DO YOU PEOPLE WANT FROM ME?
COME BACK HERE! WHERE'S DMITRI?
WHERE THE HELL AM I?
...

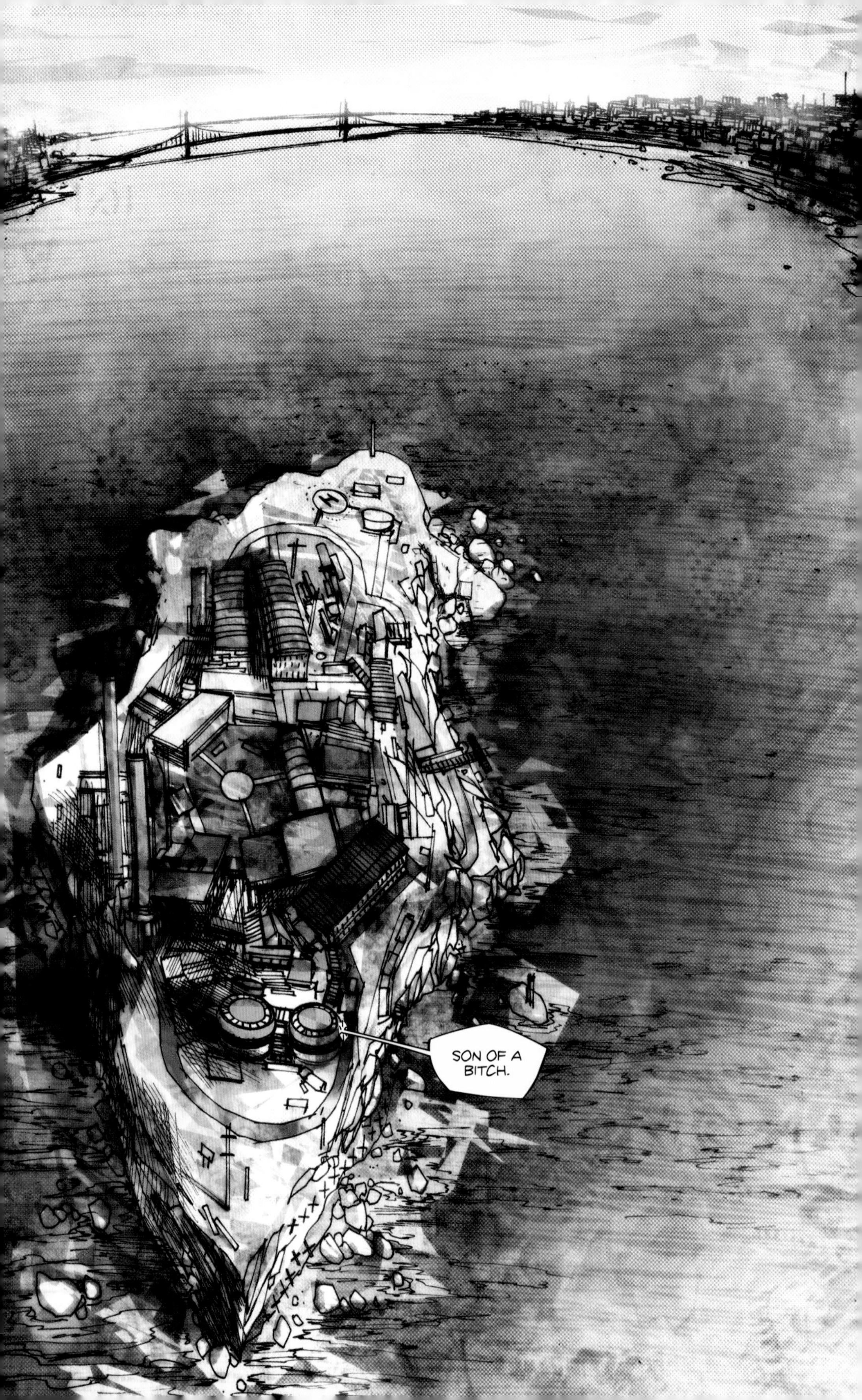
SON OF A BITCH.

ISSUE THREE COVER

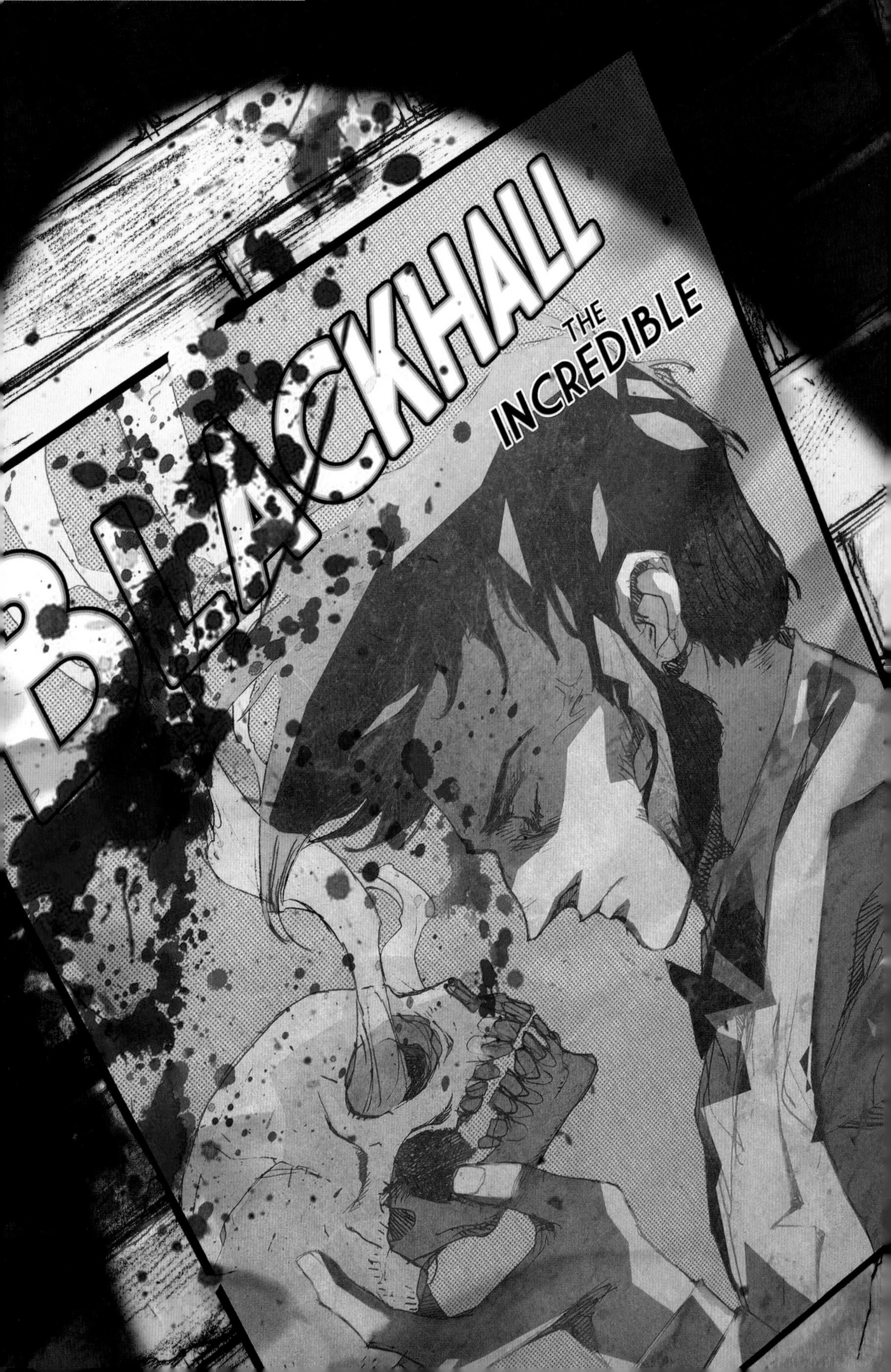
BLACKHALL
THE INCREDIBLE

CHAPTER 4: THE WORLD'S SMALLEST COUNTRY

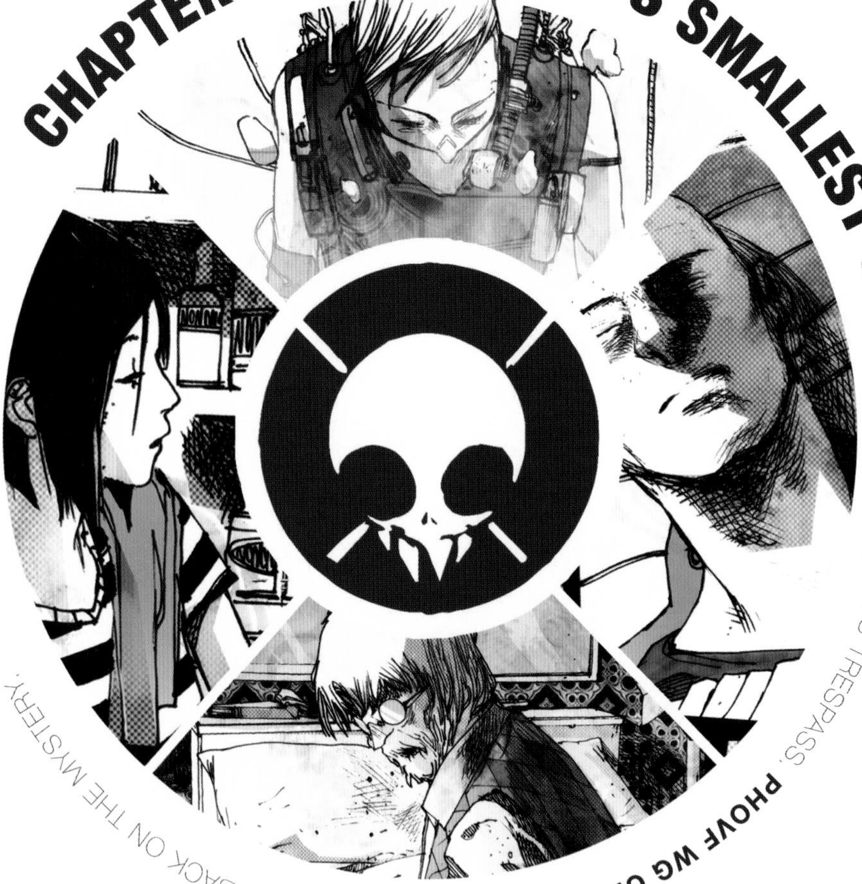

ALWAYS TRESPASS. PHOVF WG CMHVVMW. DON'T TURN YOUR BACK ON THE MYSTERY.

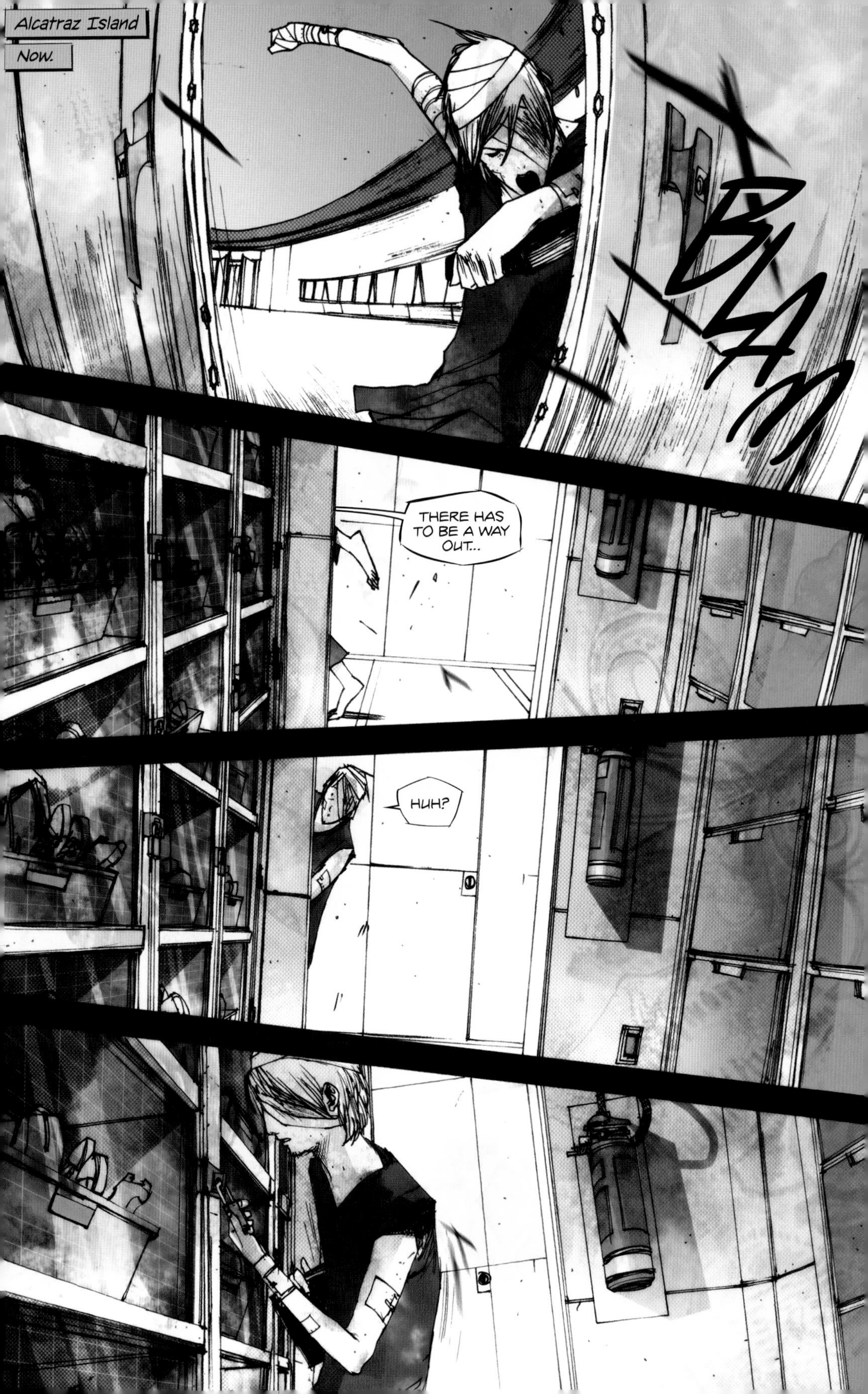

Alcatraz Island
Now.
BLAM
THERE HAS TO BE A WAY OUT...
HUH?

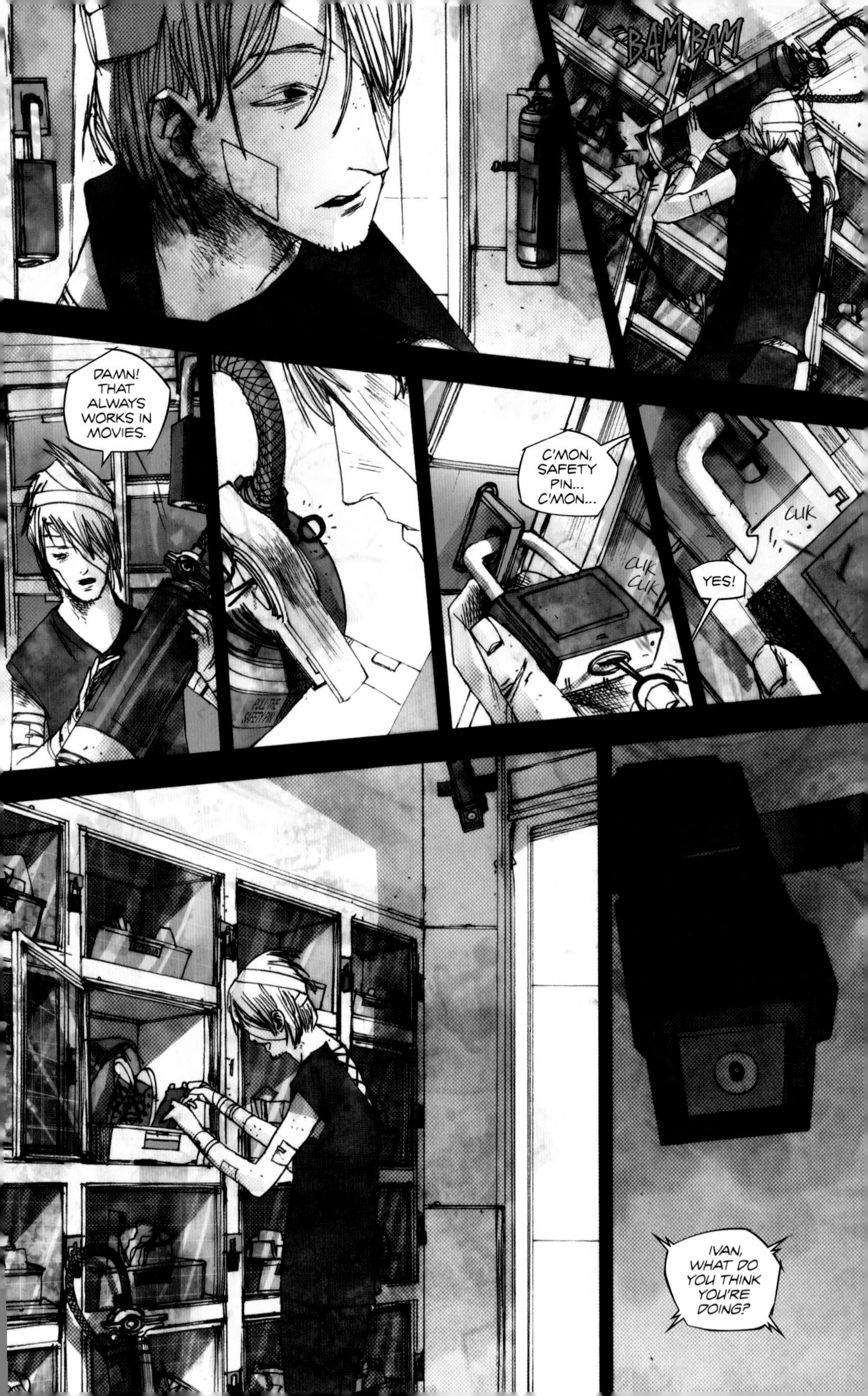

BAM BAM
DAMN! THAT ALWAYS WORKS IN MOVIES.
PULL THE SAFETY PIN
C'MON, SAFETY PIN... C'MON...
CLIK CLIK
CLIK
YES!
IVAN, WHAT DO YOU THINK YOU'RE DOING?

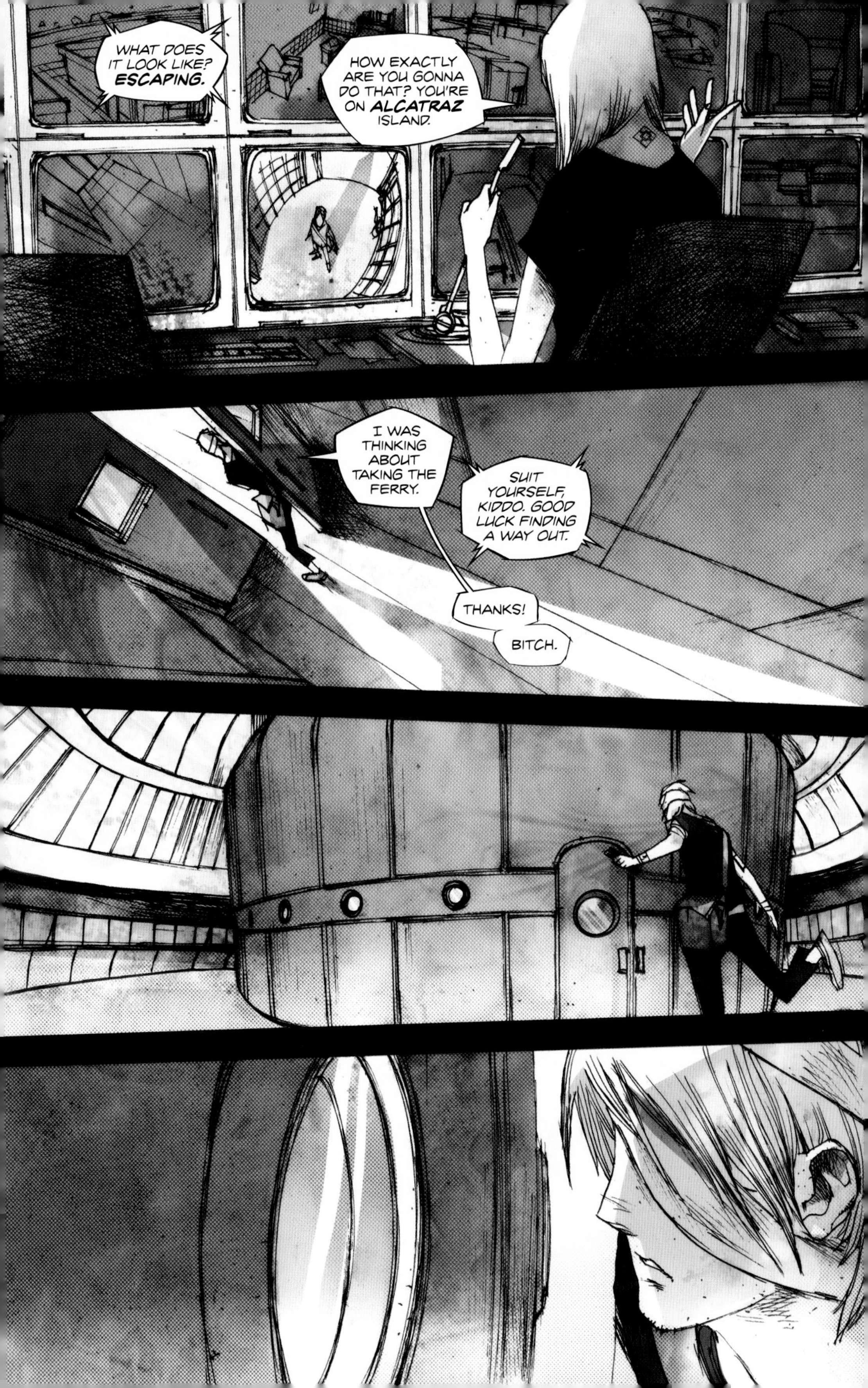
WHAT DOES IT LOOK LIKE? **ESCAPING.**
HOW EXACTLY ARE YOU GONNA DO THAT? YOU'RE ON **ALCATRAZ** ISLAND.
I WAS THINKING ABOUT TAKING THE FERRY.
SUIT YOURSELF, KIDDO. GOOD LUCK FINDING A WAY OUT.
THANKS!
BITCH.

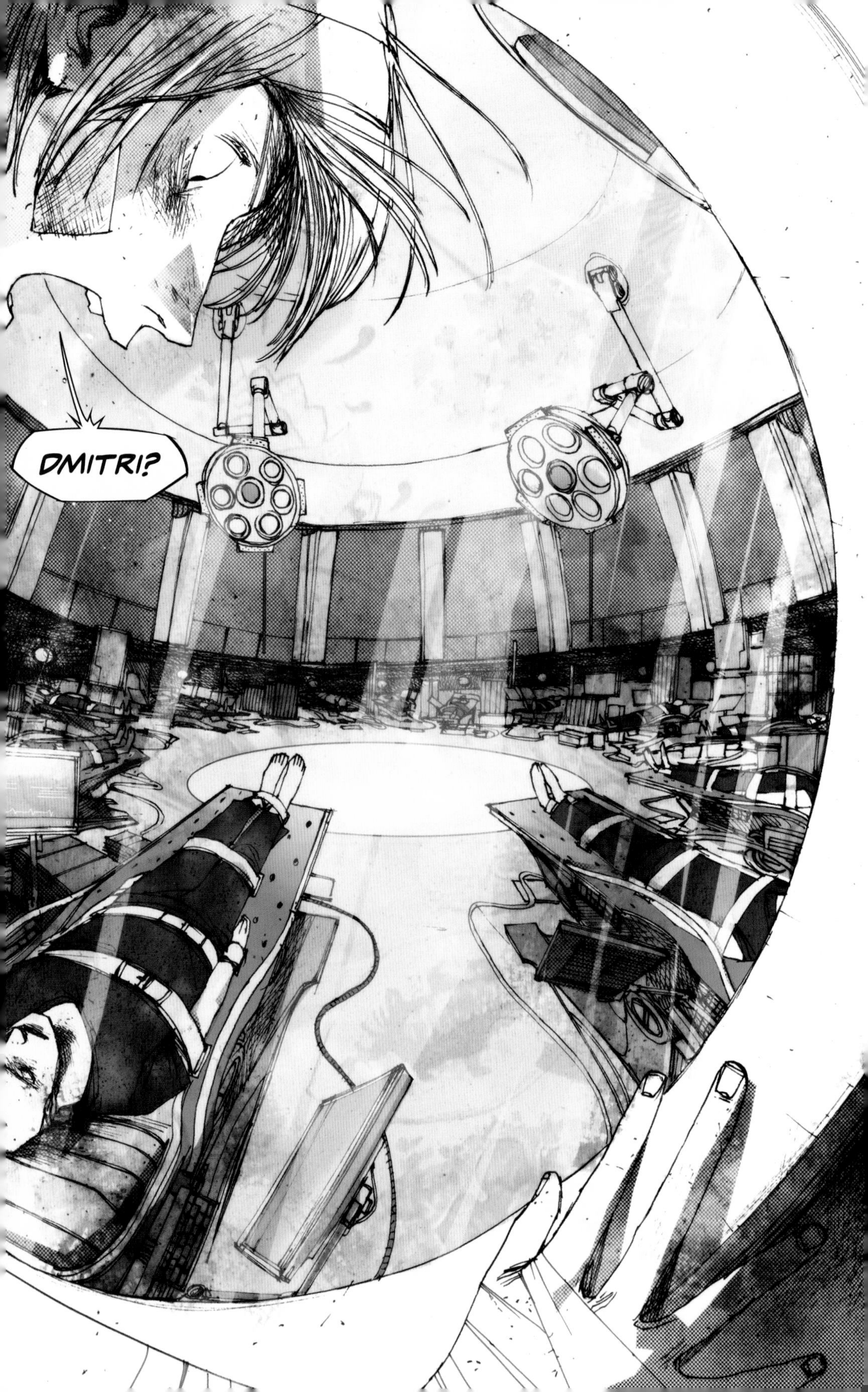
DMITRI?

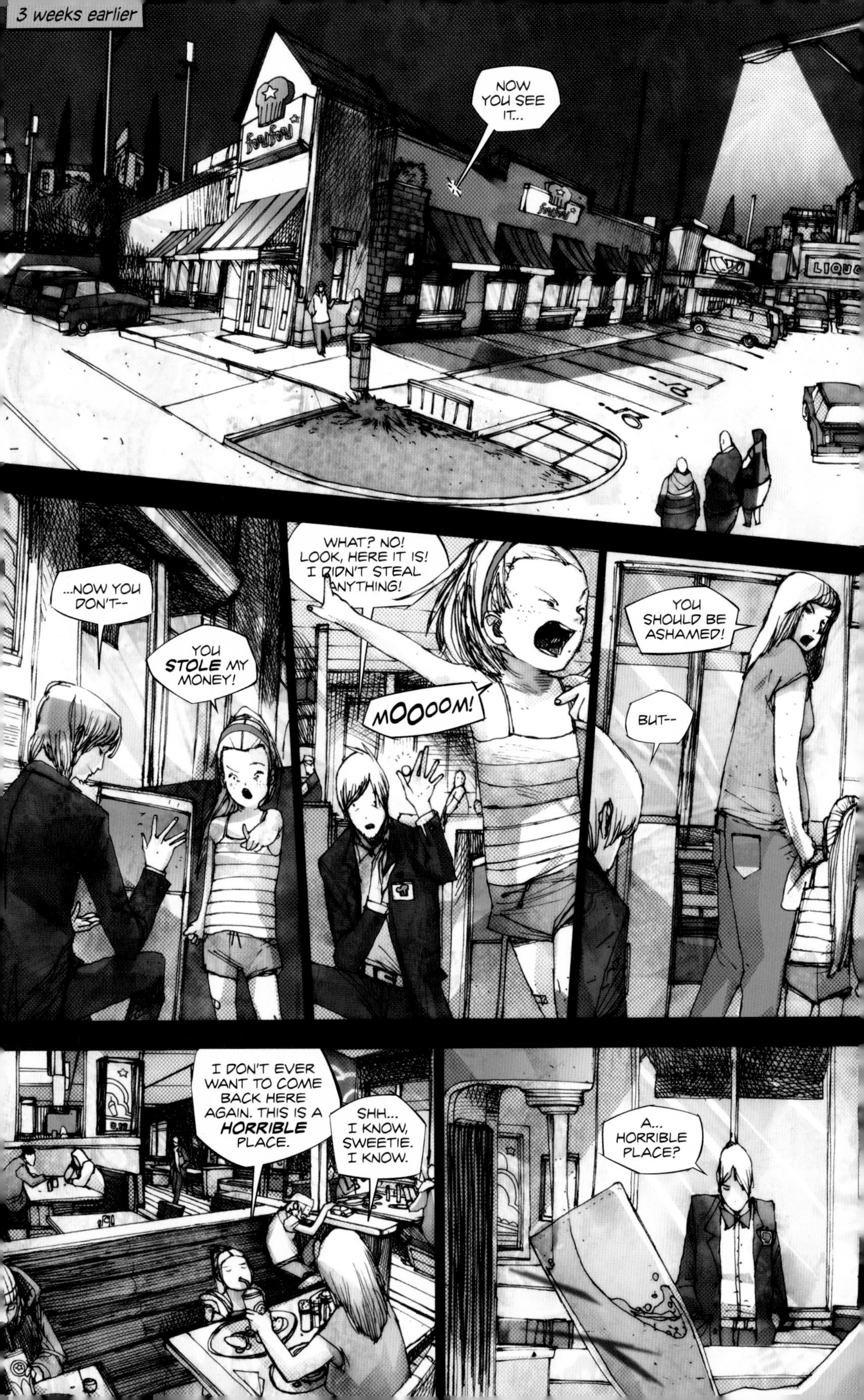
3 weeks earlier
NOW YOU SEE IT...
...NOW YOU DON'T--
YOU **STOLE** MY MONEY!
WHAT? NO! LOOK, HERE IT IS! I DIDN'T STEAL ANYTHING!
MOOOOM!
YOU SHOULD BE ASHAMED!
BUT--
I DON'T EVER WANT TO COME BACK HERE AGAIN. THIS IS A **HORRIBLE** PLACE.
SHH... I KNOW, SWEETIE. I KNOW.
A... HORRIBLE PLACE?

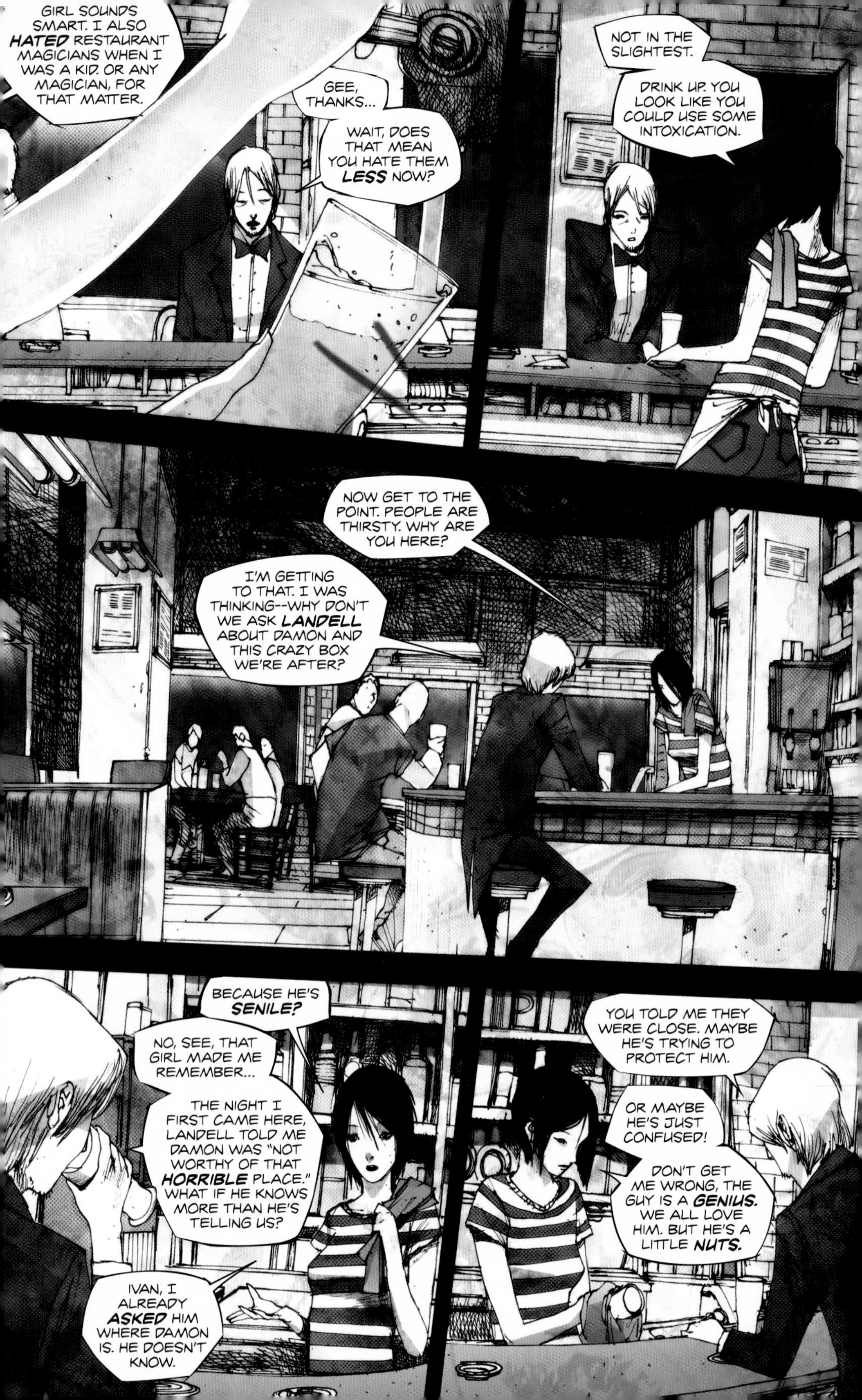
GIRL SOUNDS SMART. I ALSO HATED RESTAURANT MAGICIANS WHEN I WAS A KID. OR ANY MAGICIAN, FOR THAT MATTER.
GEE, THANKS...
WAIT, DOES THAT MEAN YOU HATE THEM LESS NOW?
NOT IN THE SLIGHTEST.
DRINK UP. YOU LOOK LIKE YOU COULD USE SOME INTOXICATION.
NOW GET TO THE POINT. PEOPLE ARE THIRSTY. WHY ARE YOU HERE?
I'M GETTING TO THAT. I WAS THINKING--WHY DON'T WE ASK LANDELL ABOUT DAMON AND THIS CRAZY BOX WE'RE AFTER?
BECAUSE HE'S SENILE?
NO, SEE, THAT GIRL MADE ME REMEMBER...
THE NIGHT I FIRST CAME HERE, LANDELL TOLD ME DAMON WAS "NOT WORTHY OF THAT HORRIBLE PLACE." WHAT IF HE KNOWS MORE THAN HE'S TELLING US?
IVAN, I ALREADY ASKED HIM WHERE DAMON IS. HE DOESN'T KNOW.
YOU TOLD ME THEY WERE CLOSE. MAYBE HE'S TRYING TO PROTECT HIM.
OR MAYBE HE'S JUST CONFUSED!
DON'T GET ME WRONG, THE GUY IS A GENIUS. WE ALL LOVE HIM. BUT HE'S A LITTLE NUTS.

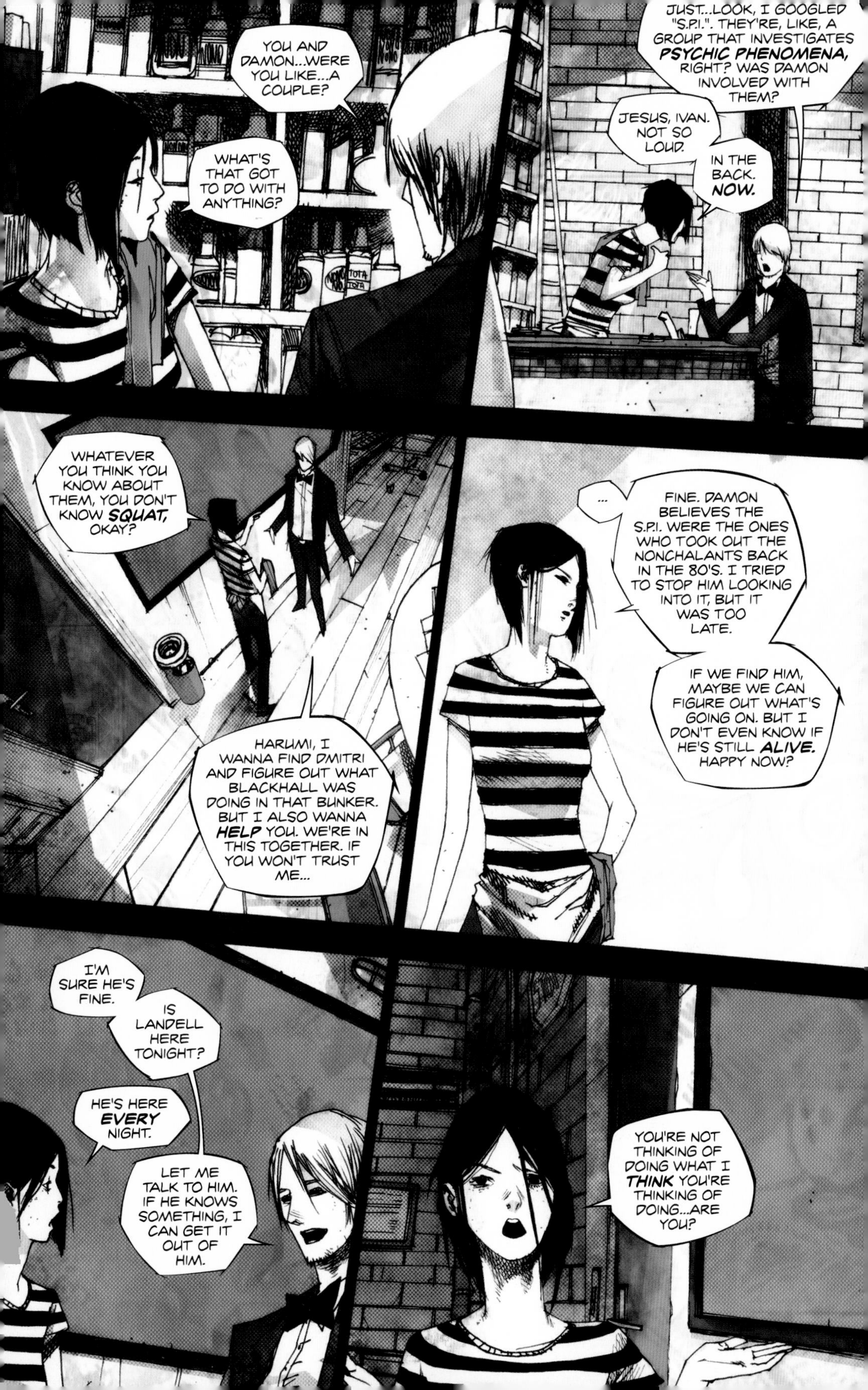
YOU AND DAMON...WERE YOU LIKE...A COUPLE?
WHAT'S THAT GOT TO DO WITH ANYTHING?
JUST...LOOK, I GOOGLED "S.P.I.". THEY'RE, LIKE, A GROUP THAT INVESTIGATES PSYCHIC PHENOMENA, RIGHT? WAS DAMON INVOLVED WITH THEM?
JESUS, IVAN. NOT SO LOUD.
IN THE BACK. NOW.
WHATEVER YOU THINK YOU KNOW ABOUT THEM, YOU DON'T KNOW SQUAT, OKAY?
HARUMI, I WANNA FIND DMITRI AND FIGURE OUT WHAT BLACKHALL WAS DOING IN THAT BUNKER. BUT I ALSO WANNA HELP YOU. WE'RE IN THIS TOGETHER. IF YOU WON'T TRUST ME...
...
FINE. DAMON BELIEVES THE S.P.I. WERE THE ONES WHO TOOK OUT THE NONCHALANTS BACK IN THE 80'S. I TRIED TO STOP HIM LOOKING INTO IT, BUT IT WAS TOO LATE.
IF WE FIND HIM, MAYBE WE CAN FIGURE OUT WHAT'S GOING ON. BUT I DON'T EVEN KNOW IF HE'S STILL ALIVE. HAPPY NOW?
I'M SURE HE'S FINE.
IS LANDELL HERE TONIGHT?
HE'S HERE EVERY NIGHT.
LET ME TALK TO HIM. IF HE KNOWS SOMETHING, I CAN GET IT OUT OF HIM.
YOU'RE NOT THINKING OF DOING WHAT I THINK YOU'RE THINKING OF DOING...ARE YOU?

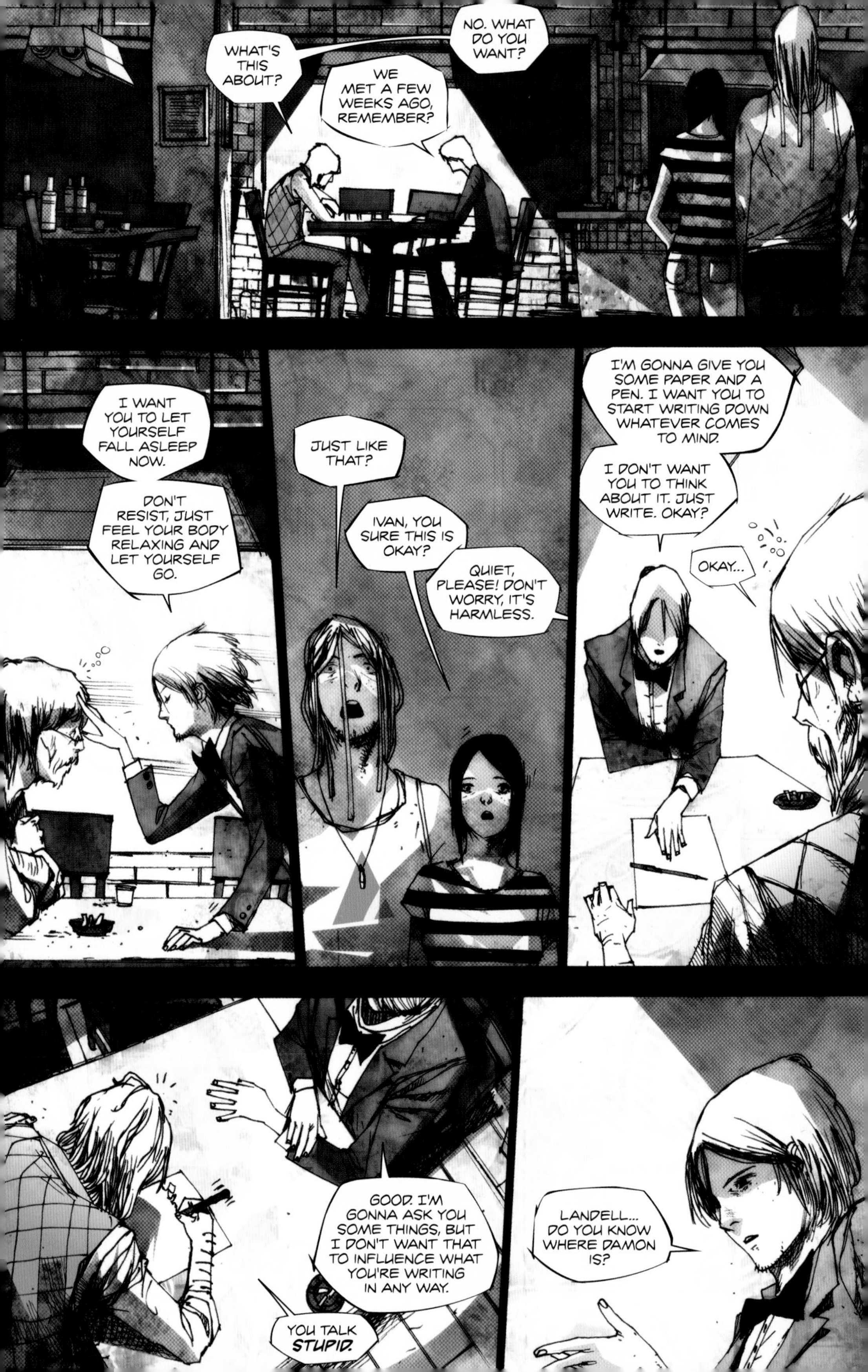
WHAT'S THIS ABOUT?
NO. WHAT DO YOU WANT?
WE MET A FEW WEEKS AGO, REMEMBER?
I WANT YOU TO LET YOURSELF FALL ASLEEP NOW.
DON'T RESIST, JUST FEEL YOUR BODY RELAXING AND LET YOURSELF GO.
JUST LIKE THAT?
IVAN, YOU SURE THIS IS OKAY?
QUIET, PLEASE! DON'T WORRY, IT'S HARMLESS.
I'M GONNA GIVE YOU SOME PAPER AND A PEN. I WANT YOU TO START WRITING DOWN WHATEVER COMES TO MIND.
I DON'T WANT YOU TO THINK ABOUT IT. JUST WRITE. OKAY?
OKAY...
GOOD. I'M GONNA ASK YOU SOME THINGS, BUT I DON'T WANT THAT TO INFLUENCE WHAT YOU'RE WRITING IN ANY WAY.
YOU TALK **STUPID.**
LANDELL... DO YOU KNOW WHERE DAMON IS?

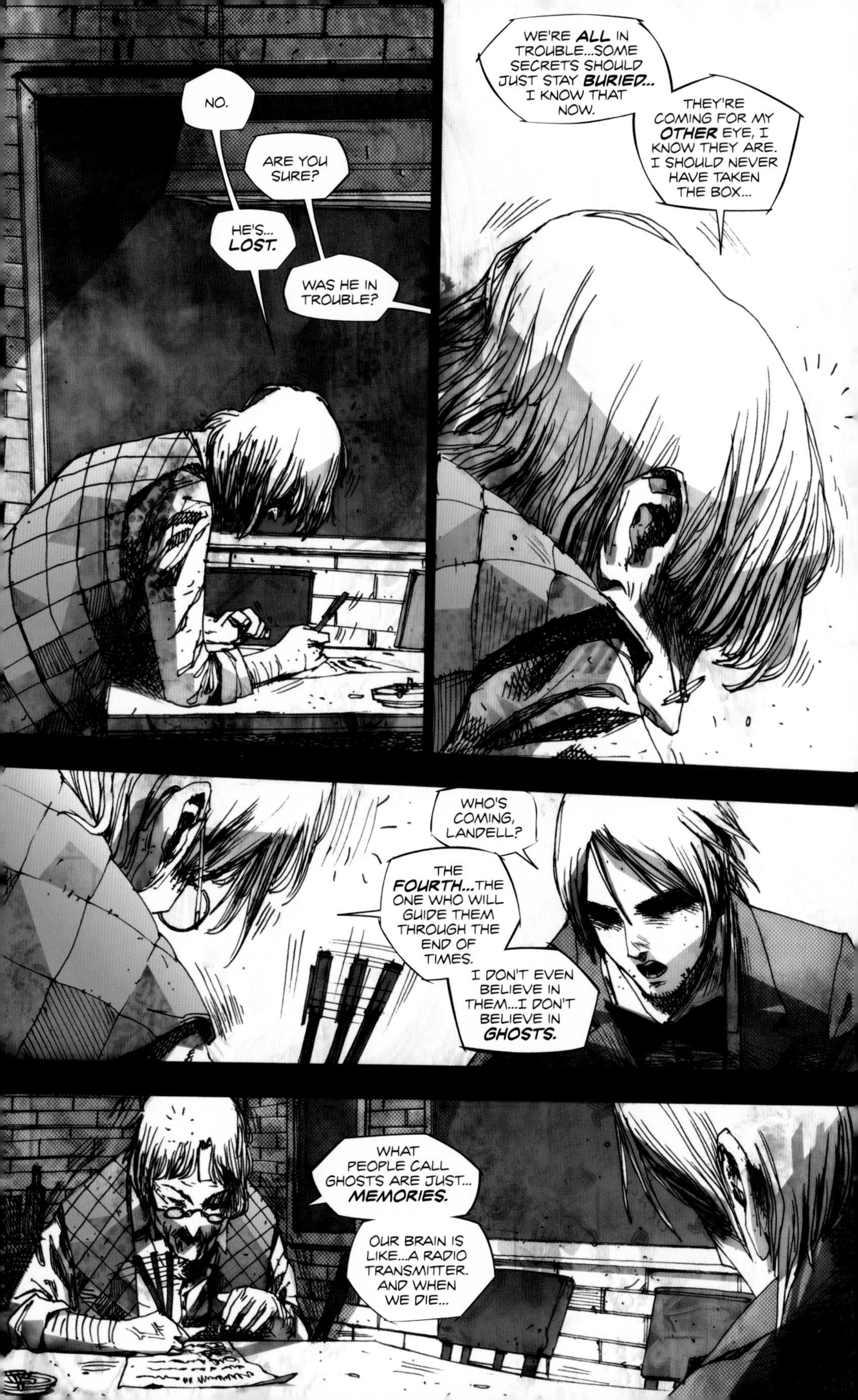
NO.
ARE YOU SURE?
HE'S... LOST.
WAS HE IN TROUBLE?
WE'RE ALL IN TROUBLE...SOME SECRETS SHOULD JUST STAY BURIED... I KNOW THAT NOW.
THEY'RE COMING FOR MY OTHER EYE, I KNOW THEY ARE. I SHOULD NEVER HAVE TAKEN THE BOX...
WHO'S COMING, LANDELL?
THE FOURTH...THE ONE WHO WILL GUIDE THEM THROUGH THE END OF TIMES.
I DON'T EVEN BELIEVE IN THEM...I DON'T BELIEVE IN GHOSTS.
WHAT PEOPLE CALL GHOSTS ARE JUST... MEMORIES.
OUR BRAIN IS LIKE...A RADIO TRANSMITTER. AND WHEN WE DIE...

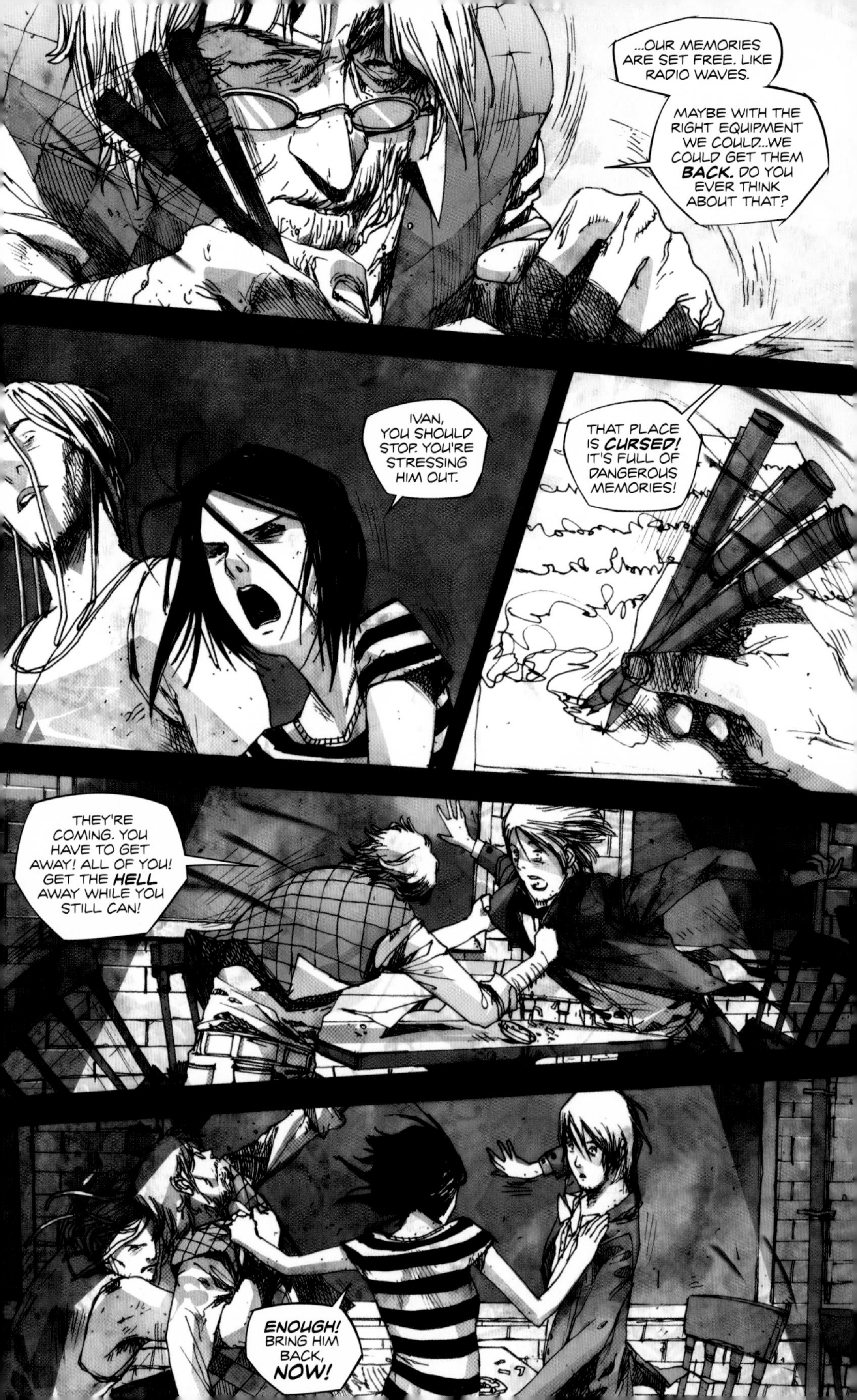
...OUR MEMORIES ARE SET FREE. LIKE RADIO WAVES.
MAYBE WITH THE RIGHT EQUIPMENT WE COULD...WE COULD GET THEM **BACK.** DO YOU EVER THINK ABOUT THAT?
IVAN, YOU SHOULD STOP. YOU'RE STRESSING HIM OUT.
THAT PLACE IS ***CURSED!*** IT'S FULL OF DANGEROUS MEMORIES!
THEY'RE COMING. YOU HAVE TO GET AWAY! ALL OF YOU! GET THE ***HELL*** AWAY WHILE YOU STILL CAN!
ENOUGH! BRING HIM BACK, ***NOW!***

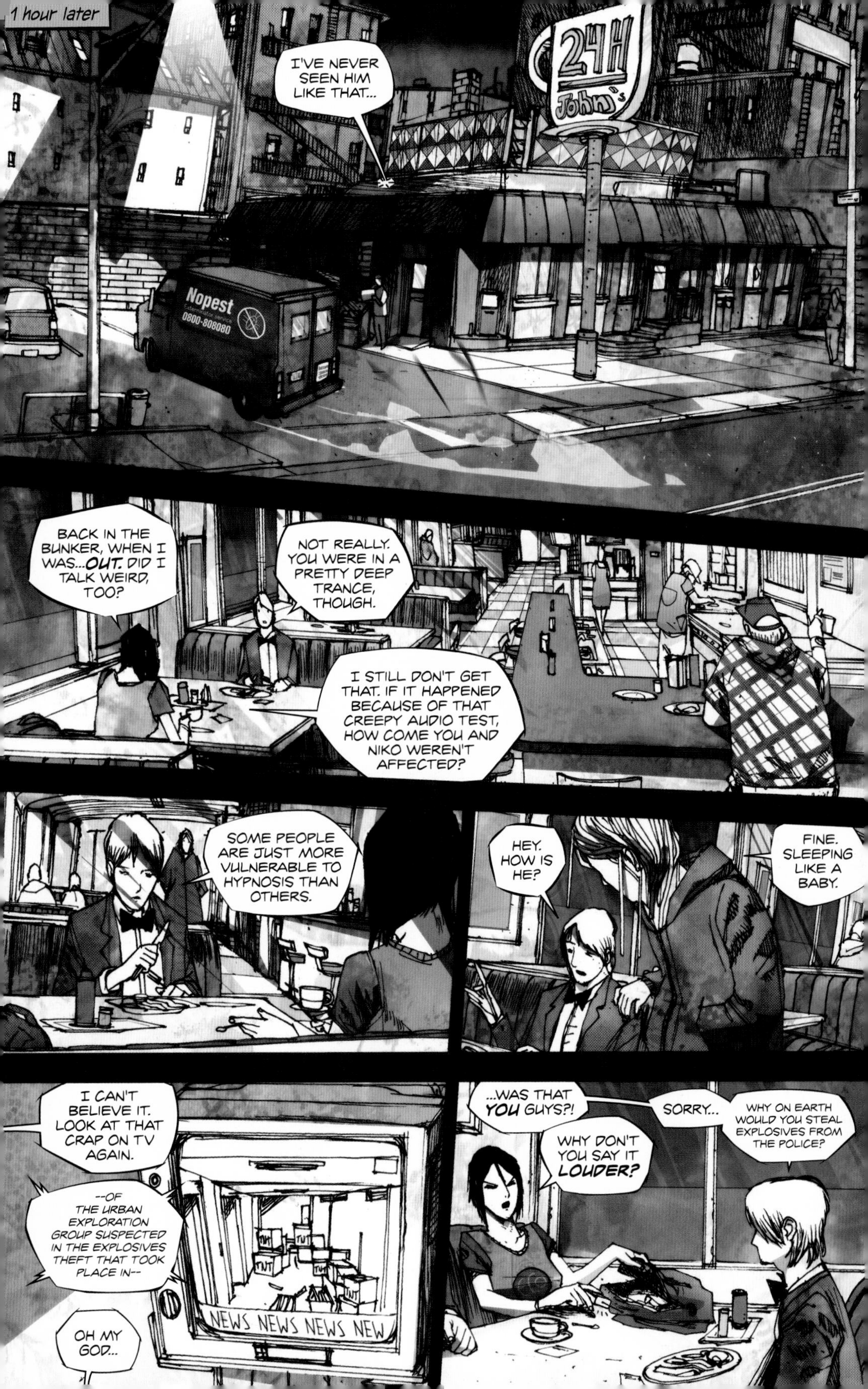
1 hour later
I'VE NEVER SEEN HIM LIKE THAT...
24H
John's
Nopest
0800-808080
BACK IN THE BUNKER, WHEN I WAS...OUT. DID I TALK WEIRD, TOO?
NOT REALLY. YOU WERE IN A PRETTY DEEP TRANCE, THOUGH.
I STILL DON'T GET THAT. IF IT HAPPENED BECAUSE OF THAT CREEPY AUDIO TEST, HOW COME YOU AND NIKO WEREN'T AFFECTED?
SOME PEOPLE ARE JUST MORE VULNERABLE TO HYPNOSIS THAN OTHERS.
HEY. HOW IS HE?
FINE. SLEEPING LIKE A BABY.
I CAN'T BELIEVE IT. LOOK AT THAT CRAP ON TV AGAIN.
--OF THE URBAN EXPLORATION GROUP SUSPECTED IN THE EXPLOSIVES THEFT THAT TOOK PLACE IN--
NEWS NEWS NEWS NEW
OH MY GOD...
...WAS THAT YOU GUYS?!
SORRY...
WHY ON EARTH WOULD YOU STEAL EXPLOSIVES FROM THE POLICE?
WHY DON'T YOU SAY IT LOUDER?

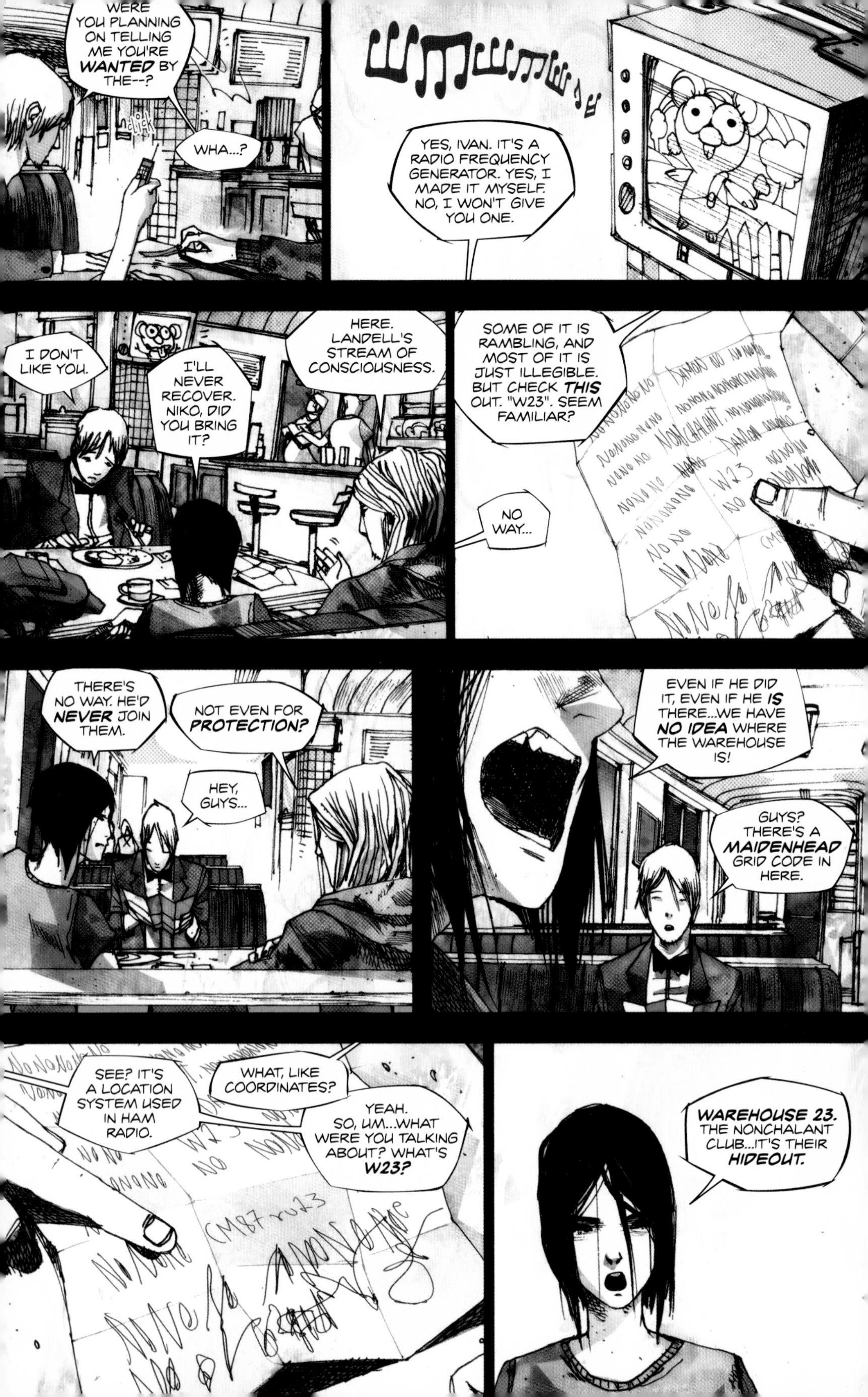
WERE YOU PLANNING ON TELLING ME YOU'RE **WANTED** BY THE--?
WHA...?
YES, IVAN. IT'S A RADIO FREQUENCY GENERATOR. YES, I MADE IT MYSELF. NO, I WON'T GIVE YOU ONE.
I DON'T LIKE YOU.
I'LL NEVER RECOVER. NIKO, DID YOU BRING IT?
HERE. LANDELL'S STREAM OF CONSCIOUSNESS.
SOME OF IT IS RAMBLING, AND MOST OF IT IS JUST ILLEGIBLE. BUT CHECK **THIS** OUT. "W23". SEEM FAMILIAR?
NO WAY...
THERE'S NO WAY. HE'D **NEVER** JOIN THEM.
NOT EVEN FOR **PROTECTION?**
HEY, GUYS...
EVEN IF HE DID IT, EVEN IF HE **IS** THERE...WE HAVE **NO IDEA** WHERE THE WAREHOUSE IS!
GUYS? THERE'S A **MAIDENHEAD** GRID CODE IN HERE.
SEE? IT'S A LOCATION SYSTEM USED IN HAM RADIO.
WHAT, LIKE COORDINATES?
YEAH. SO, UM...WHAT WERE YOU TALKING ABOUT? WHAT'S **W23?**
WAREHOUSE 23. THE NONCHALANT CLUB...IT'S THEIR **HIDEOUT.**

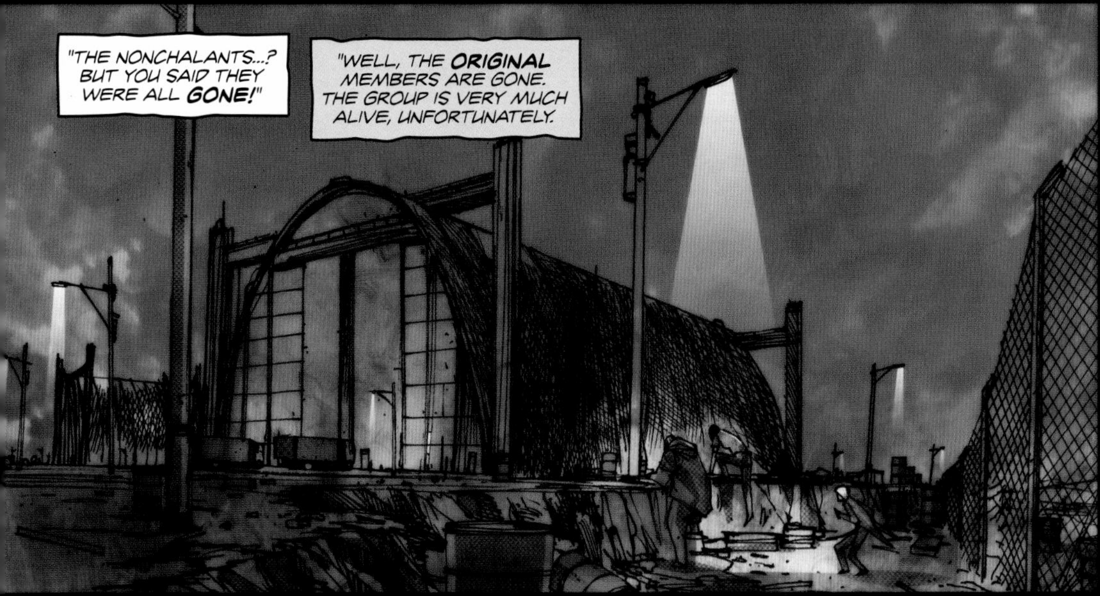
"THE NONCHALANTS...? BUT YOU SAID THEY WERE ALL GONE!"
"WELL, THE ORIGINAL MEMBERS ARE GONE. THE GROUP IS VERY MUCH ALIVE, UNFORTUNATELY.

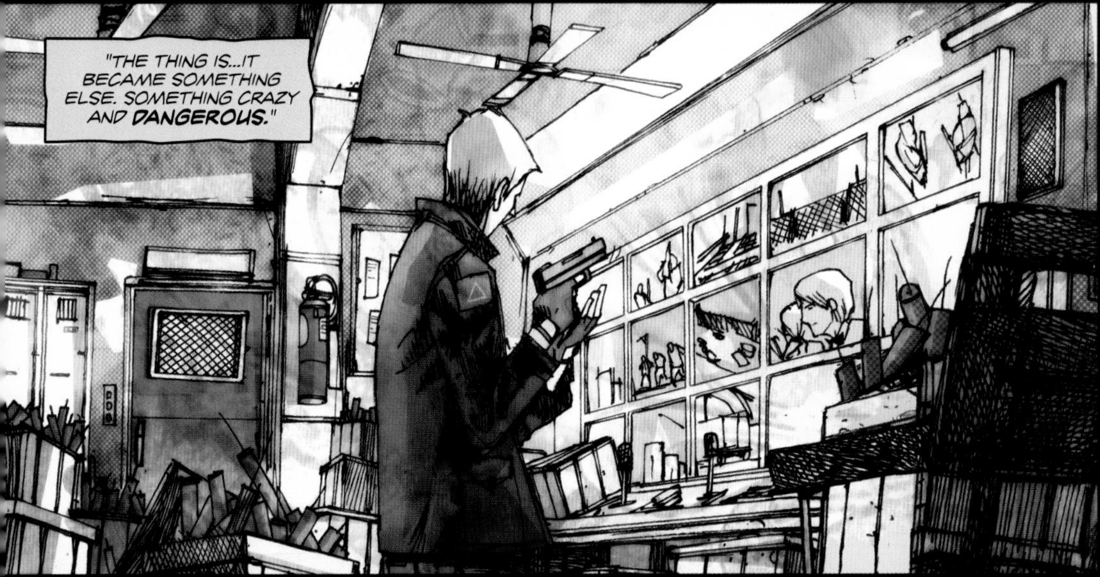
"THE THING IS...IT BECAME SOMETHING ELSE. SOMETHING CRAZY AND DANGEROUS."

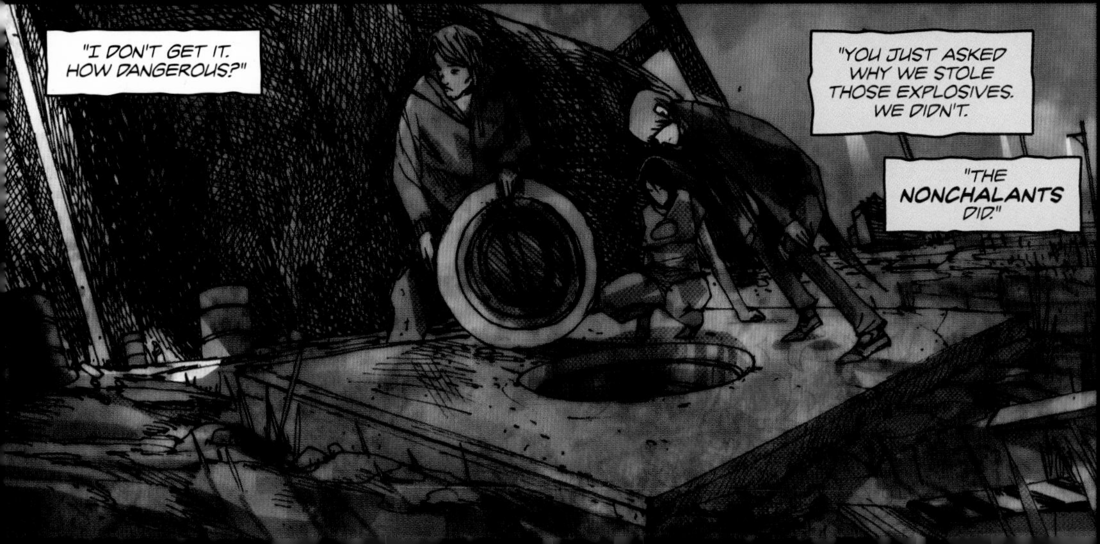
"I DON'T GET IT. HOW DANGEROUS?"
"YOU JUST ASKED WHY WE STOLE THOSE EXPLOSIVES. WE DIDN'T.
"THE NONCHALANTS DID."

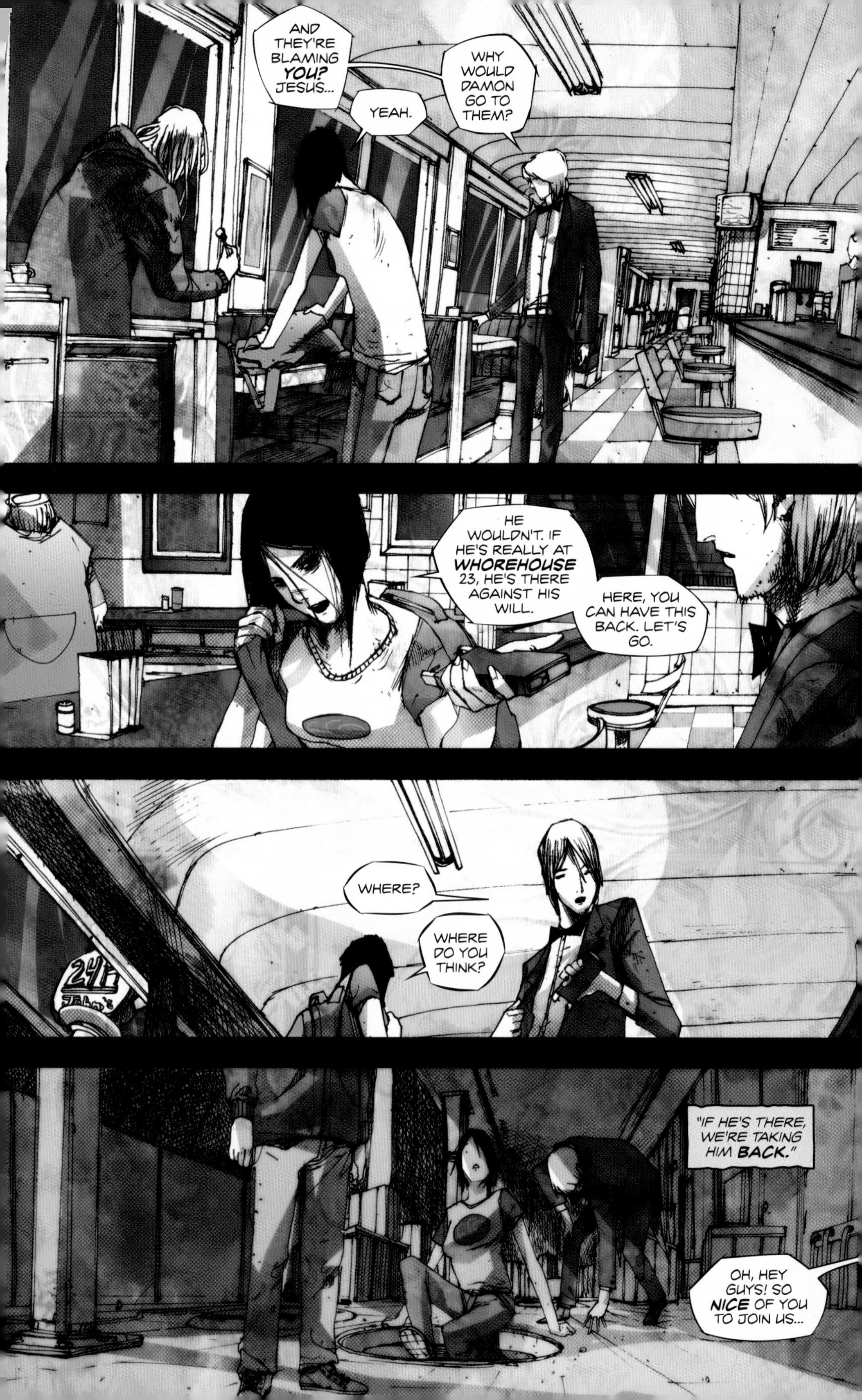
AND THEY'RE BLAMING ***YOU?*** JESUS...
WHY WOULD DAMON GO TO THEM?
YEAH.
HE WOULDN'T. IF HE'S REALLY AT ***WHOREHOUSE*** 23, HE'S THERE AGAINST HIS WILL.
HERE, YOU CAN HAVE THIS BACK. LET'S GO.
WHERE?
WHERE DO YOU THINK?
"IF HE'S THERE, WE'RE TAKING HIM ***BACK.***"
OH, HEY GUYS! SO ***NICE*** OF YOU TO JOIN US...

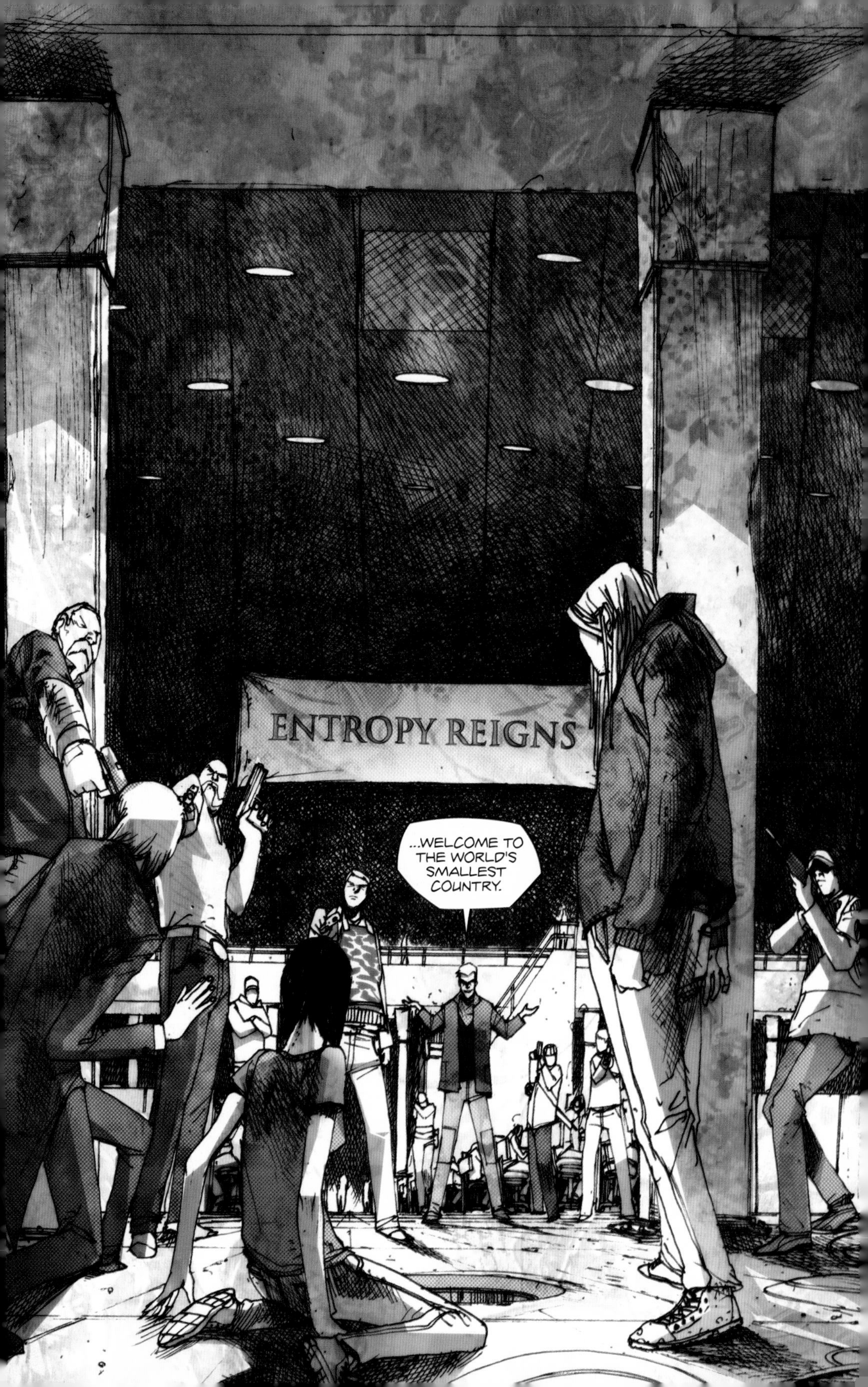
ENTROPY REIGNS
...WELCOME TO THE WORLD'S SMALLEST COUNTRY.

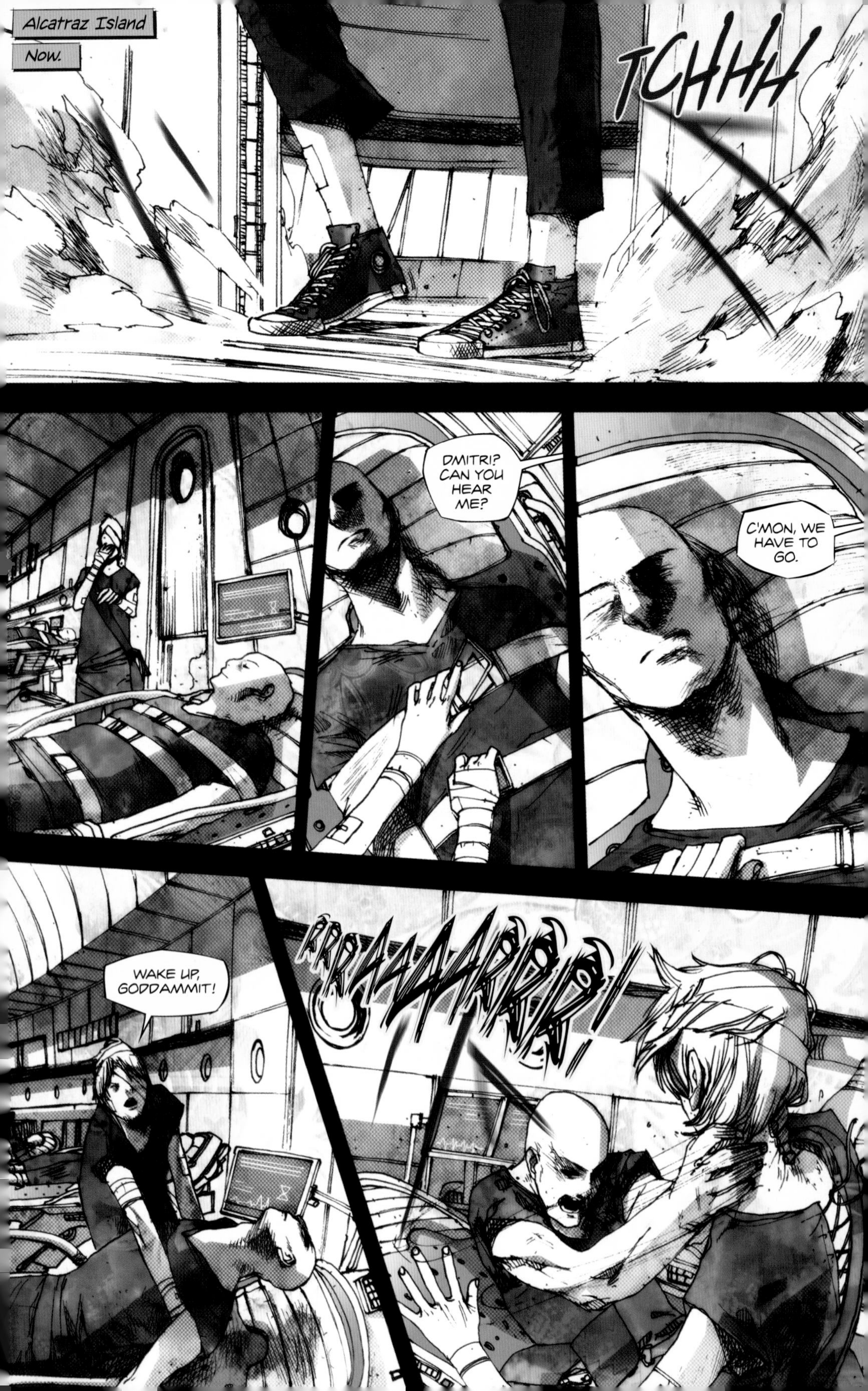
Alcatraz Island
Now.
TCHHH
DMITRI? CAN YOU HEAR ME?
C'MON, WE HAVE TO GO.
WAKE UP, GODDAMMIT!
RRRAAAARRRR!

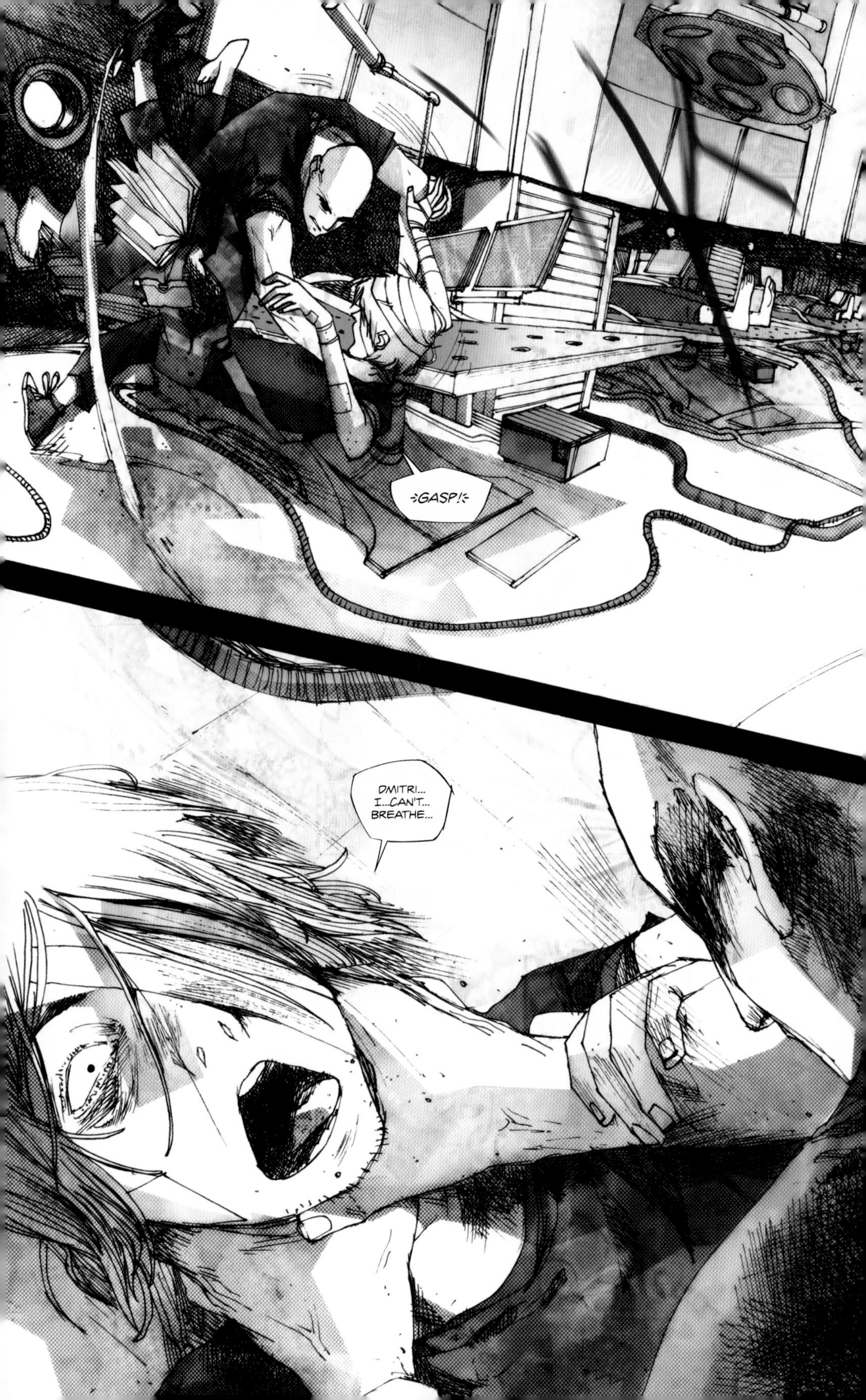
GASP!
DMITRI... I...CAN'T... BREATHE...

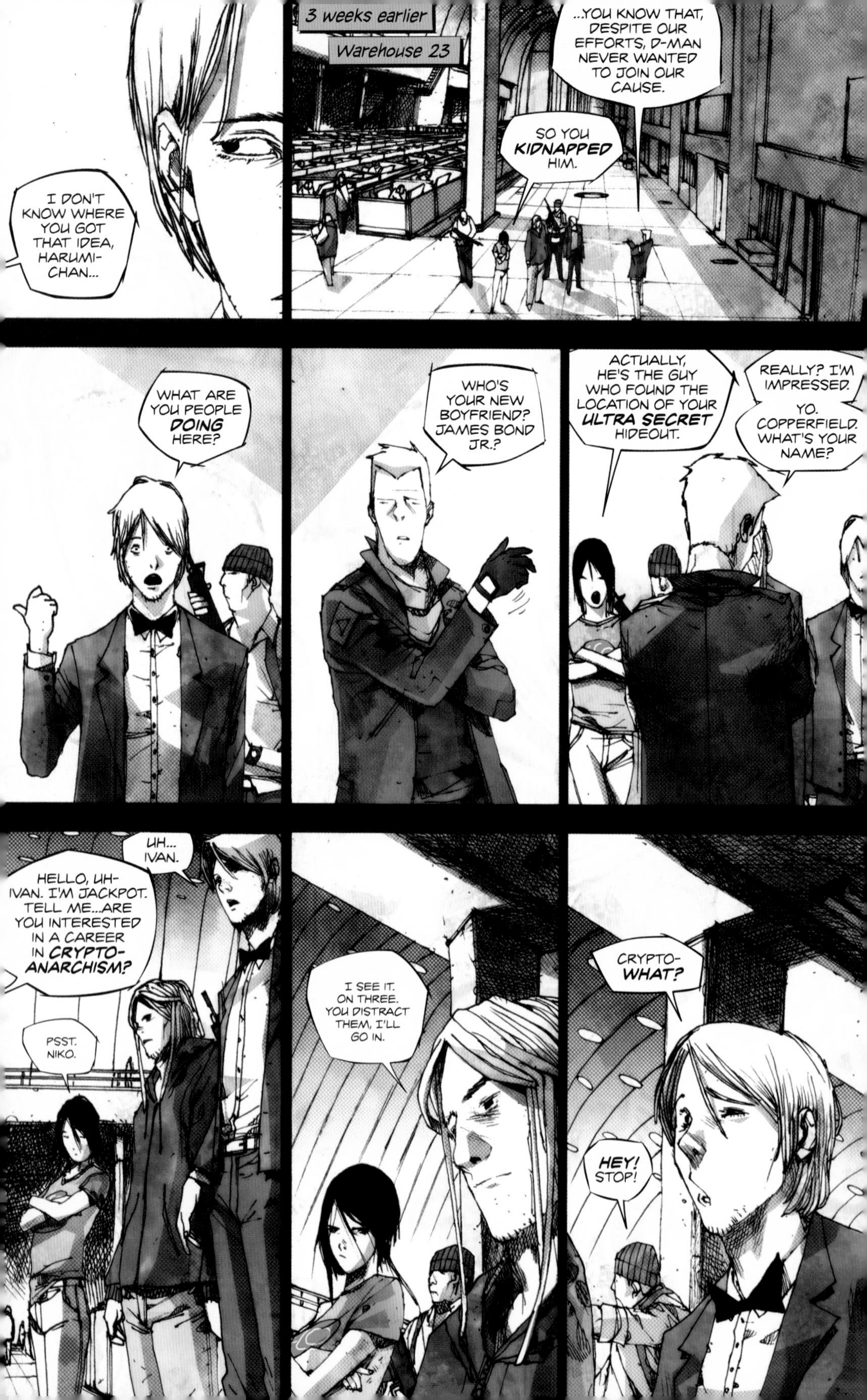
I DON'T KNOW WHERE YOU GOT THAT IDEA, HARUMI-CHAN...
3 weeks earlier
Warehouse 23
...YOU KNOW THAT, DESPITE OUR EFFORTS, D-MAN NEVER WANTED TO JOIN OUR CAUSE.
SO YOU KIDNAPPED HIM.
WHAT ARE YOU PEOPLE DOING HERE?
WHO'S YOUR NEW BOYFRIEND? JAMES BOND JR.?
ACTUALLY, HE'S THE GUY WHO FOUND THE LOCATION OF YOUR ULTRA SECRET HIDEOUT.
REALLY? I'M IMPRESSED.
YO. COPPERFIELD. WHAT'S YOUR NAME?
UH... IVAN.
HELLO, UH-IVAN. I'M JACKPOT. TELL ME...ARE YOU INTERESTED IN A CAREER IN CRYPTO-ANARCHISM?
PSST. NIKO.
I SEE IT. ON THREE. YOU DISTRACT THEM, I'LL GO IN.
CRYPTO-WHAT?
HEY! STOP!

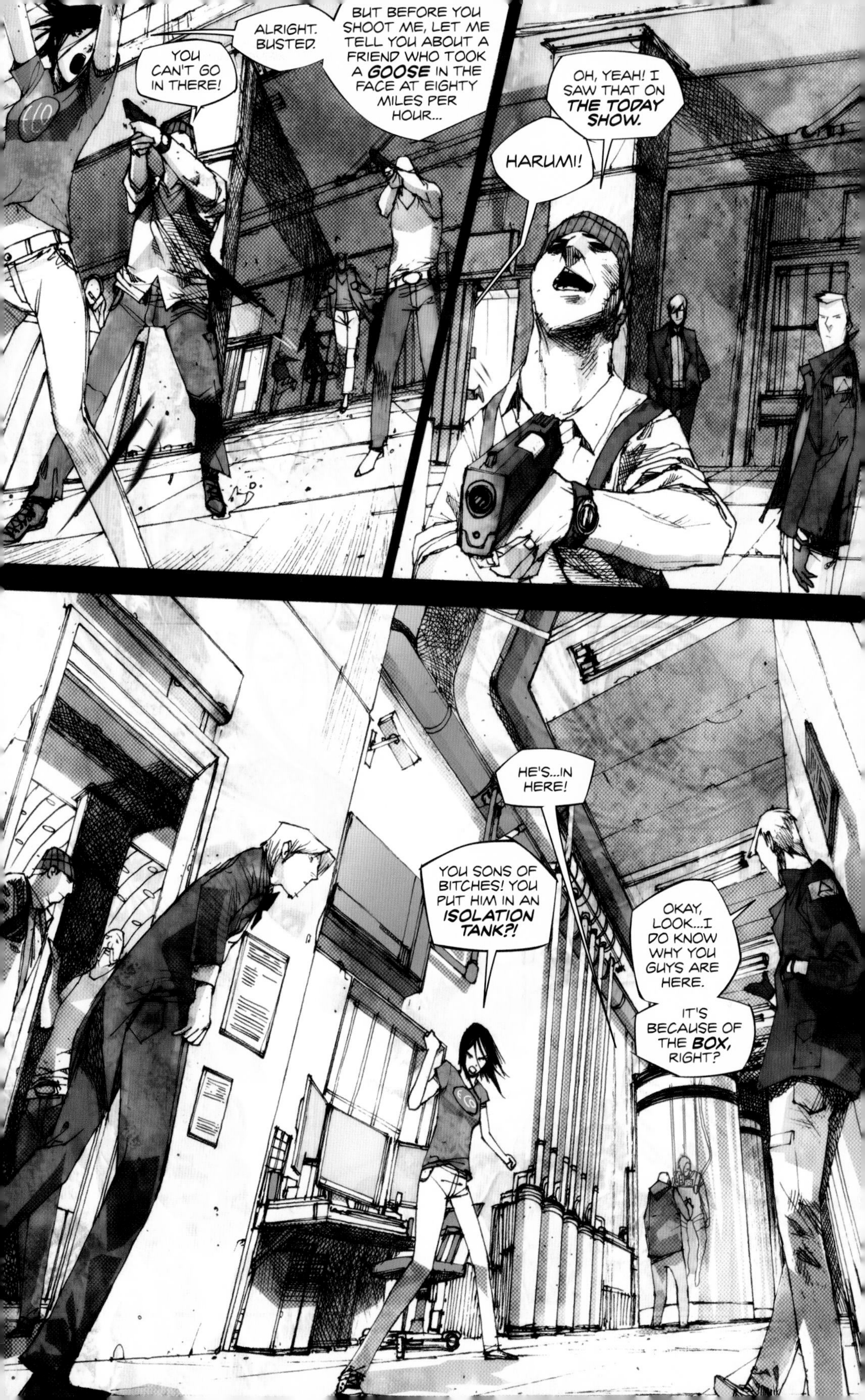
YOU CAN'T GO IN THERE!
ALRIGHT. BUSTED.
BUT BEFORE YOU SHOOT ME, LET ME TELL YOU ABOUT A FRIEND WHO TOOK A GOOSE IN THE FACE AT EIGHTY MILES PER HOUR...
OH, YEAH! I SAW THAT ON THE TODAY SHOW.
HARUMI!
HE'S...IN HERE!
YOU SONS OF BITCHES! YOU PUT HIM IN AN ISOLATION TANK?!
OKAY, LOOK...I DO KNOW WHY YOU GUYS ARE HERE.
IT'S BECAUSE OF THE BOX, RIGHT?

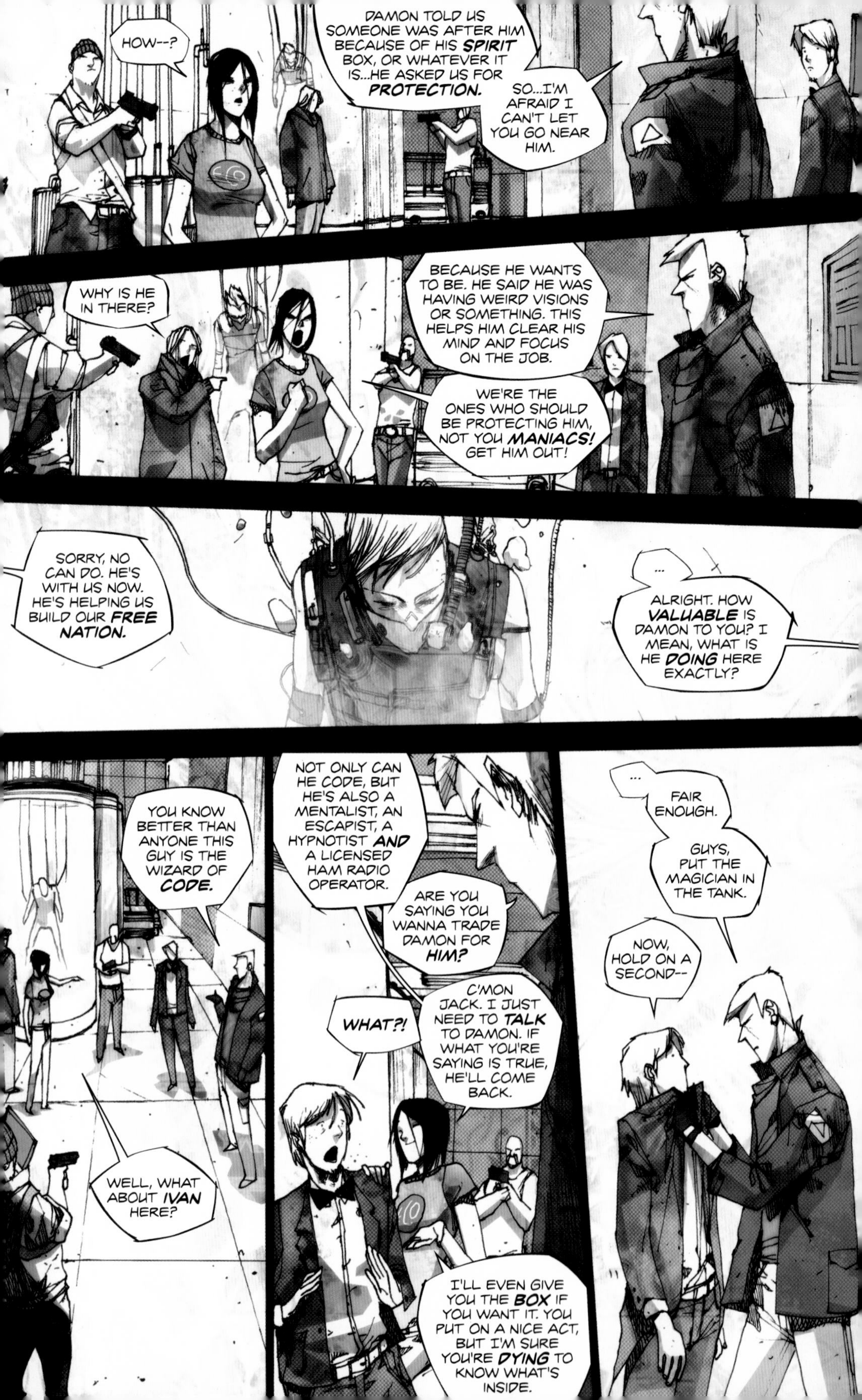
HOW--?
DAMON TOLD US SOMEONE WAS AFTER HIM BECAUSE OF HIS **SPIRIT** BOX, OR WHATEVER IT IS...HE ASKED US FOR **PROTECTION.**
SO...I'M AFRAID I CAN'T LET YOU GO NEAR HIM.
WHY IS HE IN THERE?
BECAUSE HE WANTS TO BE. HE SAID HE WAS HAVING WEIRD VISIONS OR SOMETHING. THIS HELPS HIM CLEAR HIS MIND AND FOCUS ON THE JOB.
WE'RE THE ONES WHO SHOULD BE PROTECTING HIM, NOT YOU **MANIACS!** GET HIM OUT!
SORRY, NO CAN DO. HE'S WITH US NOW. HE'S HELPING US BUILD OUR **FREE NATION.**
...
ALRIGHT. HOW **VALUABLE** IS DAMON TO YOU? I MEAN, WHAT IS HE **DOING** HERE EXACTLY?
YOU KNOW BETTER THAN ANYONE THIS GUY IS THE WIZARD OF **CODE.**
WELL, WHAT ABOUT **IVAN** HERE?
NOT ONLY CAN HE CODE, BUT HE'S ALSO A MENTALIST, AN ESCAPIST, A HYPNOTIST **AND** A LICENSED HAM RADIO OPERATOR.
ARE YOU SAYING YOU WANNA TRADE DAMON FOR **HIM?**
WHAT?!
C'MON JACK. I JUST NEED TO **TALK** TO DAMON. IF WHAT YOU'RE SAYING IS TRUE, HE'LL COME BACK.
I'LL EVEN GIVE YOU THE **BOX** IF YOU WANT IT. YOU PUT ON A NICE ACT, BUT I'M SURE YOU'RE **DYING** TO KNOW WHAT'S INSIDE.
...
FAIR ENOUGH.
GUYS, PUT THE MAGICIAN IN THE TANK.
NOW, HOLD ON A SECOND--

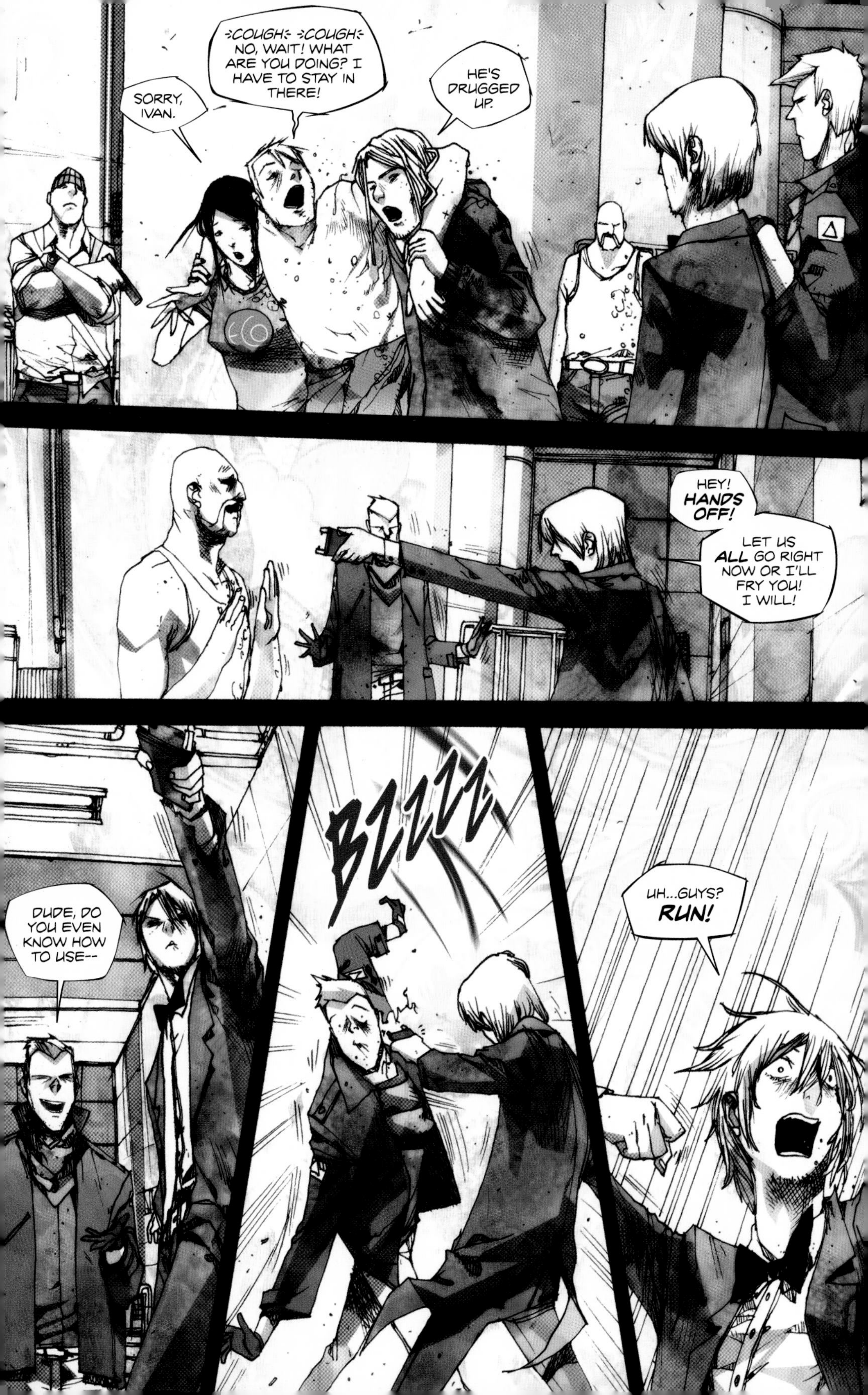
SORRY, IVAN.
>COUGH< >COUGH< NO, WAIT! WHAT ARE YOU DOING? I HAVE TO STAY IN THERE!
HE'S DRUGGED UP.
HEY! HANDS OFF!
LET US ALL GO RIGHT NOW OR I'LL FRY YOU! I WILL!
DUDE, DO YOU EVEN KNOW HOW TO USE--
BZZZZ
UH...GUYS? RUN!

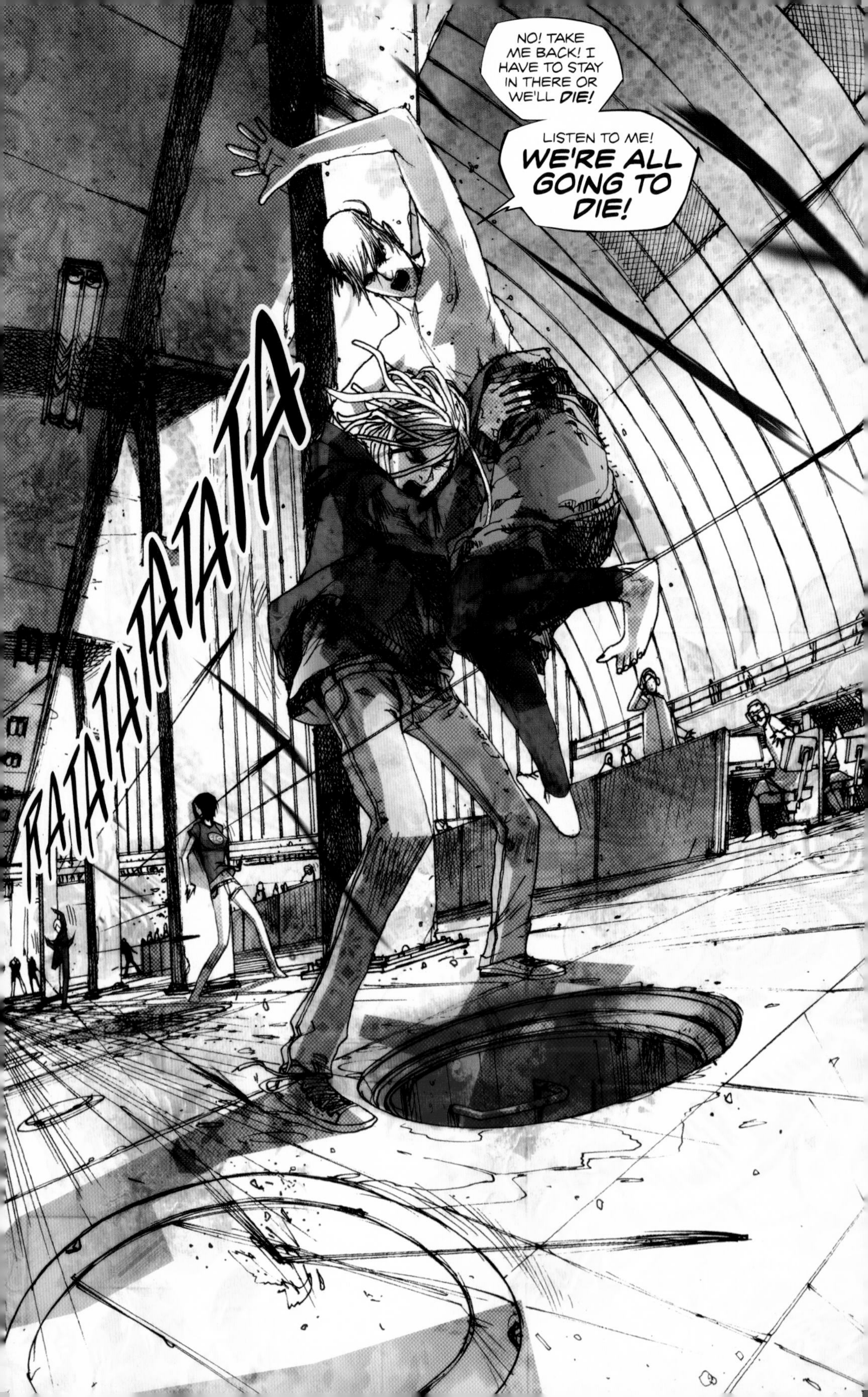
NO! TAKE ME BACK! I HAVE TO STAY IN THERE OR WE'LL DIE!
LISTEN TO ME! WE'RE ALL GOING TO DIE!
RATATATATATA

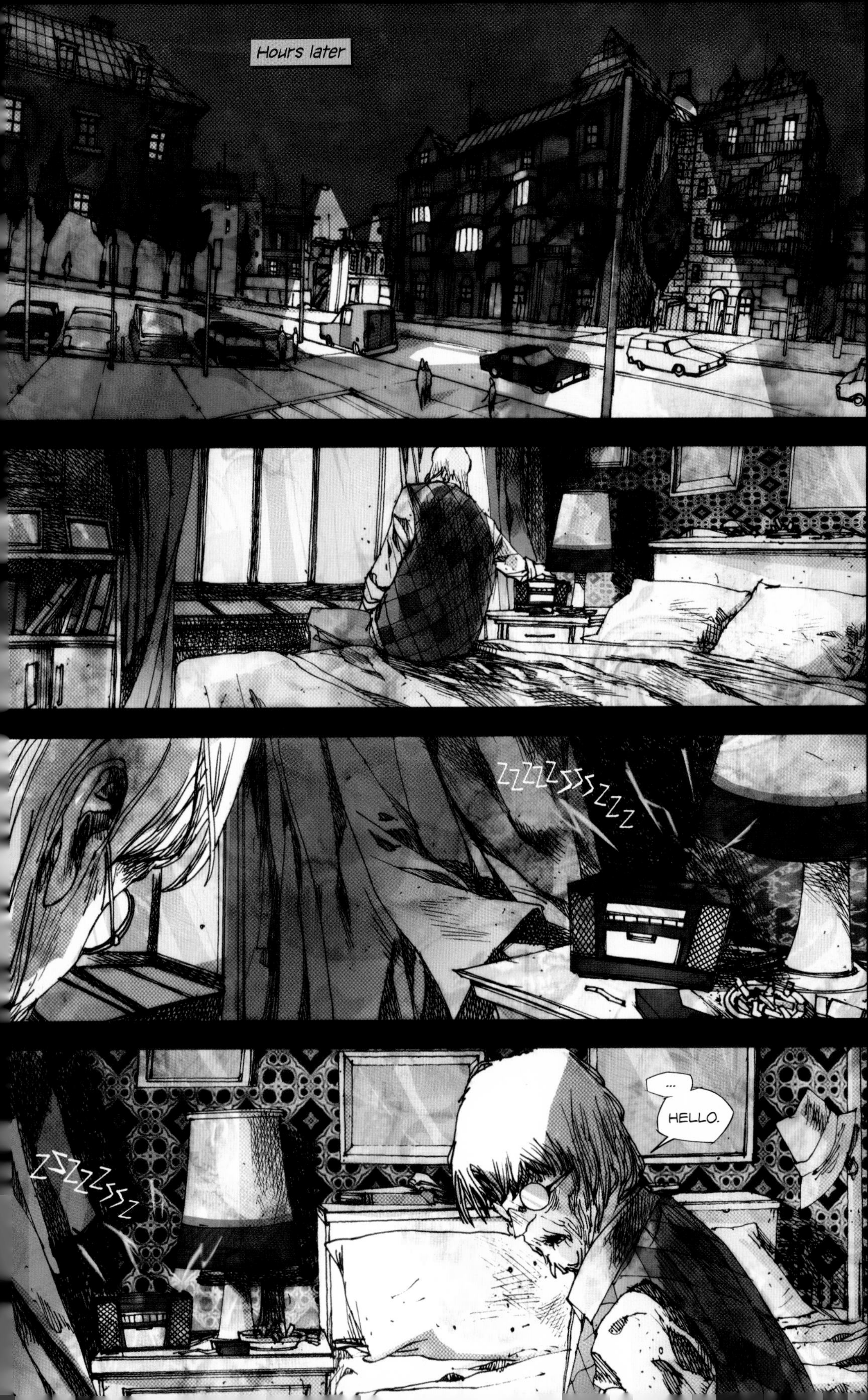
Hours later
ZZZZZSSSZZZ
...
HELLO.
ZZZZZSSSZ

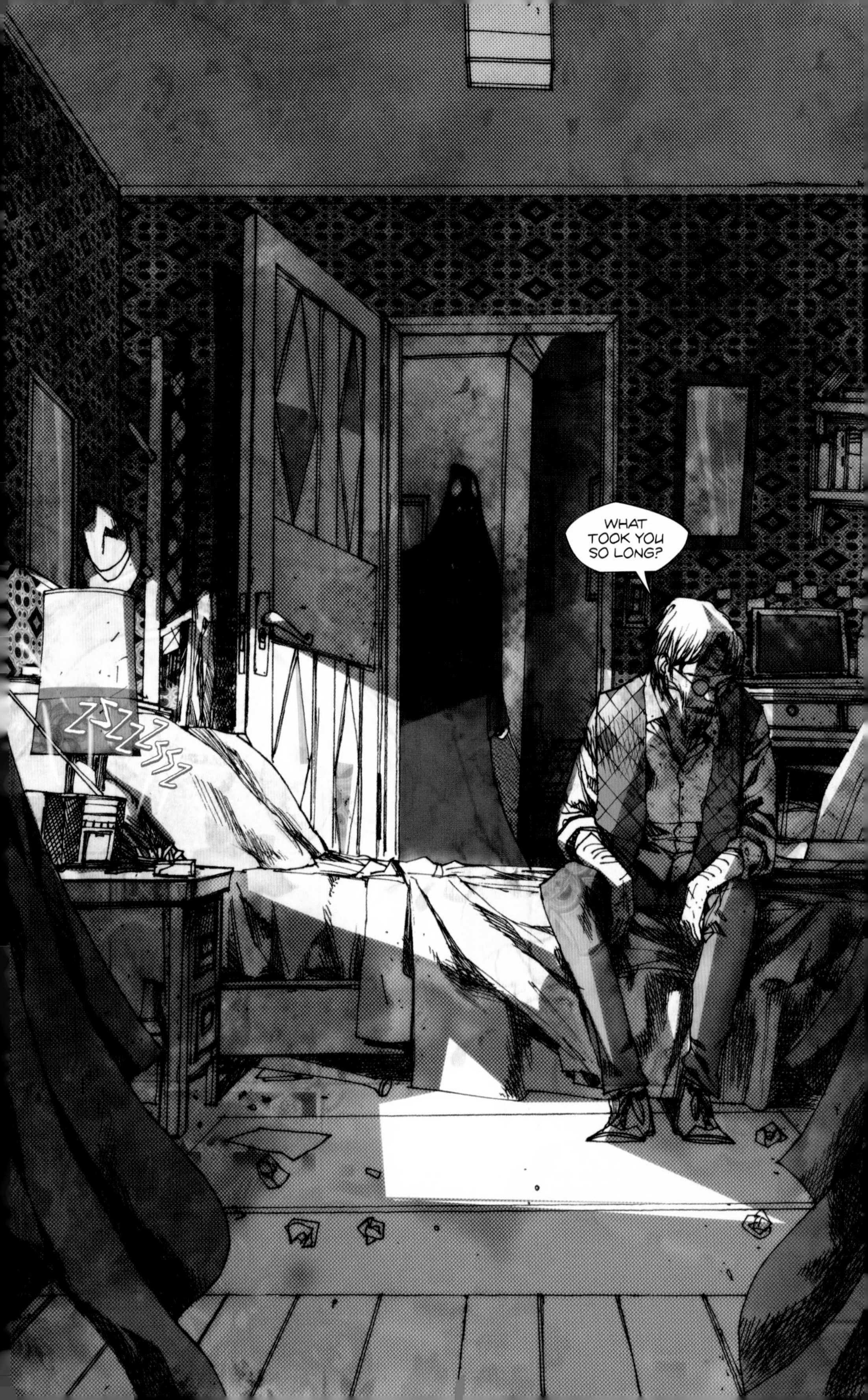
ZZZZZZZZ
WHAT TOOK YOU SO LONG?

ISSUE FOUR COVER

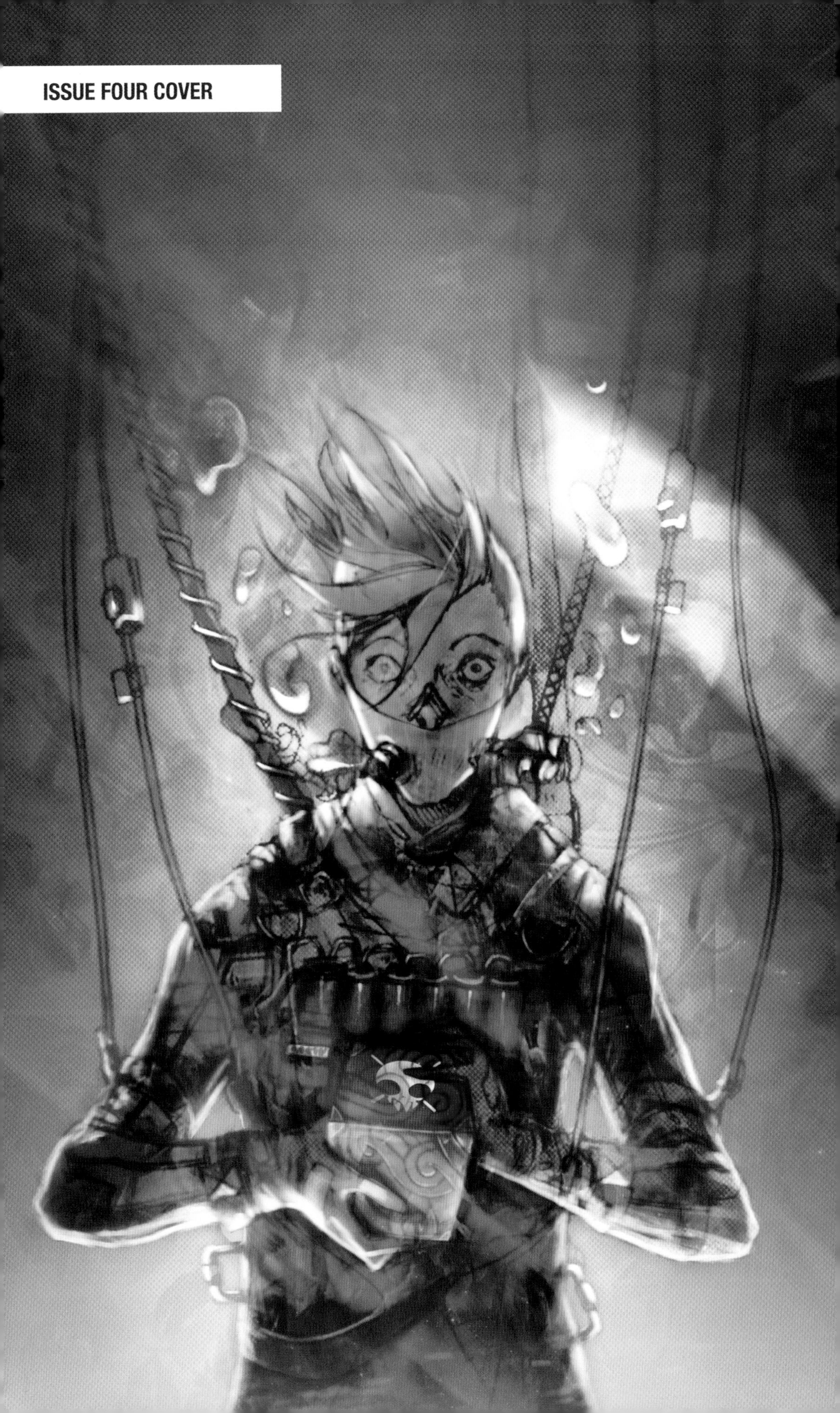

CHAPTER 5: TERMA

ALWAYS TRESPASS. TNN OOOY DAL TNIVC. DON'T TURN YOUR BACK ON THE MYSTERY.

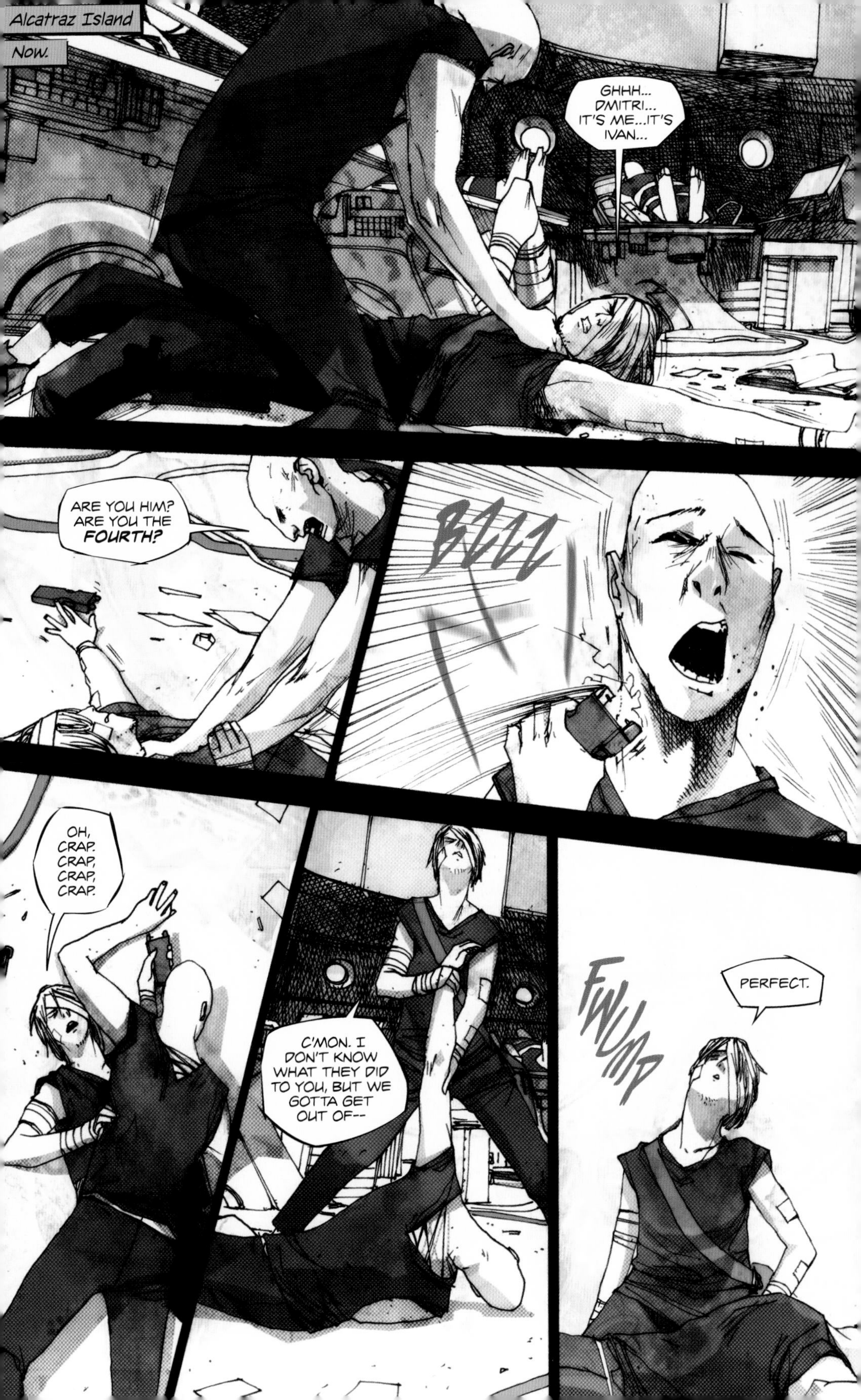

Alcatraz Island
Now.
GHHH... DMITRI... IT'S ME...IT'S IVAN...
ARE YOU HIM? ARE YOU THE FOURTH?
BZZZ
OH, CRAP. CRAP, CRAP, CRAP.
C'MON. I DON'T KNOW WHAT THEY DID TO YOU, BUT WE GOTTA GET OUT OF--
FWUMP
PERFECT.

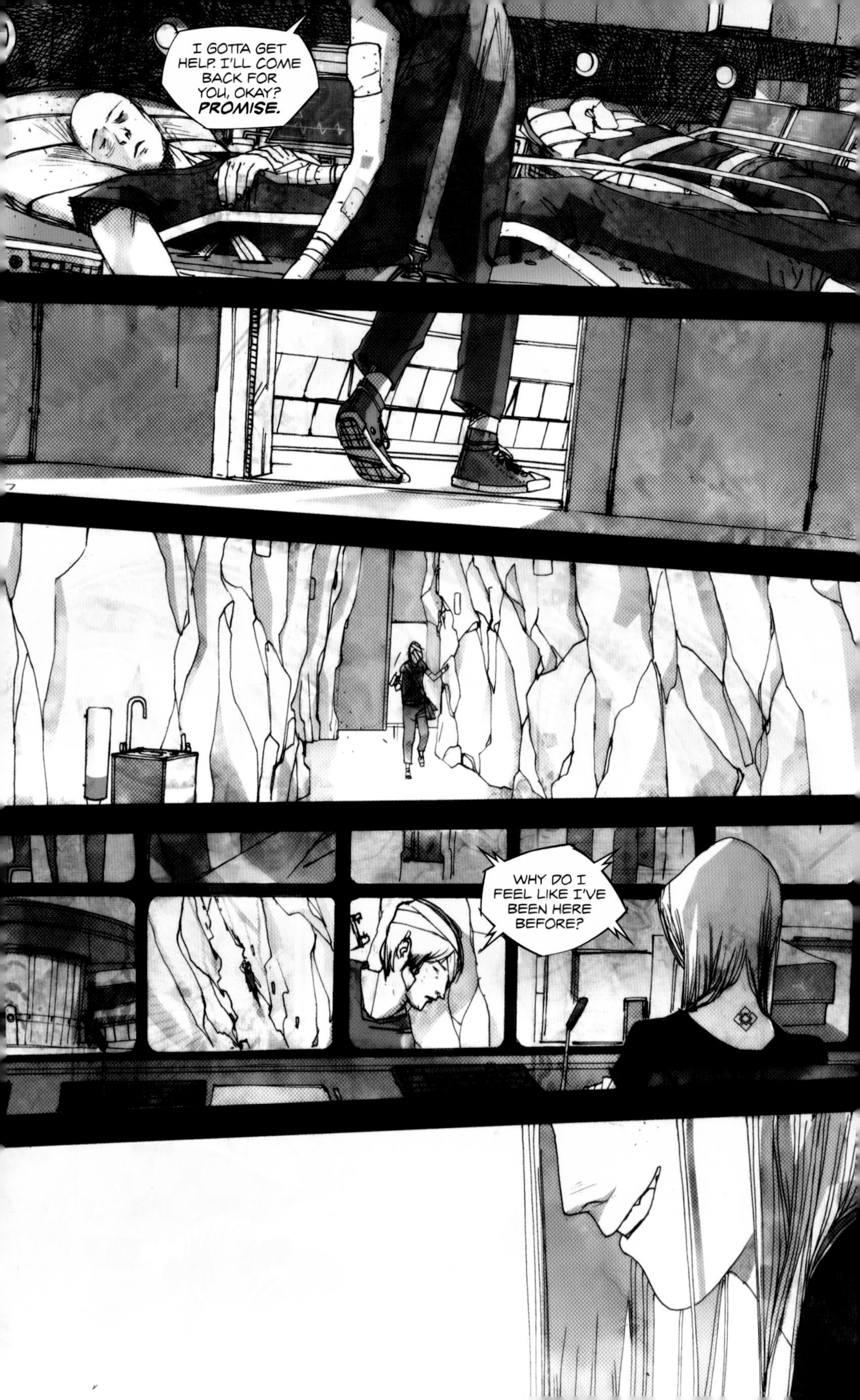
I GOTTA GET HELP. I'LL COME BACK FOR YOU, OKAY? PROMISE.
WHY DO I FEEL LIKE I'VE BEEN HERE BEFORE?

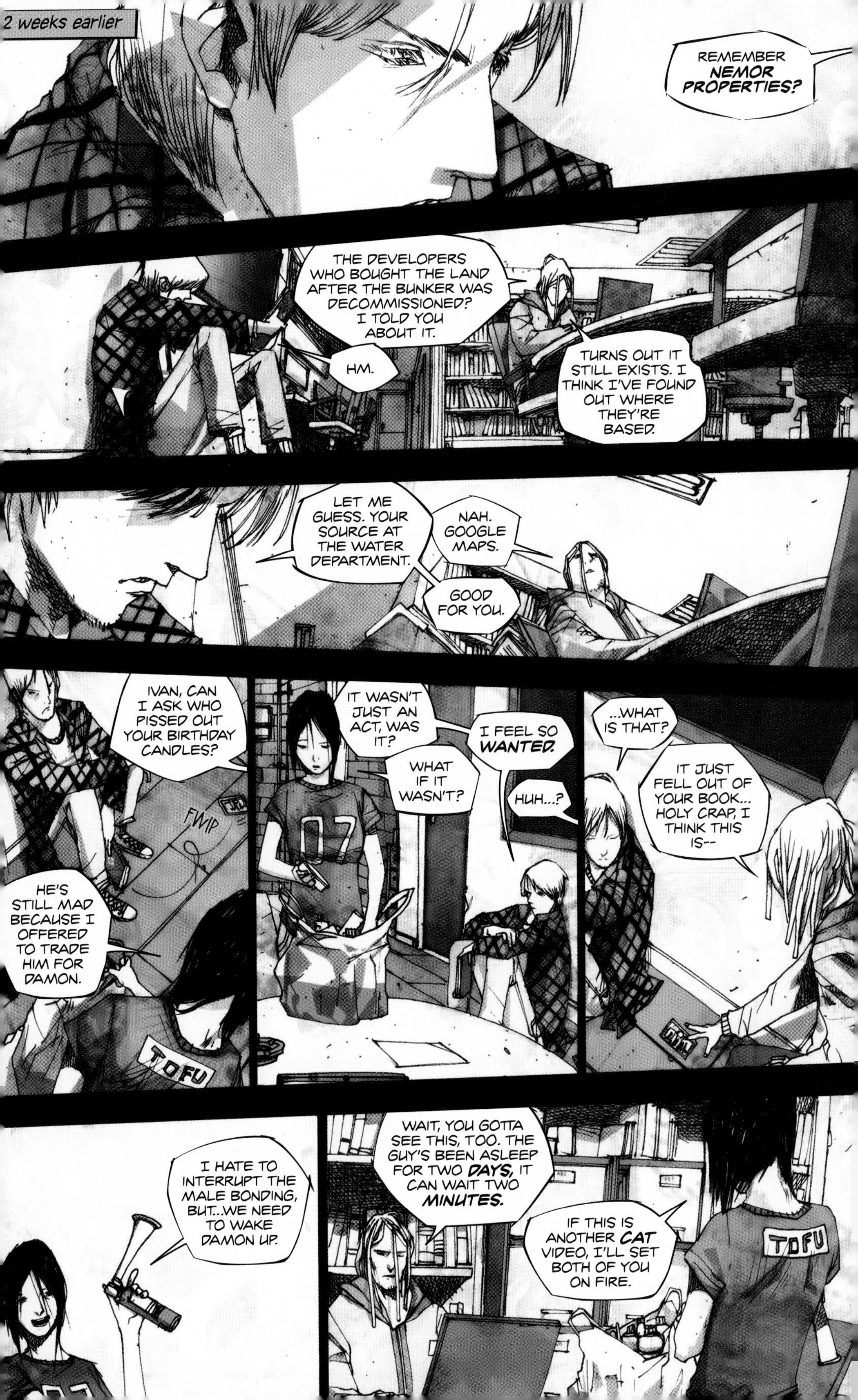
2 weeks earlier
REMEMBER **NEMOR PROPERTIES?**
THE DEVELOPERS WHO BOUGHT THE LAND AFTER THE BUNKER WAS DECOMMISSIONED? I TOLD YOU ABOUT IT.
HM.
TURNS OUT IT STILL EXISTS. I THINK I'VE FOUND OUT WHERE THEY'RE BASED.
LET ME GUESS. YOUR SOURCE AT THE WATER DEPARTMENT.
NAH. GOOGLE MAPS.
GOOD FOR YOU.
IVAN, CAN I ASK WHO PISSED OUT YOUR BIRTHDAY CANDLES?
FWIP
HE'S STILL MAD BECAUSE I OFFERED TO TRADE HIM FOR DAMON.
TOFU
IT WASN'T JUST AN ACT, WAS IT?
I FEEL SO ***WANTED.***
WHAT IF IT WASN'T?
HUH...?
...WHAT IS THAT?
IT JUST FELL OUT OF YOUR BOOK... HOLY CRAP, I THINK THIS IS--
I HATE TO INTERRUPT THE MALE BONDING, BUT...WE NEED TO WAKE DAMON UP.
WAIT, YOU GOTTA SEE THIS, TOO. THE GUY'S BEEN ASLEEP FOR TWO ***DAYS,*** IT CAN WAIT TWO ***MINUTES.***
IF THIS IS ANOTHER ***CAT*** VIDEO, I'LL SET BOTH OF YOU ON FIRE.
TOFU

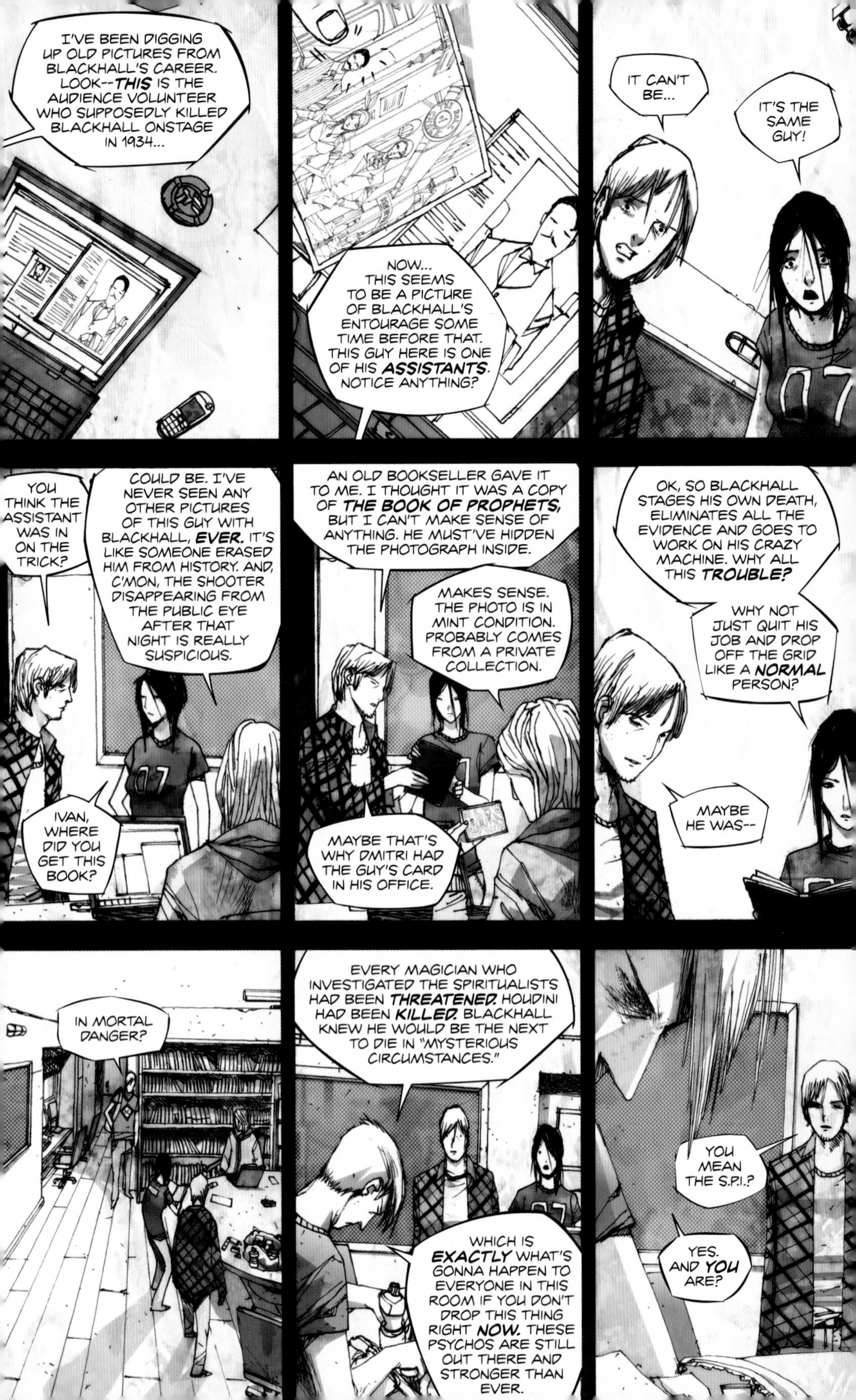

I'VE BEEN DIGGING UP OLD PICTURES FROM BLACKHALL'S CAREER. LOOK--THIS IS THE AUDIENCE VOLUNTEER WHO SUPPOSEDLY KILLED BLACKHALL ONSTAGE IN 1934...
NOW... THIS SEEMS TO BE A PICTURE OF BLACKHALL'S ENTOURAGE SOME TIME BEFORE THAT. THIS GUY HERE IS ONE OF HIS ASSISTANTS. NOTICE ANYTHING?
IT CAN'T BE...
IT'S THE SAME GUY!
YOU THINK THE ASSISTANT WAS IN ON THE TRICK?
COULD BE. I'VE NEVER SEEN ANY OTHER PICTURES OF THIS GUY WITH BLACKHALL, EVER. IT'S LIKE SOMEONE ERASED HIM FROM HISTORY. AND, C'MON, THE SHOOTER DISAPPEARING FROM THE PUBLIC EYE AFTER THAT NIGHT IS REALLY SUSPICIOUS.
IVAN, WHERE DID YOU GET THIS BOOK?
AN OLD BOOKSELLER GAVE IT TO ME. I THOUGHT IT WAS A COPY OF THE BOOK OF PROPHETS, BUT I CAN'T MAKE SENSE OF ANYTHING. HE MUST'VE HIDDEN THE PHOTOGRAPH INSIDE.
MAKES SENSE. THE PHOTO IS IN MINT CONDITION. PROBABLY COMES FROM A PRIVATE COLLECTION.
MAYBE THAT'S WHY DMITRI HAD THE GUY'S CARD IN HIS OFFICE.
OK, SO BLACKHALL STAGES HIS OWN DEATH, ELIMINATES ALL THE EVIDENCE AND GOES TO WORK ON HIS CRAZY MACHINE. WHY ALL THIS TROUBLE?
WHY NOT JUST QUIT HIS JOB AND DROP OFF THE GRID LIKE A NORMAL PERSON?
MAYBE HE WAS--
IN MORTAL DANGER?
EVERY MAGICIAN WHO INVESTIGATED THE SPIRITUALISTS HAD BEEN THREATENED. HOUDINI HAD BEEN KILLED. BLACKHALL KNEW HE WOULD BE THE NEXT TO DIE IN "MYSTERIOUS CIRCUMSTANCES."
WHICH IS EXACTLY WHAT'S GONNA HAPPEN TO EVERYONE IN THIS ROOM IF YOU DON'T DROP THIS THING RIGHT NOW. THESE PSYCHOS ARE STILL OUT THERE AND STRONGER THAN EVER.
YOU MEAN THE S.P.I.?
YES. AND YOU ARE?

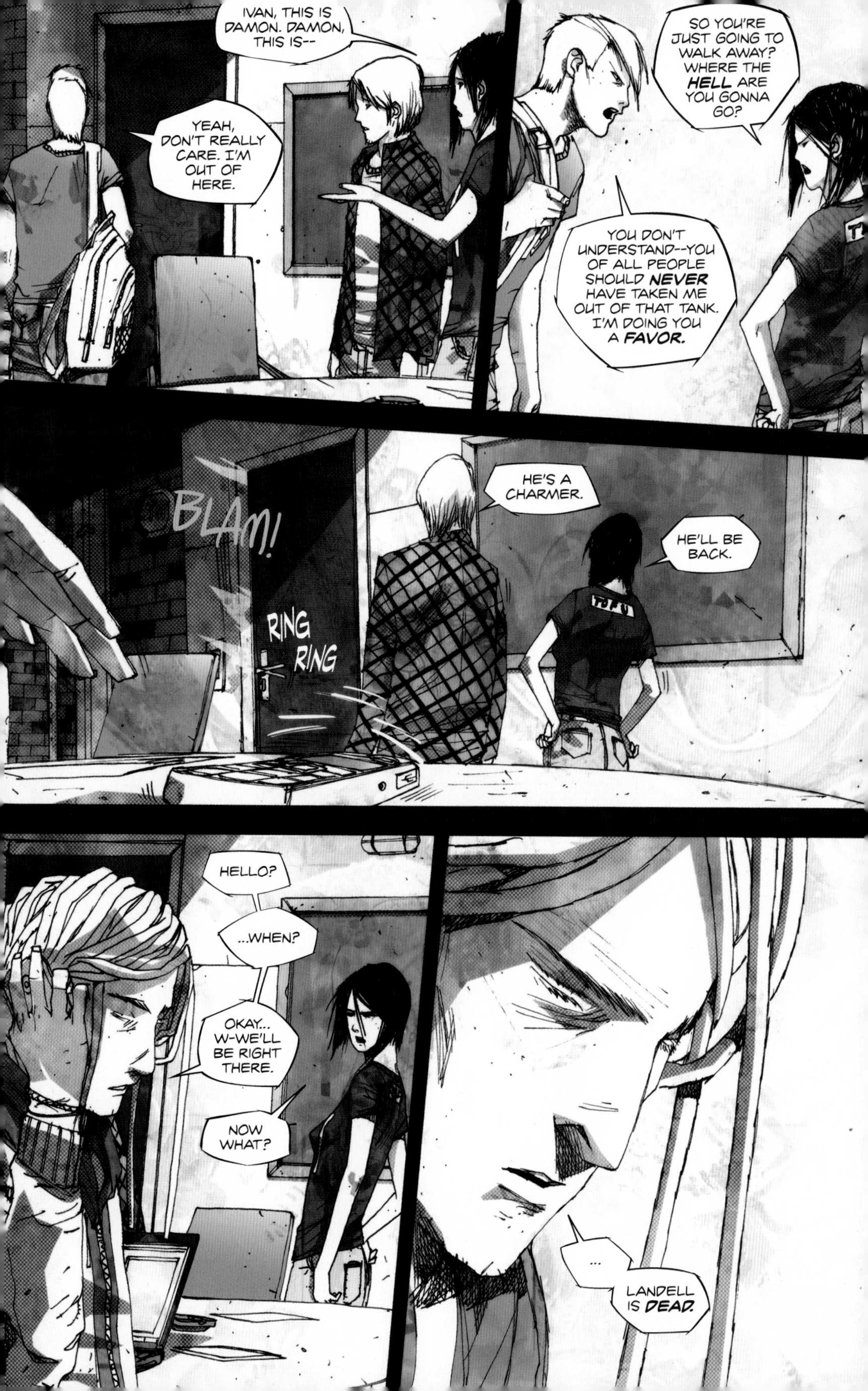
IVAN, THIS IS DAMON. DAMON, THIS IS--
YEAH, DON'T REALLY CARE. I'M OUT OF HERE.
SO YOU'RE JUST GOING TO WALK AWAY? WHERE THE HELL ARE YOU GONNA GO?
YOU DON'T UNDERSTAND--YOU OF ALL PEOPLE SHOULD NEVER HAVE TAKEN ME OUT OF THAT TANK. I'M DOING YOU A FAVOR.
BLAM!
RING RING
HE'S A CHARMER.
HE'LL BE BACK.
HELLO?
...WHEN?
OKAY... W-WE'LL BE RIGHT THERE.
NOW WHAT?
...
LANDELL IS DEAD.

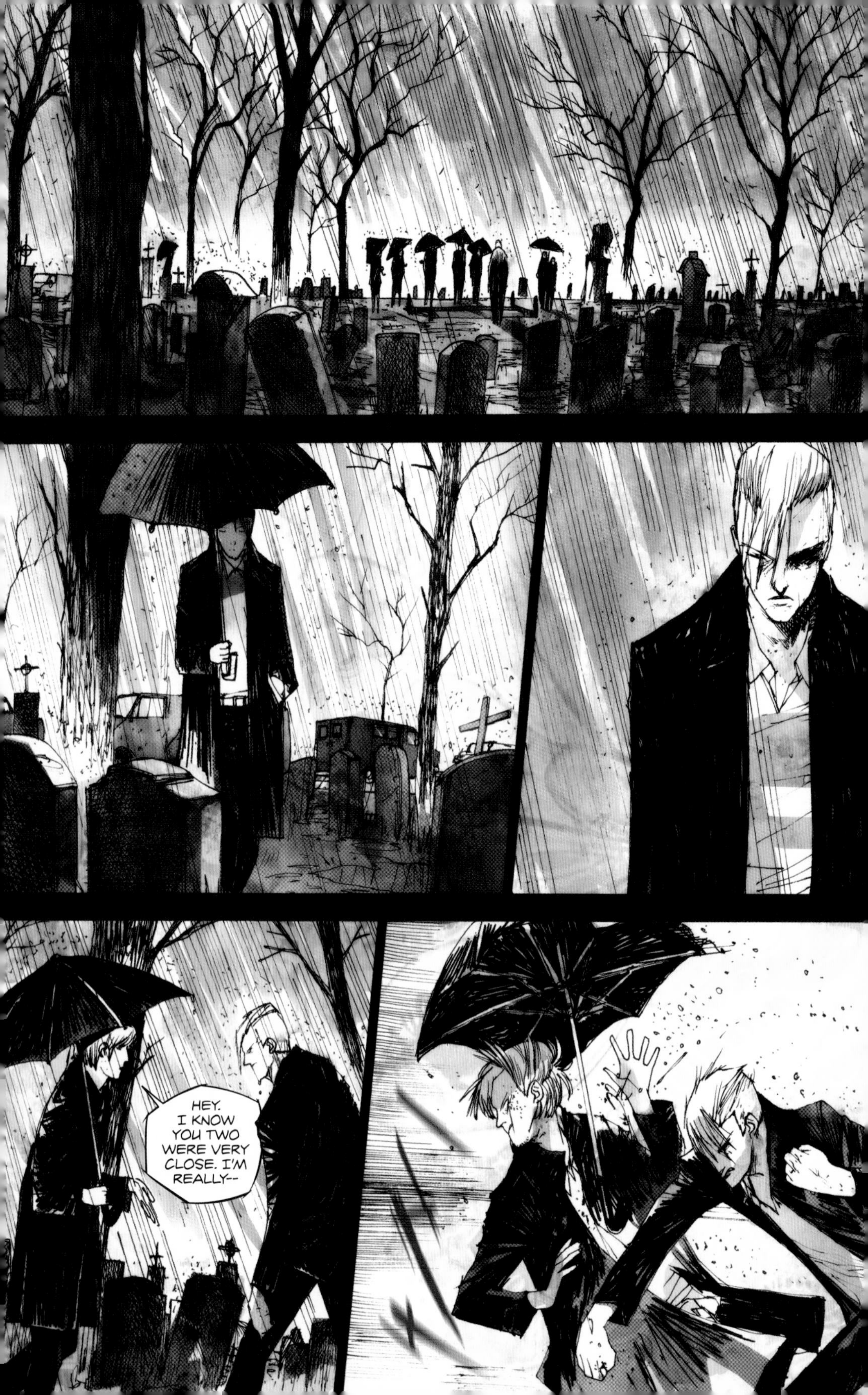
HEY. I KNOW YOU TWO WERE VERY CLOSE. I'M REALLY--

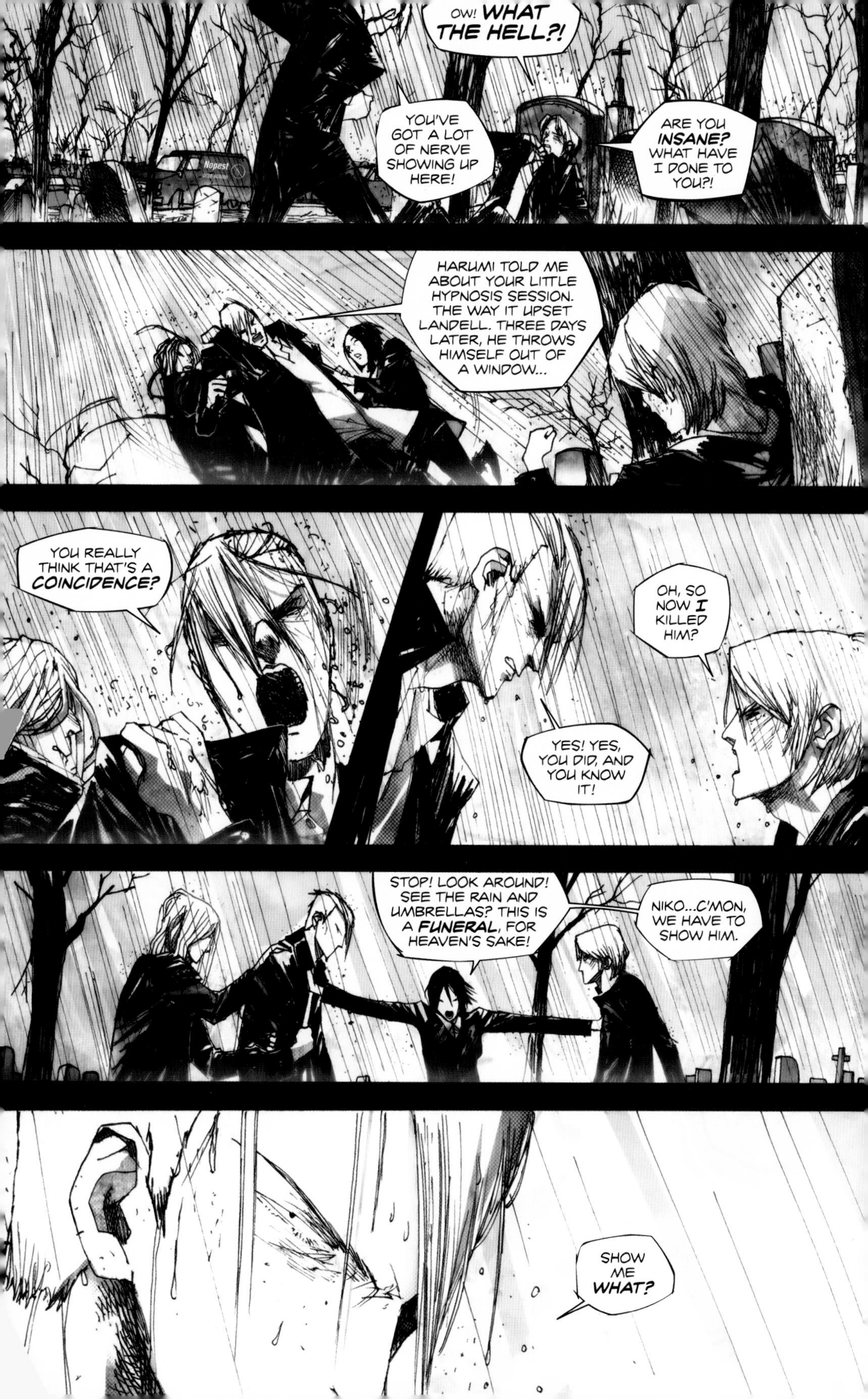
OW! WHAT THE HELL?!
YOU'VE GOT A LOT OF NERVE SHOWING UP HERE!
ARE YOU INSANE? WHAT HAVE I DONE TO YOU?!
HARUMI TOLD ME ABOUT YOUR LITTLE HYPNOSIS SESSION. THE WAY IT UPSET LANDELL. THREE DAYS LATER, HE THROWS HIMSELF OUT OF A WINDOW...
YOU REALLY THINK THAT'S A COINCIDENCE?
OH, SO NOW I KILLED HIM?
YES! YES, YOU DID, AND YOU KNOW IT!
STOP! LOOK AROUND! SEE THE RAIN AND UMBRELLAS? THIS IS A FUNERAL, FOR HEAVEN'S SAKE!
NIKO...C'MON, WE HAVE TO SHOW HIM.
SHOW ME WHAT?

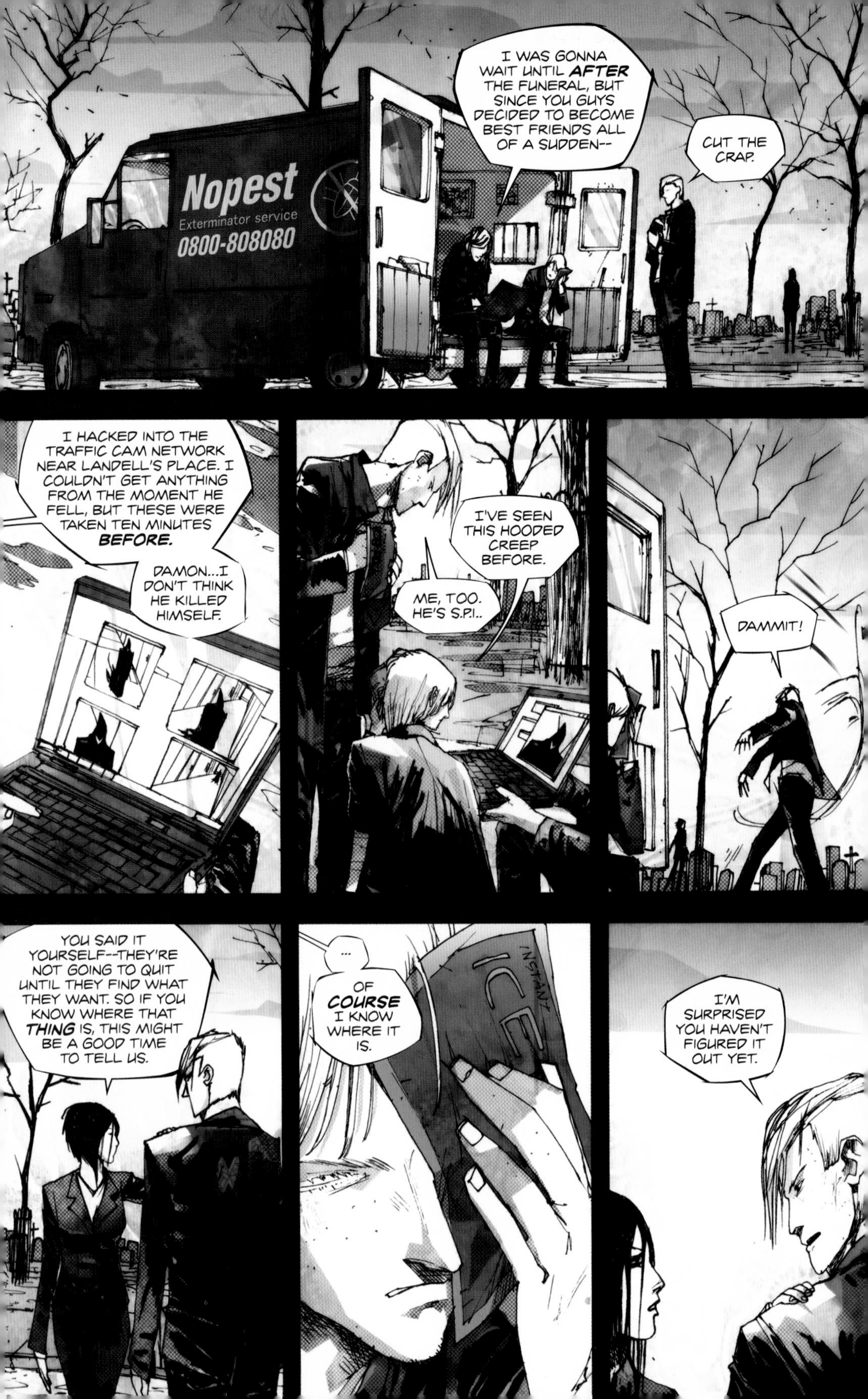

Nopest
Exterminator service
0800-808080
I WAS GONNA WAIT UNTIL **AFTER** THE FUNERAL, BUT SINCE YOU GUYS DECIDED TO BECOME BEST FRIENDS ALL OF A SUDDEN--
CUT THE CRAP.
I HACKED INTO THE TRAFFIC CAM NETWORK NEAR LANDELL'S PLACE. I COULDN'T GET ANYTHING FROM THE MOMENT HE FELL, BUT THESE WERE TAKEN TEN MINUTES **BEFORE.**
DAMON...I DON'T THINK HE KILLED HIMSELF.
I'VE SEEN THIS HOODED CREEP BEFORE.
ME, TOO. HE'S S.P.I..
DAMMIT!
YOU SAID IT YOURSELF--THEY'RE NOT GOING TO QUIT UNTIL THEY FIND WHAT THEY WANT. SO IF YOU KNOW WHERE THAT **THING** IS, THIS MIGHT BE A GOOD TIME TO TELL US.
...
OF **COURSE** I KNOW WHERE IT IS.
INSTANT
ICE
I'M SURPRISED YOU HAVEN'T FIGURED IT OUT YET.

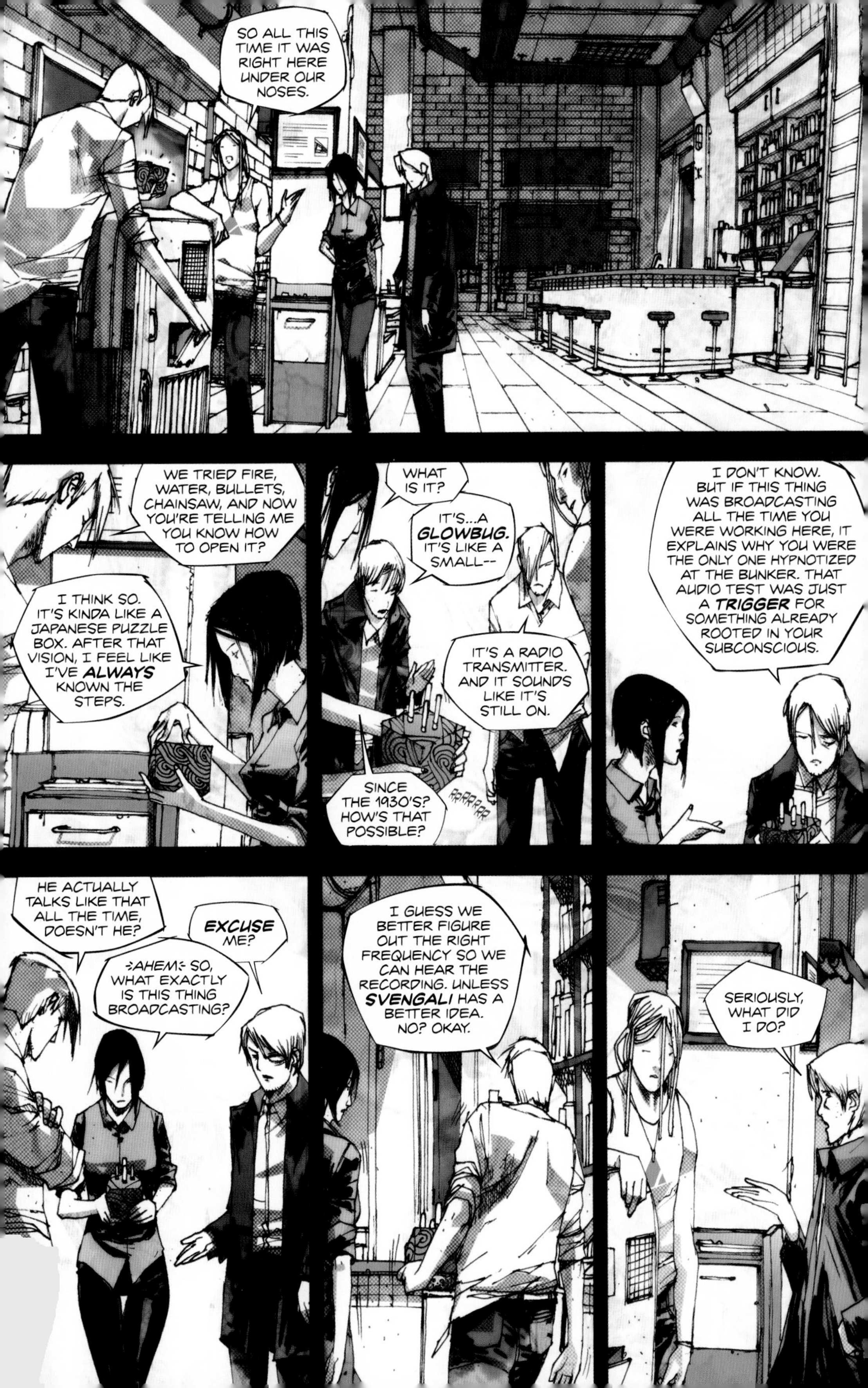
SO ALL THIS TIME IT WAS RIGHT HERE UNDER OUR NOSES.
WE TRIED FIRE, WATER, BULLETS, CHAINSAW, AND NOW YOU'RE TELLING ME YOU KNOW HOW TO OPEN IT?
I THINK SO. IT'S KINDA LIKE A JAPANESE PUZZLE BOX. AFTER THAT VISION, I FEEL LIKE I'VE ALWAYS KNOWN THE STEPS.
WHAT IS IT?
IT'S...A GLOWBUG. IT'S LIKE A SMALL--
IT'S A RADIO TRANSMITTER. AND IT SOUNDS LIKE IT'S STILL ON.
SINCE THE 1930'S? HOW'S THAT POSSIBLE?
RRRRRRR
I DON'T KNOW. BUT IF THIS THING WAS BROADCASTING ALL THE TIME YOU WERE WORKING HERE, IT EXPLAINS WHY YOU WERE THE ONLY ONE HYPNOTIZED AT THE BUNKER. THAT AUDIO TEST WAS JUST A TRIGGER FOR SOMETHING ALREADY ROOTED IN YOUR SUBCONSCIOUS.
HE ACTUALLY TALKS LIKE THAT ALL THE TIME, DOESN'T HE?
EXCUSE ME?
AHEM SO, WHAT EXACTLY IS THIS THING BROADCASTING?
I GUESS WE BETTER FIGURE OUT THE RIGHT FREQUENCY SO WE CAN HEAR THE RECORDING. UNLESS SVENGALI HAS A BETTER IDEA. NO? OKAY.
SERIOUSLY, WHAT DID I DO?

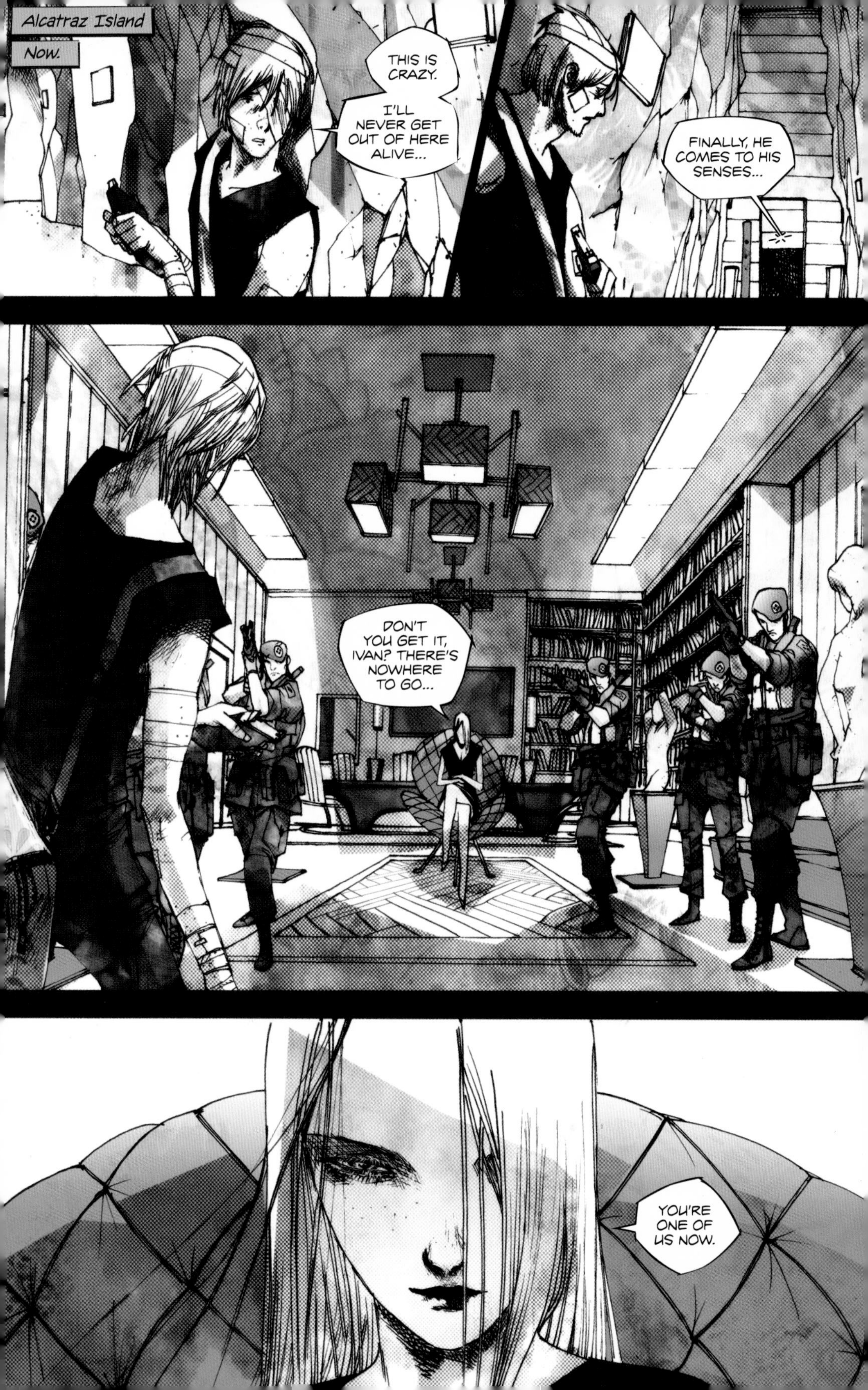
Alcatraz Island
Now.
THIS IS CRAZY.
I'LL NEVER GET OUT OF HERE ALIVE...
FINALLY, HE COMES TO HIS SENSES...
DON'T YOU GET IT, IVAN? THERE'S NOWHERE TO GO...
YOU'RE ONE OF US NOW.

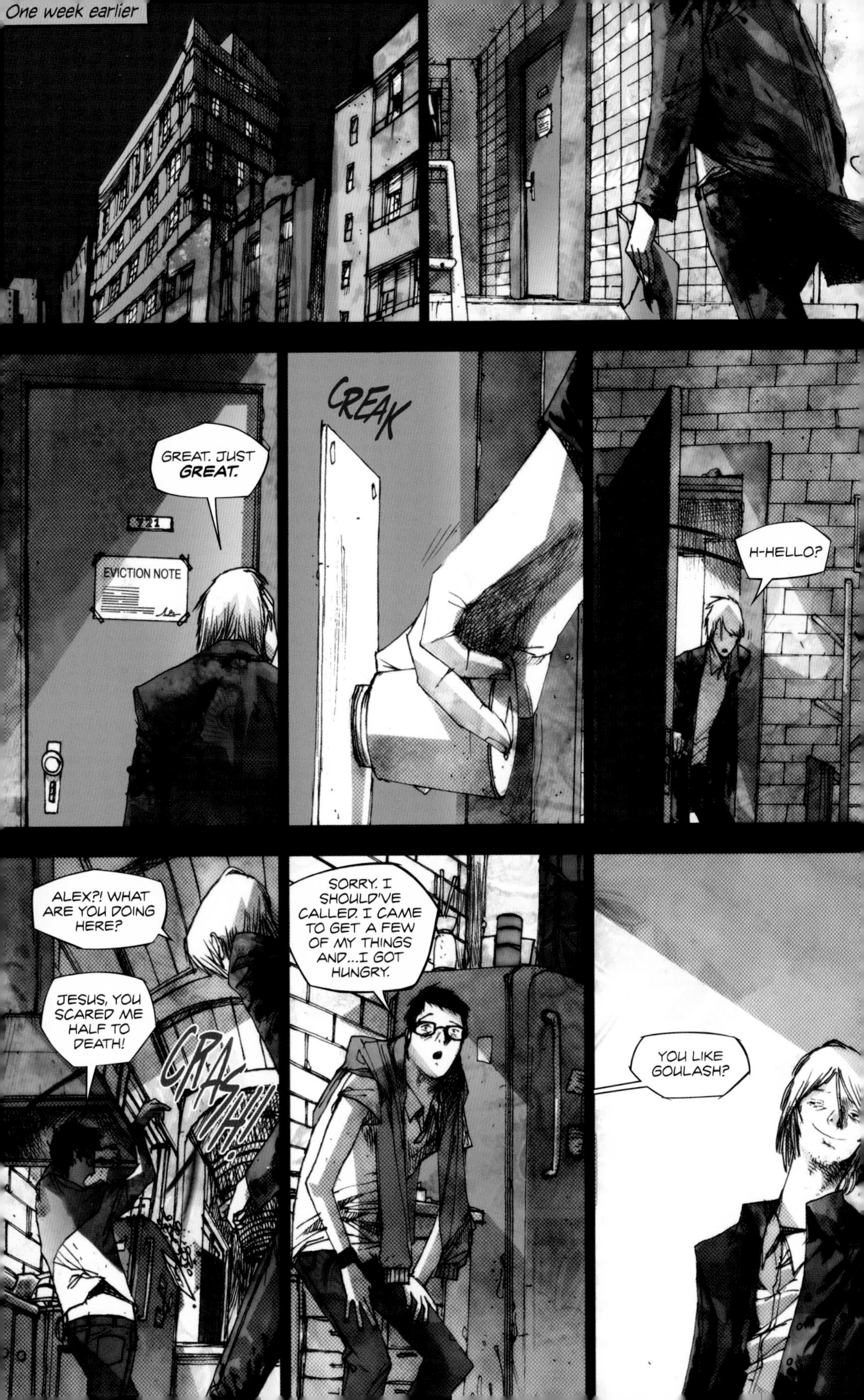
One week earlier
GREAT. JUST GREAT.
721
EVICTION NOTE
CREAK
H-HELLO?
ALEX?! WHAT ARE YOU DOING HERE?
JESUS, YOU SCARED ME HALF TO DEATH!
CRASH!
SORRY. I SHOULD'VE CALLED. I CAME TO GET A FEW OF MY THINGS AND...I GOT HUNGRY.
YOU LIKE GOULASH?

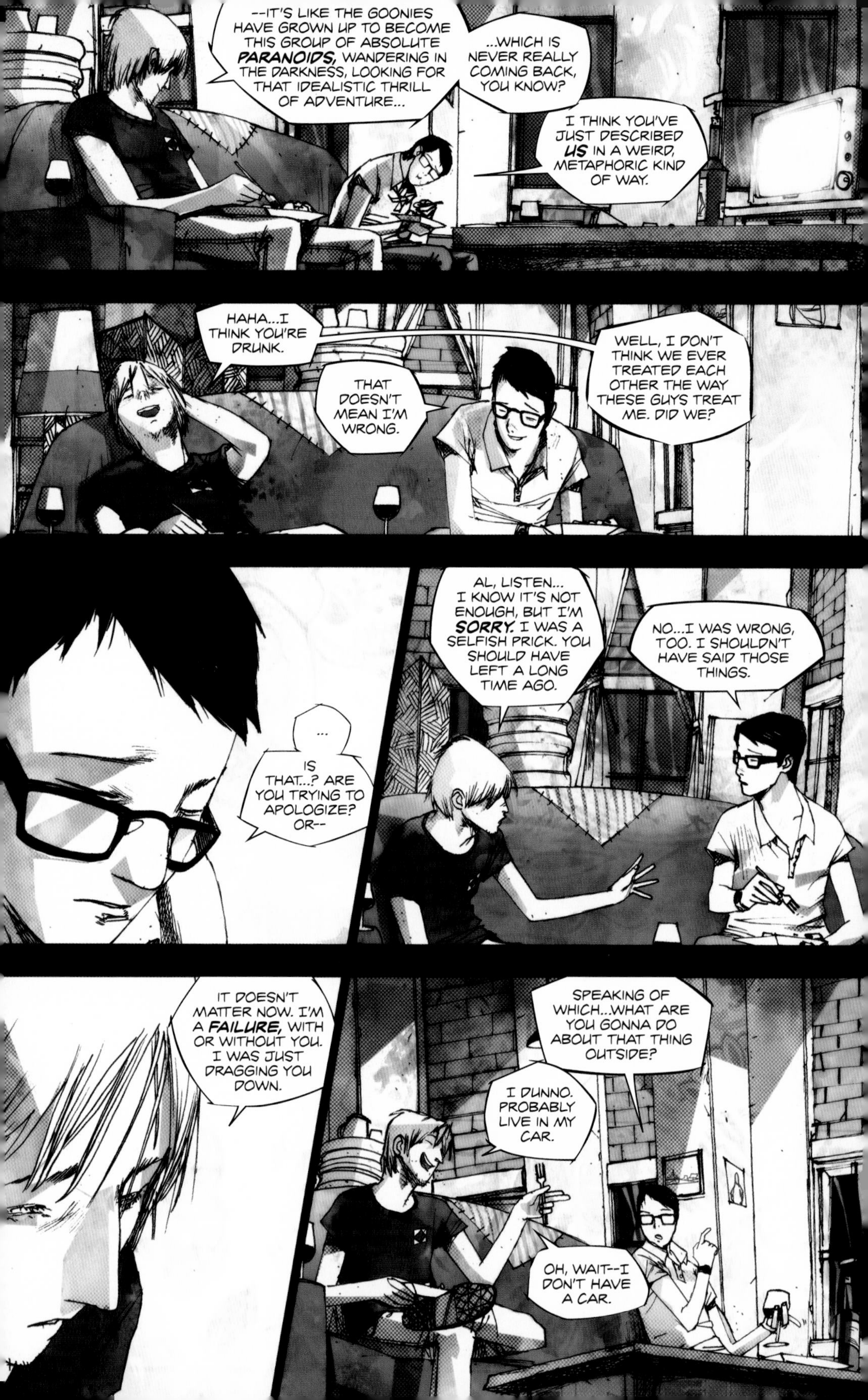
--IT'S LIKE THE GOONIES HAVE GROWN UP TO BECOME THIS GROUP OF ABSOLUTE PARANOIDS, WANDERING IN THE DARKNESS, LOOKING FOR THAT IDEALISTIC THRILL OF ADVENTURE...
...WHICH IS NEVER REALLY COMING BACK, YOU KNOW?
I THINK YOU'VE JUST DESCRIBED US IN A WEIRD, METAPHORIC KIND OF WAY.
HAHA...I THINK YOU'RE DRUNK.
THAT DOESN'T MEAN I'M WRONG.
WELL, I DON'T THINK WE EVER TREATED EACH OTHER THE WAY THESE GUYS TREAT ME. DID WE?
...
IS THAT...? ARE YOU TRYING TO APOLOGIZE? OR--
AL, LISTEN... I KNOW IT'S NOT ENOUGH, BUT I'M SORRY. I WAS A SELFISH PRICK. YOU SHOULD HAVE LEFT A LONG TIME AGO.
NO...I WAS WRONG, TOO. I SHOULDN'T HAVE SAID THOSE THINGS.
IT DOESN'T MATTER NOW. I'M A FAILURE, WITH OR WITHOUT YOU. I WAS JUST DRAGGING YOU DOWN.
SPEAKING OF WHICH...WHAT ARE YOU GONNA DO ABOUT THAT THING OUTSIDE?
I DUNNO. PROBABLY LIVE IN MY CAR.
OH, WAIT--I DON'T HAVE A CAR.

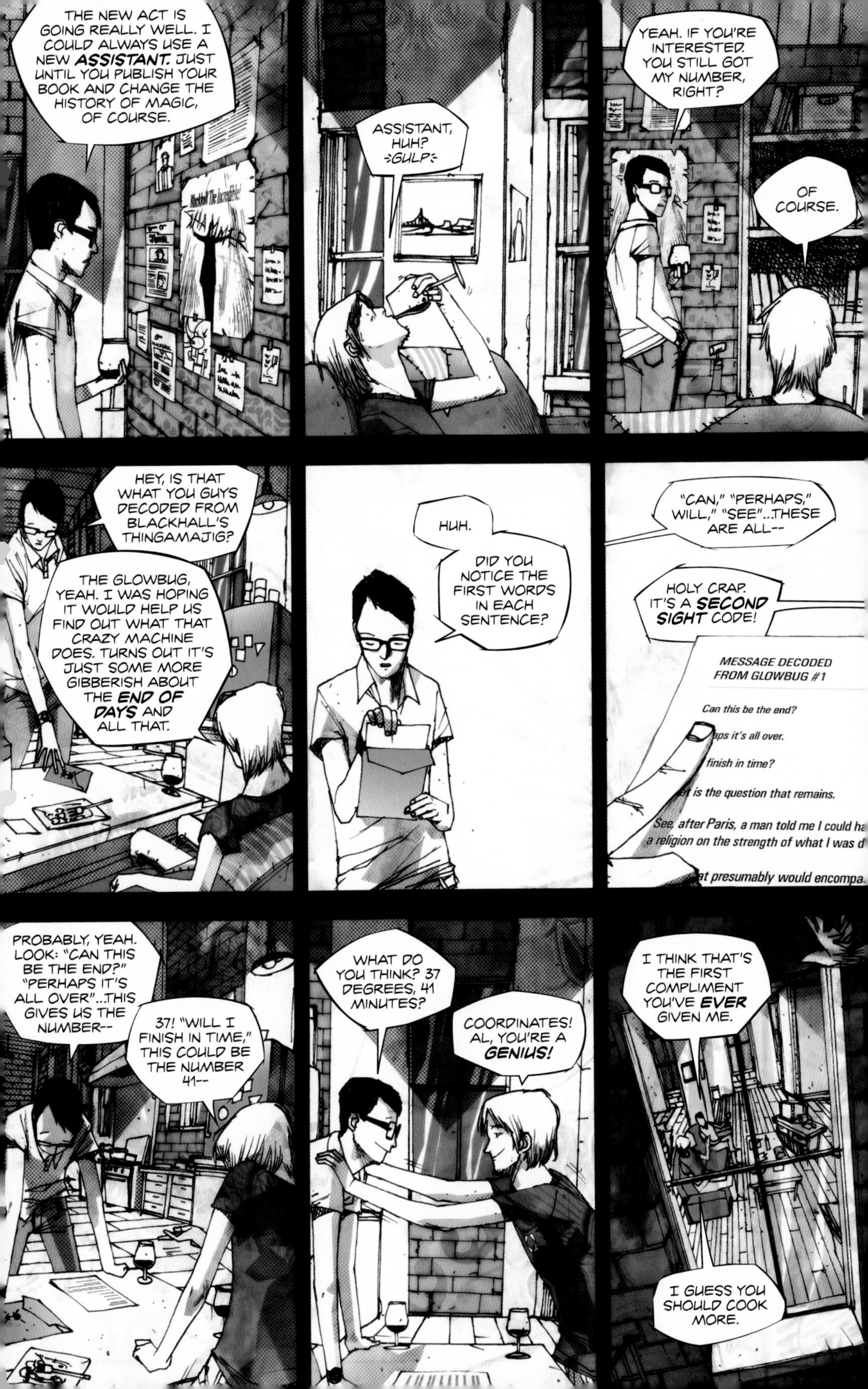
THE NEW ACT IS GOING REALLY WELL. I COULD ALWAYS USE A NEW **ASSISTANT.** JUST UNTIL YOU PUBLISH YOUR BOOK AND CHANGE THE HISTORY OF MAGIC, OF COURSE.
ASSISTANT, HUH? *GULP*
YEAH. IF YOU'RE INTERESTED. YOU STILL GOT MY NUMBER, RIGHT?
OF COURSE.
HEY, IS THAT WHAT YOU GUYS DECODED FROM BLACKHALL'S THINGAMAJIG?
THE GLOWBUG, YEAH. I WAS HOPING IT WOULD HELP US FIND OUT WHAT THAT CRAZY MACHINE DOES. TURNS OUT IT'S JUST SOME MORE GIBBERISH ABOUT THE **END OF DAYS** AND ALL THAT.
HUH.
DID YOU NOTICE THE FIRST WORDS IN EACH SENTENCE?
"CAN," "PERHAPS," WILL," "SEE"...THESE ARE ALL--
HOLY CRAP. IT'S A **SECOND SIGHT** CODE!
MESSAGE DECODED FROM GLOWBUG #1
Can this be the end?
aps it's all over.
finish in time?
t is the question that remains.
See, after Paris, a man told me I could ha
a religion on the strength of what I was d
at presumably would encompa
PROBABLY, YEAH. LOOK: "CAN THIS BE THE END?" "PERHAPS IT'S ALL OVER"...THIS GIVES US THE NUMBER--
37! "WILL I FINISH IN TIME," THIS COULD BE THE NUMBER 41--
WHAT DO YOU THINK? 37 DEGREES, 41 MINUTES?
COORDINATES! AL, YOU'RE A **GENIUS!**
I THINK THAT'S THE FIRST COMPLIMENT YOU'VE **EVER** GIVEN ME.
I GUESS YOU SHOULD COOK MORE.

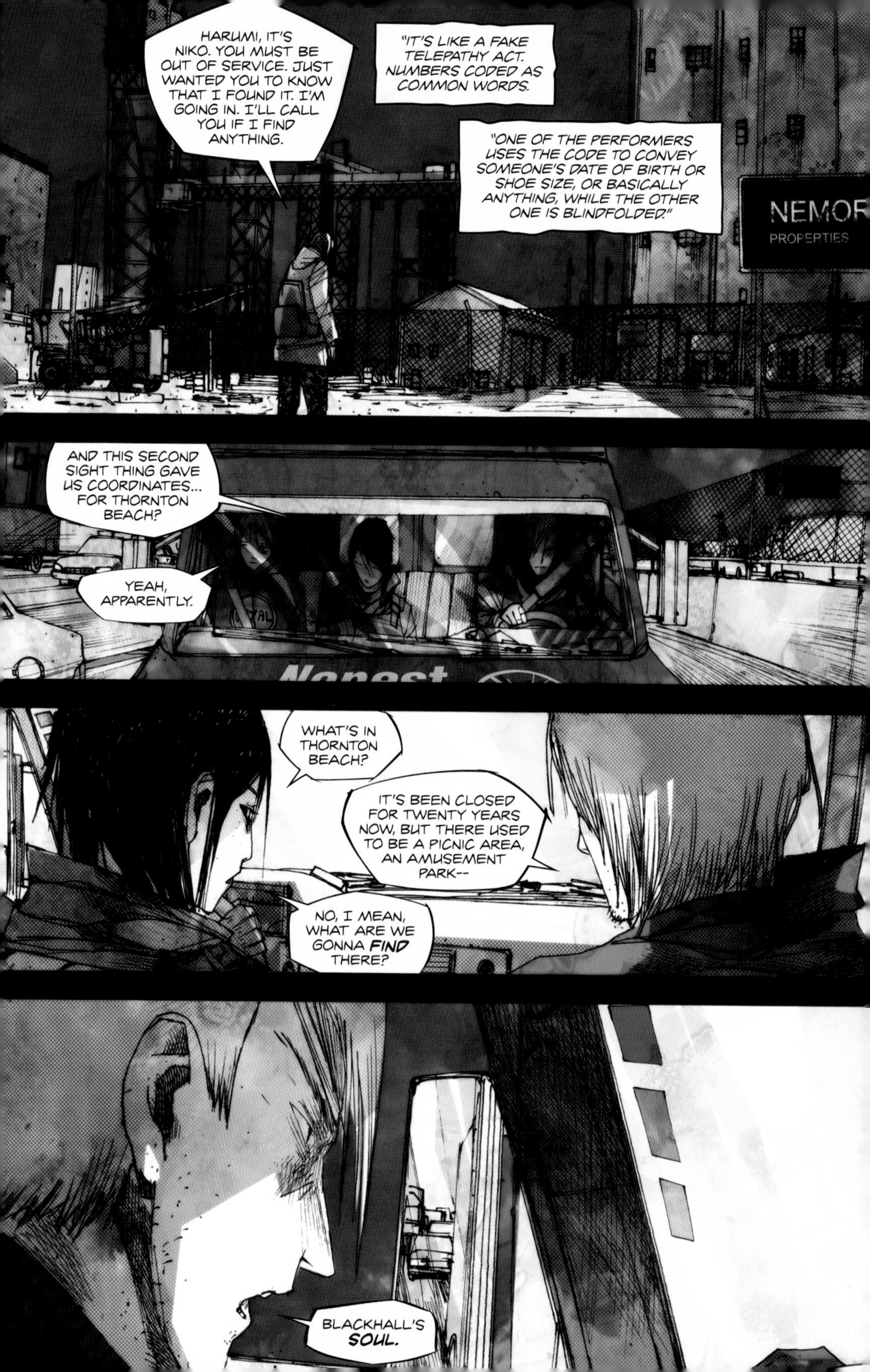
HARUMI, IT'S NIKO. YOU MUST BE OUT OF SERVICE. JUST WANTED YOU TO KNOW THAT I FOUND IT. I'M GOING IN. I'LL CALL YOU IF I FIND ANYTHING.
"IT'S LIKE A FAKE TELEPATHY ACT. NUMBERS CODED AS COMMON WORDS.
"ONE OF THE PERFORMERS USES THE CODE TO CONVEY SOMEONE'S DATE OF BIRTH OR SHOE SIZE, OR BASICALLY ANYTHING, WHILE THE OTHER ONE IS BLINDFOLDED."
NEMOR
PROPERTIES
AND THIS SECOND SIGHT THING GAVE US COORDINATES... FOR THORNTON BEACH?
YEAH, APPARENTLY.
WHAT'S IN THORNTON BEACH?
IT'S BEEN CLOSED FOR TWENTY YEARS NOW, BUT THERE USED TO BE A PICNIC AREA, AN AMUSEMENT PARK--
NO, I MEAN, WHAT ARE WE GONNA **FIND** THERE?
BLACKHALL'S **SOUL.**

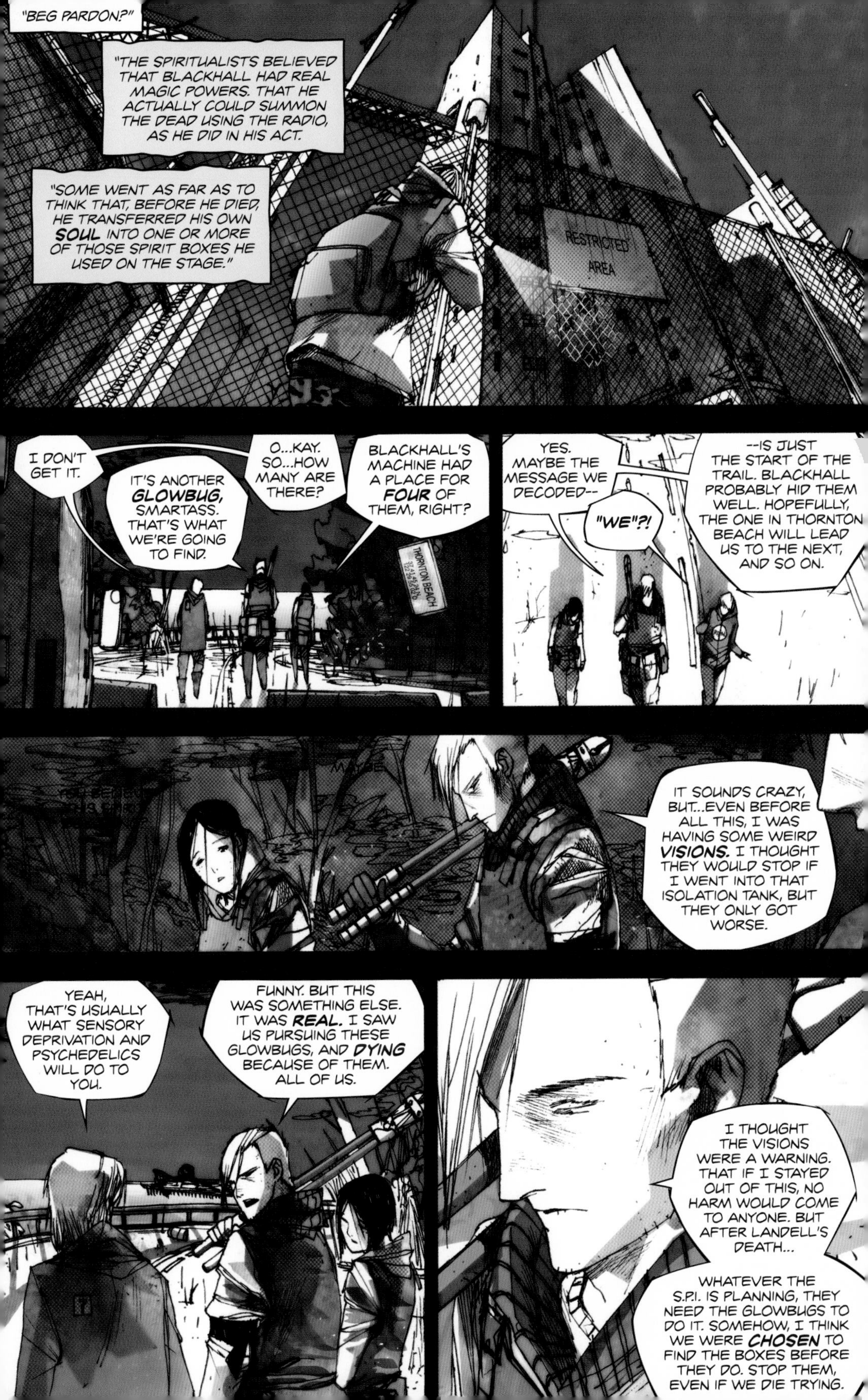
"BEG PARDON?"
"THE SPIRITUALISTS BELIEVED THAT BLACKHALL HAD REAL MAGIC POWERS. THAT HE ACTUALLY COULD SUMMON THE DEAD USING THE RADIO, AS HE DID IN HIS ACT.
"SOME WENT AS FAR AS TO THINK THAT, BEFORE HE DIED, HE TRANSFERRED HIS OWN **SOUL** INTO ONE OR MORE OF THOSE SPIRIT BOXES HE USED ON THE STAGE."
RESTRICTED AREA
I DON'T GET IT.
IT'S ANOTHER ***GLOWBUG,*** SMARTASS. THAT'S WHAT WE'RE GOING TO FIND.
O...KAY. SO...HOW MANY ARE THERE?
BLACKHALL'S MACHINE HAD A PLACE FOR ***FOUR*** OF THEM, RIGHT?
THORNTON BEACH
YES. MAYBE THE MESSAGE WE DECODED--
"WE"?!
--IS JUST THE START OF THE TRAIL. BLACKHALL PROBABLY HID THEM WELL. HOPEFULLY, THE ONE IN THORNTON BEACH WILL LEAD US TO THE NEXT, AND SO ON.
IT SOUNDS CRAZY, BUT...EVEN BEFORE ALL THIS, I WAS HAVING SOME WEIRD ***VISIONS.*** I THOUGHT THEY WOULD STOP IF I WENT INTO THAT ISOLATION TANK, BUT THEY ONLY GOT WORSE.
YEAH, THAT'S USUALLY WHAT SENSORY DEPRIVATION AND PSYCHEDELICS WILL DO TO YOU.
FUNNY. BUT THIS WAS SOMETHING ELSE. IT WAS ***REAL.*** I SAW US PURSUING THESE GLOWBUGS, AND ***DYING*** BECAUSE OF THEM. ALL OF US.
I THOUGHT THE VISIONS WERE A WARNING. THAT IF I STAYED OUT OF THIS, NO HARM WOULD COME TO ANYONE. BUT AFTER LANDELL'S DEATH...
WHATEVER THE S.P.I. IS PLANNING, THEY NEED THE GLOWBUGS TO DO IT. SOMEHOW, I THINK WE WERE ***CHOSEN*** TO FIND THE BOXES BEFORE THEY DO. STOP THEM, EVEN IF WE DIE TRYING.

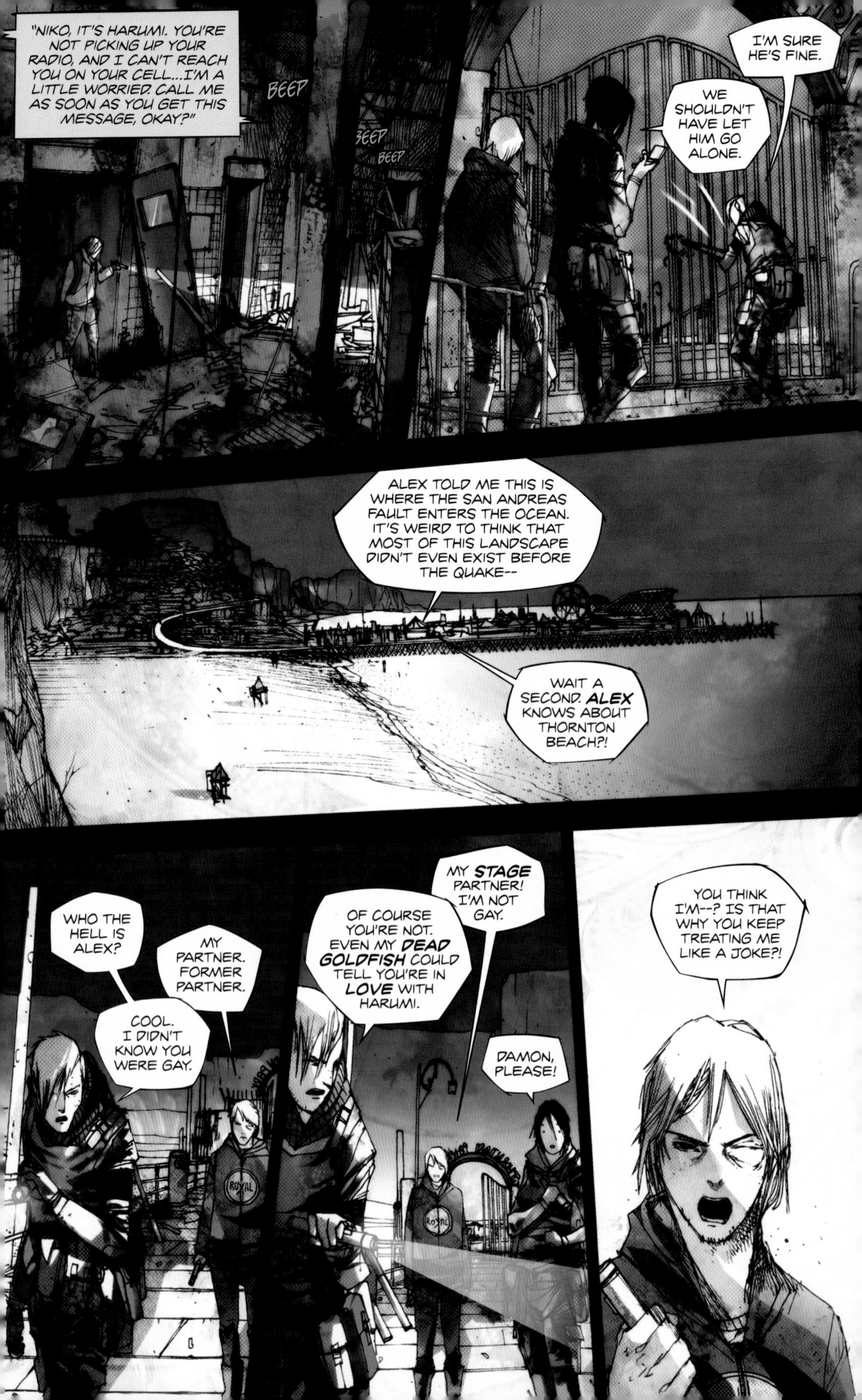
"NIKO, IT'S HARUMI. YOU'RE NOT PICKING UP YOUR RADIO, AND I CAN'T REACH YOU ON YOUR CELL...I'M A LITTLE WORRIED. CALL ME AS SOON AS YOU GET THIS MESSAGE, OKAY?"
BEEP
BEEP
BEEP
I'M SURE HE'S FINE.
WE SHOULDN'T HAVE LET HIM GO ALONE.
ALEX TOLD ME THIS IS WHERE THE SAN ANDREAS FAULT ENTERS THE OCEAN. IT'S WEIRD TO THINK THAT MOST OF THIS LANDSCAPE DIDN'T EVEN EXIST BEFORE THE QUAKE--
WAIT A SECOND. ALEX KNOWS ABOUT THORNTON BEACH?!
WHO THE HELL IS ALEX?
MY PARTNER. FORMER PARTNER.
COOL. I DIDN'T KNOW YOU WERE GAY.
MY STAGE PARTNER! I'M NOT GAY.
OF COURSE YOU'RE NOT. EVEN MY DEAD GOLDFISH COULD TELL YOU'RE IN LOVE WITH HARUMI.
DAMON, PLEASE!
YOU THINK I'M--? IS THAT WHY YOU KEEP TREATING ME LIKE A JOKE?!

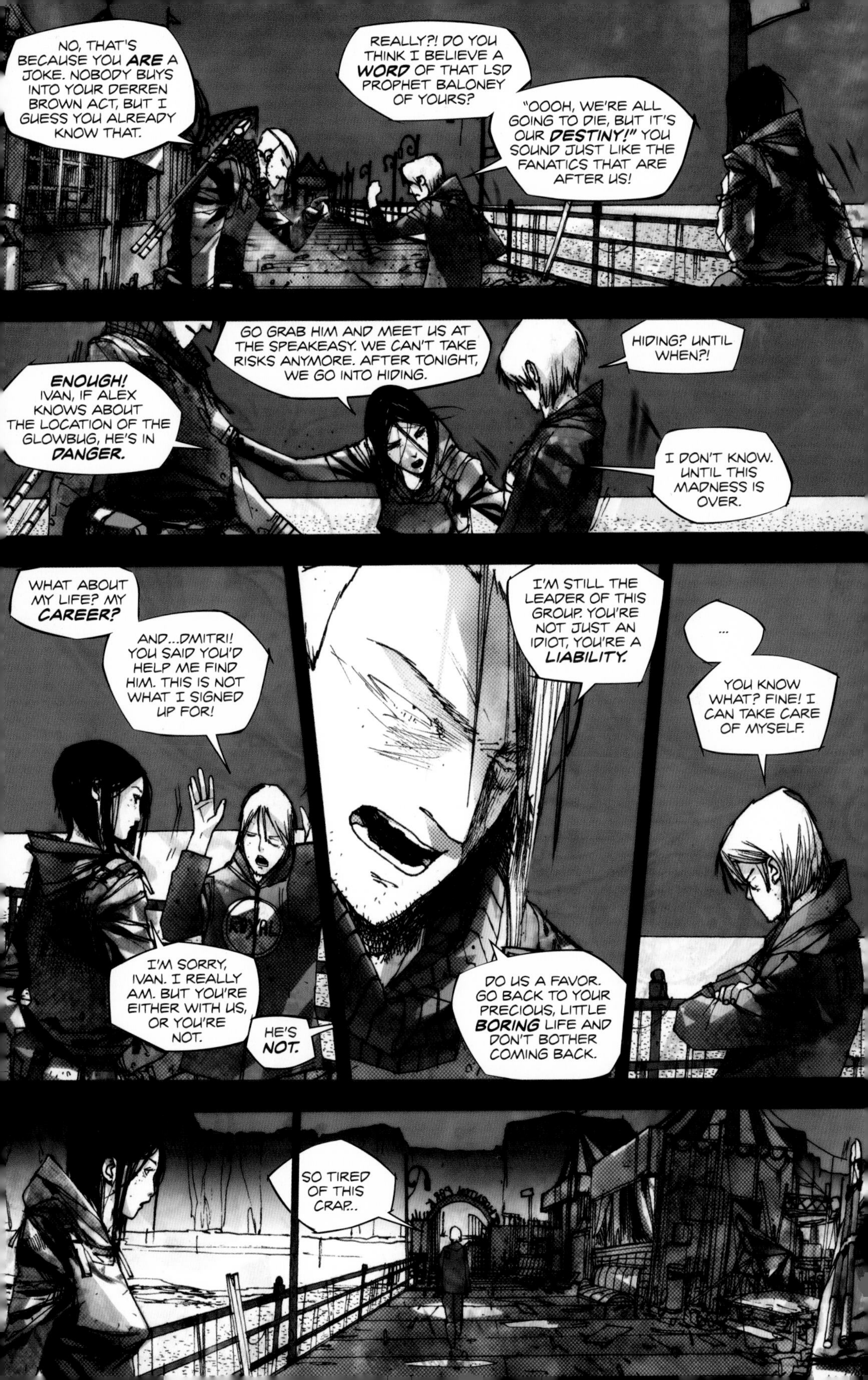
NO, THAT'S BECAUSE YOU **ARE** A JOKE. NOBODY BUYS INTO YOUR DERREN BROWN ACT, BUT I GUESS YOU ALREADY KNOW THAT.
REALLY?! DO YOU THINK I BELIEVE A **WORD** OF THAT LSD PROPHET BALONEY OF YOURS?
"OOOH, WE'RE ALL GOING TO DIE, BUT IT'S OUR **DESTINY!**" YOU SOUND JUST LIKE THE FANATICS THAT ARE AFTER US!
ENOUGH! IVAN, IF ALEX KNOWS ABOUT THE LOCATION OF THE GLOWBUG, HE'S IN **DANGER.**
GO GRAB HIM AND MEET US AT THE SPEAKEASY. WE CAN'T TAKE RISKS ANYMORE. AFTER TONIGHT, WE GO INTO HIDING.
HIDING? UNTIL WHEN?!
I DON'T KNOW. UNTIL THIS MADNESS IS OVER.
WHAT ABOUT MY LIFE? MY **CAREER?**
AND...DMITRI! YOU SAID YOU'D HELP ME FIND HIM. THIS IS NOT WHAT I SIGNED UP FOR!
I'M SORRY, IVAN. I REALLY AM. BUT YOU'RE EITHER WITH US, OR YOU'RE NOT.
HE'S **NOT.**
I'M STILL THE LEADER OF THIS GROUP. YOU'RE NOT JUST AN IDIOT, YOU'RE A **LIABILITY.**
DO US A FAVOR. GO BACK TO YOUR PRECIOUS, LITTLE **BORING** LIFE AND DON'T BOTHER COMING BACK.
...
YOU KNOW WHAT? FINE! I CAN TAKE CARE OF MYSELF.
SO TIRED OF THIS CRAP...

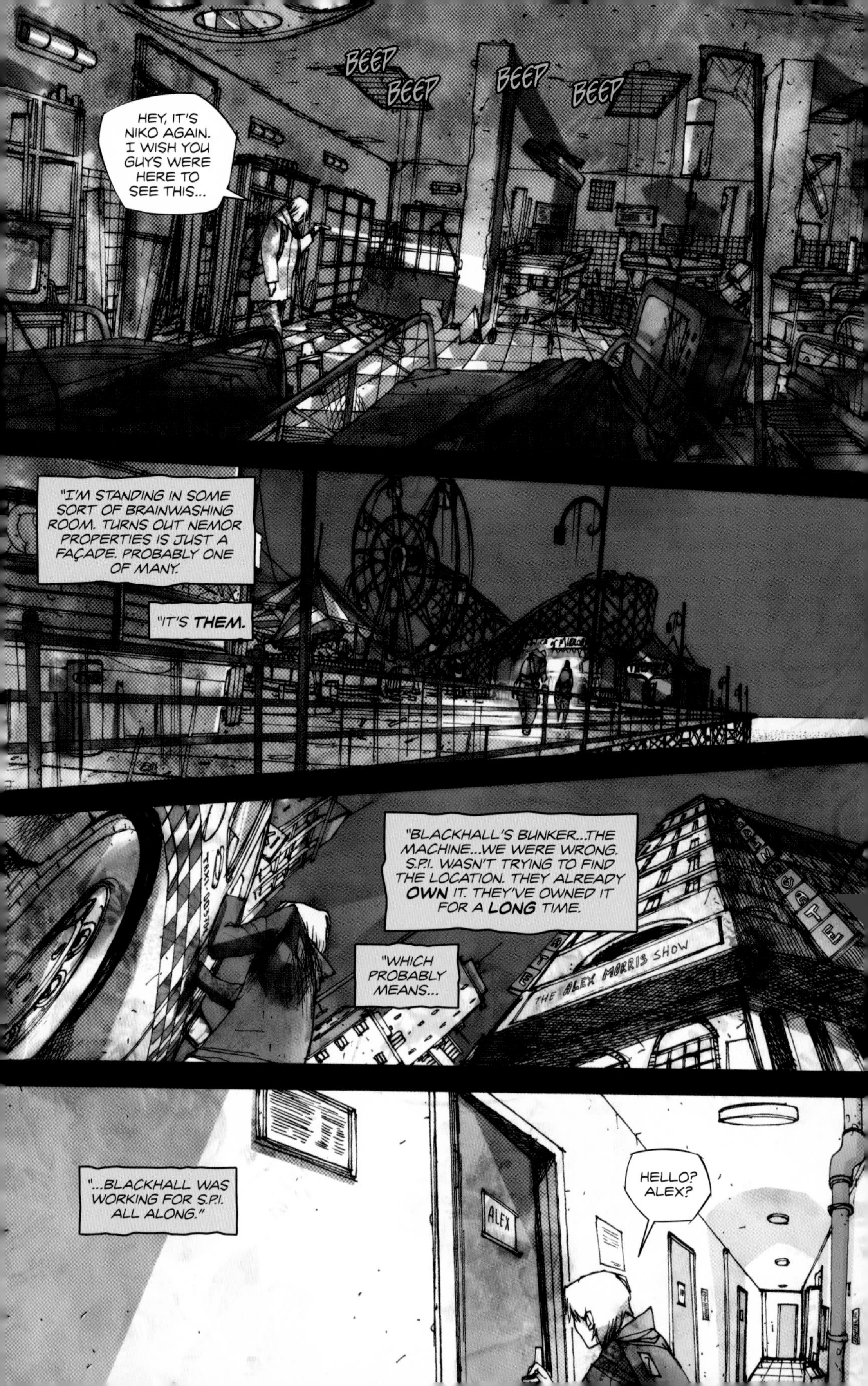
BEEP
BEEP
BEEP
BEEP
HEY, IT'S NIKO AGAIN. I WISH YOU GUYS WERE HERE TO SEE THIS...
"I'M STANDING IN SOME SORT OF BRAINWASHING ROOM. TURNS OUT NEMOR PROPERTIES IS JUST A FAÇADE. PROBABLY ONE OF MANY.
"IT'S THEM.
"BLACKHALL'S BUNKER...THE MACHINE...WE WERE WRONG. S.P.I. WASN'T TRYING TO FIND THE LOCATION. THEY ALREADY OWN IT. THEY'VE OWNED IT FOR A LONG TIME.
"WHICH PROBABLY MEANS...
THE ALEX MORRIS SHOW
"...BLACKHALL WAS WORKING FOR S.P.I. ALL ALONG."
ALEX
HELLO? ALEX?

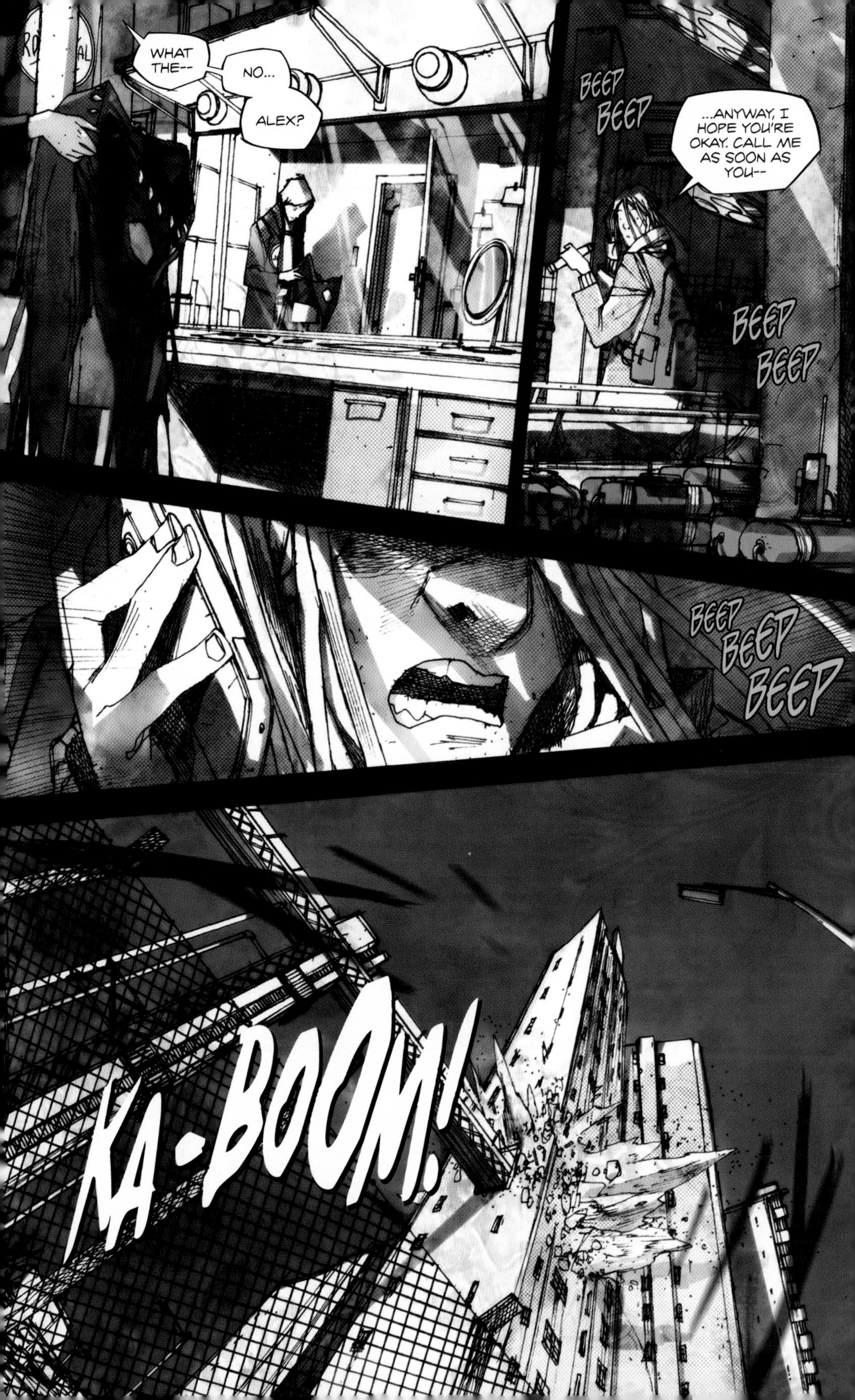
WHAT THE--
NO...
ALEX?
BEEP BEEP
...ANYWAY, I HOPE YOU'RE OKAY. CALL ME AS SOON AS YOU--
BEEP BEEP
BEEP BEEP BEEP
KA-BOOM!

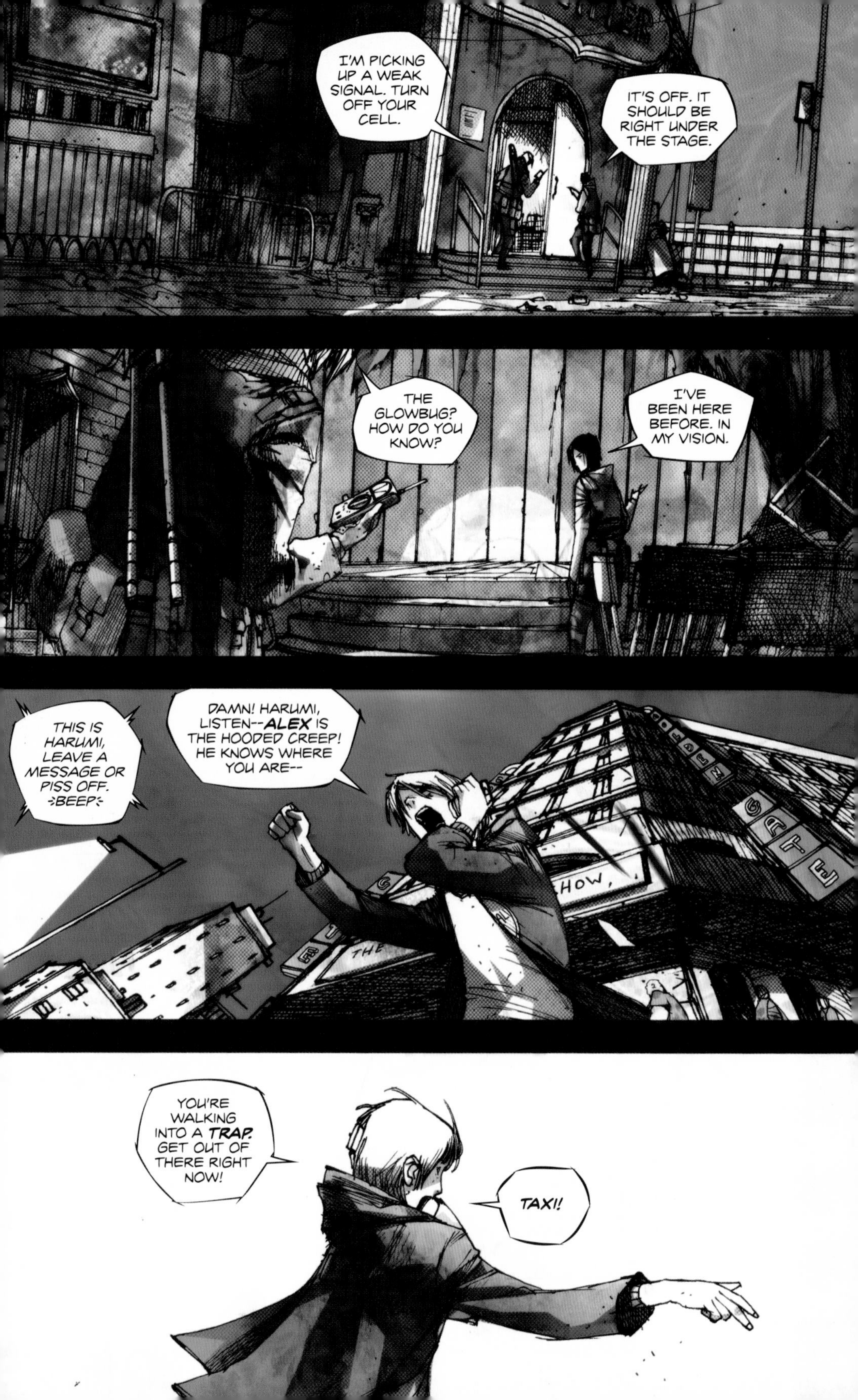
I'M PICKING UP A WEAK SIGNAL. TURN OFF YOUR CELL.
IT'S OFF. IT SHOULD BE RIGHT UNDER THE STAGE.
THE GLOWBUG? HOW DO YOU KNOW?
I'VE BEEN HERE BEFORE. IN MY VISION.
THIS IS HARUMI, LEAVE A MESSAGE OR PISS OFF. BEEP
DAMN! HARUMI, LISTEN--ALEX IS THE HOODED CREEP! HE KNOWS WHERE YOU ARE--
YOU'RE WALKING INTO A TRAP. GET OUT OF THERE RIGHT NOW!
TAXI!

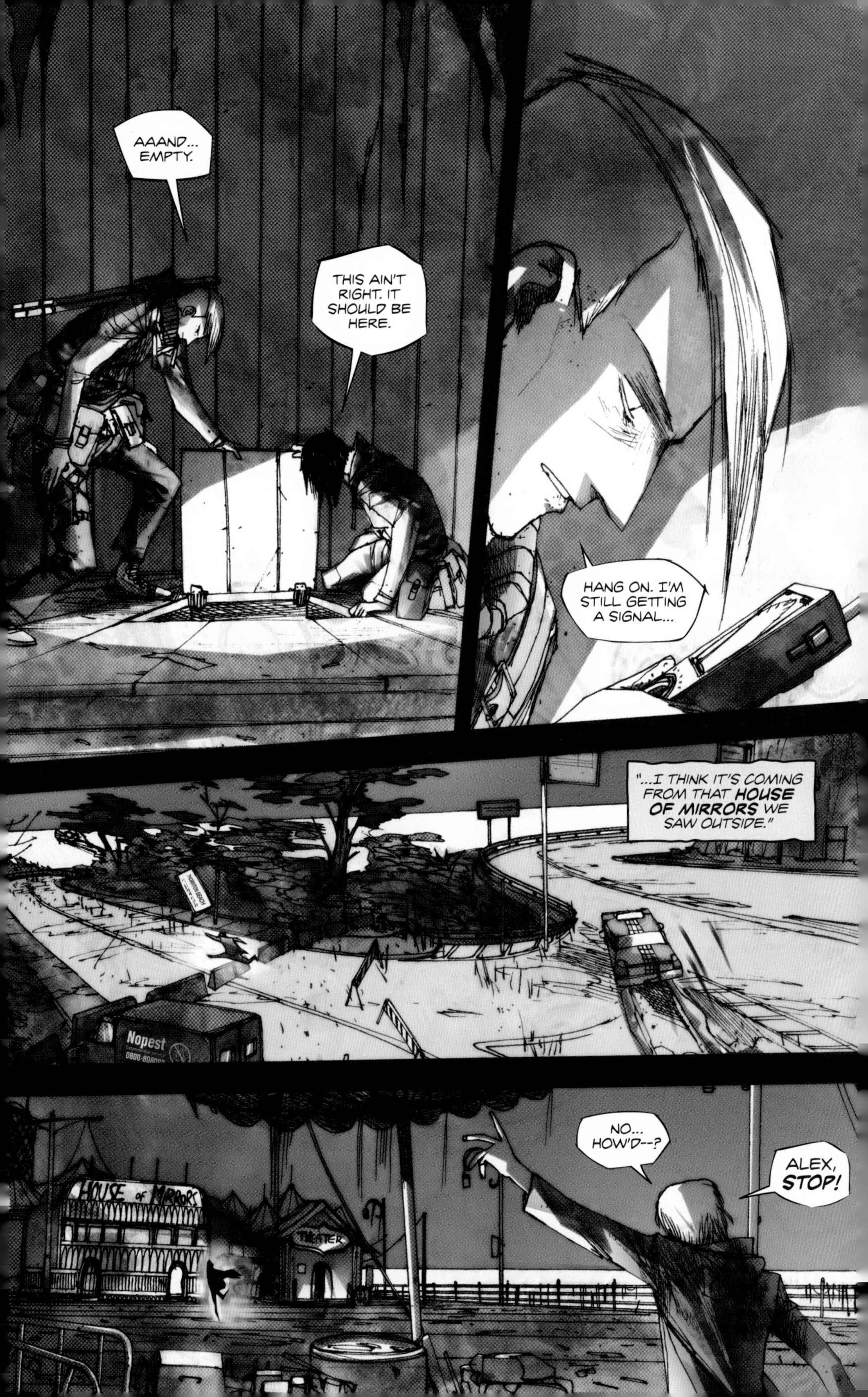
AAAND... EMPTY.
THIS AIN'T RIGHT. IT SHOULD BE HERE.
HANG ON. I'M STILL GETTING A SIGNAL...
"...I THINK IT'S COMING FROM THAT HOUSE OF MIRRORS WE SAW OUTSIDE."
Nopest
NO... HOW'D--?
ALEX, STOP!
HOUSE of MIRRORS
THEATER

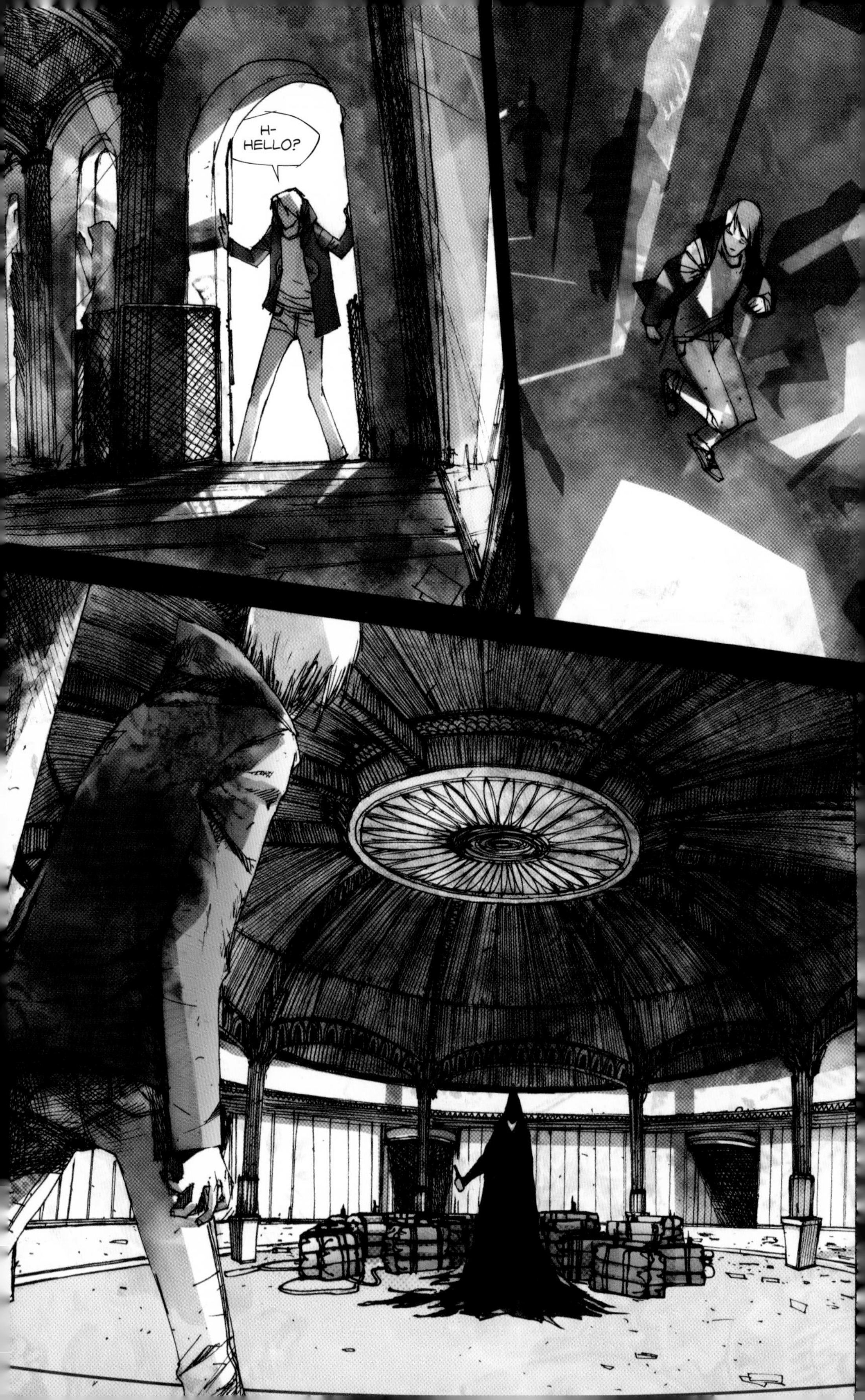
H-
HELLO?

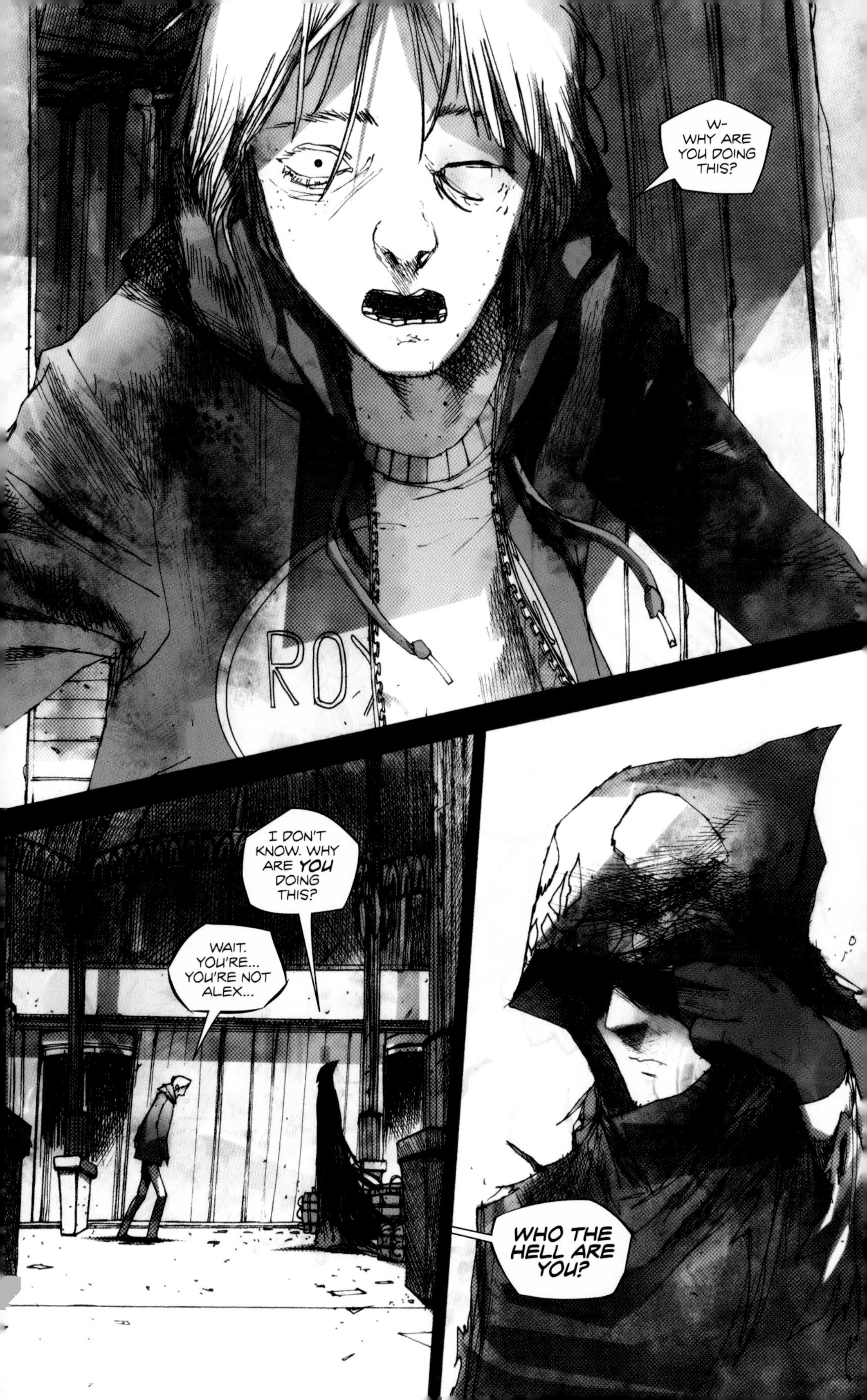
W-
WHY ARE YOU DOING THIS?
ROX
I DON'T KNOW. WHY ARE YOU DOING THIS?
WAIT. YOU'RE... YOU'RE NOT ALEX...
WHO THE HELL ARE YOU?

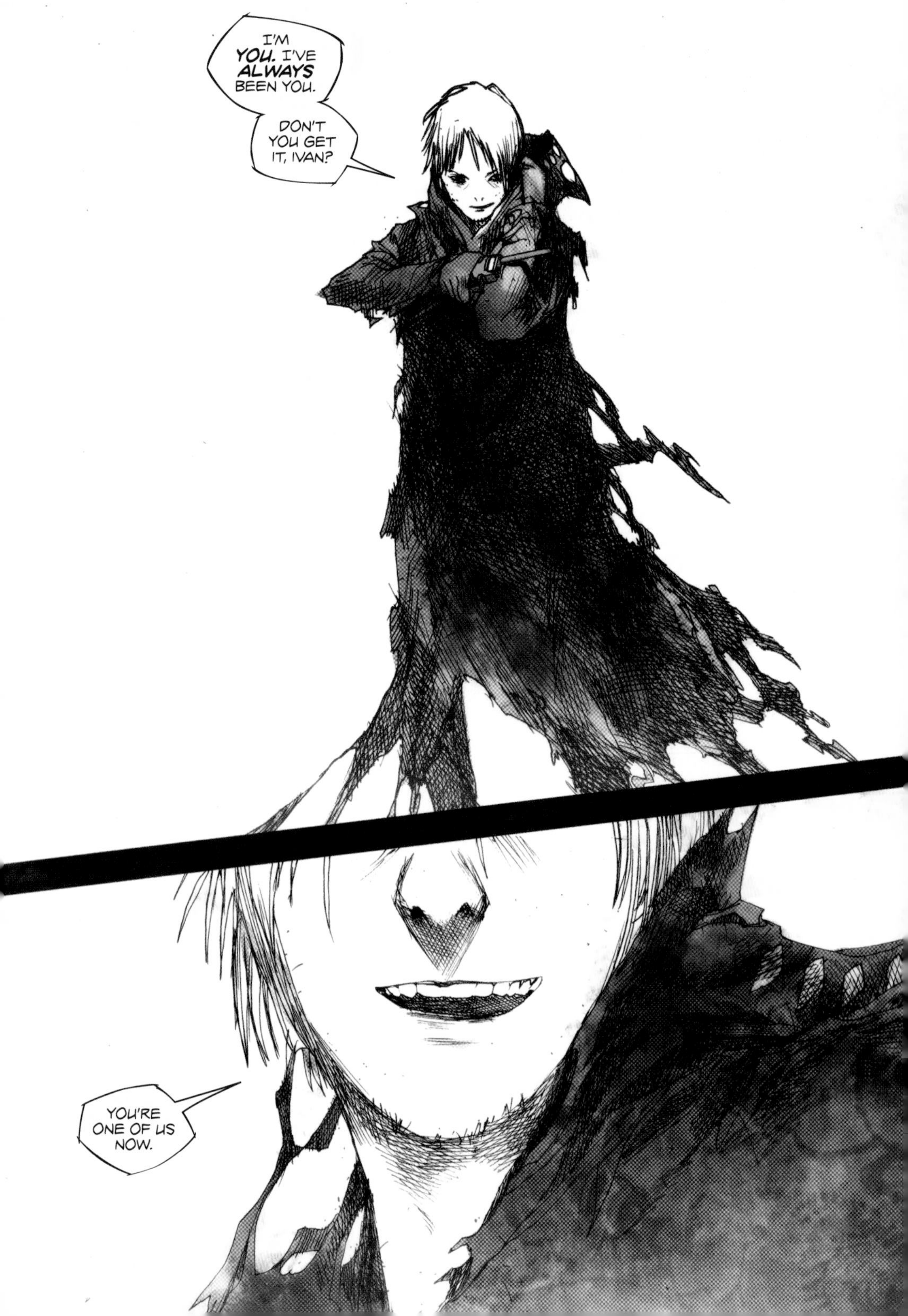
I'M YOU. I'VE ALWAYS BEEN YOU.
DON'T YOU GET IT, IVAN?
YOU'RE ONE OF US NOW.

ISSUE FIVE COVER

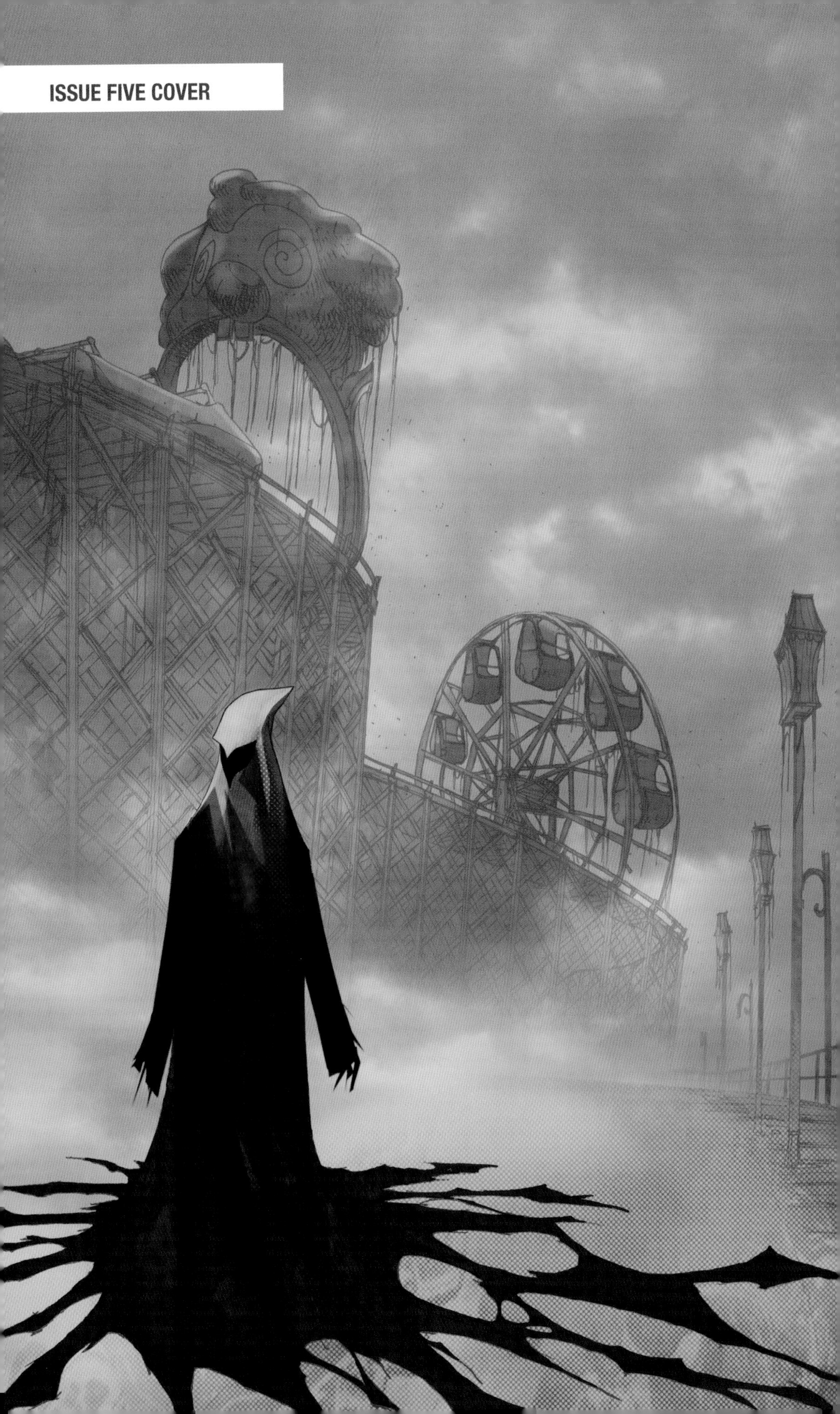

CHAPTER 6: THE FOURTH PROPHET

ALWAYS TRESPASS. YOB XIE HSKZX VQFC. DON'T TURN YOUR BACK ON THE MYSTERY.

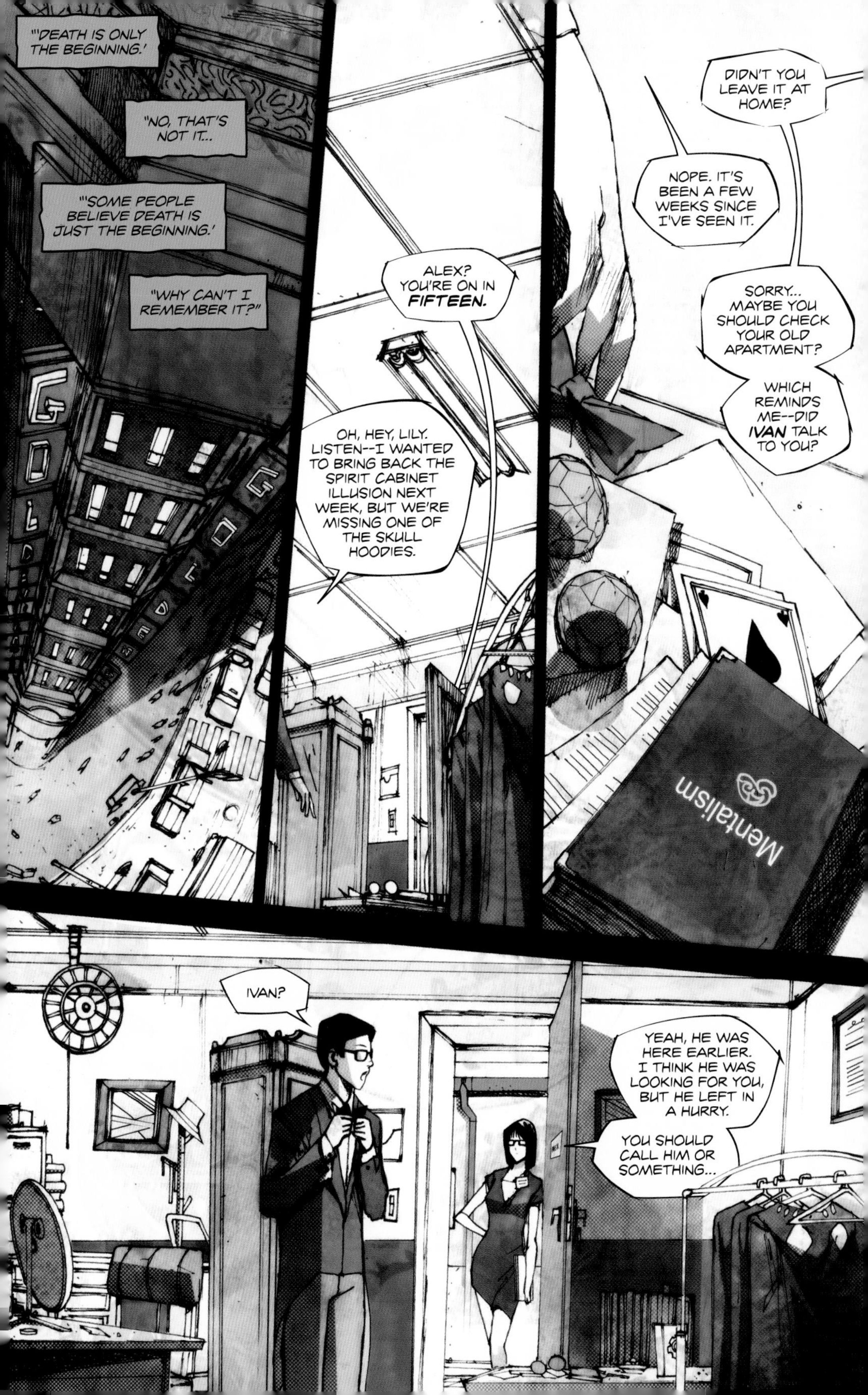
"'DEATH IS ONLY THE BEGINNING.'
"NO, THAT'S NOT IT...
"'SOME PEOPLE BELIEVE DEATH IS JUST THE BEGINNING.'
"WHY CAN'T I REMEMBER IT?"
GOLD
GOLDEN
ALEX? YOU'RE ON IN FIFTEEN.
OH, HEY, LILY. LISTEN--I WANTED TO BRING BACK THE SPIRIT CABINET ILLUSION NEXT WEEK, BUT WE'RE MISSING ONE OF THE SKULL HOODIES.
DIDN'T YOU LEAVE IT AT HOME?
NOPE. IT'S BEEN A FEW WEEKS SINCE I'VE SEEN IT.
SORRY... MAYBE YOU SHOULD CHECK YOUR OLD APARTMENT?
WHICH REMINDS ME--DID IVAN TALK TO YOU?
Mentalism
IVAN?
YEAH, HE WAS HERE EARLIER. I THINK HE WAS LOOKING FOR YOU, BUT HE LEFT IN A HURRY.
YOU SHOULD CALL HIM OR SOMETHING...

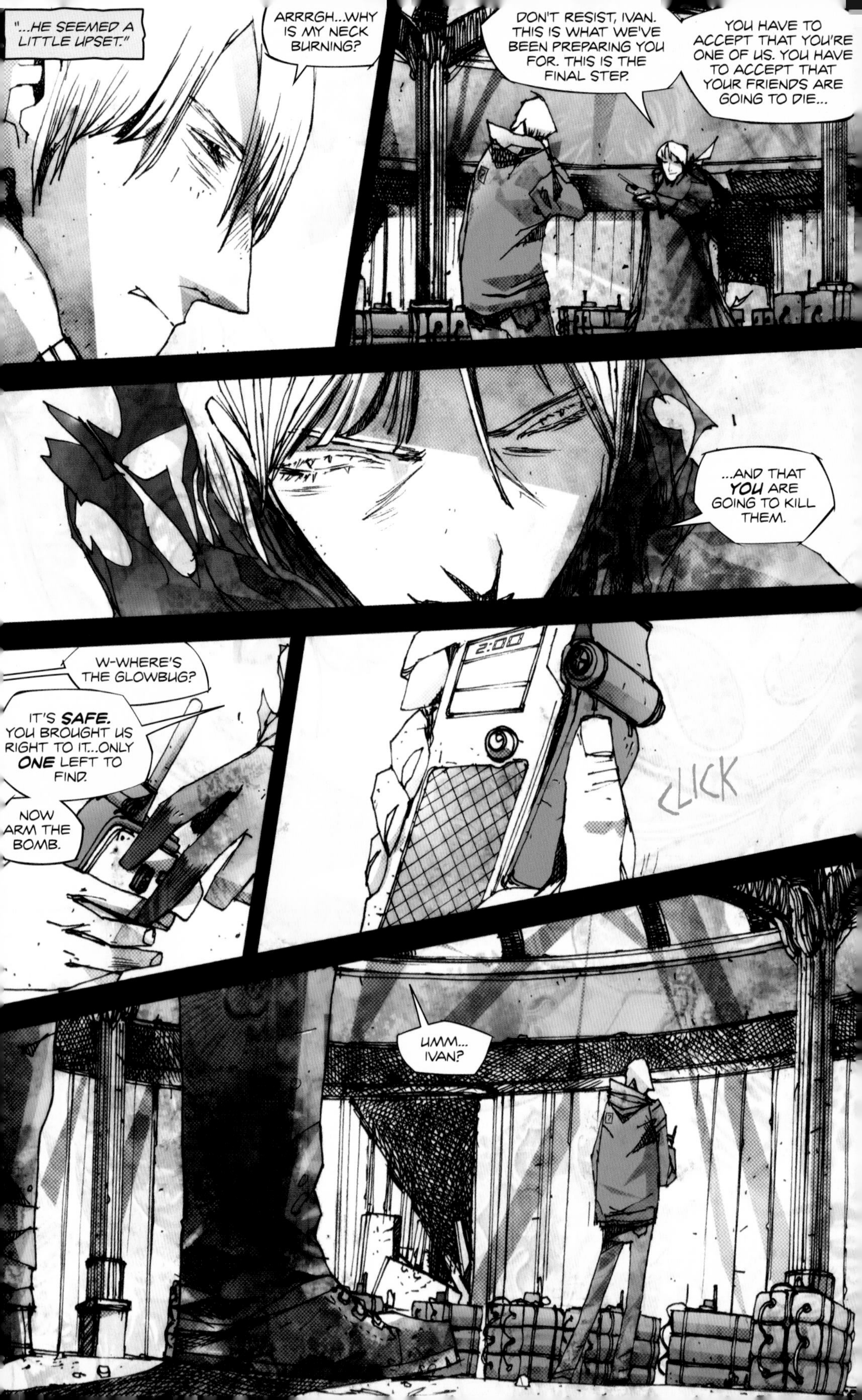
"...HE SEEMED A LITTLE UPSET."
ARRRGH...WHY IS MY NECK BURNING?
DON'T RESIST, IVAN. THIS IS WHAT WE'VE BEEN PREPARING YOU FOR. THIS IS THE FINAL STEP.
YOU HAVE TO ACCEPT THAT YOU'RE ONE OF US. YOU HAVE TO ACCEPT THAT YOUR FRIENDS ARE GOING TO DIE...
...AND THAT YOU ARE GOING TO KILL THEM.
W-WHERE'S THE GLOWBUG?
IT'S SAFE. YOU BROUGHT US RIGHT TO IT...ONLY ONE LEFT TO FIND.
NOW ARM THE BOMB.
2:00
CLICK
UMM... IVAN?

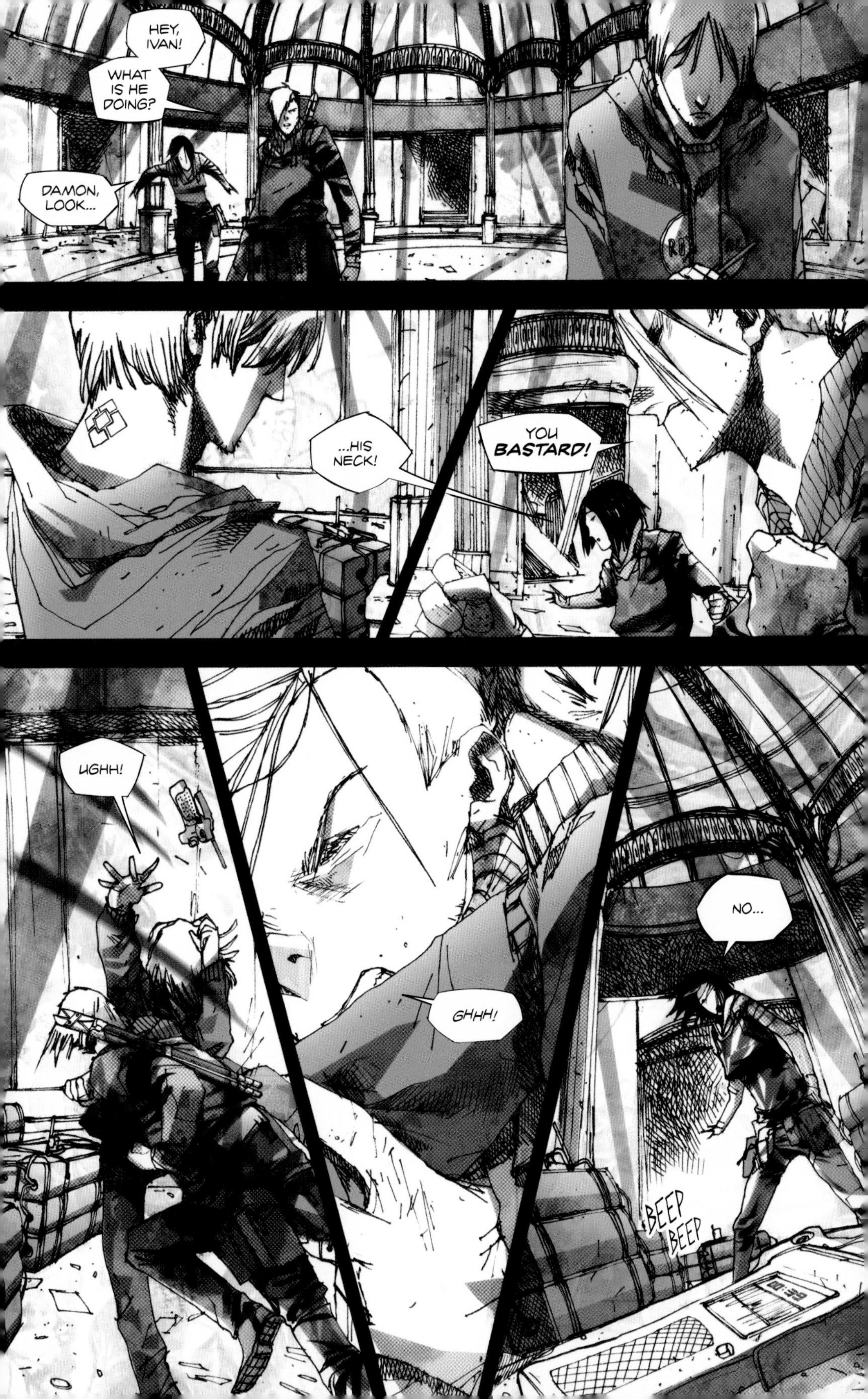
HEY, IVAN!
WHAT IS HE DOING?
DAMON, LOOK...
...HIS NECK!
YOU BASTARD!
UGHH!
GHHH!
NO...
BEEP BEEP

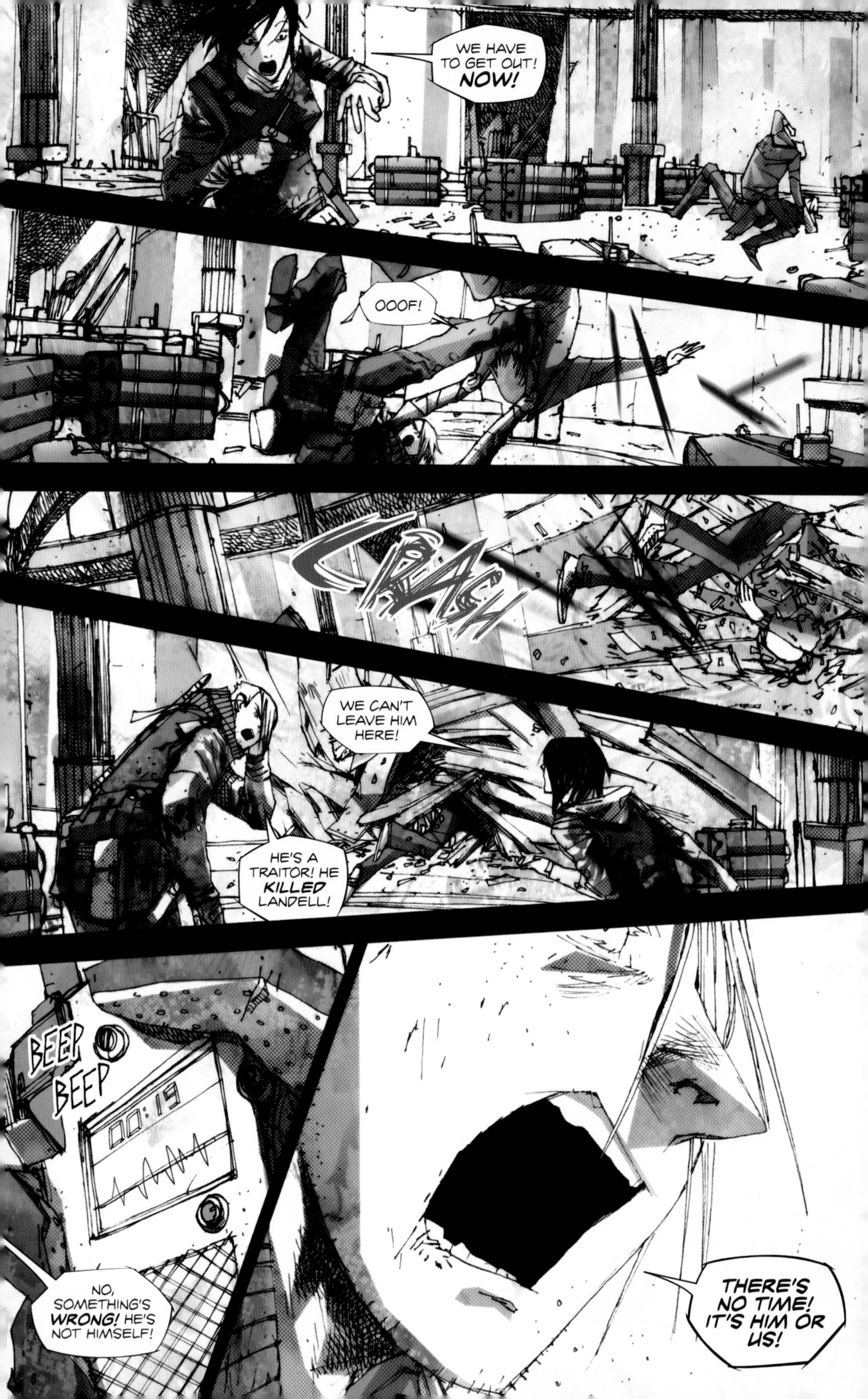

WE HAVE TO GET OUT! NOW!
OOOF!
CRASH
WE CAN'T LEAVE HIM HERE!
HE'S A TRAITOR! HE KILLED LANDELL!
BEEP BEEP
00:19
NO, SOMETHING'S WRONG! HE'S NOT HIMSELF!
THERE'S NO TIME! IT'S HIM OR US!

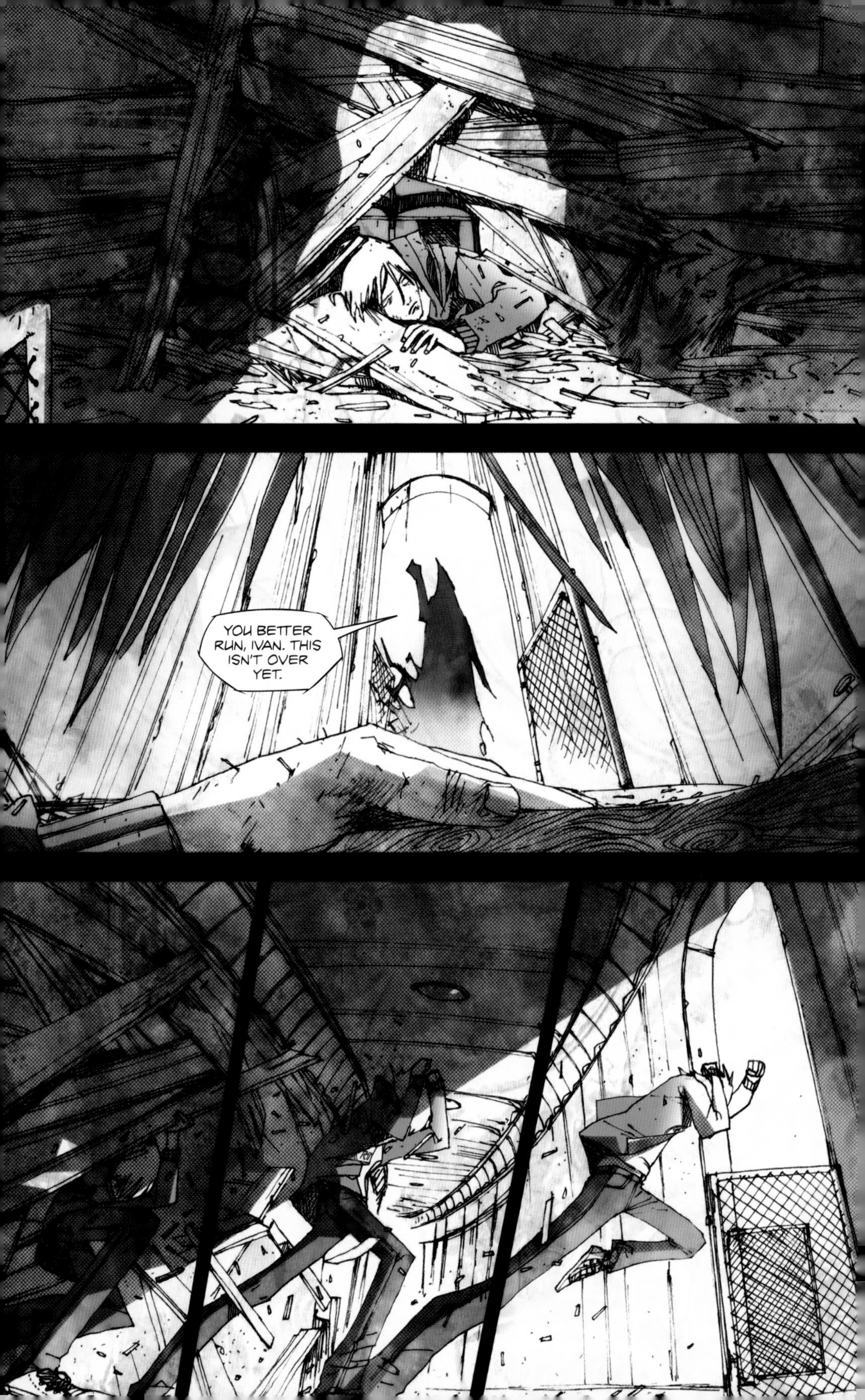
YOU BETTER RUN, IVAN. THIS ISN'T OVER YET.

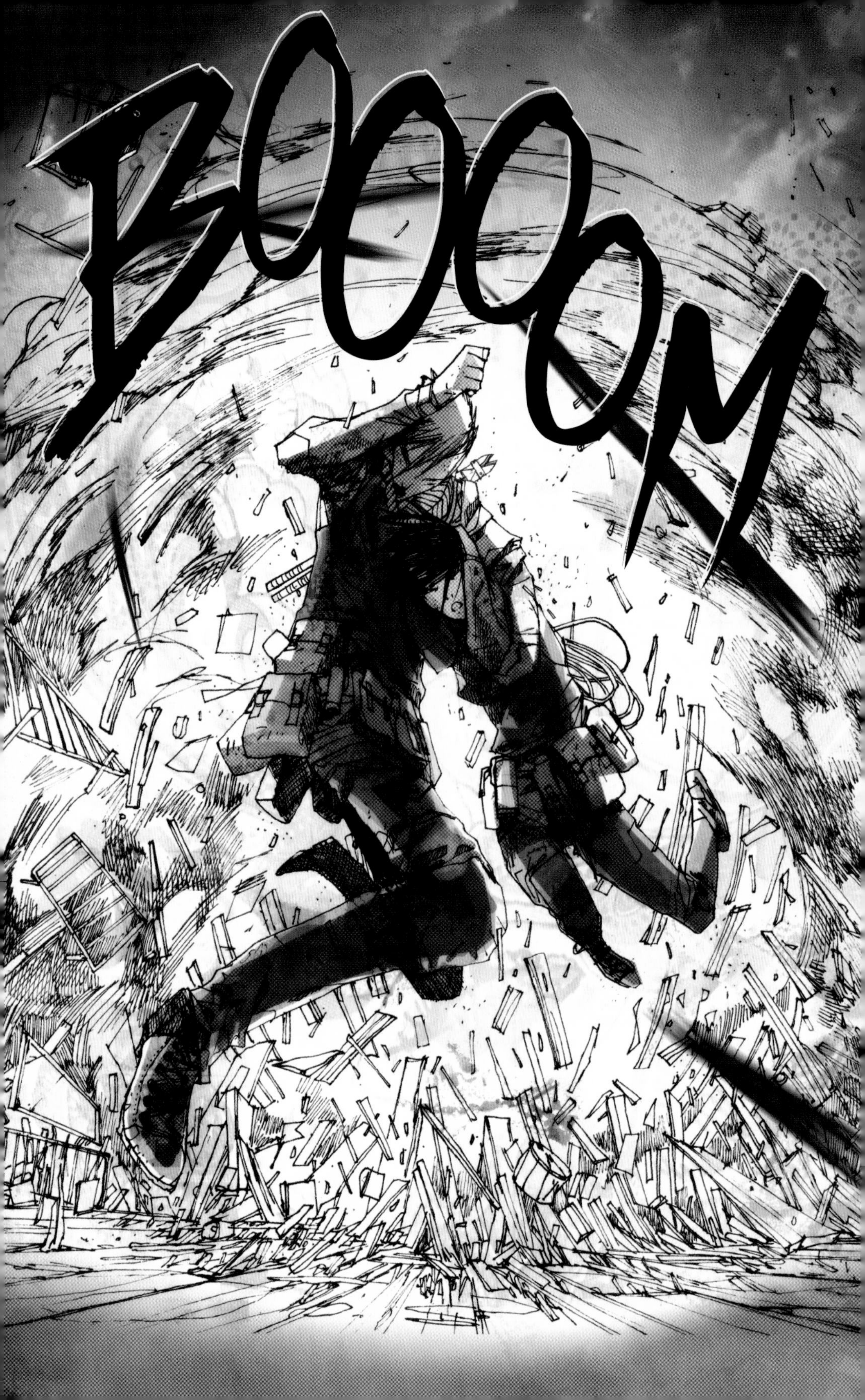
BOOOOM

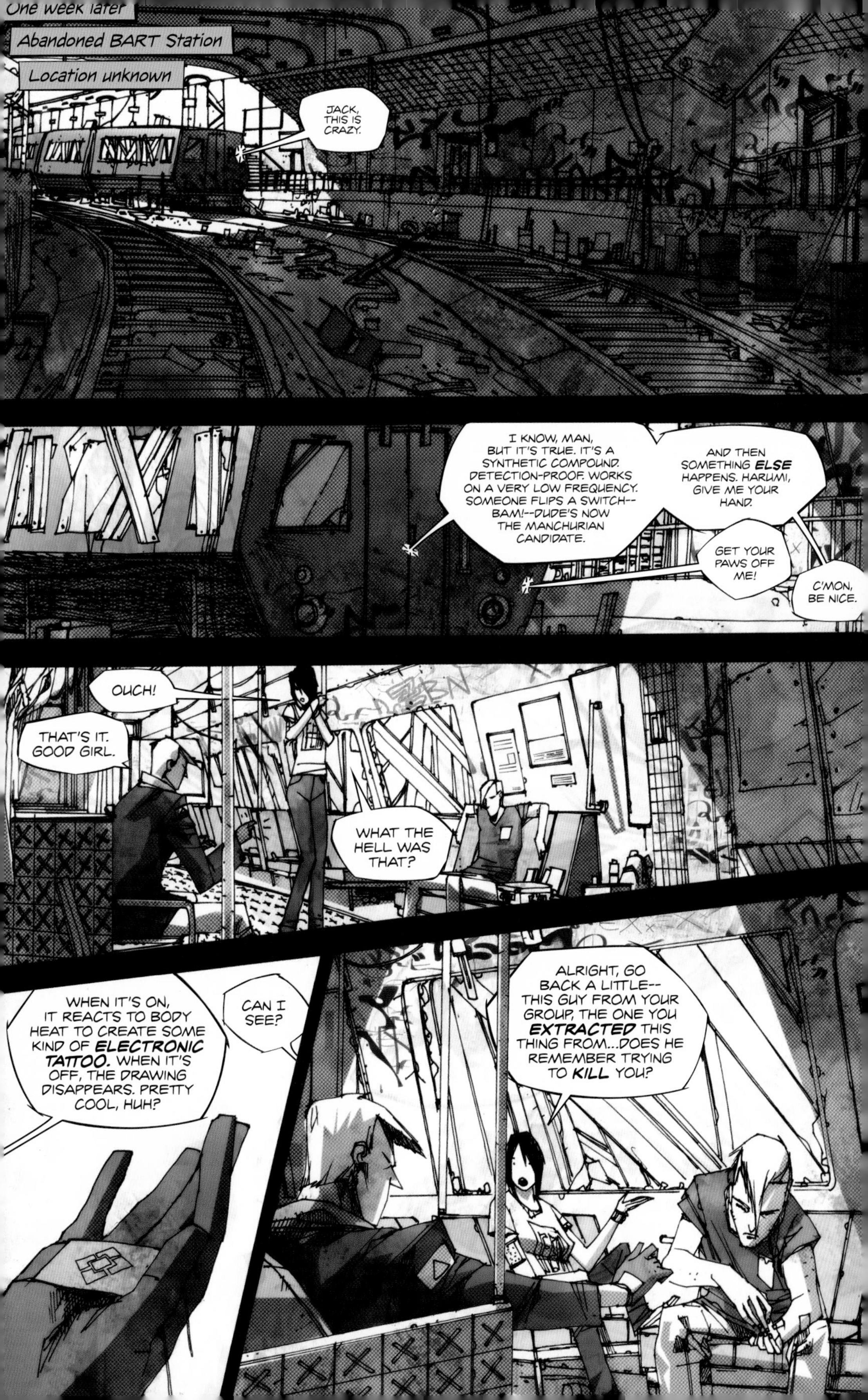
One week later
Abandoned BART Station
Location unknown
JACK, THIS IS CRAZY.
I KNOW, MAN, BUT IT'S TRUE. IT'S A SYNTHETIC COMPOUND. DETECTION-PROOF. WORKS ON A VERY LOW FREQUENCY. SOMEONE FLIPS A SWITCH--BAM!--DUDE'S NOW THE MANCHURIAN CANDIDATE.
AND THEN SOMETHING ELSE HAPPENS. HARUMI, GIVE ME YOUR HAND.
GET YOUR PAWS OFF ME!
C'MON, BE NICE.
OUCH!
THAT'S IT. GOOD GIRL.
WHAT THE HELL WAS THAT?
WHEN IT'S ON, IT REACTS TO BODY HEAT TO CREATE SOME KIND OF ELECTRONIC TATTOO. WHEN IT'S OFF, THE DRAWING DISAPPEARS. PRETTY COOL, HUH?
CAN I SEE?
ALRIGHT, GO BACK A LITTLE-- THIS GUY FROM YOUR GROUP, THE ONE YOU EXTRACTED THIS THING FROM...DOES HE REMEMBER TRYING TO KILL YOU?

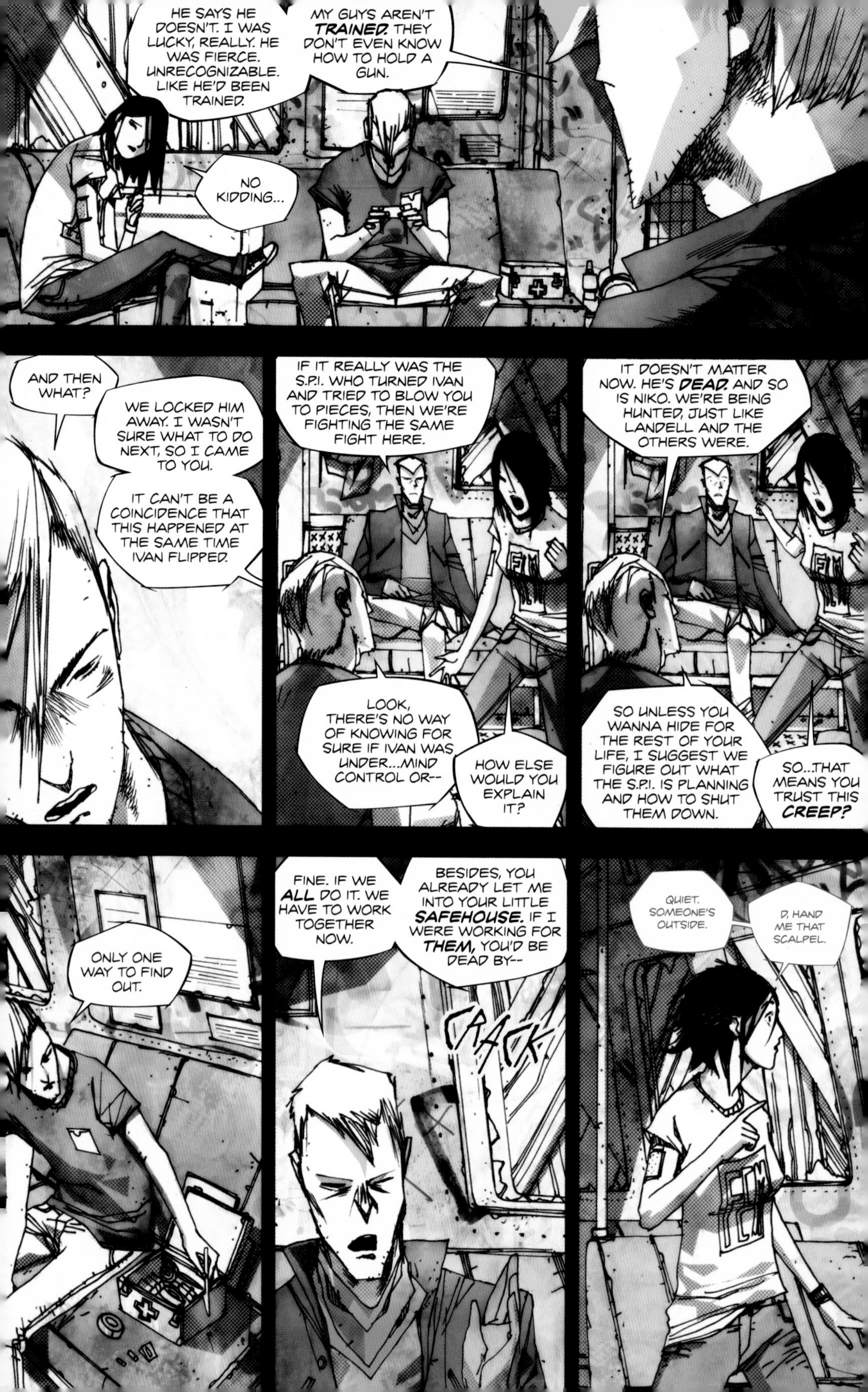
HE SAYS HE DOESN'T. I WAS LUCKY, REALLY. HE WAS FIERCE. UNRECOGNIZABLE. LIKE HE'D BEEN TRAINED.
MY GUYS AREN'T TRAINED. THEY DON'T EVEN KNOW HOW TO HOLD A GUN.
NO KIDDING...
AND THEN WHAT?
WE LOCKED HIM AWAY. I WASN'T SURE WHAT TO DO NEXT, SO I CAME TO YOU.
IT CAN'T BE A COINCIDENCE THAT THIS HAPPENED AT THE SAME TIME IVAN FLIPPED.
IF IT REALLY WAS THE S.P.I. WHO TURNED IVAN AND TRIED TO BLOW YOU TO PIECES, THEN WE'RE FIGHTING THE SAME FIGHT HERE.
LOOK, THERE'S NO WAY OF KNOWING FOR SURE IF IVAN WAS UNDER...MIND CONTROL OR--
HOW ELSE WOULD YOU EXPLAIN IT?
IT DOESN'T MATTER NOW. HE'S DEAD. AND SO IS NIKO. WE'RE BEING HUNTED, JUST LIKE LANDELL AND THE OTHERS WERE.
SO UNLESS YOU WANNA HIDE FOR THE REST OF YOUR LIFE, I SUGGEST WE FIGURE OUT WHAT THE S.P.I. IS PLANNING AND HOW TO SHUT THEM DOWN.
SO...THAT MEANS YOU TRUST THIS CREEP?
ONLY ONE WAY TO FIND OUT.
FINE. IF WE ALL DO IT. WE HAVE TO WORK TOGETHER NOW.
BESIDES, YOU ALREADY LET ME INTO YOUR LITTLE SAFEHOUSE. IF I WERE WORKING FOR THEM, YOU'D BE DEAD BY--
CRACK
QUIET. SOMEONE'S OUTSIDE.
D, HAND ME THAT SCALPEL.

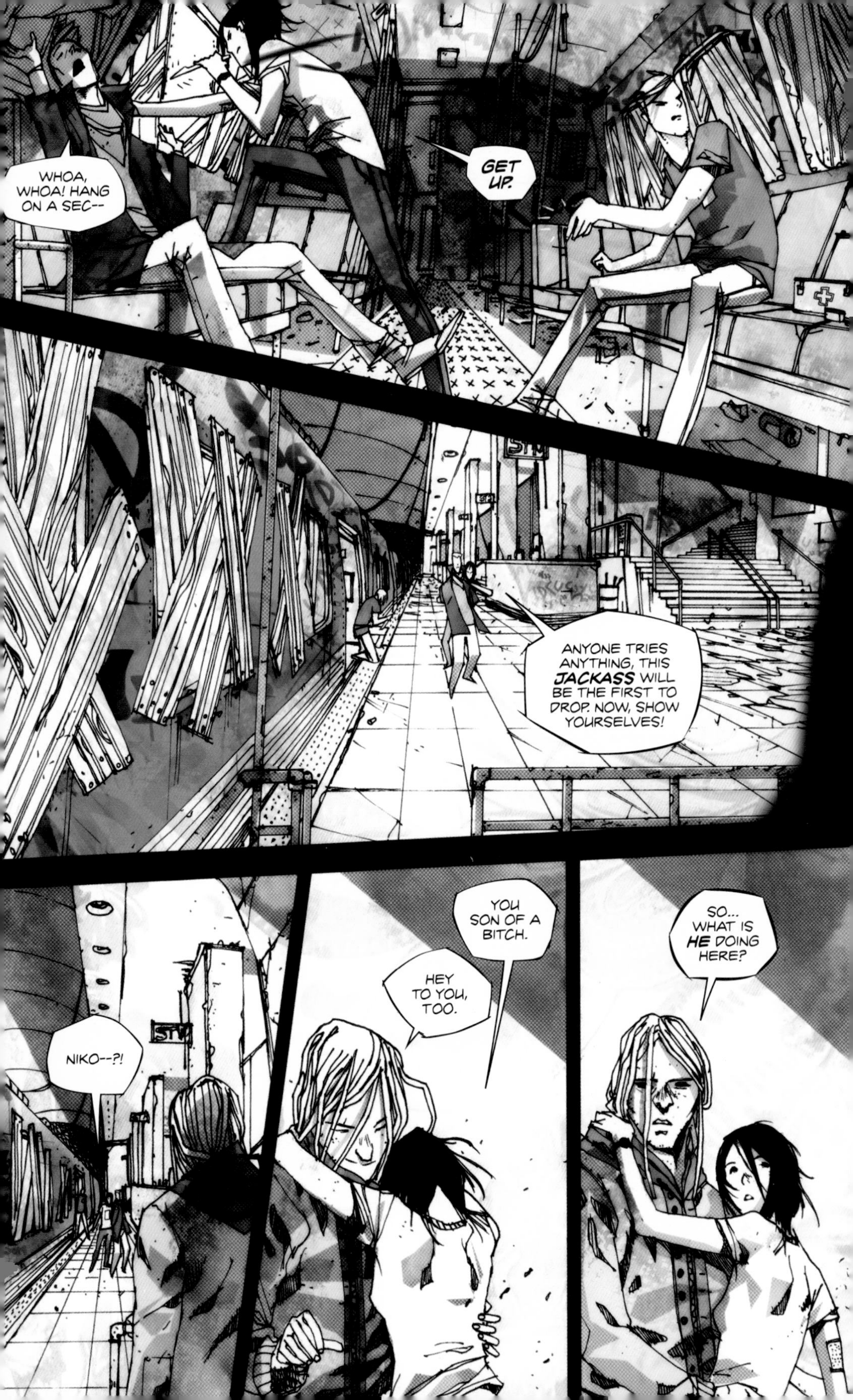
WHOA, WHOA! HANG ON A SEC--
GET UP.
ANYONE TRIES ANYTHING, THIS **JACKASS** WILL BE THE FIRST TO DROP. NOW, SHOW YOURSELVES!
NIKO--?!
YOU SON OF A BITCH.
HEY TO YOU, TOO.
SO... WHAT IS **HE** DOING HERE?

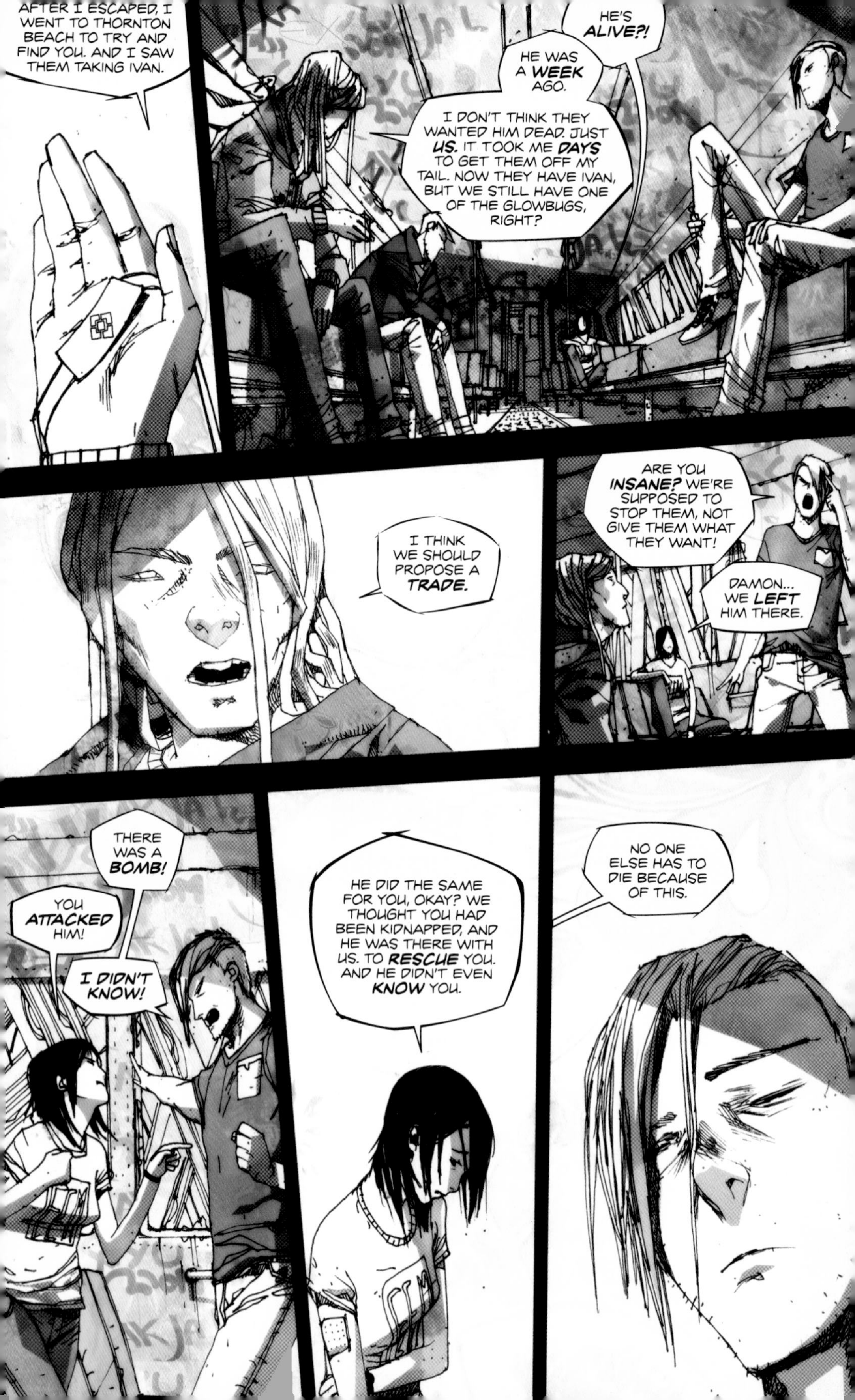
AFTER I ESCAPED, I WENT TO THORNTON BEACH TO TRY AND FIND YOU. AND I SAW THEM TAKING IVAN.
HE'S ALIVE?!
HE WAS A WEEK AGO.
I DON'T THINK THEY WANTED HIM DEAD. JUST US. IT TOOK ME DAYS TO GET THEM OFF MY TAIL. NOW THEY HAVE IVAN, BUT WE STILL HAVE ONE OF THE GLOWBUGS, RIGHT?
I THINK WE SHOULD PROPOSE A TRADE.
ARE YOU INSANE? WE'RE SUPPOSED TO STOP THEM, NOT GIVE THEM WHAT THEY WANT!
DAMON... WE LEFT HIM THERE.
THERE WAS A BOMB!
YOU ATTACKED HIM!
I DIDN'T KNOW!
HE DID THE SAME FOR YOU, OKAY? WE THOUGHT YOU HAD BEEN KIDNAPPED, AND HE WAS THERE WITH US. TO RESCUE YOU. AND HE DIDN'T EVEN KNOW YOU.
NO ONE ELSE HAS TO DIE BECAUSE OF THIS.

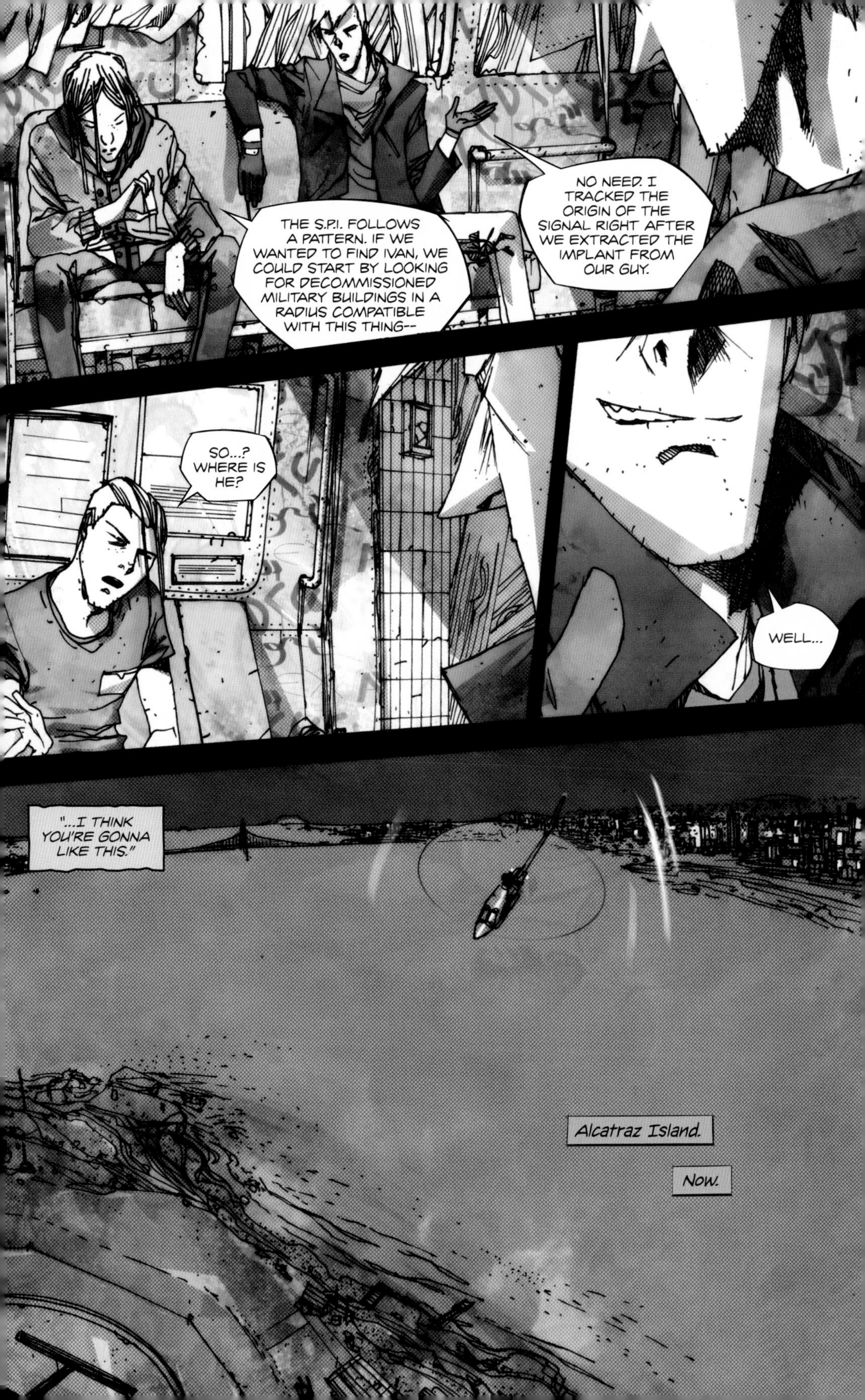
THE S.P.I. FOLLOWS A PATTERN. IF WE WANTED TO FIND IVAN, WE COULD START BY LOOKING FOR DECOMMISSIONED MILITARY BUILDINGS IN A RADIUS COMPATIBLE WITH THIS THING--
NO NEED. I TRACKED THE ORIGIN OF THE SIGNAL RIGHT AFTER WE EXTRACTED THE IMPLANT FROM OUR GUY.
SO...? WHERE IS HE?
WELL...
"...I THINK YOU'RE GONNA LIKE THIS."
Alcatraz Island.
Now.

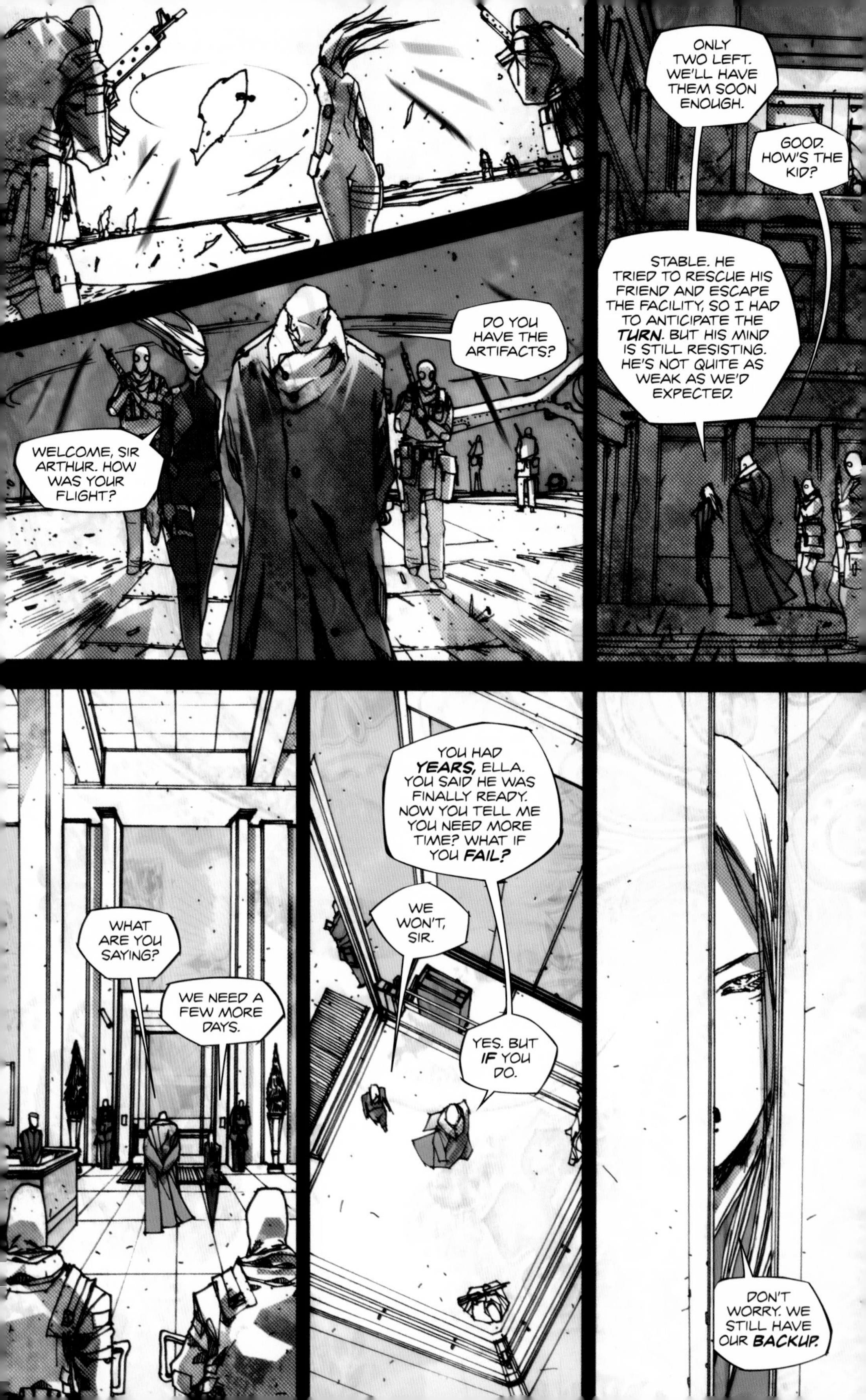
DO YOU HAVE THE ARTIFACTS?
WELCOME, SIR ARTHUR. HOW WAS YOUR FLIGHT?
ONLY TWO LEFT. WE'LL HAVE THEM SOON ENOUGH.
GOOD. HOW'S THE KID?
STABLE. HE TRIED TO RESCUE HIS FRIEND AND ESCAPE THE FACILITY, SO I HAD TO ANTICIPATE THE **TURN**. BUT HIS MIND IS STILL RESISTING. HE'S NOT QUITE AS WEAK AS WE'D EXPECTED.
WHAT ARE YOU SAYING?
WE NEED A FEW MORE DAYS.
YOU HAD **YEARS,** ELLA. YOU SAID HE WAS FINALLY READY. NOW YOU TELL ME YOU NEED MORE TIME? WHAT IF YOU **FAIL?**
WE WON'T, SIR.
YES. BUT **IF** YOU DO.
DON'T WORRY. WE STILL HAVE OUR **BACKUP.**

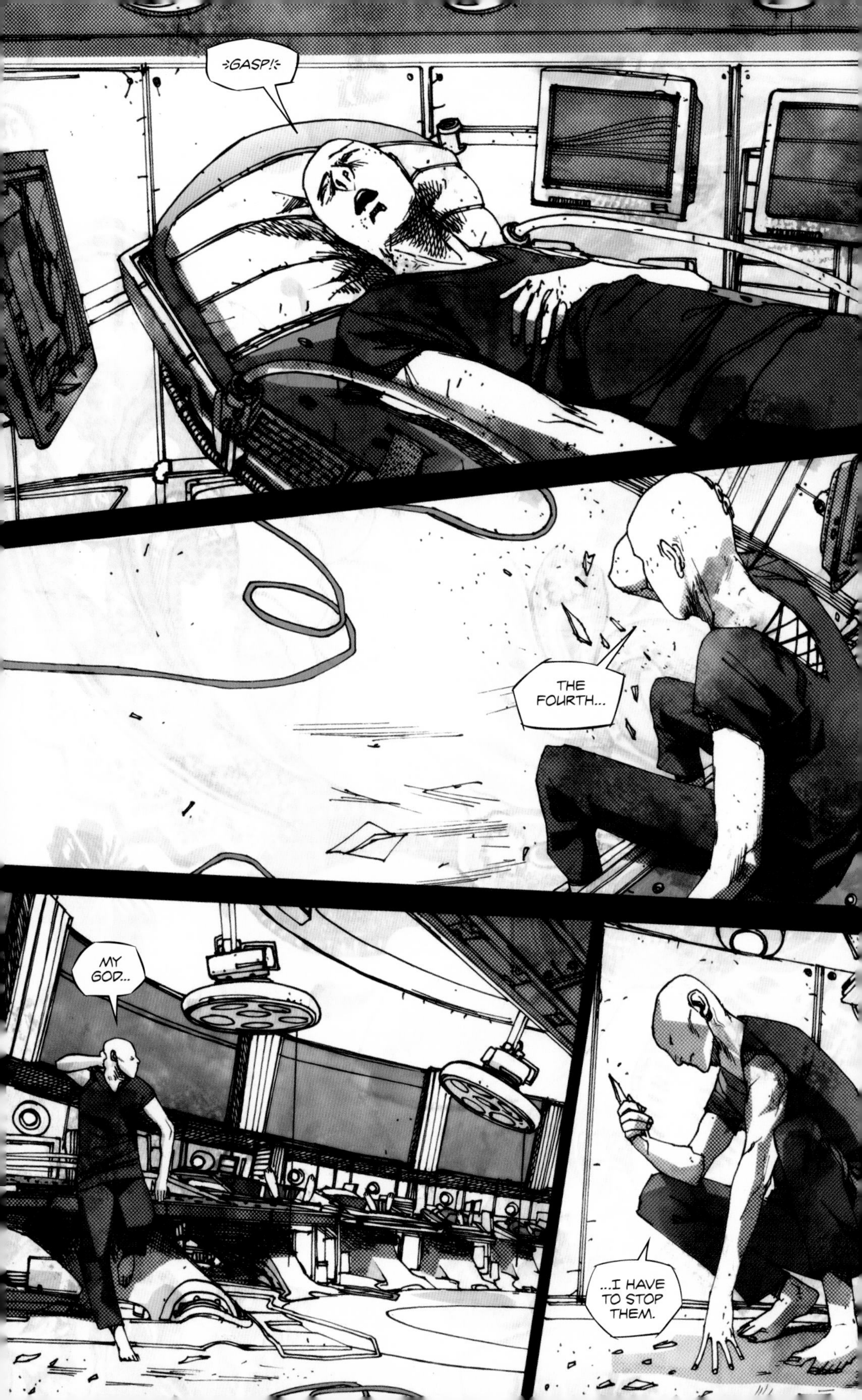

GASP!
THE FOURTH...
MY GOD...
...I HAVE TO STOP THEM.

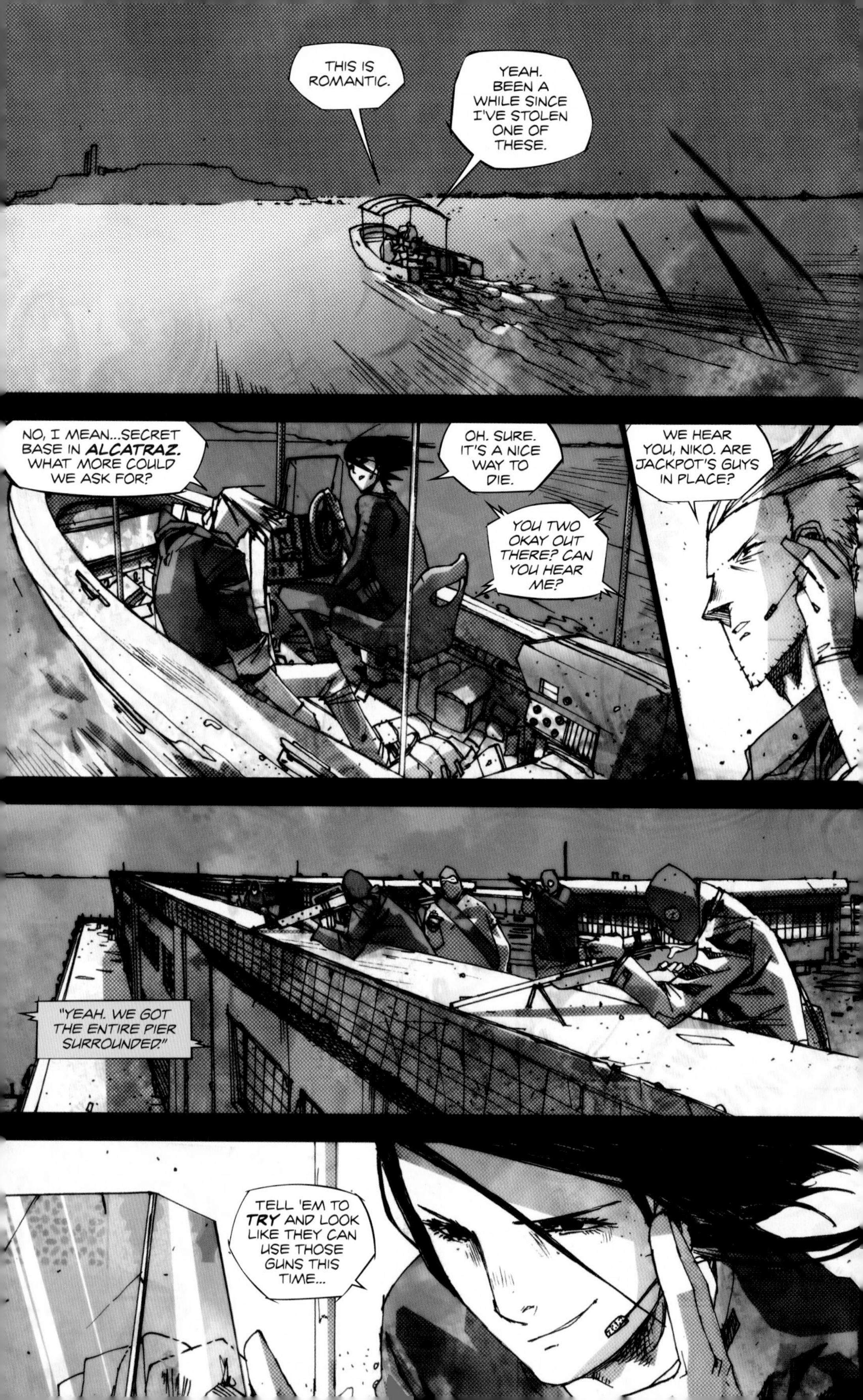
THIS IS ROMANTIC.
YEAH. BEEN A WHILE SINCE I'VE STOLEN ONE OF THESE.
NO, I MEAN...SECRET BASE IN ALCATRAZ. WHAT MORE COULD WE ASK FOR?
OH. SURE. IT'S A NICE WAY TO DIE.
YOU TWO OKAY OUT THERE? CAN YOU HEAR ME?
WE HEAR YOU, NIKO. ARE JACKPOT'S GUYS IN PLACE?
"YEAH. WE GOT THE ENTIRE PIER SURROUNDED."
TELL 'EM TO TRY AND LOOK LIKE THEY CAN USE THOSE GUNS THIS TIME...

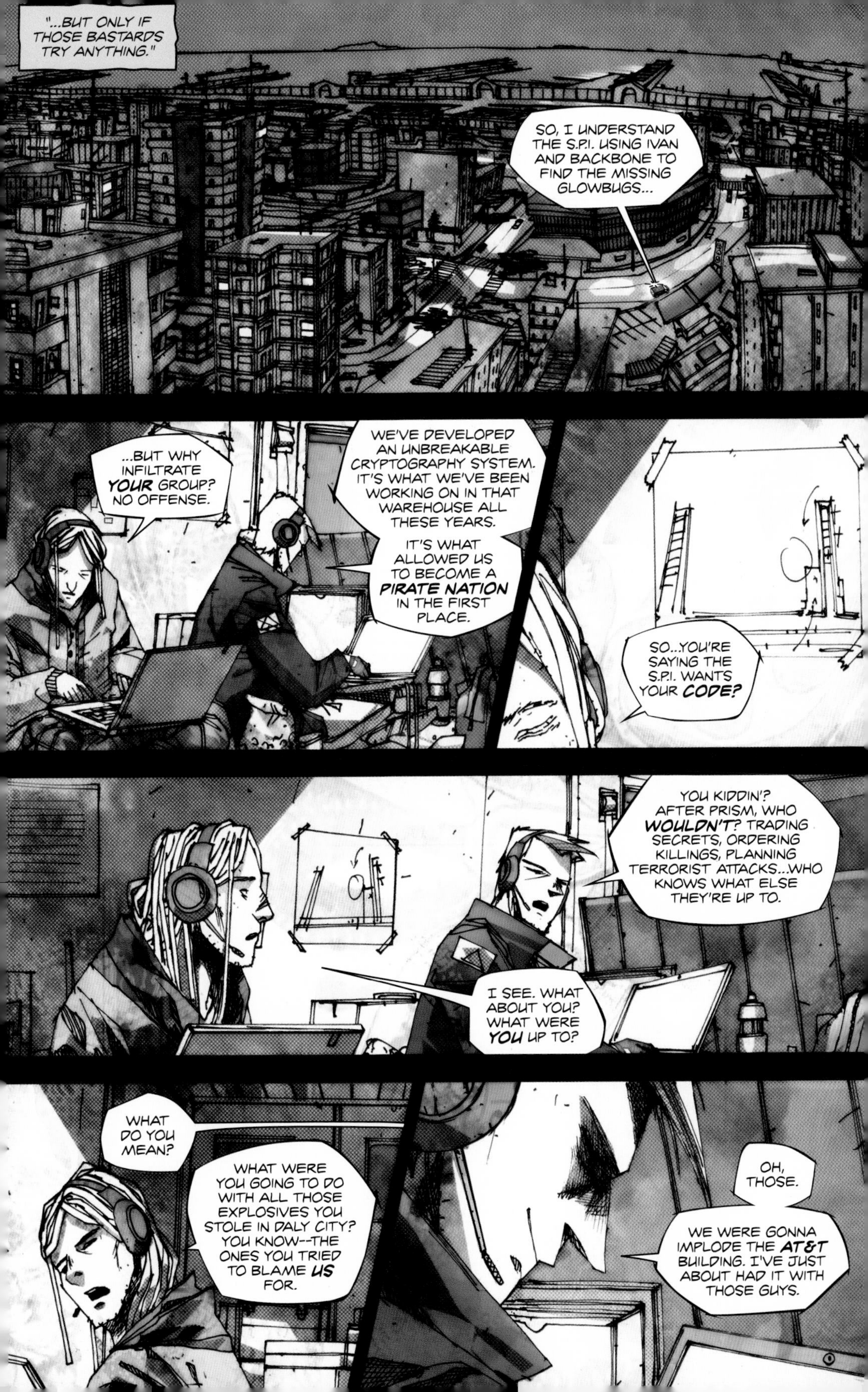
"...BUT ONLY IF THOSE BASTARDS TRY ANYTHING."
SO, I UNDERSTAND THE S.P.I. USING IVAN AND BACKBONE TO FIND THE MISSING GLOWBUGS...
...BUT WHY INFILTRATE YOUR GROUP? NO OFFENSE.
WE'VE DEVELOPED AN UNBREAKABLE CRYPTOGRAPHY SYSTEM. IT'S WHAT WE'VE BEEN WORKING ON IN THAT WAREHOUSE ALL THESE YEARS.
IT'S WHAT ALLOWED US TO BECOME A PIRATE NATION IN THE FIRST PLACE.
SO...YOU'RE SAYING THE S.P.I. WANTS YOUR CODE?
YOU KIDDIN'? AFTER PRISM, WHO WOULDN'T? TRADING SECRETS, ORDERING KILLINGS, PLANNING TERRORIST ATTACKS...WHO KNOWS WHAT ELSE THEY'RE UP TO.
I SEE. WHAT ABOUT YOU? WHAT WERE YOU UP TO?
WHAT DO YOU MEAN?
WHAT WERE YOU GOING TO DO WITH ALL THOSE EXPLOSIVES YOU STOLE IN DALY CITY? YOU KNOW--THE ONES YOU TRIED TO BLAME US FOR.
OH, THOSE.
WE WERE GONNA IMPLODE THE AT&T BUILDING. I'VE JUST ABOUT HAD IT WITH THOSE GUYS.

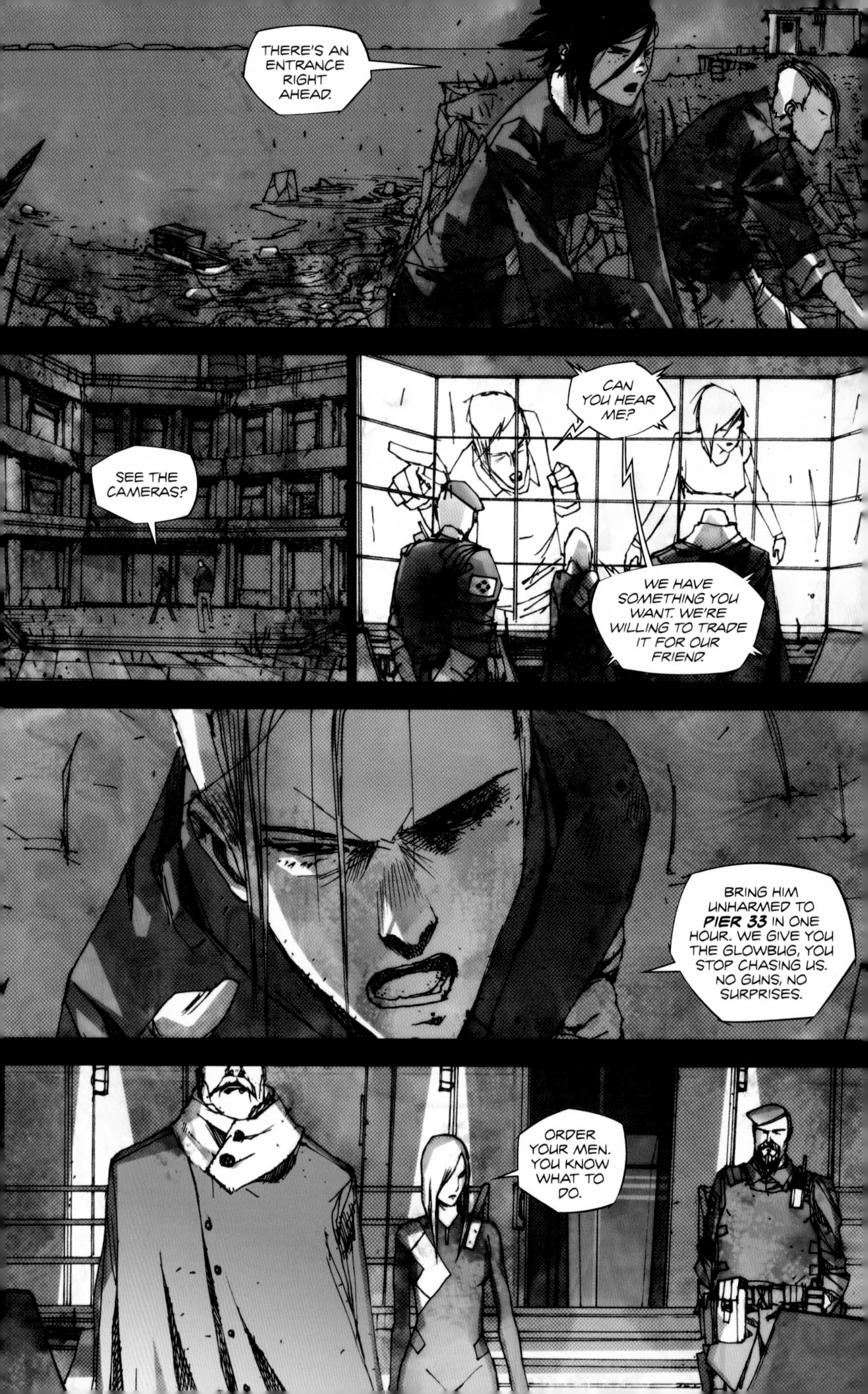
THERE'S AN ENTRANCE RIGHT AHEAD.
SEE THE CAMERAS?
CAN YOU HEAR ME?
WE HAVE SOMETHING YOU WANT. WE'RE WILLING TO TRADE IT FOR OUR FRIEND.
BRING HIM UNHARMED TO **PIER 33** IN ONE HOUR. WE GIVE YOU THE GLOWBUG, YOU STOP CHASING US. NO GUNS, NO SURPRISES.
ORDER YOUR MEN. YOU KNOW WHAT TO DO.

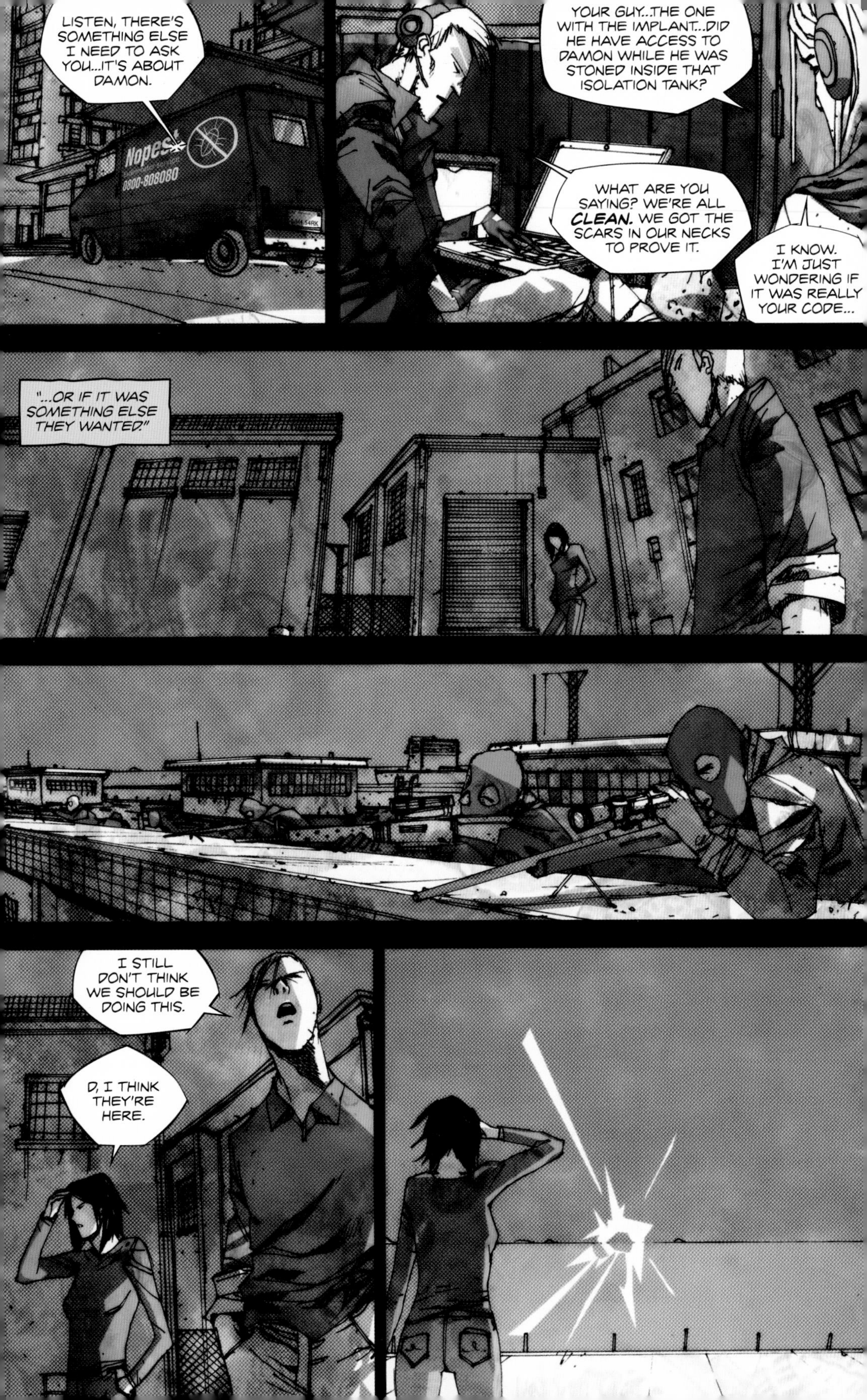
LISTEN, THERE'S SOMETHING ELSE I NEED TO ASK YOU...IT'S ABOUT DAMON.
Nopest
0800-808080
YOUR GUY...THE ONE WITH THE IMPLANT...DID HE HAVE ACCESS TO DAMON WHILE HE WAS STONED INSIDE THAT ISOLATION TANK?
WHAT ARE YOU SAYING? WE'RE ALL **CLEAN.** WE GOT THE SCARS IN OUR NECKS TO PROVE IT.
I KNOW. I'M JUST WONDERING IF IT WAS REALLY YOUR CODE...
"...OR IF IT WAS SOMETHING ELSE THEY WANTED."
I STILL DON'T THINK WE SHOULD BE DOING THIS.
D, I THINK THEY'RE HERE.

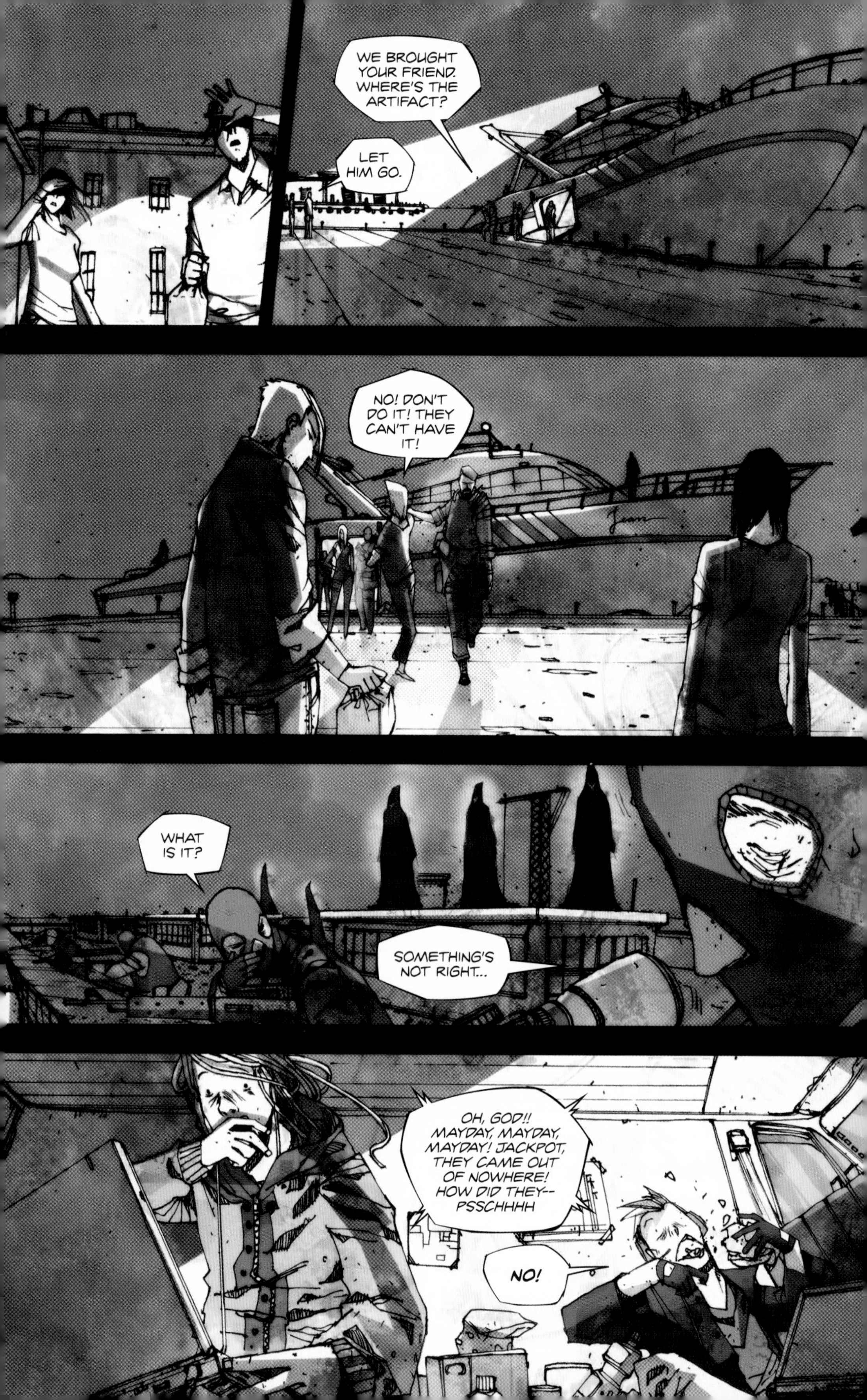
WE BROUGHT YOUR FRIEND. WHERE'S THE ARTIFACT?
LET HIM GO.
NO! DON'T DO IT! THEY CAN'T HAVE IT!
WHAT IS IT?
SOMETHING'S NOT RIGHT...
OH, GOD!! MAYDAY, MAYDAY, MAYDAY! JACKPOT, THEY CAME OUT OF NOWHERE! HOW DID THEY-- PSSCHHHH
NO!

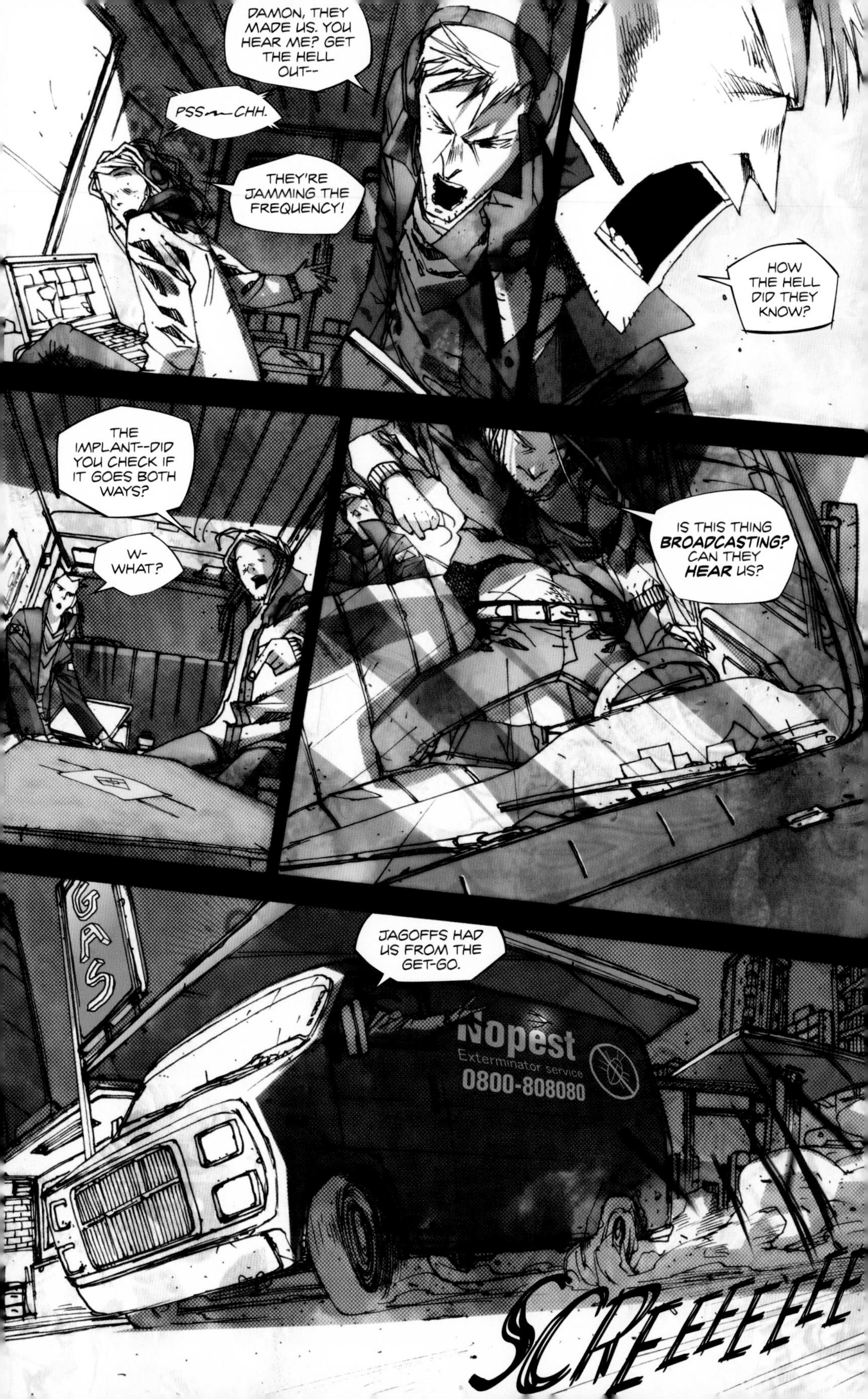
DAMON, THEY MADE US. YOU HEAR ME? GET THE HELL OUT--
PSS~CHH.
THEY'RE JAMMING THE FREQUENCY!
HOW THE HELL DID THEY KNOW?
THE IMPLANT--DID YOU CHECK IF IT GOES BOTH WAYS?
W- WHAT?
IS THIS THING **BROADCASTING?** CAN THEY **HEAR** US?
GAS
JAGOFFS HAD US FROM THE GET-GO.
Nopest
Exterminator service
0800-808080
SCREEEEEEE

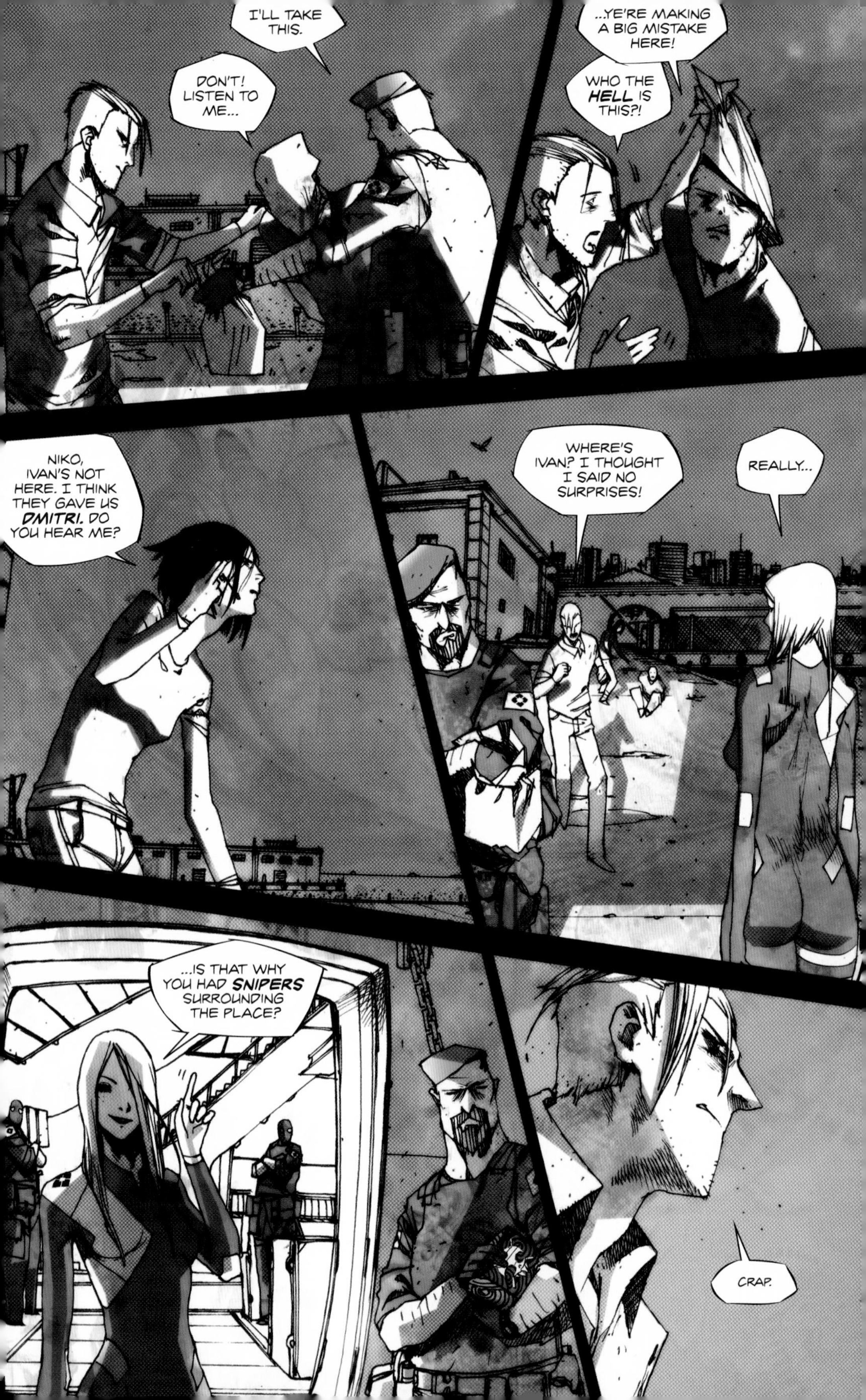
I'LL TAKE THIS.
DON'T! LISTEN TO ME...
...YE'RE MAKING A BIG MISTAKE HERE!
WHO THE HELL IS THIS?!
NIKO, IVAN'S NOT HERE. I THINK THEY GAVE US DMITRI. DO YOU HEAR ME?
WHERE'S IVAN? I THOUGHT I SAID NO SURPRISES!
REALLY...
...IS THAT WHY YOU HAD SNIPERS SURROUNDING THE PLACE?
CRAP.

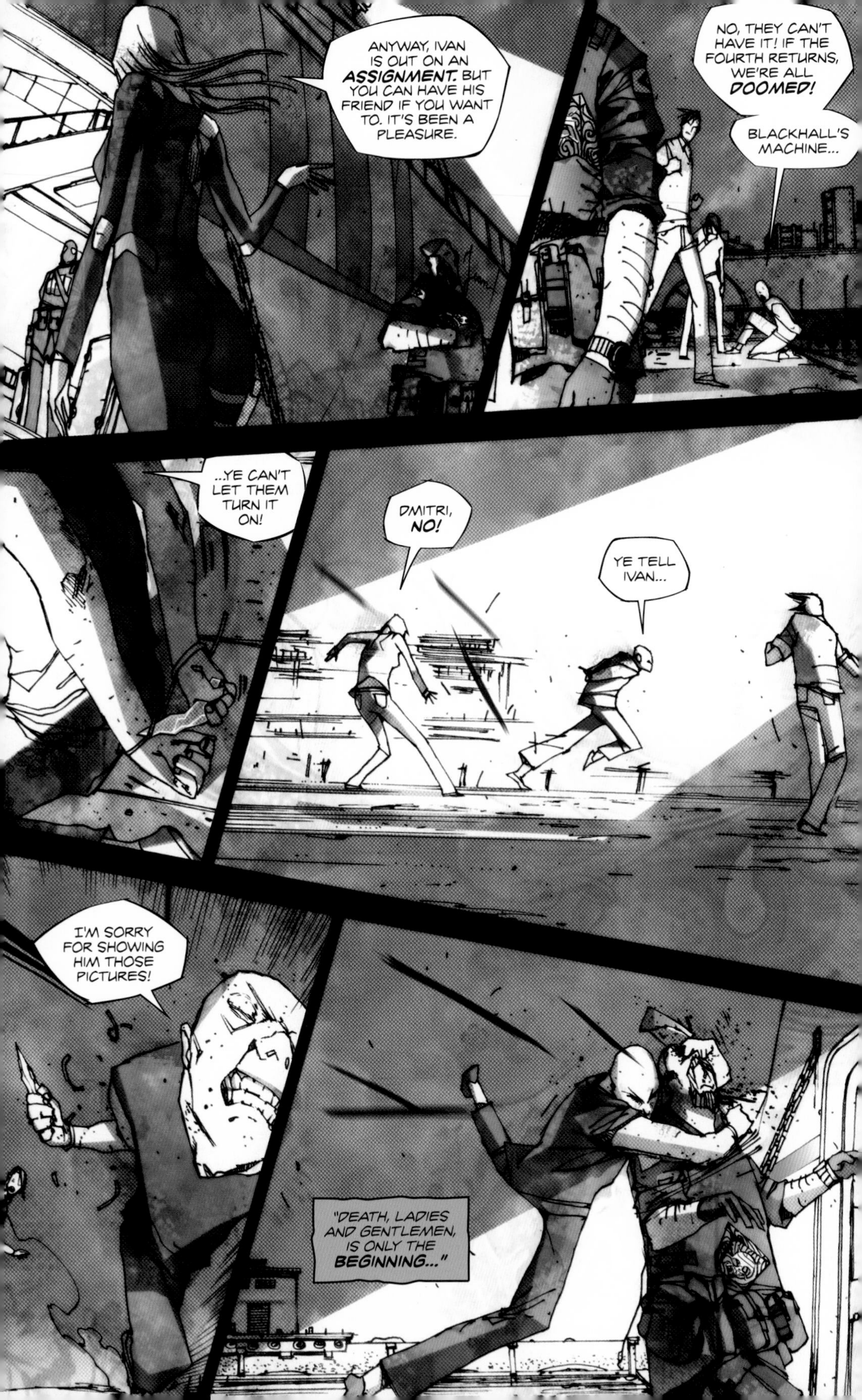
ANYWAY, IVAN IS OUT ON AN **ASSIGNMENT.** BUT YOU CAN HAVE HIS FRIEND IF YOU WANT TO. IT'S BEEN A PLEASURE.
NO, THEY CAN'T HAVE IT! IF THE FOURTH RETURNS, WE'RE ALL ***DOOMED!***
BLACKHALL'S MACHINE...
...YE CAN'T LET THEM TURN IT ON!
DMITRI, **NO!**
YE TELL IVAN...
I'M SORRY FOR SHOWING HIM THOSE PICTURES!
"DEATH, LADIES AND GENTLEMEN, IS ONLY THE **BEGINNING...**"

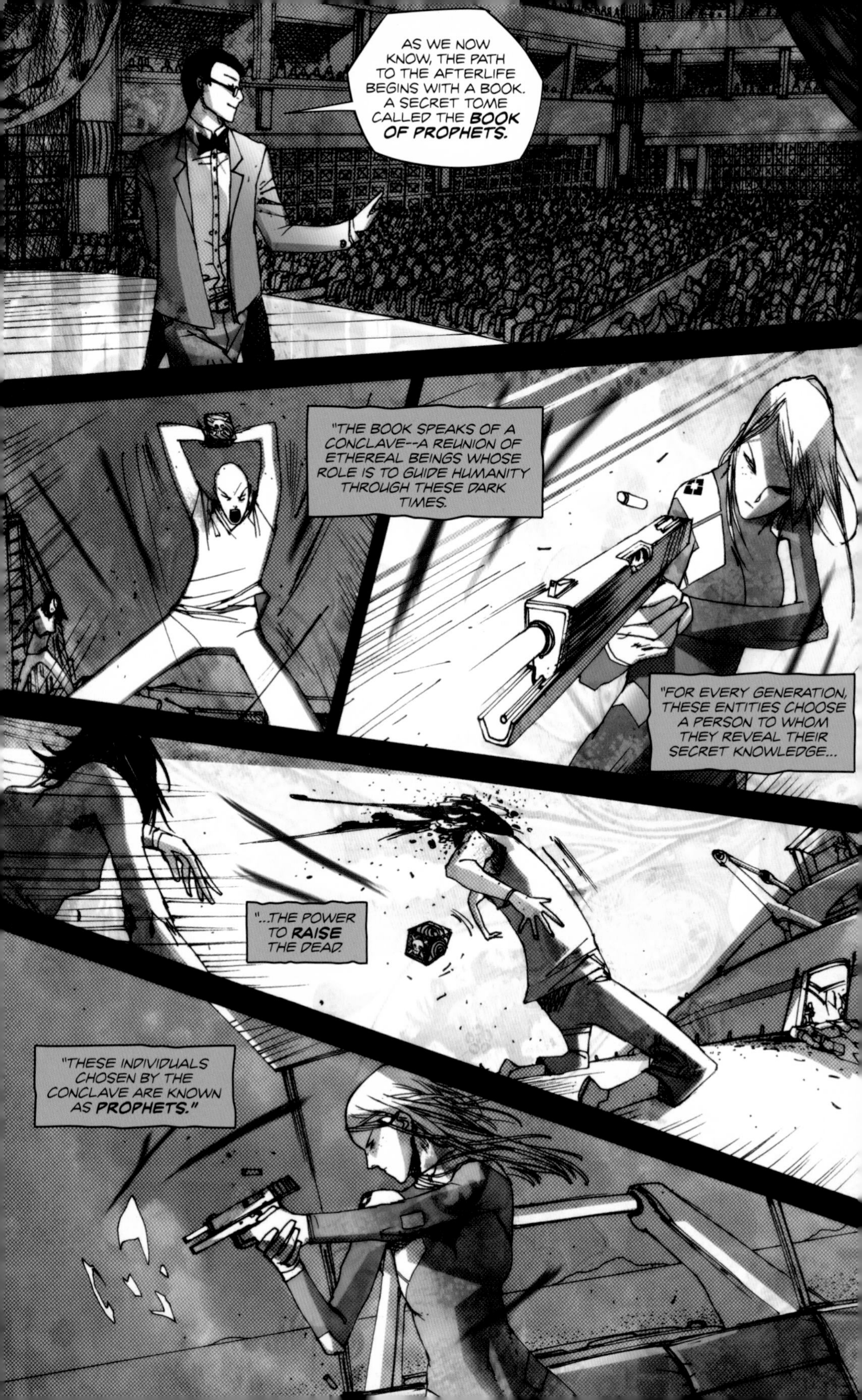
AS WE NOW KNOW, THE PATH TO THE AFTERLIFE BEGINS WITH A BOOK. A SECRET TOME CALLED THE **BOOK OF PROPHETS.**
"THE BOOK SPEAKS OF A CONCLAVE--A REUNION OF ETHEREAL BEINGS WHOSE ROLE IS TO GUIDE HUMANITY THROUGH THESE DARK TIMES.
"FOR EVERY GENERATION, THESE ENTITIES CHOOSE A PERSON TO WHOM THEY REVEAL THEIR SECRET KNOWLEDGE...
"...THE POWER TO **RAISE** THE DEAD.
"THESE INDIVIDUALS CHOSEN BY THE CONCLAVE ARE KNOWN AS **PROPHETS.**"

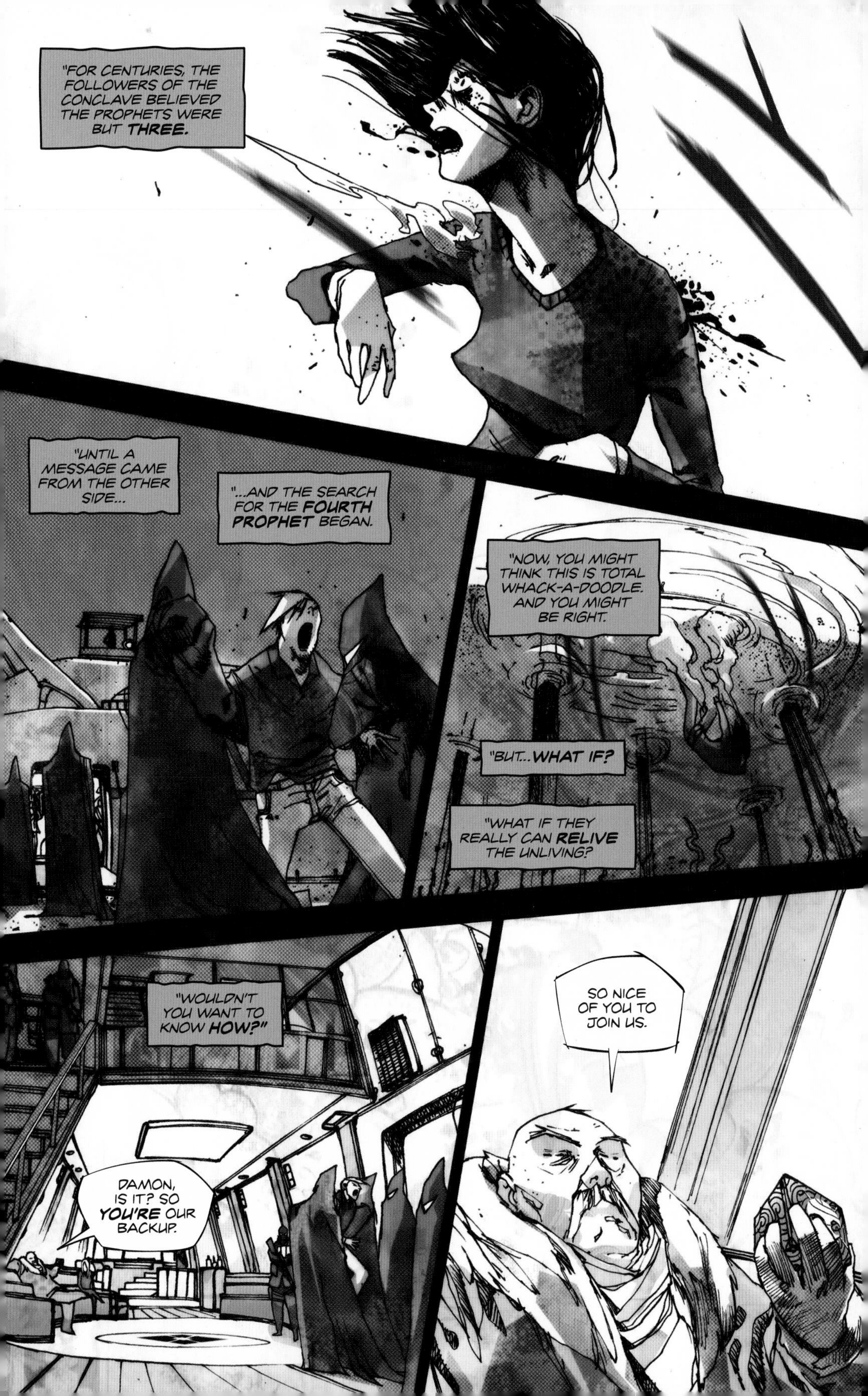
"FOR CENTURIES, THE FOLLOWERS OF THE CONCLAVE BELIEVED THE PROPHETS WERE BUT THREE.
"UNTIL A MESSAGE CAME FROM THE OTHER SIDE...
"...AND THE SEARCH FOR THE FOURTH PROPHET BEGAN.
"NOW, YOU MIGHT THINK THIS IS TOTAL WHACK-A-DOODLE. AND YOU MIGHT BE RIGHT.
"BUT...WHAT IF?
"WHAT IF THEY REALLY CAN RELIVE THE UNLIVING?
"WOULDN'T YOU WANT TO KNOW HOW?"
SO NICE OF YOU TO JOIN US.
DAMON, IS IT? SO YOU'RE OUR BACKUP.

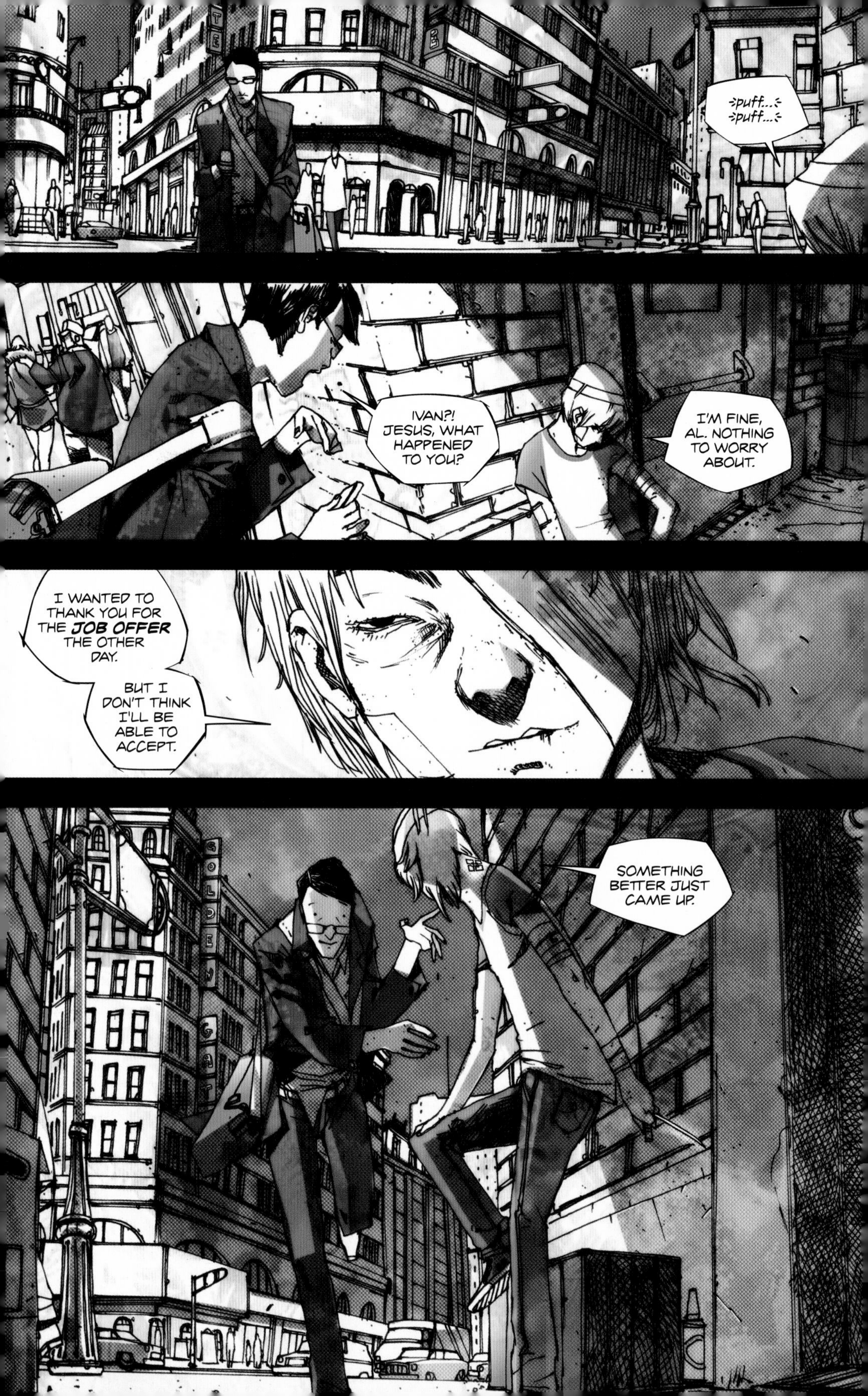
puff... puff...
IVAN?! JESUS, WHAT HAPPENED TO YOU?
I'M FINE, AL. NOTHING TO WORRY ABOUT.
I WANTED TO THANK YOU FOR THE JOB OFFER THE OTHER DAY.
BUT I DON'T THINK I'LL BE ABLE TO ACCEPT.
SOMETHING BETTER JUST CAME UP.

ISSUE SIX COVER

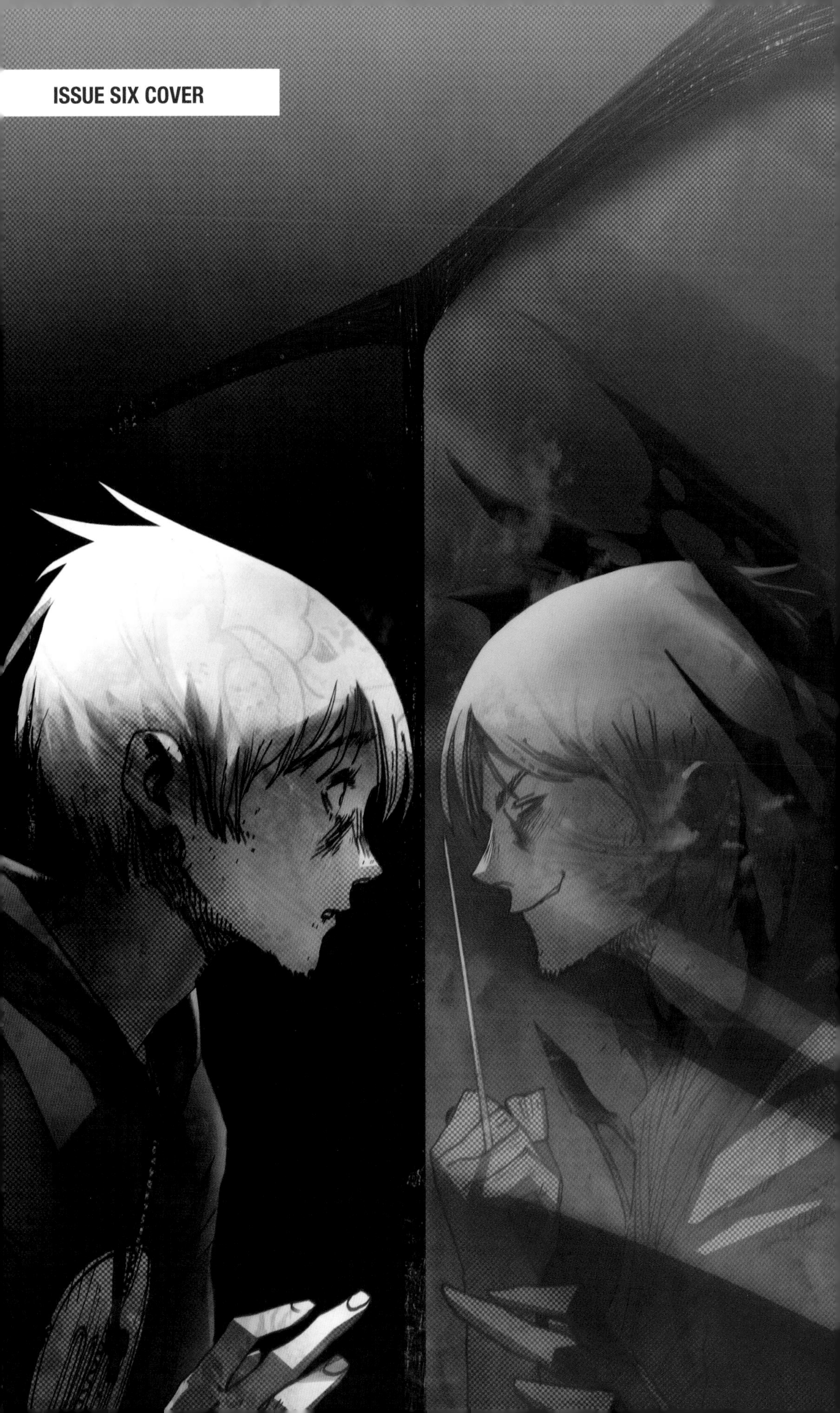

CHAPTER 7: SMOKE AND MIRRORS

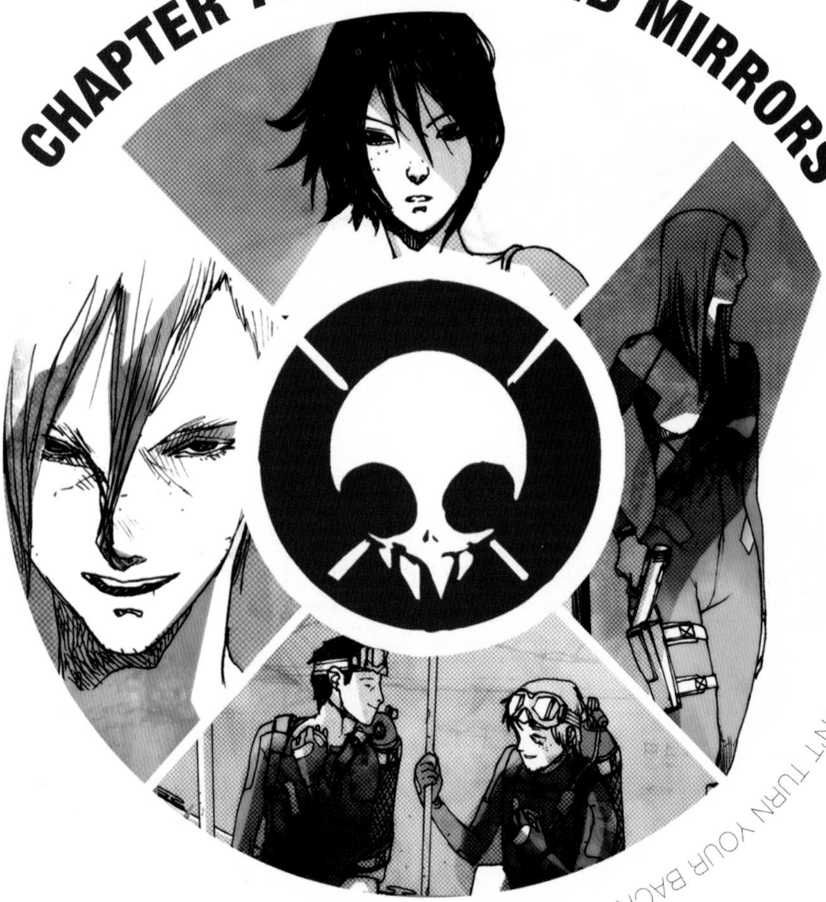

ALWAYS TRESPASS. --M.S. OPJOV. DON'T TURN YOUR BACK ON THE MYSTERY.

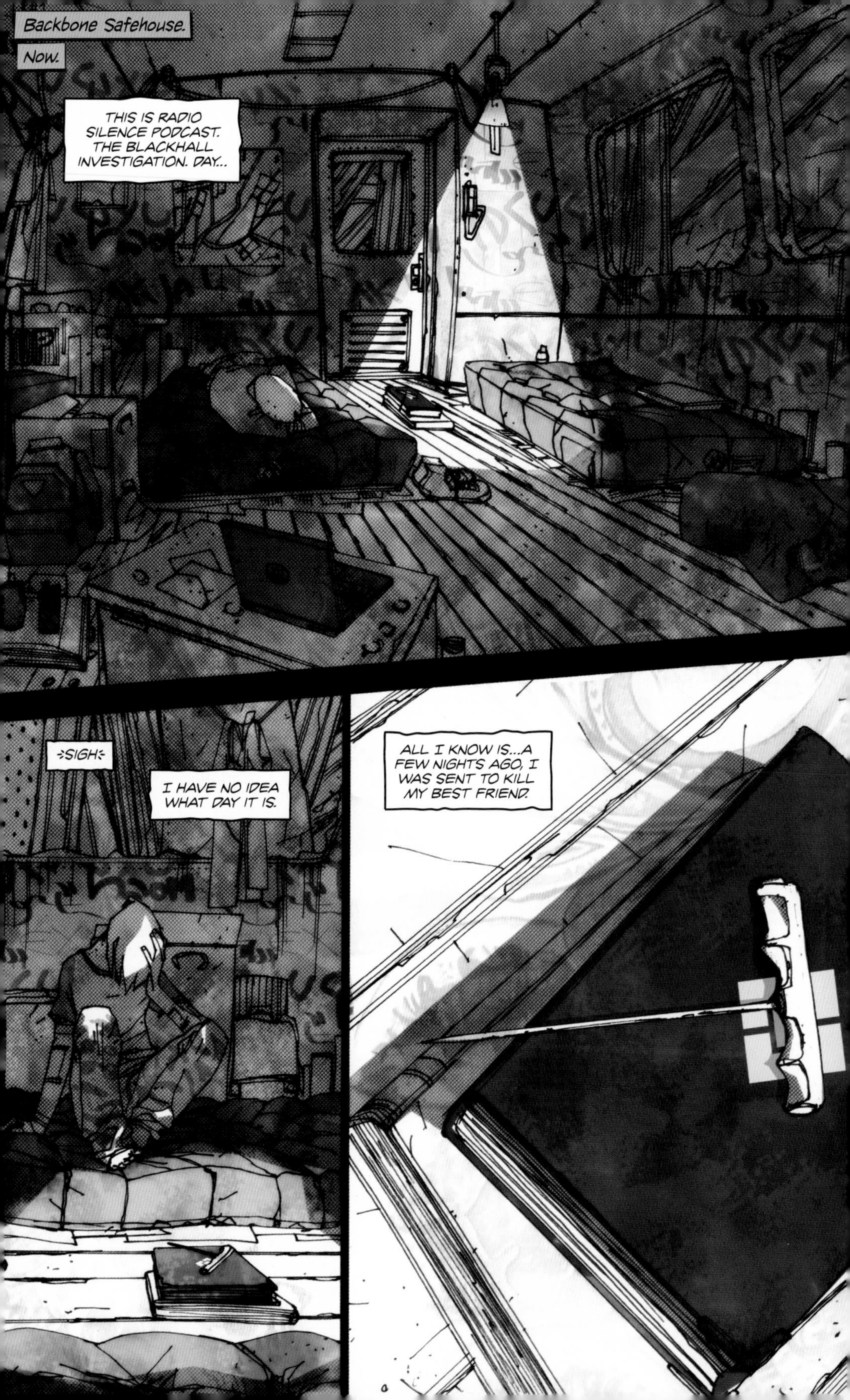

Backbone Safehouse.
Now.
THIS IS RADIO SILENCE PODCAST. THE BLACKHALL INVESTIGATION. DAY...
SIGH
I HAVE NO IDEA WHAT DAY IT IS.
ALL I KNOW IS...A FEW NIGHTS AGO, I WAS SENT TO KILL MY BEST FRIEND.

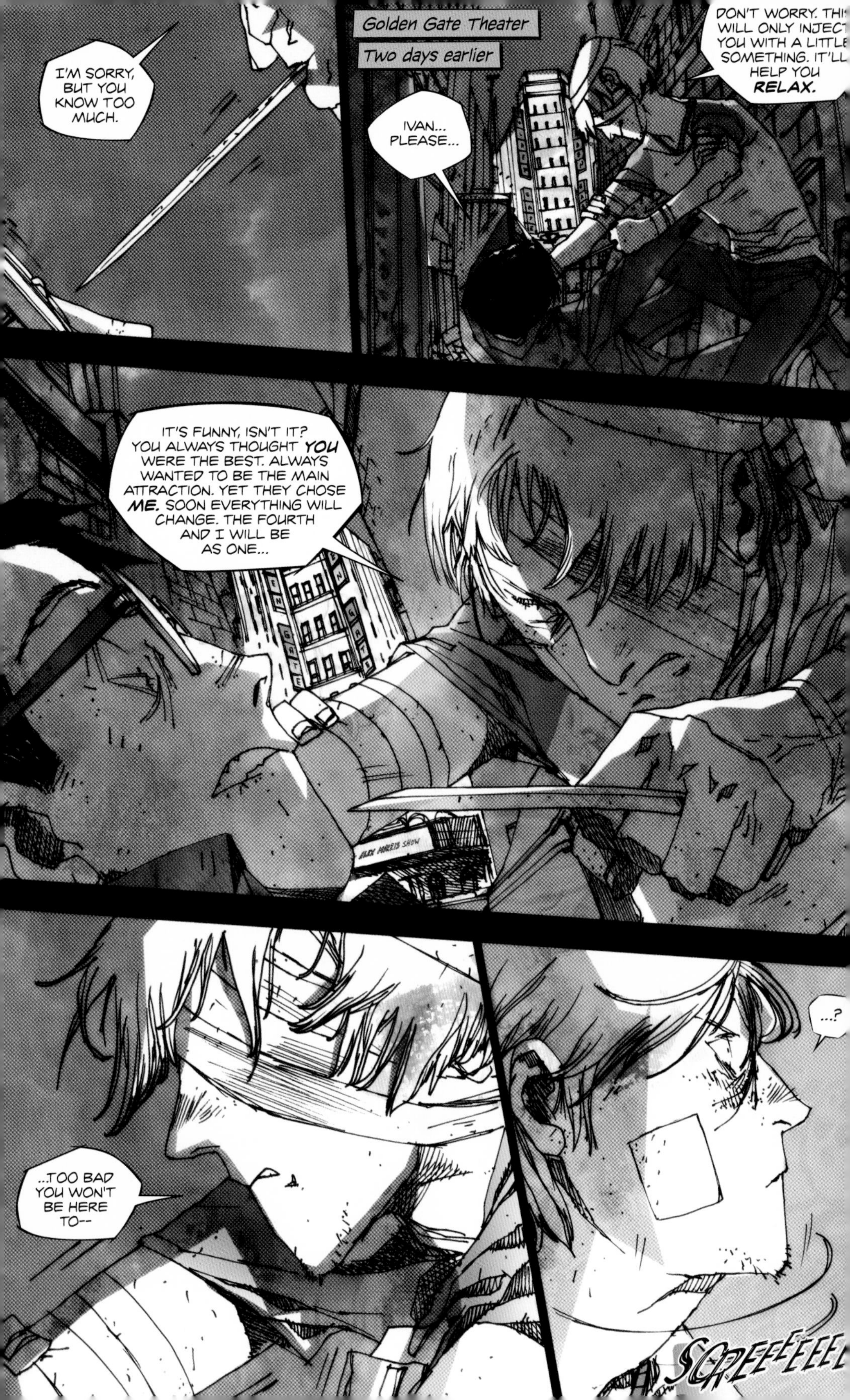
I'M SORRY, BUT YOU KNOW TOO MUCH.
Golden Gate Theater
Two days earlier
IVAN... PLEASE...
DON'T WORRY. THIS WILL ONLY INJECT YOU WITH A LITTLE SOMETHING. IT'LL HELP YOU **RELAX.**
IT'S FUNNY, ISN'T IT? YOU ALWAYS THOUGHT **YOU** WERE THE BEST. ALWAYS WANTED TO BE THE MAIN ATTRACTION. YET THEY CHOSE **ME.** SOON EVERYTHING WILL CHANGE. THE FOURTH AND I WILL BE AS ONE...
...TOO BAD YOU WON'T BE HERE TO--
...?
SCREEEEEE

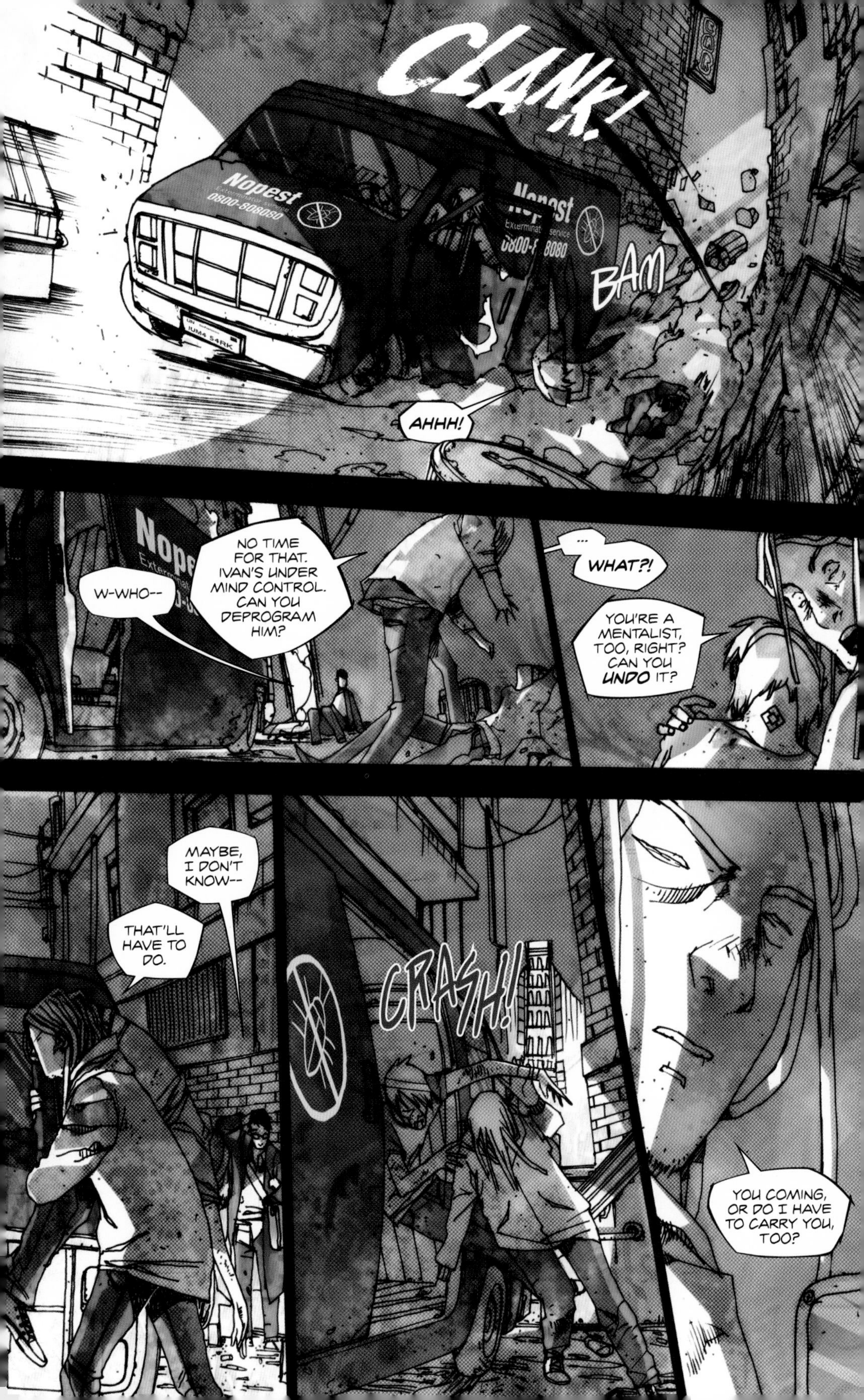
CLANK!
Nopest
0800-808080
Nopest
Exterminator service
BAM
AHHH!
W-WHO--
NO TIME FOR THAT. IVAN'S UNDER MIND CONTROL. CAN YOU DEPROGRAM HIM?
... WHAT?!
YOU'RE A MENTALIST, TOO, RIGHT? CAN YOU UNDO IT?
MAYBE, I DON'T KNOW--
THAT'LL HAVE TO DO.
CRASH!
YOU COMING, OR DO I HAVE TO CARRY YOU, TOO?

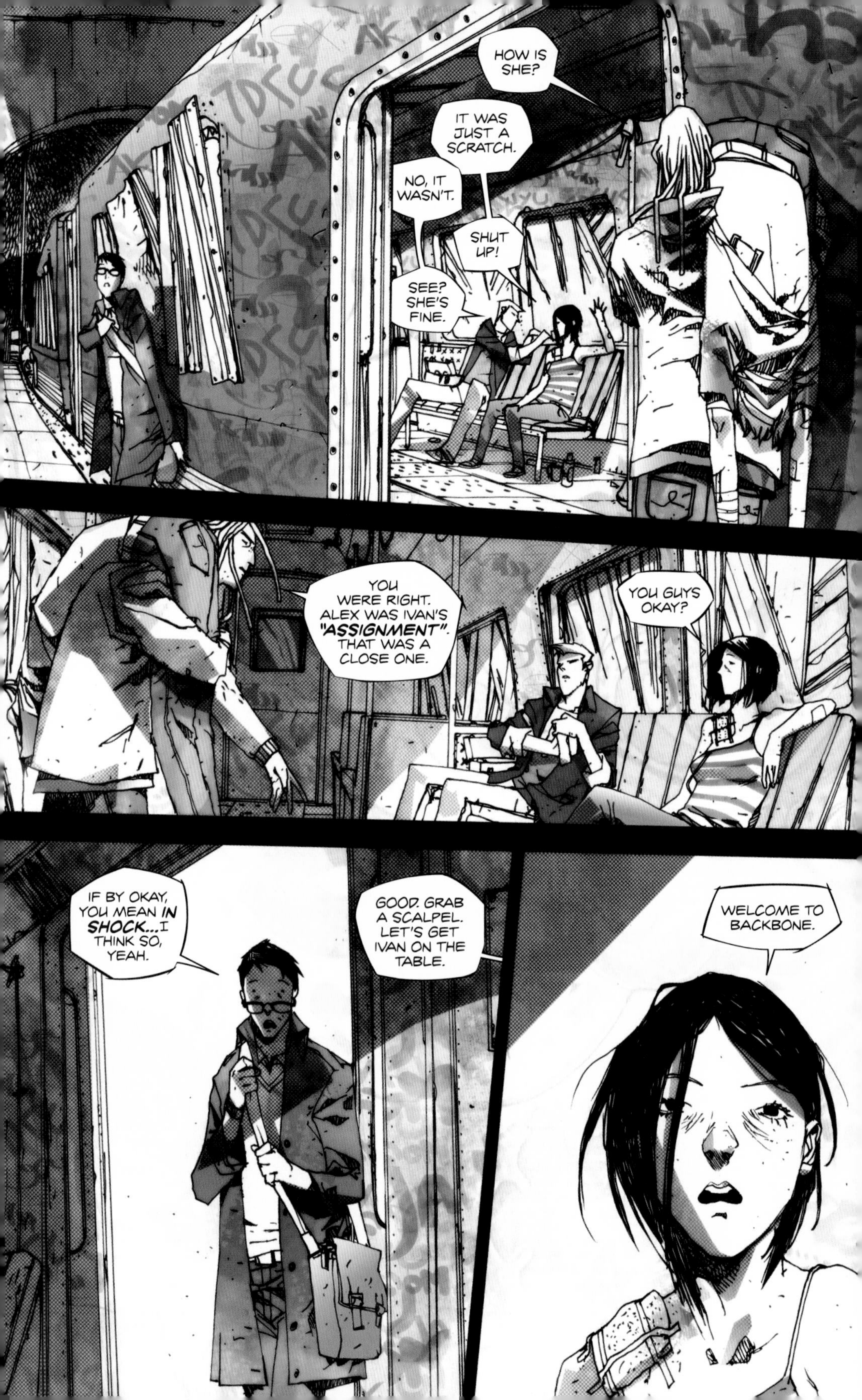
HOW IS SHE?
IT WAS JUST A SCRATCH.
NO, IT WASN'T.
SHUT UP!
SEE? SHE'S FINE.
YOU WERE RIGHT. ALEX WAS IVAN'S "ASSIGNMENT". THAT WAS A CLOSE ONE.
YOU GUYS OKAY?
IF BY OKAY, YOU MEAN IN SHOCK... I THINK SO, YEAH.
GOOD. GRAB A SCALPEL. LET'S GET IVAN ON THE TABLE.
WELCOME TO BACKBONE.

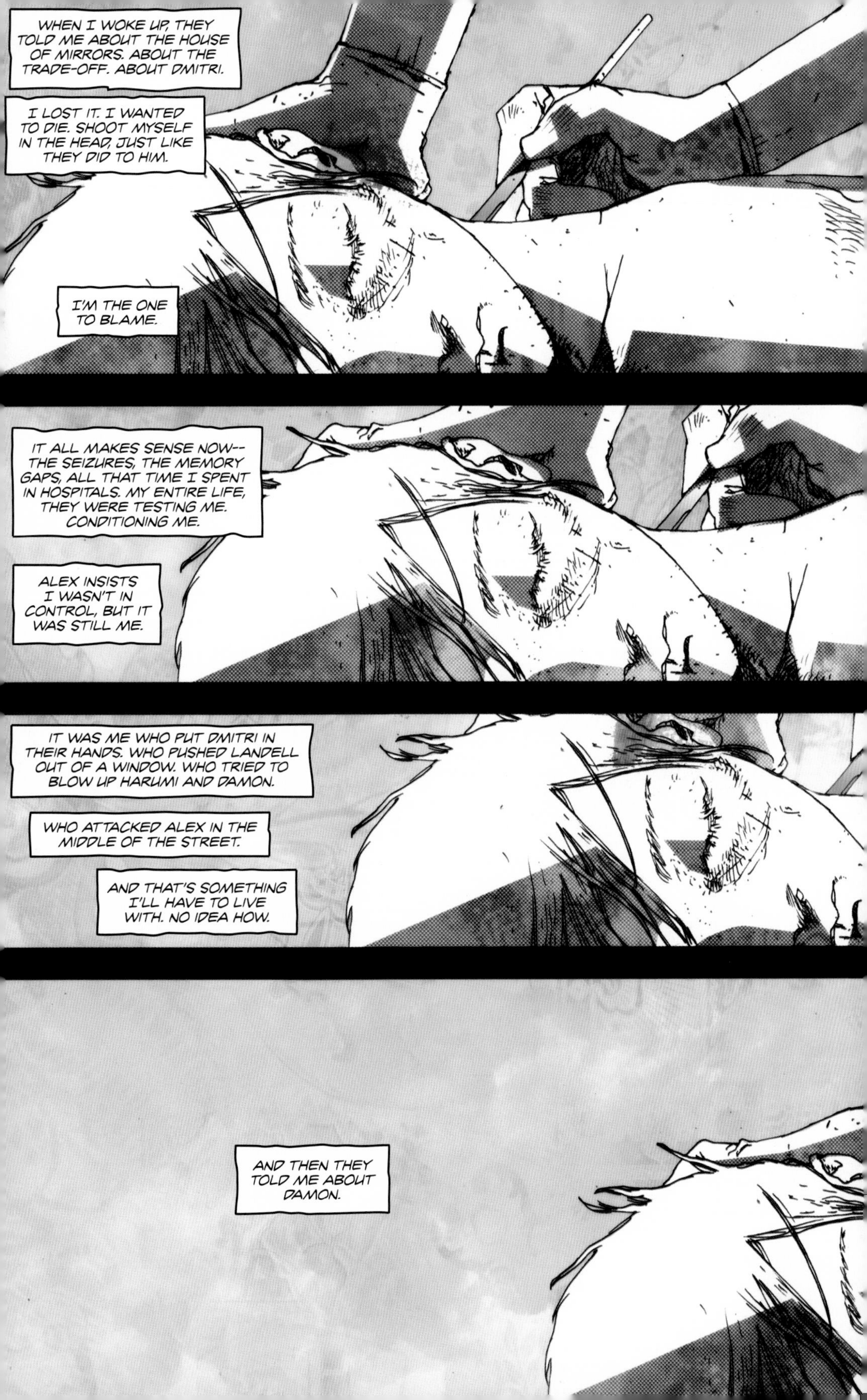
WHEN I WOKE UP, THEY TOLD ME ABOUT THE HOUSE OF MIRRORS. ABOUT THE TRADE-OFF. ABOUT DMITRI.
I LOST IT. I WANTED TO DIE. SHOOT MYSELF IN THE HEAD, JUST LIKE THEY DID TO HIM.
I'M THE ONE TO BLAME.
IT ALL MAKES SENSE NOW-- THE SEIZURES, THE MEMORY GAPS, ALL THAT TIME I SPENT IN HOSPITALS. MY ENTIRE LIFE, THEY WERE TESTING ME. CONDITIONING ME.
ALEX INSISTS I WASN'T IN CONTROL, BUT IT WAS STILL ME.
IT WAS ME WHO PUT DMITRI IN THEIR HANDS. WHO PUSHED LANDELL OUT OF A WINDOW. WHO TRIED TO BLOW UP HARUMI AND DAMON.
WHO ATTACKED ALEX IN THE MIDDLE OF THE STREET.
AND THAT'S SOMETHING I'LL HAVE TO LIVE WITH. NO IDEA HOW.
AND THEN THEY TOLD ME ABOUT DAMON.

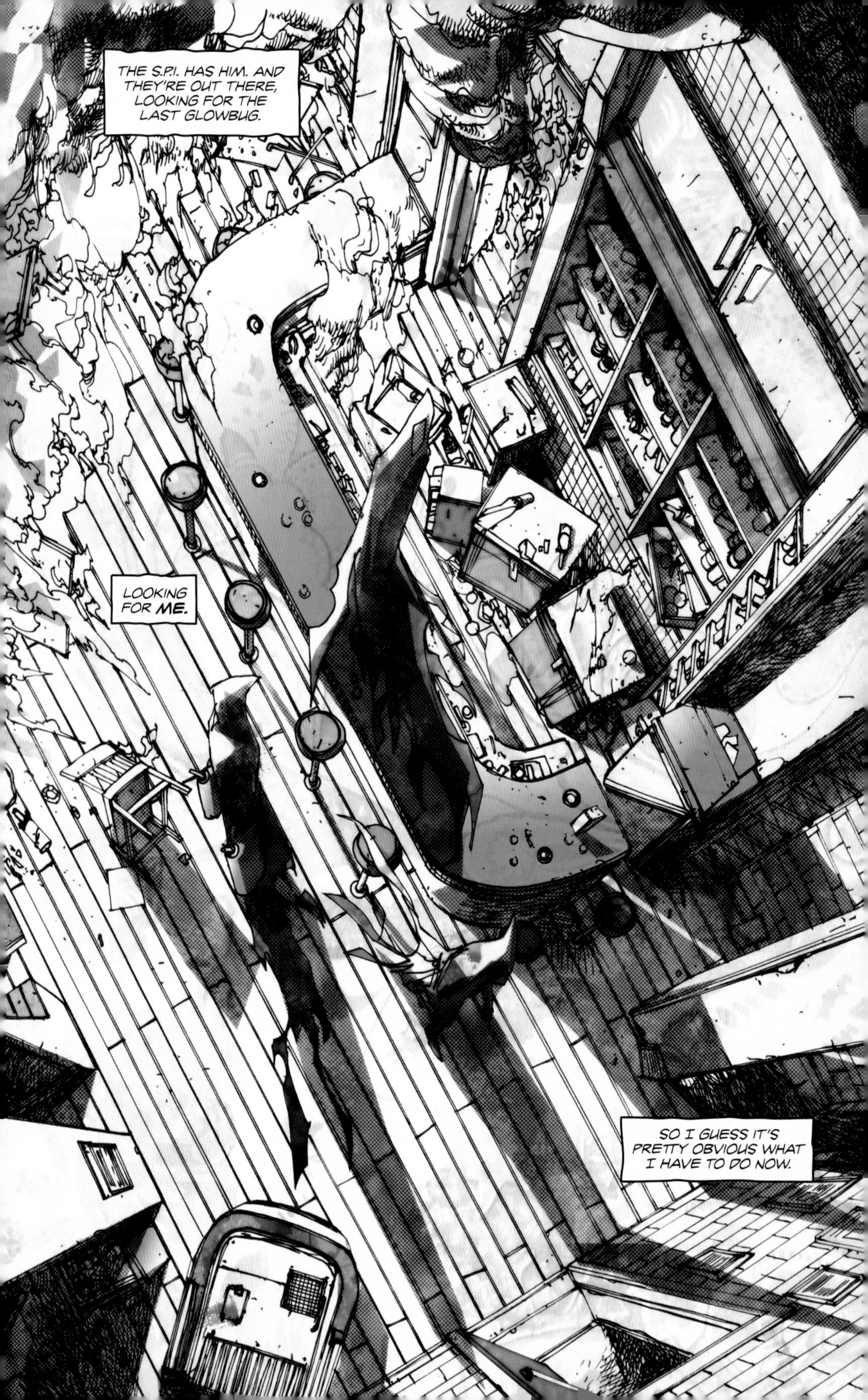
THE S.P.I. HAS HIM. AND THEY'RE OUT THERE, LOOKING FOR THE LAST GLOWBUG.
LOOKING FOR ME.
SO I GUESS IT'S PRETTY OBVIOUS WHAT I HAVE TO DO NOW.

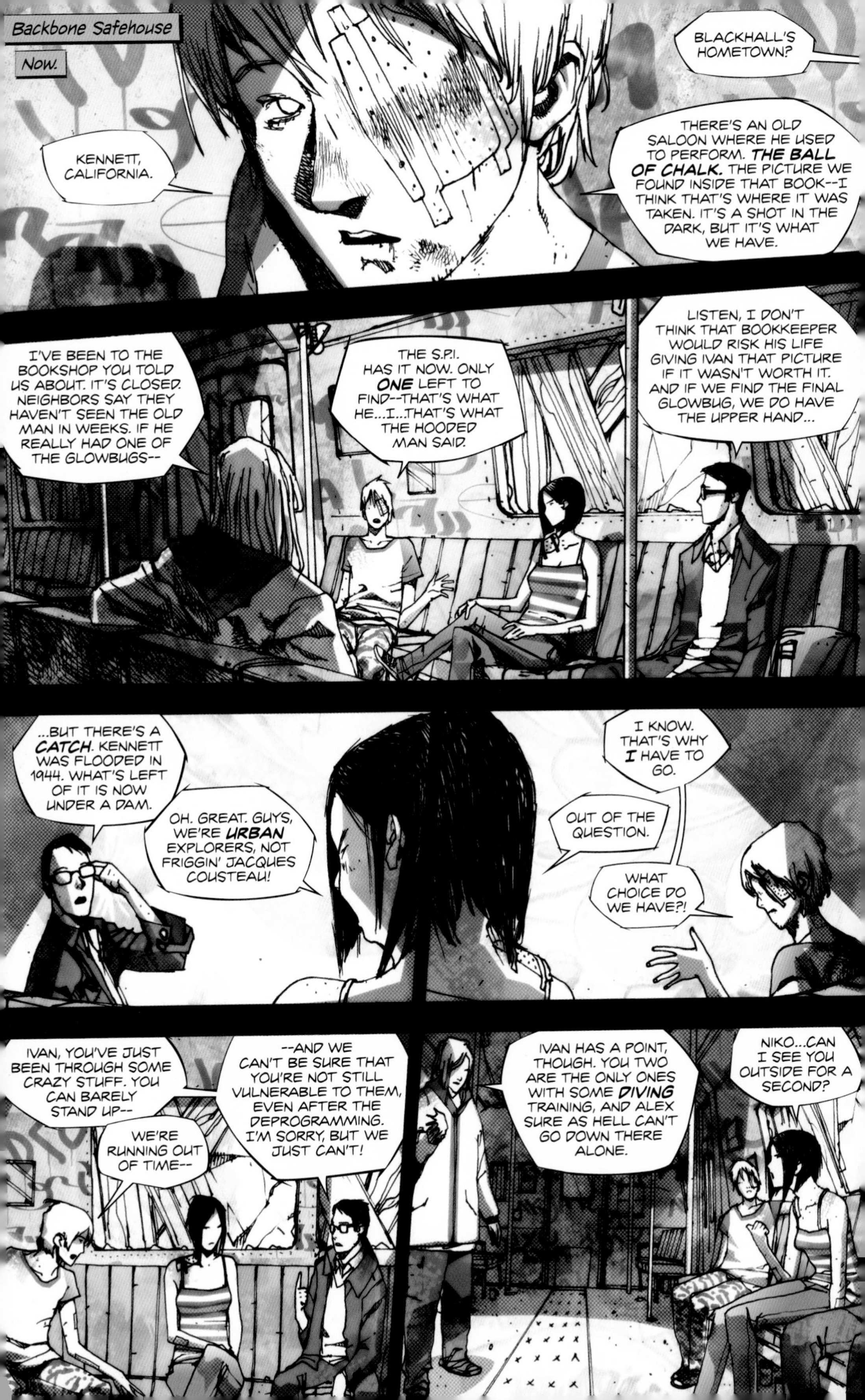
Backbone Safehouse
Now.
BLACKHALL'S HOMETOWN?
KENNETT, CALIFORNIA.
THERE'S AN OLD SALOON WHERE HE USED TO PERFORM. THE BALL OF CHALK. THE PICTURE WE FOUND INSIDE THAT BOOK--I THINK THAT'S WHERE IT WAS TAKEN. IT'S A SHOT IN THE DARK, BUT IT'S WHAT WE HAVE.
I'VE BEEN TO THE BOOKSHOP YOU TOLD US ABOUT. IT'S CLOSED. NEIGHBORS SAY THEY HAVEN'T SEEN THE OLD MAN IN WEEKS. IF HE REALLY HAD ONE OF THE GLOWBUGS--
THE S.P.I. HAS IT NOW. ONLY ONE LEFT TO FIND--THAT'S WHAT HE...I...THAT'S WHAT THE HOODED MAN SAID.
LISTEN, I DON'T THINK THAT BOOKKEEPER WOULD RISK HIS LIFE GIVING IVAN THAT PICTURE IF IT WASN'T WORTH IT. AND IF WE FIND THE FINAL GLOWBUG, WE DO HAVE THE UPPER HAND...
...BUT THERE'S A CATCH. KENNETT WAS FLOODED IN 1944. WHAT'S LEFT OF IT IS NOW UNDER A DAM.
OH. GREAT. GUYS, WE'RE URBAN EXPLORERS, NOT FRIGGIN' JACQUES COUSTEAU!
I KNOW. THAT'S WHY I HAVE TO GO.
OUT OF THE QUESTION.
WHAT CHOICE DO WE HAVE?!
IVAN, YOU'VE JUST BEEN THROUGH SOME CRAZY STUFF. YOU CAN BARELY STAND UP--
WE'RE RUNNING OUT OF TIME--
--AND WE CAN'T BE SURE THAT YOU'RE NOT STILL VULNERABLE TO THEM, EVEN AFTER THE DEPROGRAMMING. I'M SORRY, BUT WE JUST CAN'T!
IVAN HAS A POINT, THOUGH. YOU TWO ARE THE ONLY ONES WITH SOME DIVING TRAINING, AND ALEX SURE AS HELL CAN'T GO DOWN THERE ALONE.
NIKO...CAN I SEE YOU OUTSIDE FOR A SECOND?

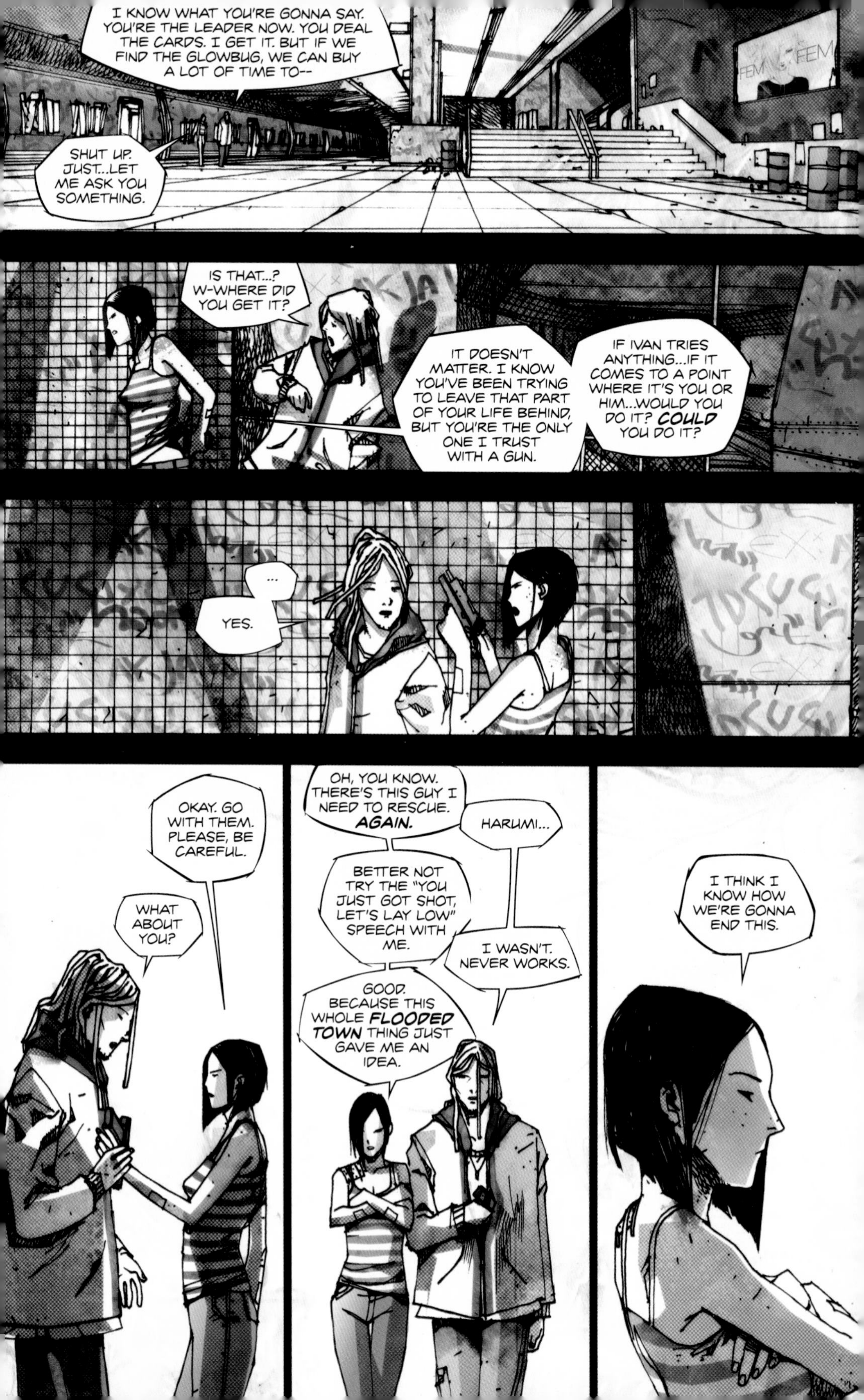
I KNOW WHAT YOU'RE GONNA SAY. YOU'RE THE LEADER NOW. YOU DEAL THE CARDS. I GET IT. BUT IF WE FIND THE GLOWBUG, WE CAN BUY A LOT OF TIME TO--
SHUT UP. JUST...LET ME ASK YOU SOMETHING.
FEM FEM
IS THAT...? W-WHERE DID YOU GET IT?
IT DOESN'T MATTER. I KNOW YOU'VE BEEN TRYING TO LEAVE THAT PART OF YOUR LIFE BEHIND, BUT YOU'RE THE ONLY ONE I TRUST WITH A GUN.
IF IVAN TRIES ANYTHING...IF IT COMES TO A POINT WHERE IT'S YOU OR HIM...WOULD YOU DO IT? COULD YOU DO IT?
...
YES.
OKAY. GO WITH THEM. PLEASE, BE CAREFUL.
WHAT ABOUT YOU?
OH, YOU KNOW. THERE'S THIS GUY I NEED TO RESCUE. AGAIN.
HARUMI...
BETTER NOT TRY THE "YOU JUST GOT SHOT, LET'S LAY LOW" SPEECH WITH ME.
I WASN'T. NEVER WORKS.
GOOD. BECAUSE THIS WHOLE FLOODED TOWN THING JUST GAVE ME AN IDEA.
I THINK I KNOW HOW WE'RE GONNA END THIS.

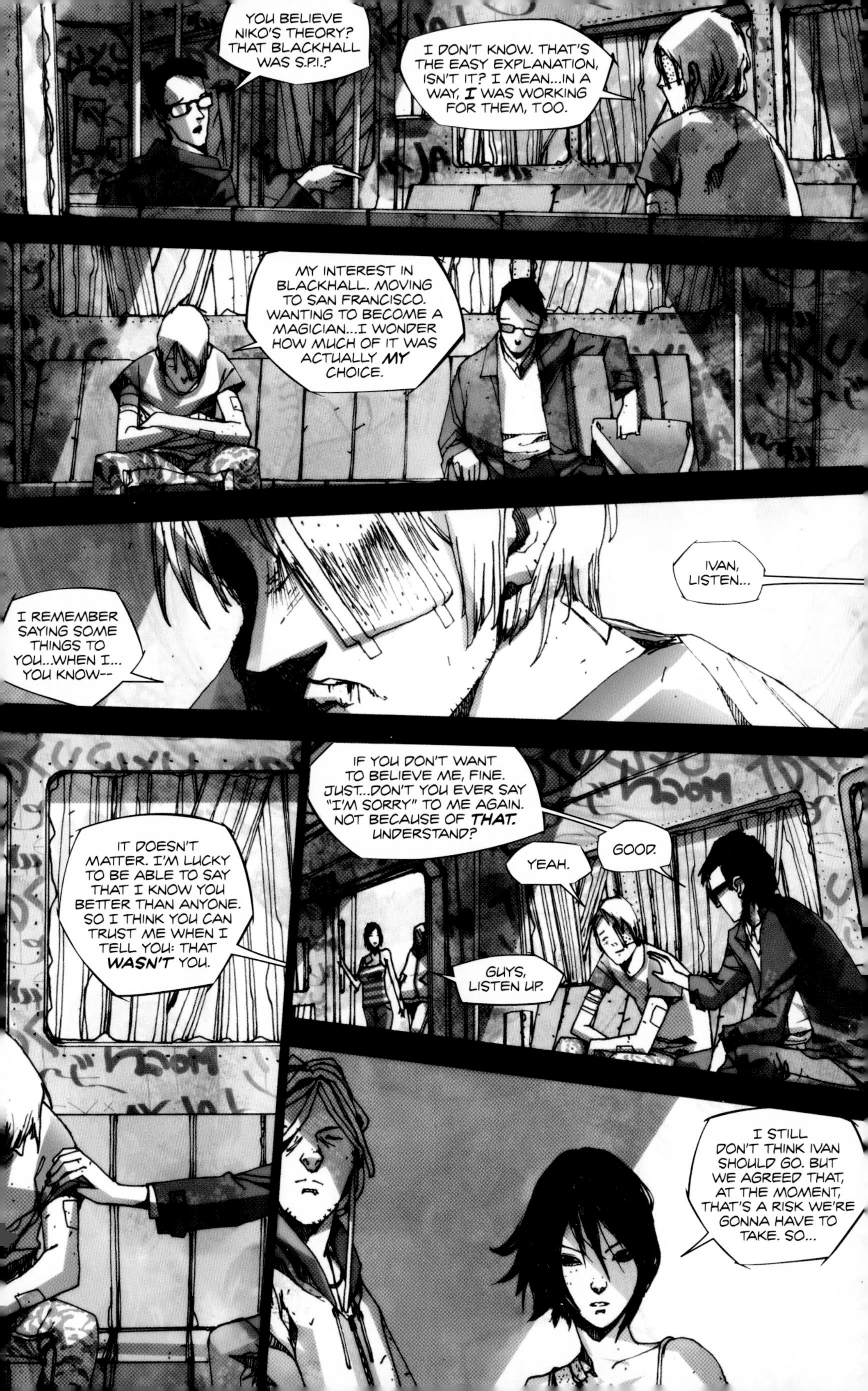
YOU BELIEVE NIKO'S THEORY? THAT BLACKHALL WAS S.P.I.?
I DON'T KNOW. THAT'S THE EASY EXPLANATION, ISN'T IT? I MEAN...IN A WAY, I WAS WORKING FOR THEM, TOO.
MY INTEREST IN BLACKHALL. MOVING TO SAN FRANCISCO. WANTING TO BECOME A MAGICIAN...I WONDER HOW MUCH OF IT WAS ACTUALLY MY CHOICE.
IVAN, LISTEN...
I REMEMBER SAYING SOME THINGS TO YOU...WHEN I... YOU KNOW--
IT DOESN'T MATTER. I'M LUCKY TO BE ABLE TO SAY THAT I KNOW YOU BETTER THAN ANYONE. SO I THINK YOU CAN TRUST ME WHEN I TELL YOU: THAT WASN'T YOU.
IF YOU DON'T WANT TO BELIEVE ME, FINE. JUST...DON'T YOU EVER SAY "I'M SORRY" TO ME AGAIN. NOT BECAUSE OF THAT. UNDERSTAND?
YEAH.
GOOD.
GUYS, LISTEN UP.
I STILL DON'T THINK IVAN SHOULD GO. BUT WE AGREED THAT, AT THE MOMENT, THAT'S A RISK WE'RE GONNA HAVE TO TAKE. SO...

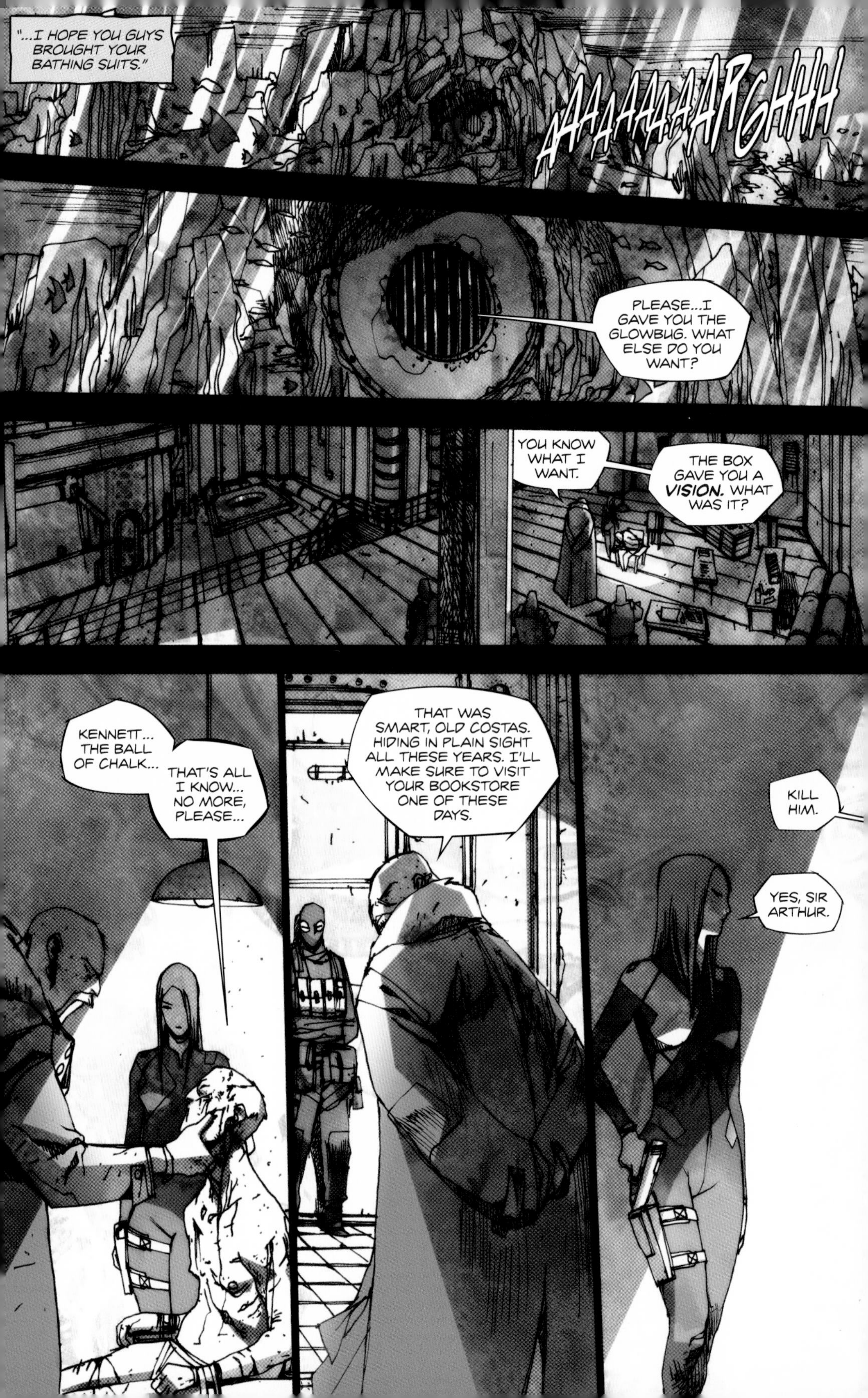
"...I HOPE YOU GUYS BROUGHT YOUR BATHING SUITS."
AAAAAAAAARGHHH
PLEASE...I GAVE YOU THE GLOWBUG. WHAT ELSE DO YOU WANT?
YOU KNOW WHAT I WANT.
THE BOX GAVE YOU A VISION. WHAT WAS IT?
KENNETT... THE BALL OF CHALK...
THAT'S ALL I KNOW... NO MORE, PLEASE...
THAT WAS SMART, OLD COSTAS. HIDING IN PLAIN SIGHT ALL THESE YEARS. I'LL MAKE SURE TO VISIT YOUR BOOKSTORE ONE OF THESE DAYS.
KILL HIM.
YES, SIR ARTHUR.

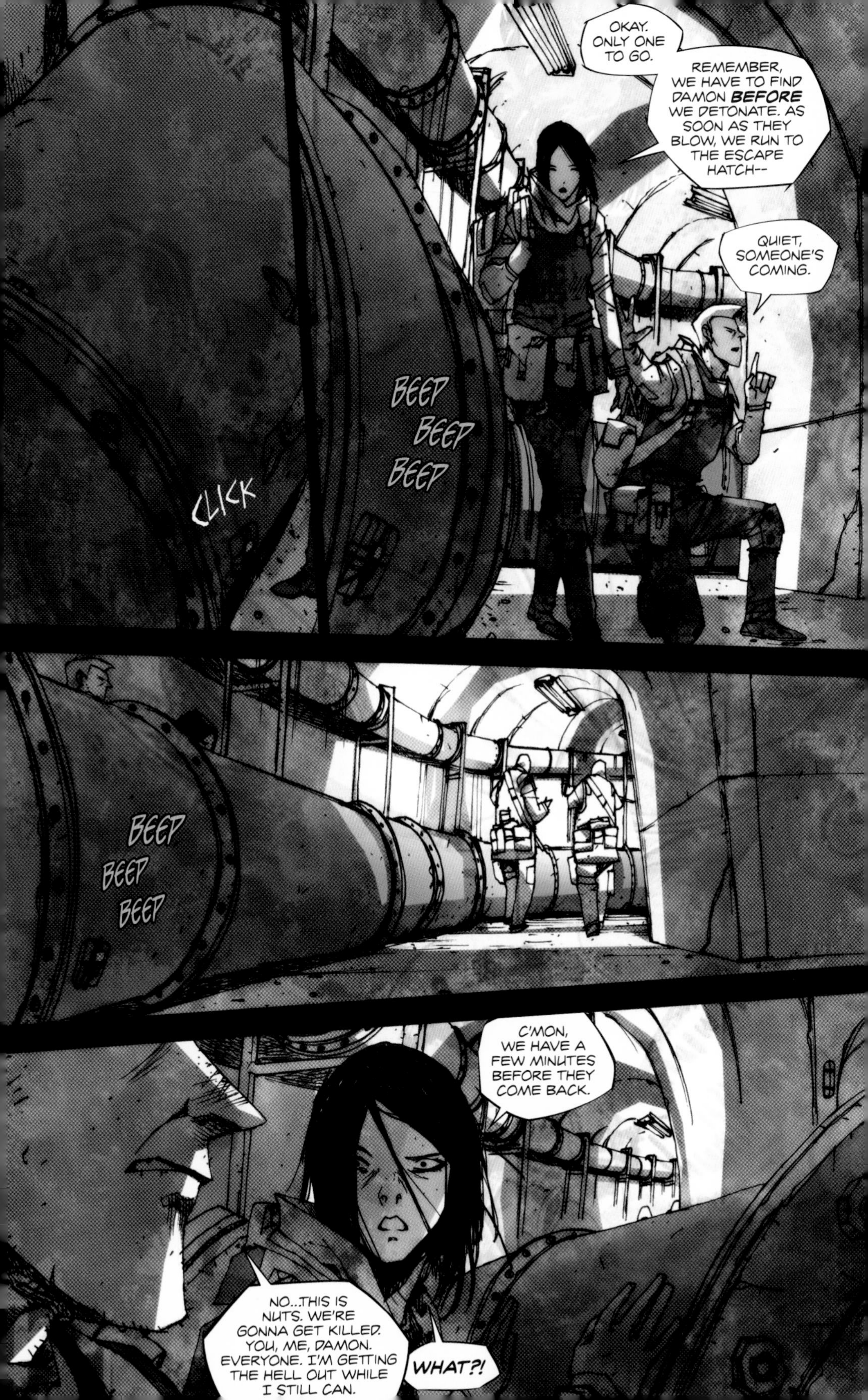
OKAY. ONLY ONE TO GO.
REMEMBER, WE HAVE TO FIND DAMON **BEFORE** WE DETONATE. AS SOON AS THEY BLOW, WE RUN TO THE ESCAPE HATCH--
QUIET, SOMEONE'S COMING.
BEEP BEEP BEEP
CLICK
BEEP BEEP BEEP
C'MON, WE HAVE A FEW MINUTES BEFORE THEY COME BACK.
NO...THIS IS NUTS. WE'RE GONNA GET KILLED. YOU, ME, DAMON. EVERYONE. I'M GETTING THE HELL OUT WHILE I STILL CAN.
WHAT?!

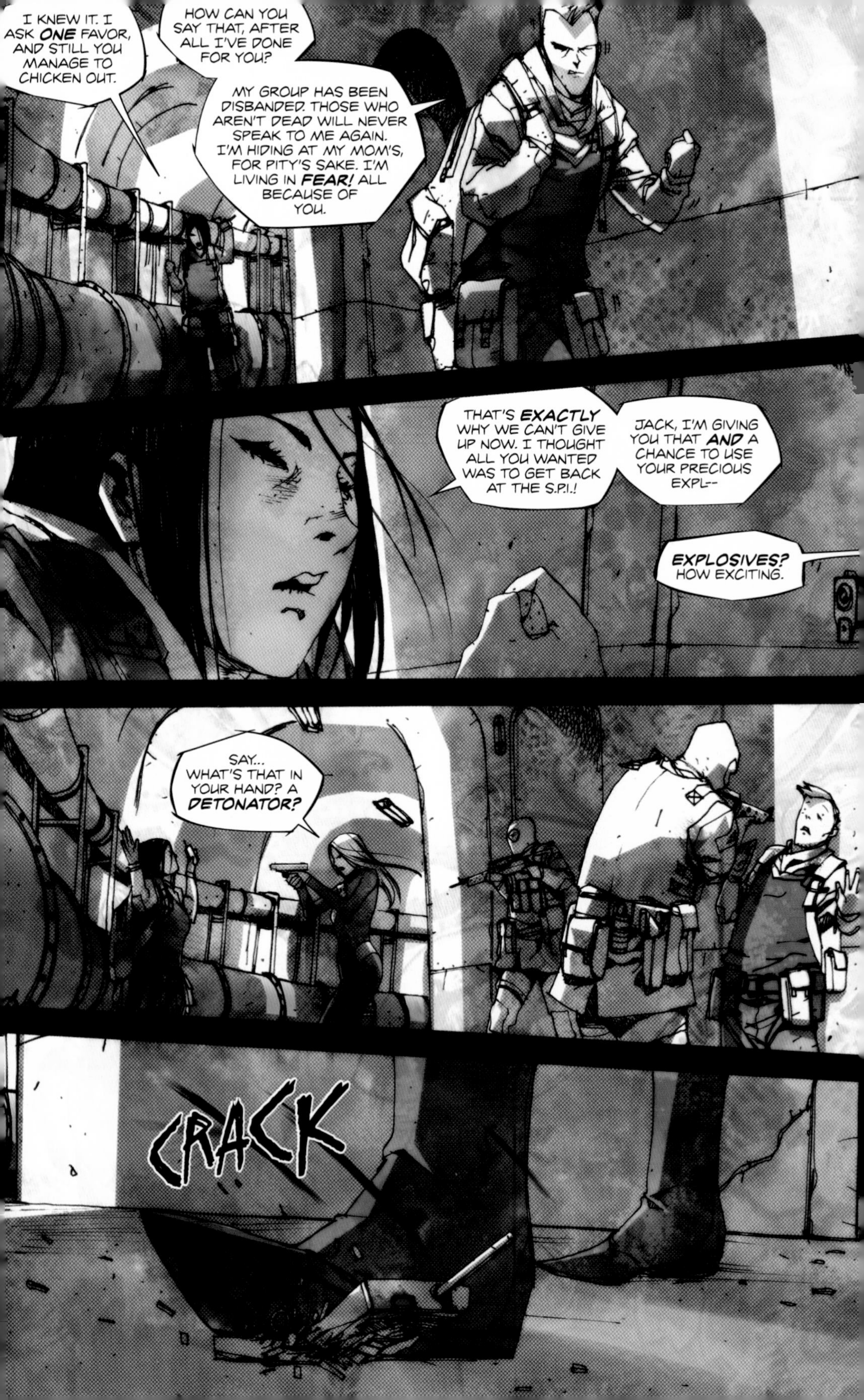
I KNEW IT. I ASK ONE FAVOR, AND STILL YOU MANAGE TO CHICKEN OUT.
HOW CAN YOU SAY THAT, AFTER ALL I'VE DONE FOR YOU?
MY GROUP HAS BEEN DISBANDED. THOSE WHO AREN'T DEAD WILL NEVER SPEAK TO ME AGAIN. I'M HIDING AT MY MOM'S, FOR PITY'S SAKE. I'M LIVING IN FEAR! ALL BECAUSE OF YOU.
THAT'S EXACTLY WHY WE CAN'T GIVE UP NOW. I THOUGHT ALL YOU WANTED WAS TO GET BACK AT THE S.P.I.!
JACK, I'M GIVING YOU THAT AND A CHANCE TO USE YOUR PRECIOUS EXPL--
EXPLOSIVES? HOW EXCITING.
SAY... WHAT'S THAT IN YOUR HAND? A DETONATOR?
CRACK

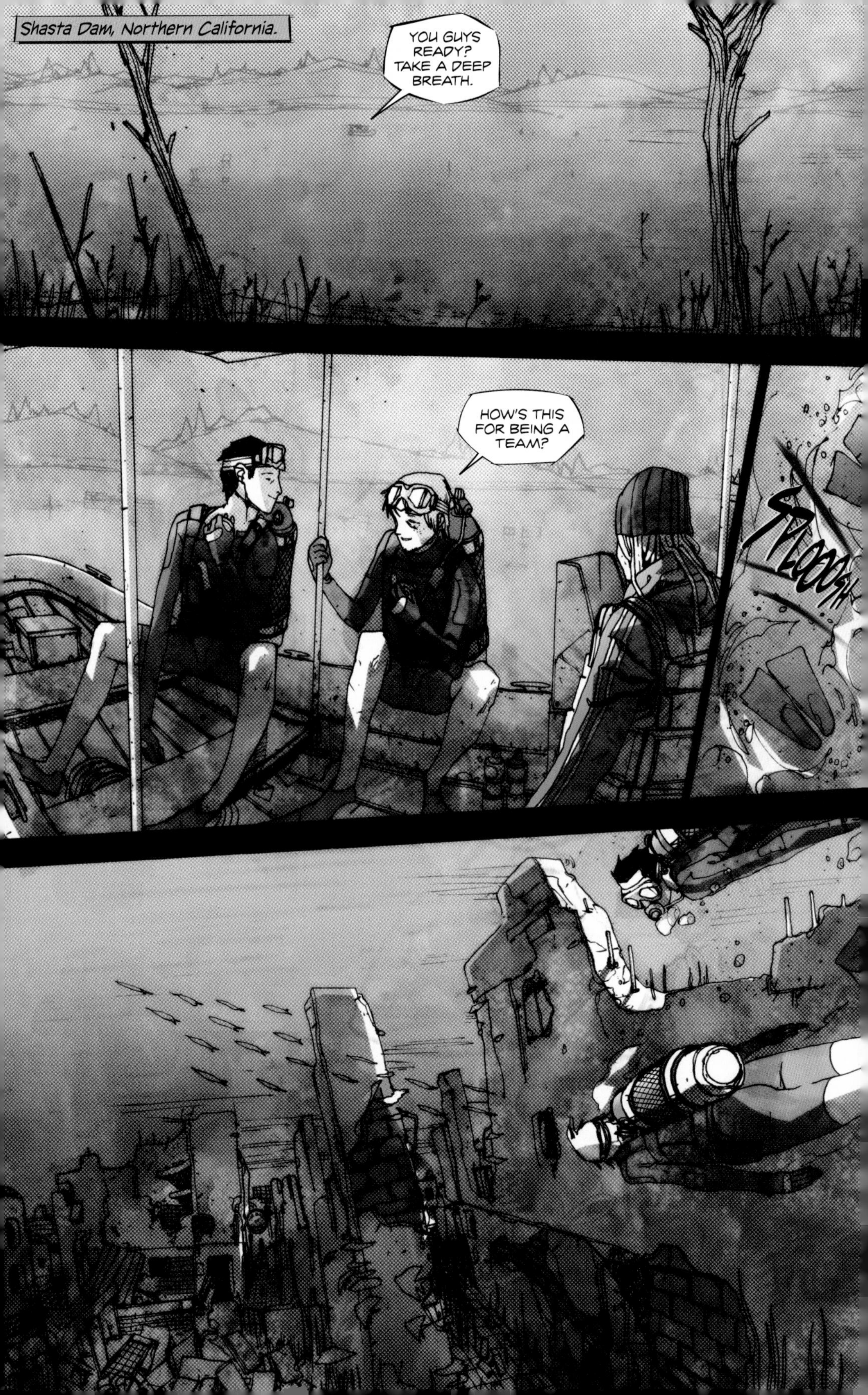
Shasta Dam, Northern California.
YOU GUYS READY? TAKE A DEEP BREATH.
HOW'S THIS FOR BEING A TEAM?
SPLOOSH

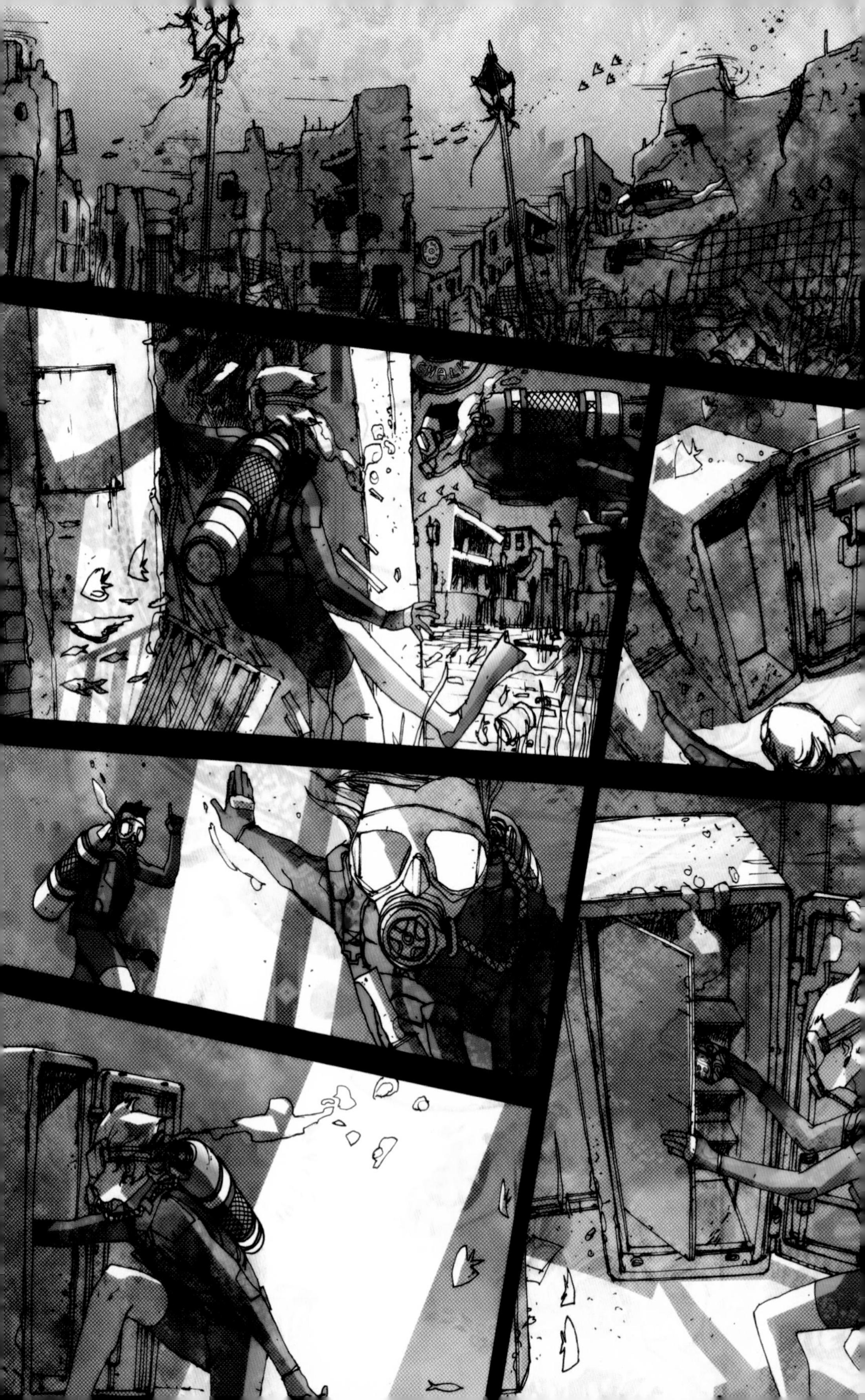
CHALK

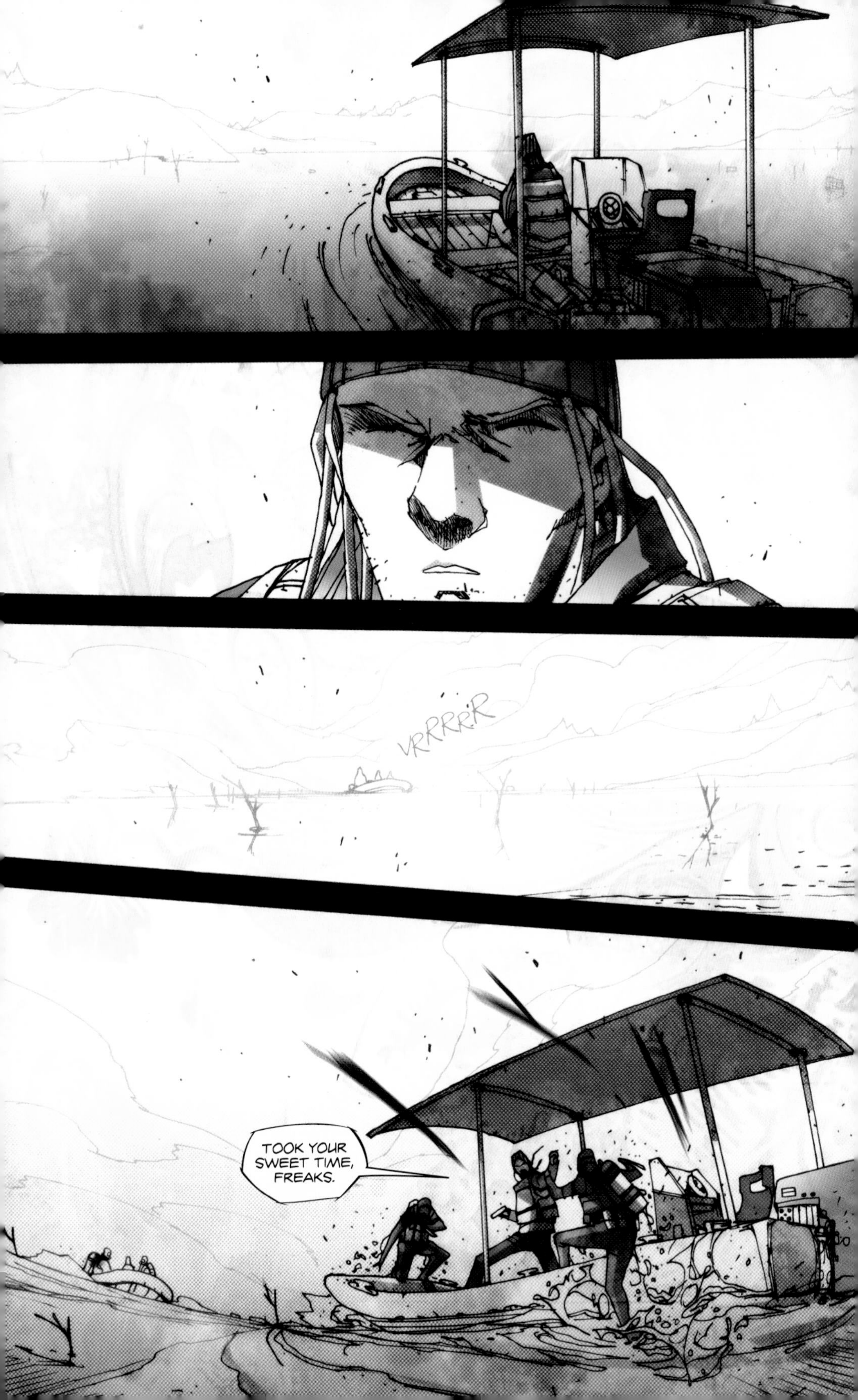
VRRRRR
TOOK YOUR SWEET TIME, FREAKS.

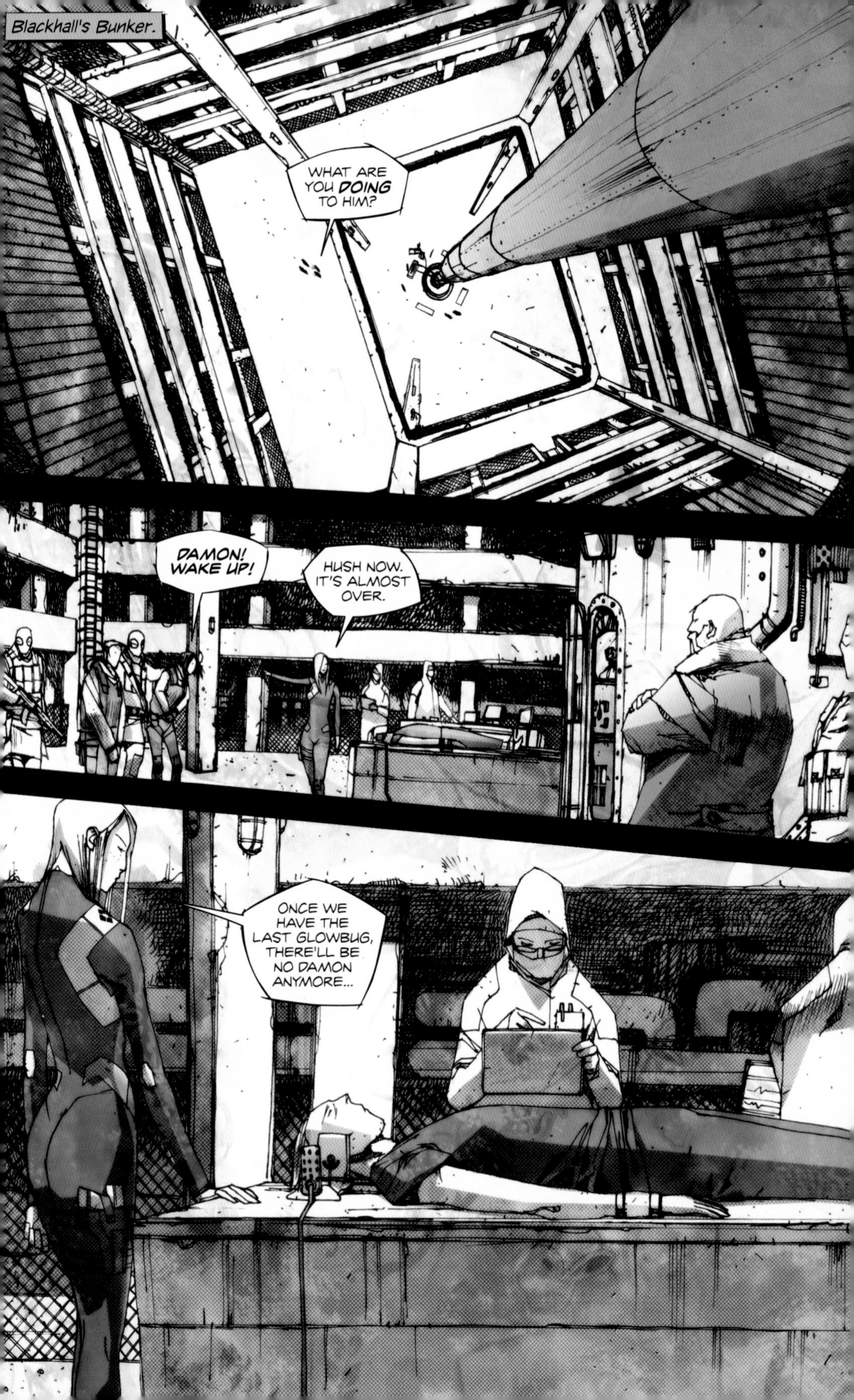
Blackhall's Bunker.
WHAT ARE YOU DOING TO HIM?
DAMON! WAKE UP!
HUSH NOW. IT'S ALMOST OVER.
ONCE WE HAVE THE LAST GLOWBUG, THERE'LL BE NO DAMON ANYMORE...

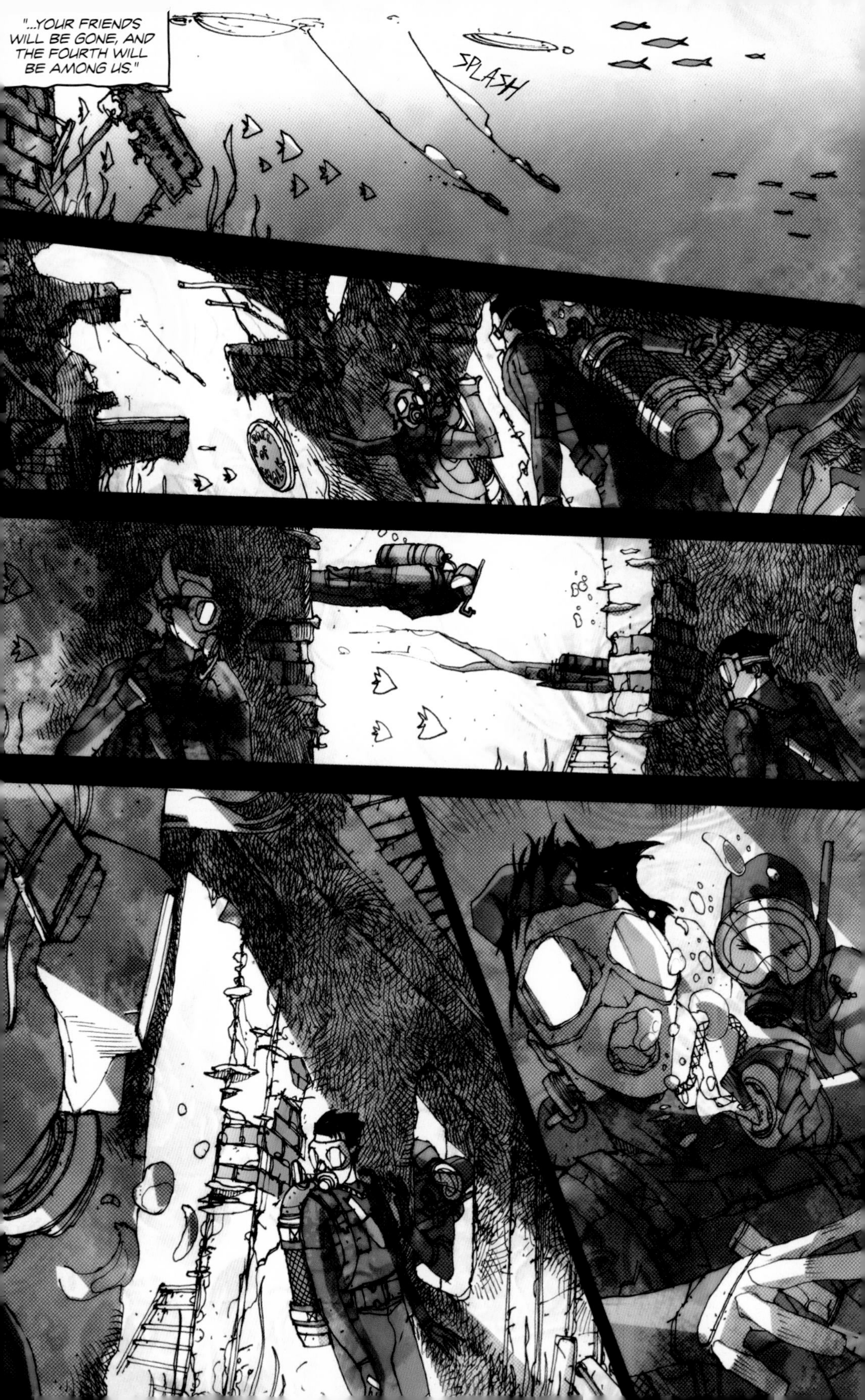
"...YOUR FRIENDS WILL BE GONE, AND THE FOURTH WILL BE AMONG US."
SPLASH

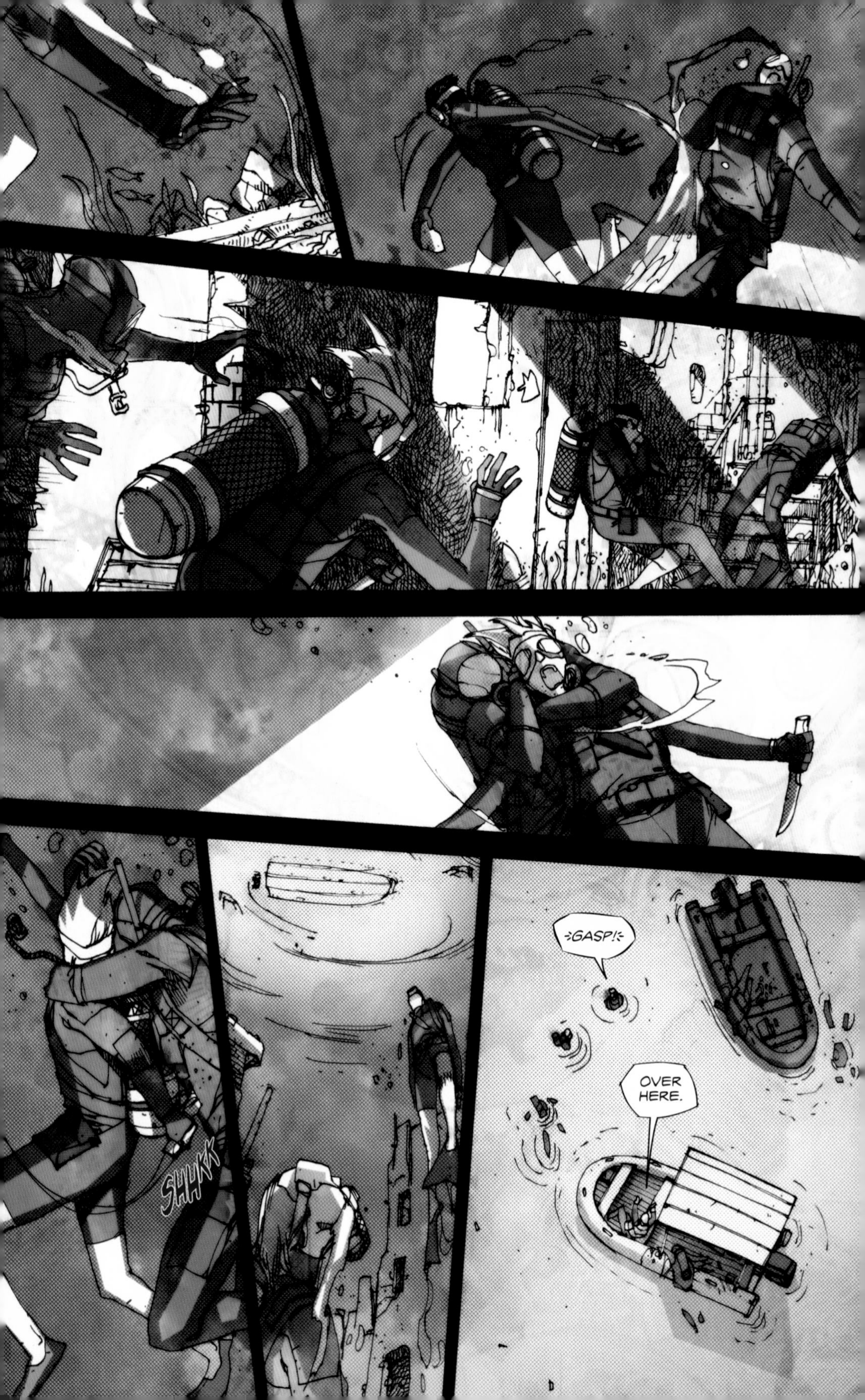
SHHKK
-GASP!-
OVER HERE.

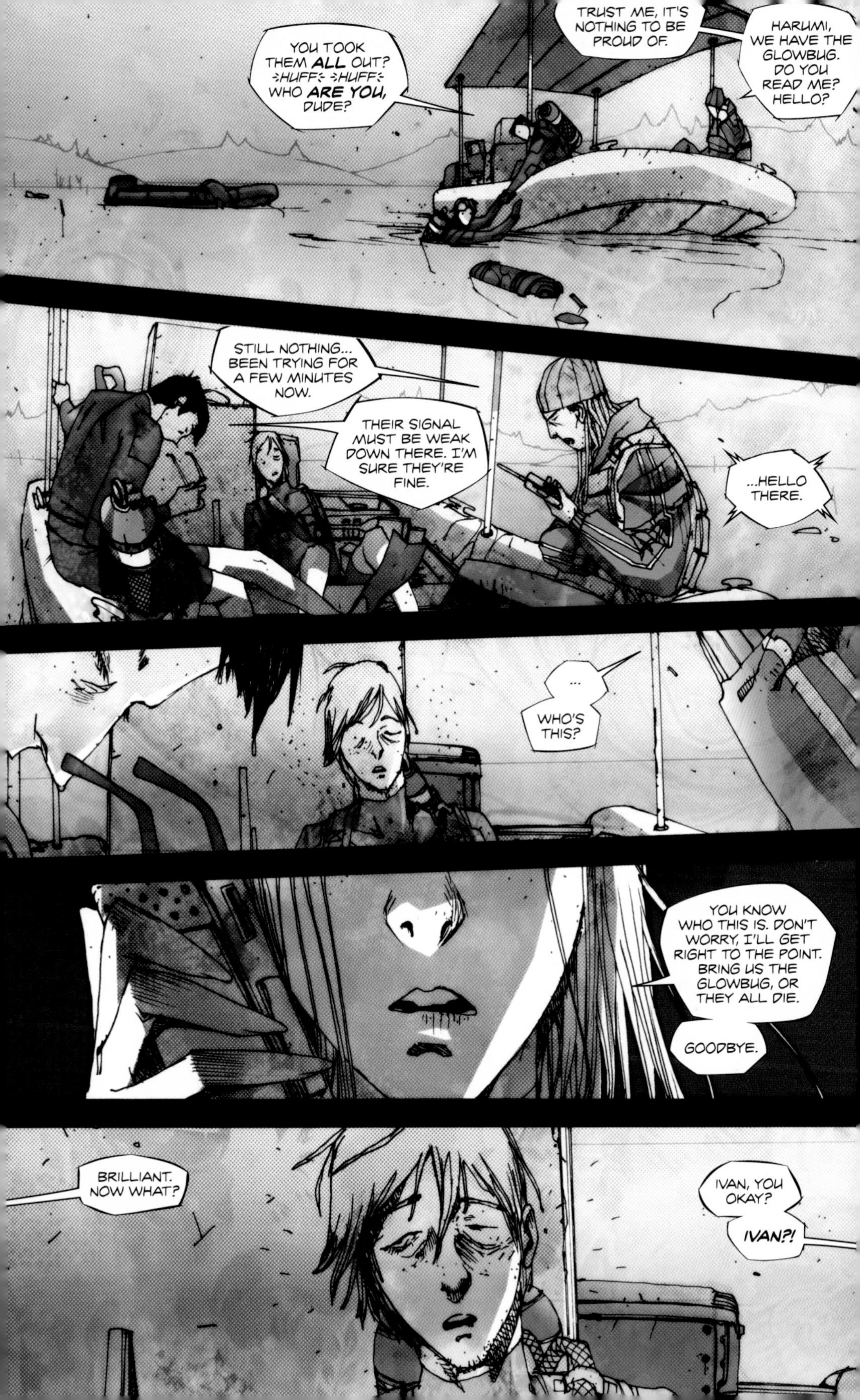
YOU TOOK THEM ALL OUT? ~HUFF~ ~HUFF~ WHO ARE YOU, DUDE?
TRUST ME, IT'S NOTHING TO BE PROUD OF.
HARUMI, WE HAVE THE GLOWBUG. DO YOU READ ME? HELLO?
STILL NOTHING... BEEN TRYING FOR A FEW MINUTES NOW.
THEIR SIGNAL MUST BE WEAK DOWN THERE. I'M SURE THEY'RE FINE.
...HELLO THERE.
...
WHO'S THIS?
YOU KNOW WHO THIS IS. DON'T WORRY, I'LL GET RIGHT TO THE POINT. BRING US THE GLOWBUG, OR THEY ALL DIE.
GOODBYE.
BRILLIANT. NOW WHAT?
IVAN, YOU OKAY?
IVAN?!

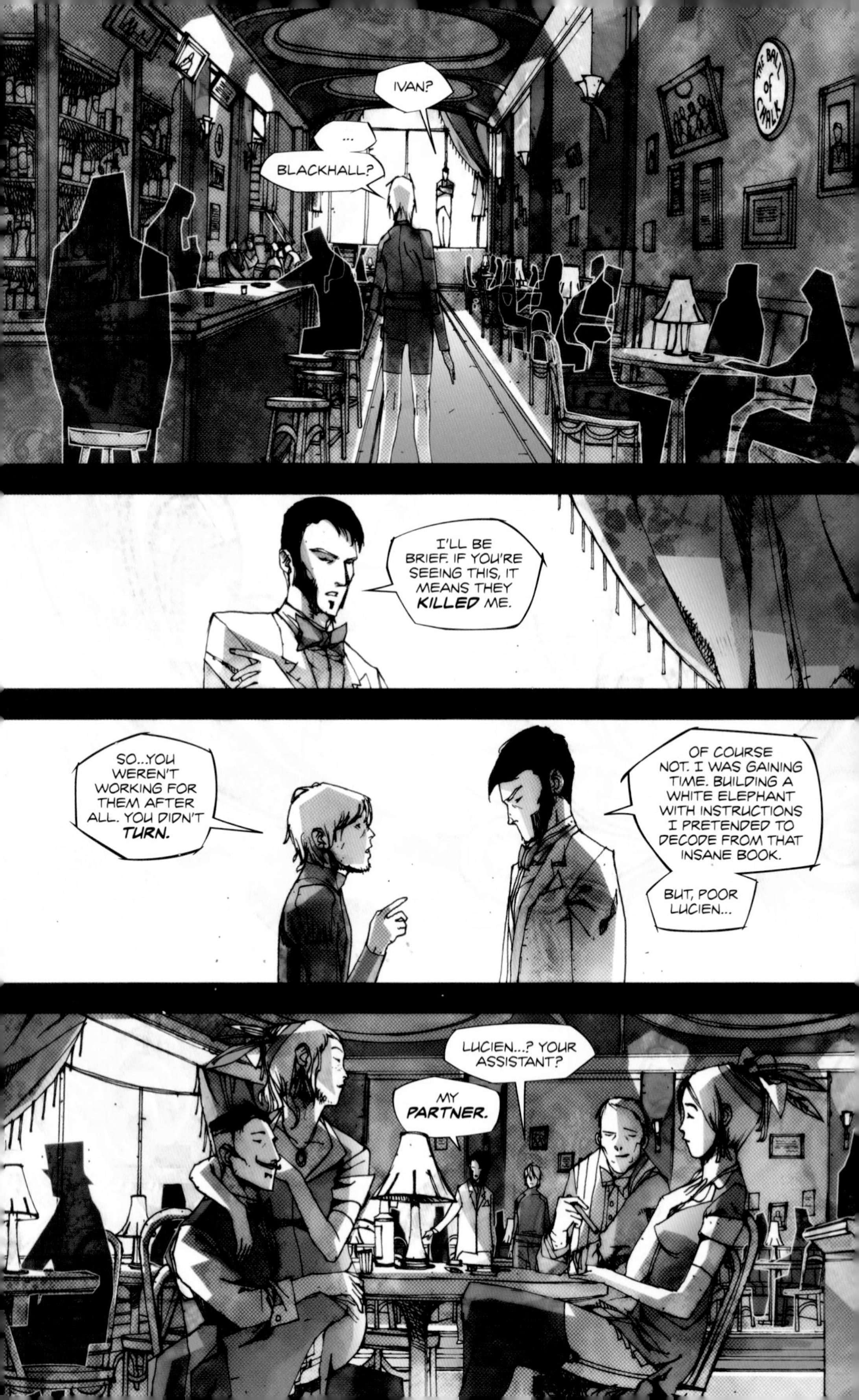
IVAN?
...
BLACKHALL?
THE BALL OF CHALK
I'LL BE BRIEF. IF YOU'RE SEEING THIS, IT MEANS THEY **KILLED** ME.
SO...YOU WEREN'T WORKING FOR THEM AFTER ALL. YOU DIDN'T **TURN.**
OF COURSE NOT. I WAS GAINING TIME. BUILDING A WHITE ELEPHANT WITH INSTRUCTIONS I PRETENDED TO DECODE FROM THAT INSANE BOOK.
BUT, POOR LUCIEN...
LUCIEN...? YOUR ASSISTANT?
MY **PARTNER.**

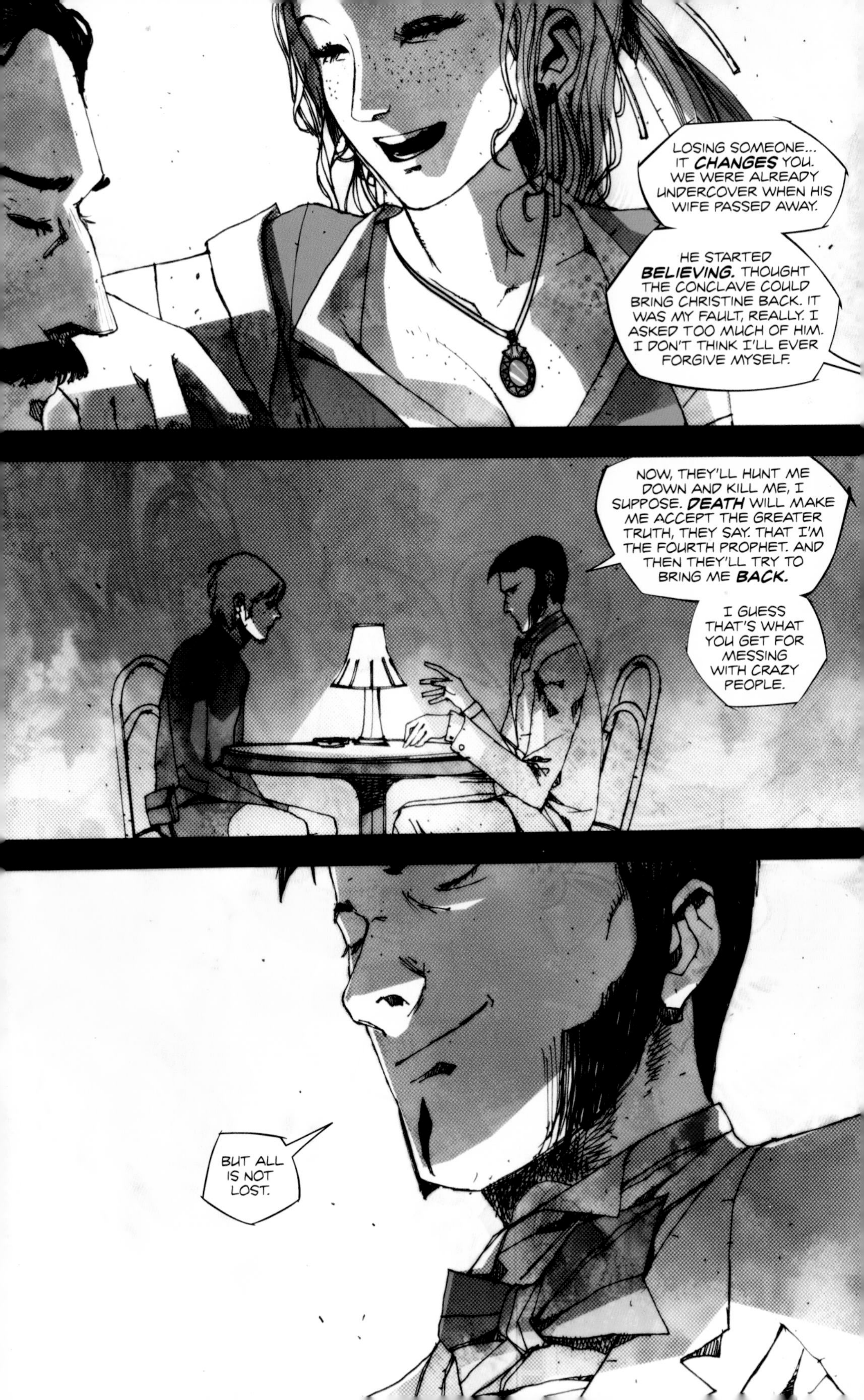
LOSING SOMEONE... IT CHANGES YOU. WE WERE ALREADY UNDERCOVER WHEN HIS WIFE PASSED AWAY.
HE STARTED BELIEVING. THOUGHT THE CONCLAVE COULD BRING CHRISTINE BACK. IT WAS MY FAULT, REALLY. I ASKED TOO MUCH OF HIM. I DON'T THINK I'LL EVER FORGIVE MYSELF.
NOW, THEY'LL HUNT ME DOWN AND KILL ME, I SUPPOSE. DEATH WILL MAKE ME ACCEPT THE GREATER TRUTH, THEY SAY. THAT I'M THE FOURTH PROPHET. AND THEN THEY'LL TRY TO BRING ME BACK.
I GUESS THAT'S WHAT YOU GET FOR MESSING WITH CRAZY PEOPLE.
BUT ALL IS NOT LOST.

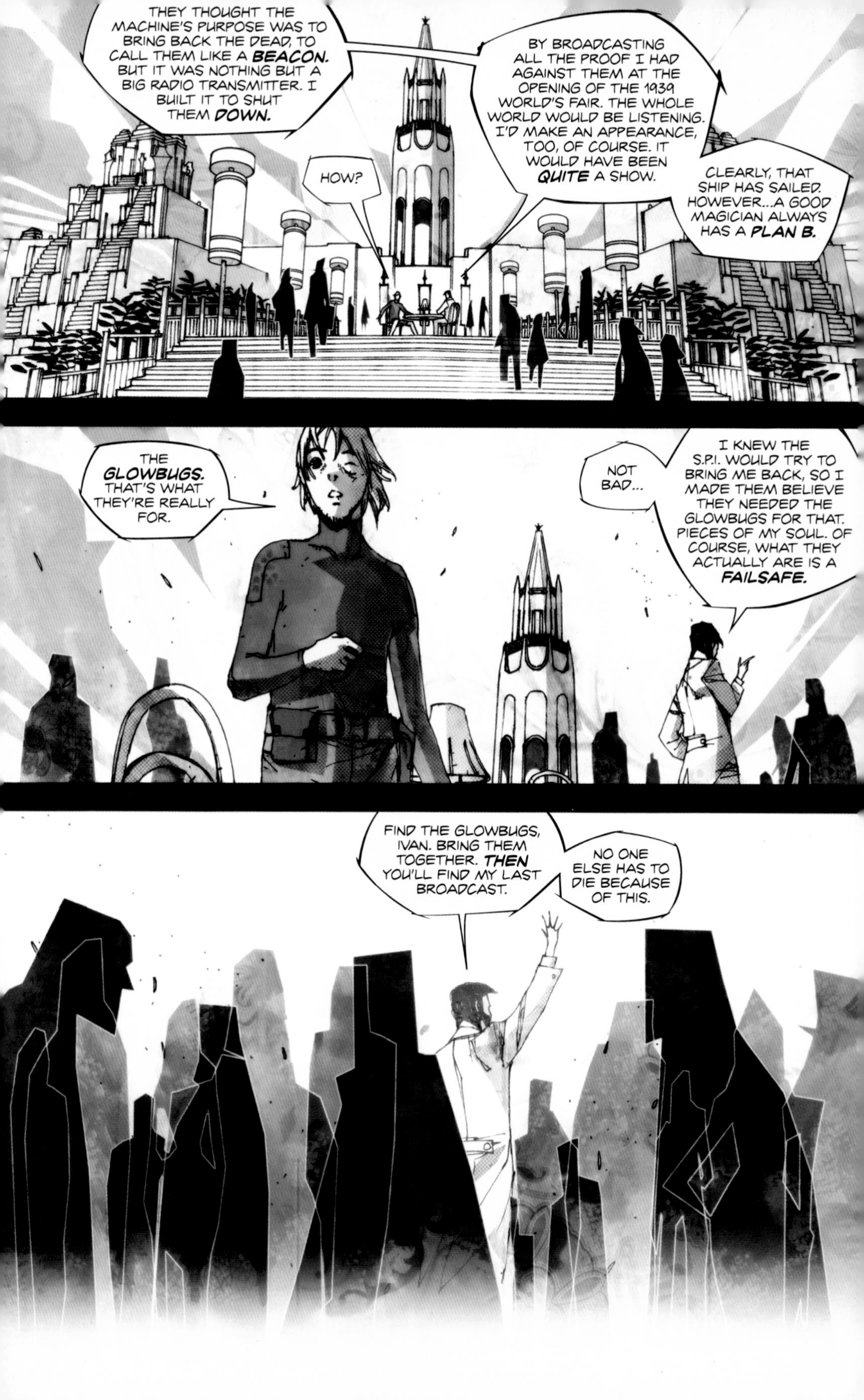
THEY THOUGHT THE MACHINE'S PURPOSE WAS TO BRING BACK THE DEAD, TO CALL THEM LIKE A **BEACON.** BUT IT WAS NOTHING BUT A BIG RADIO TRANSMITTER. I BUILT IT TO SHUT THEM **DOWN.**
HOW?
BY BROADCASTING ALL THE PROOF I HAD AGAINST THEM AT THE OPENING OF THE 1939 WORLD'S FAIR. THE WHOLE WORLD WOULD BE LISTENING. I'D MAKE AN APPEARANCE, TOO, OF COURSE. IT WOULD HAVE BEEN **QUITE** A SHOW.
CLEARLY, THAT SHIP HAS SAILED. HOWEVER...A GOOD MAGICIAN ALWAYS HAS A **PLAN B.**
THE **GLOWBUGS.** THAT'S WHAT THEY'RE REALLY FOR.
NOT BAD...
I KNEW THE S.P.I. WOULD TRY TO BRING ME BACK, SO I MADE THEM BELIEVE THEY NEEDED THE GLOWBUGS FOR THAT. PIECES OF MY SOUL. OF COURSE, WHAT THEY ACTUALLY ARE IS A **FAILSAFE.**
FIND THE GLOWBUGS, IVAN. BRING THEM TOGETHER. **THEN** YOU'LL FIND MY LAST BROADCAST.
NO ONE ELSE HAS TO DIE BECAUSE OF THIS.

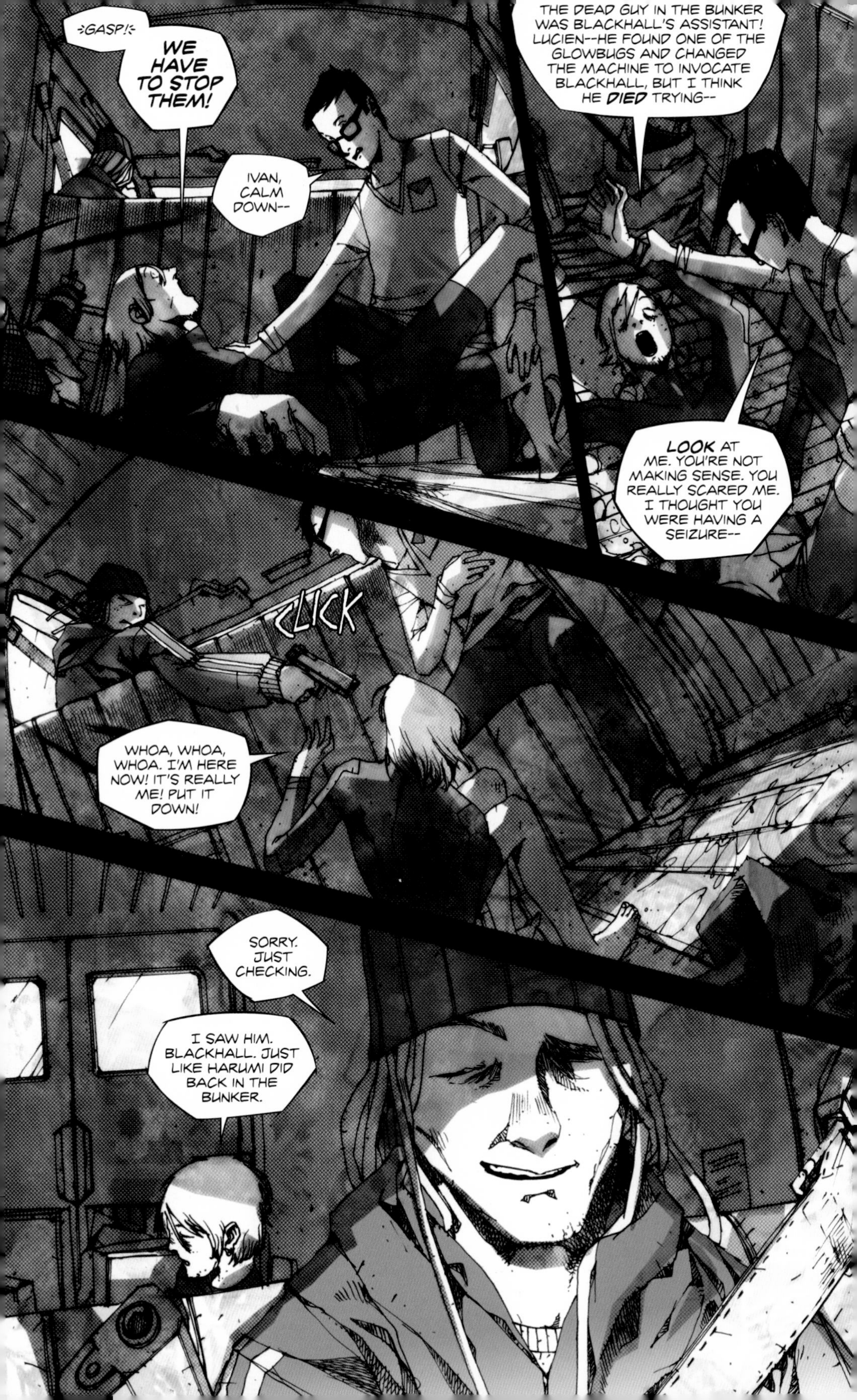
-GASP!-
WE HAVE TO STOP THEM!
IVAN, CALM DOWN--
THE DEAD GUY IN THE BUNKER WAS BLACKHALL'S ASSISTANT! LUCIEN--HE FOUND ONE OF THE GLOWBUGS AND CHANGED THE MACHINE TO INVOCATE BLACKHALL, BUT I THINK HE DIED TRYING--
LOOK AT ME. YOU'RE NOT MAKING SENSE. YOU REALLY SCARED ME. I THOUGHT YOU WERE HAVING A SEIZURE--
CLICK
WHOA, WHOA, WHOA. I'M HERE NOW! IT'S REALLY ME! PUT IT DOWN!
SORRY. JUST CHECKING.
I SAW HIM. BLACKHALL. JUST LIKE HARUMI DID BACK IN THE BUNKER.

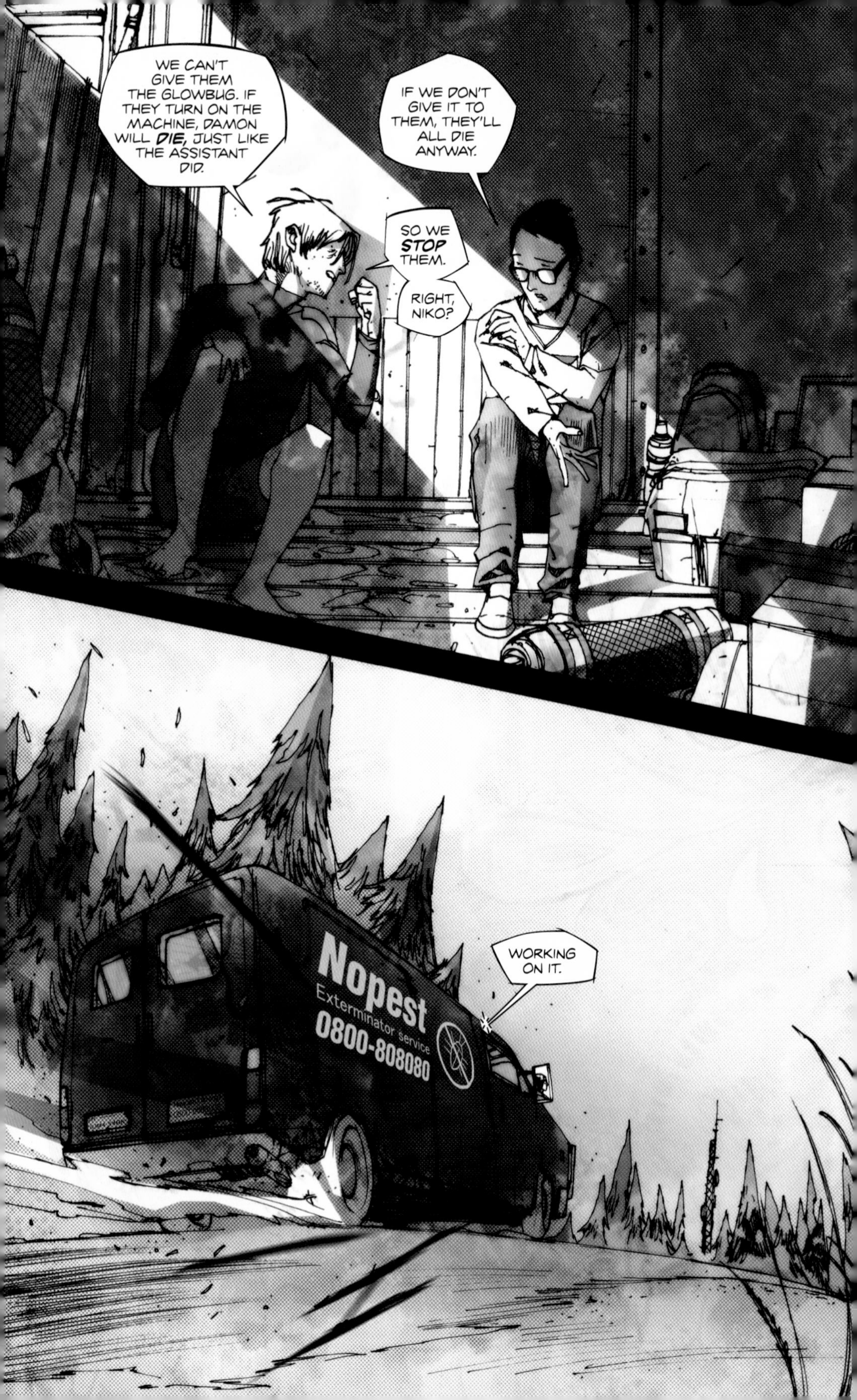
WE CAN'T GIVE THEM THE GLOWBUG. IF THEY TURN ON THE MACHINE, DAMON WILL DIE, JUST LIKE THE ASSISTANT DID.
IF WE DON'T GIVE IT TO THEM, THEY'LL ALL DIE ANYWAY.
SO WE STOP THEM.
RIGHT, NIKO?
Nopest
Exterminator service
0800-808080
WORKING ON IT.

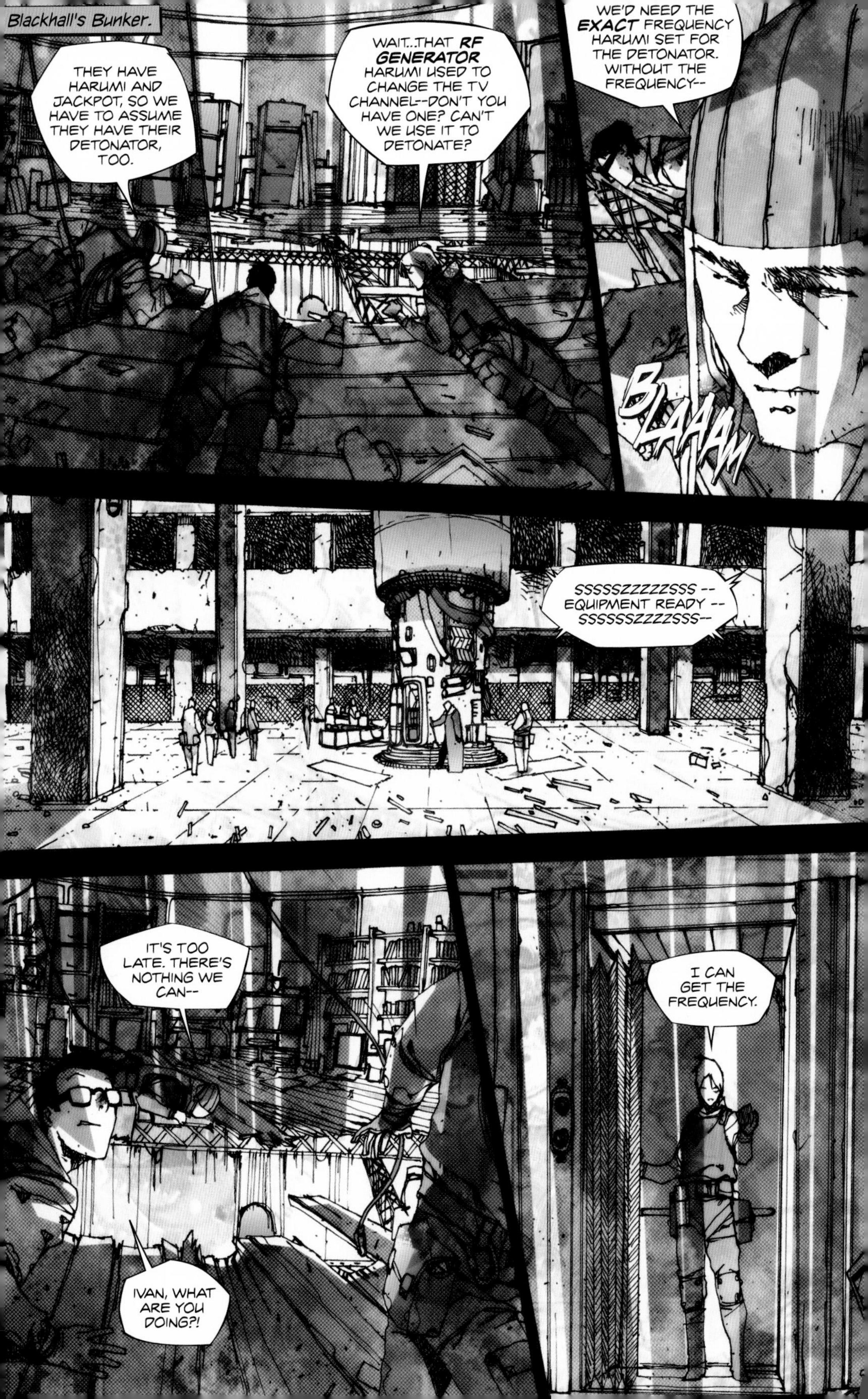
Blackhall's Bunker.
THEY HAVE HARUMI AND JACKPOT, SO WE HAVE TO ASSUME THEY HAVE THEIR DETONATOR, TOO.
WAIT..THAT RF GENERATOR HARUMI USED TO CHANGE THE TV CHANNEL--DON'T YOU HAVE ONE? CAN'T WE USE IT TO DETONATE?
WE'D NEED THE EXACT FREQUENCY HARUMI SET FOR THE DETONATOR. WITHOUT THE FREQUENCY--
BLAAAM
SSSSSZZZZZSSS -- EQUIPMENT READY -- SSSSSSZZZZSSS--
IT'S TOO LATE. THERE'S NOTHING WE CAN--
IVAN, WHAT ARE YOU DOING?!
I CAN GET THE FREQUENCY.

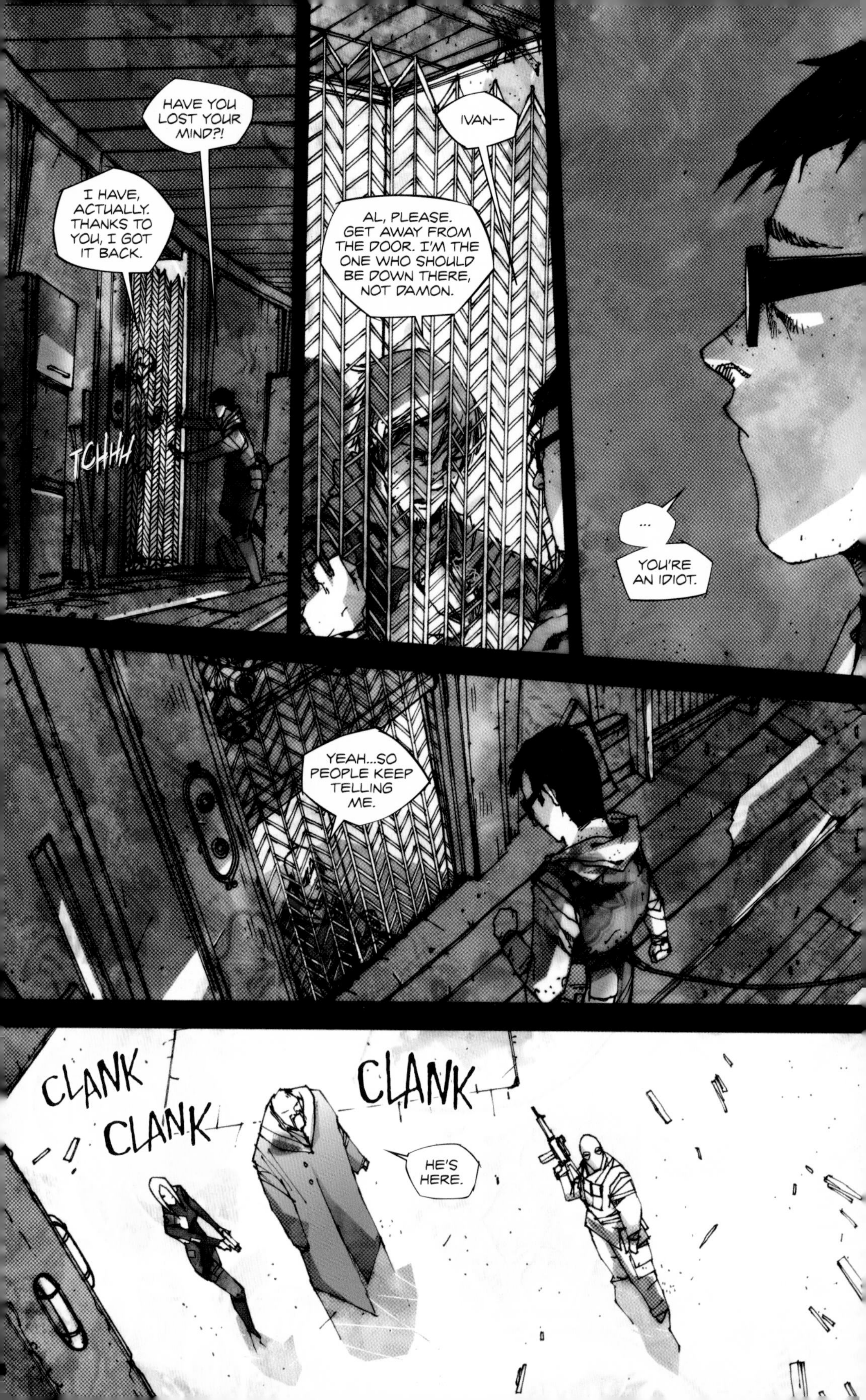
HAVE YOU LOST YOUR MIND?!
I HAVE, ACTUALLY. THANKS TO YOU, I GOT IT BACK.
TCHHH
IVAN--
AL, PLEASE. GET AWAY FROM THE DOOR. I'M THE ONE WHO SHOULD BE DOWN THERE, NOT DAMON.
...
YOU'RE AN IDIOT.
YEAH...SO PEOPLE KEEP TELLING ME.
CLANK
CLANK
CLANK
HE'S HERE.

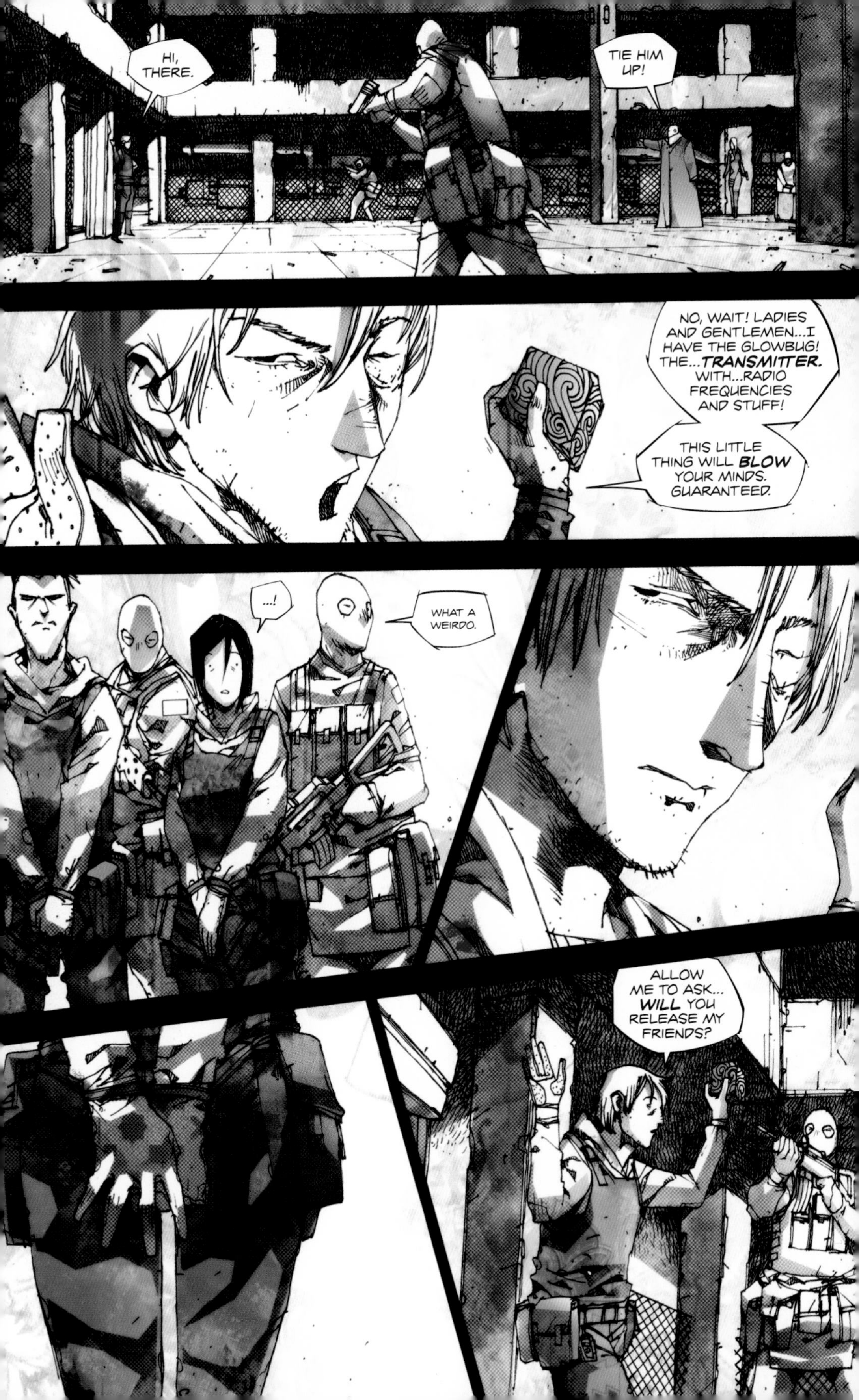
HI, THERE.
TIE HIM UP!
NO, WAIT! LADIES AND GENTLEMEN...I HAVE THE GLOWBUG! THE...TRANSMITTER. WITH...RADIO FREQUENCIES AND STUFF!
THIS LITTLE THING WILL BLOW YOUR MINDS. GUARANTEED.
...!
WHAT A WEIRDO.
ALLOW ME TO ASK... WILL YOU RELEASE MY FRIENDS?

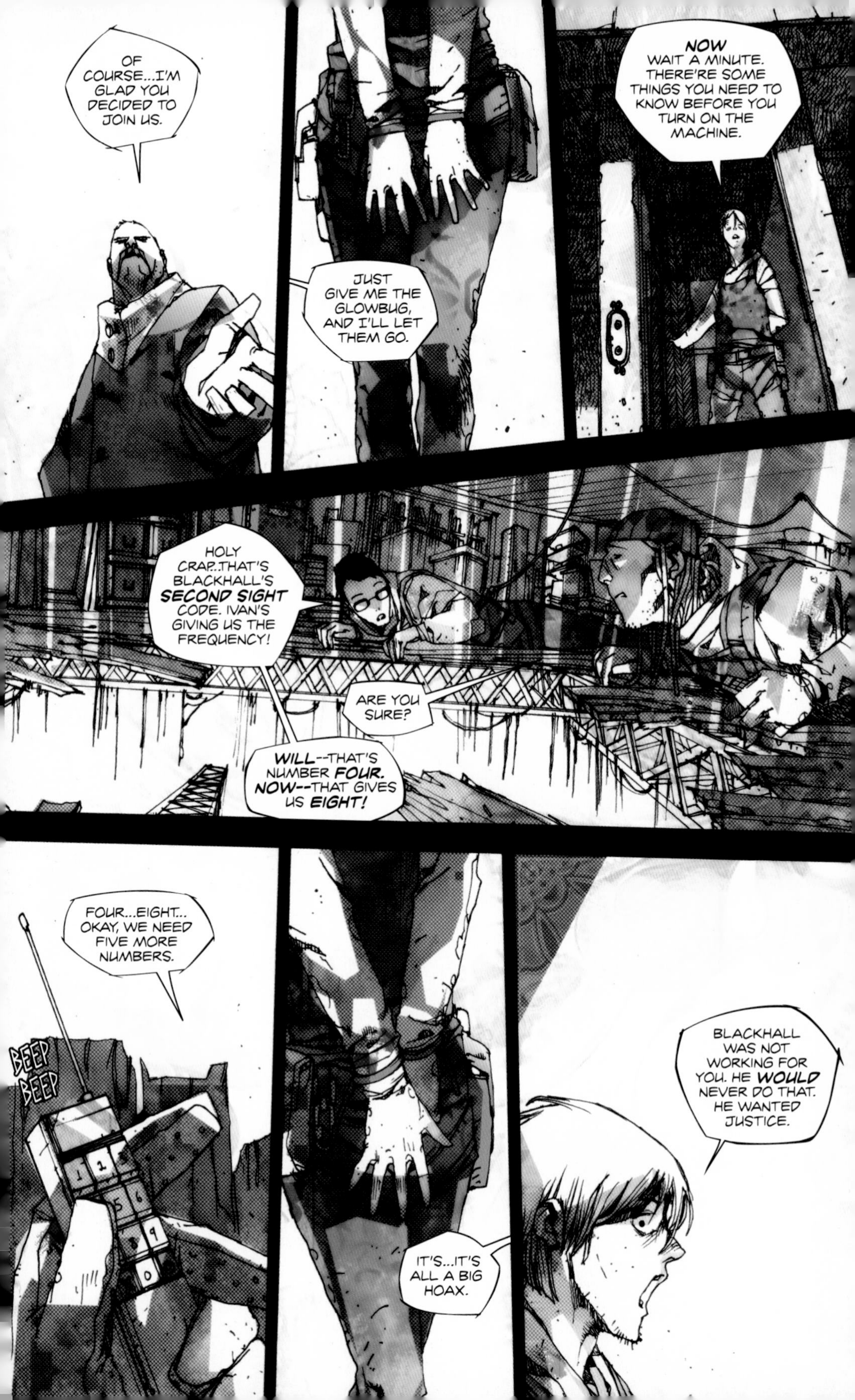
OF COURSE...I'M GLAD YOU DECIDED TO JOIN US.
JUST GIVE ME THE GLOWBUG, AND I'LL LET THEM GO.
NOW WAIT A MINUTE. THERE'RE SOME THINGS YOU NEED TO KNOW BEFORE YOU TURN ON THE MACHINE.
HOLY CRAP..THAT'S BLACKHALL'S SECOND SIGHT CODE. IVAN'S GIVING US THE FREQUENCY!
ARE YOU SURE?
WILL--THAT'S NUMBER FOUR. NOW--THAT GIVES US EIGHT!
FOUR...EIGHT... OKAY, WE NEED FIVE MORE NUMBERS.
BEEP BEEP
IT'S...IT'S ALL A BIG HOAX.
BLACKHALL WAS NOT WORKING FOR YOU. HE WOULD NEVER DO THAT. HE WANTED JUSTICE.

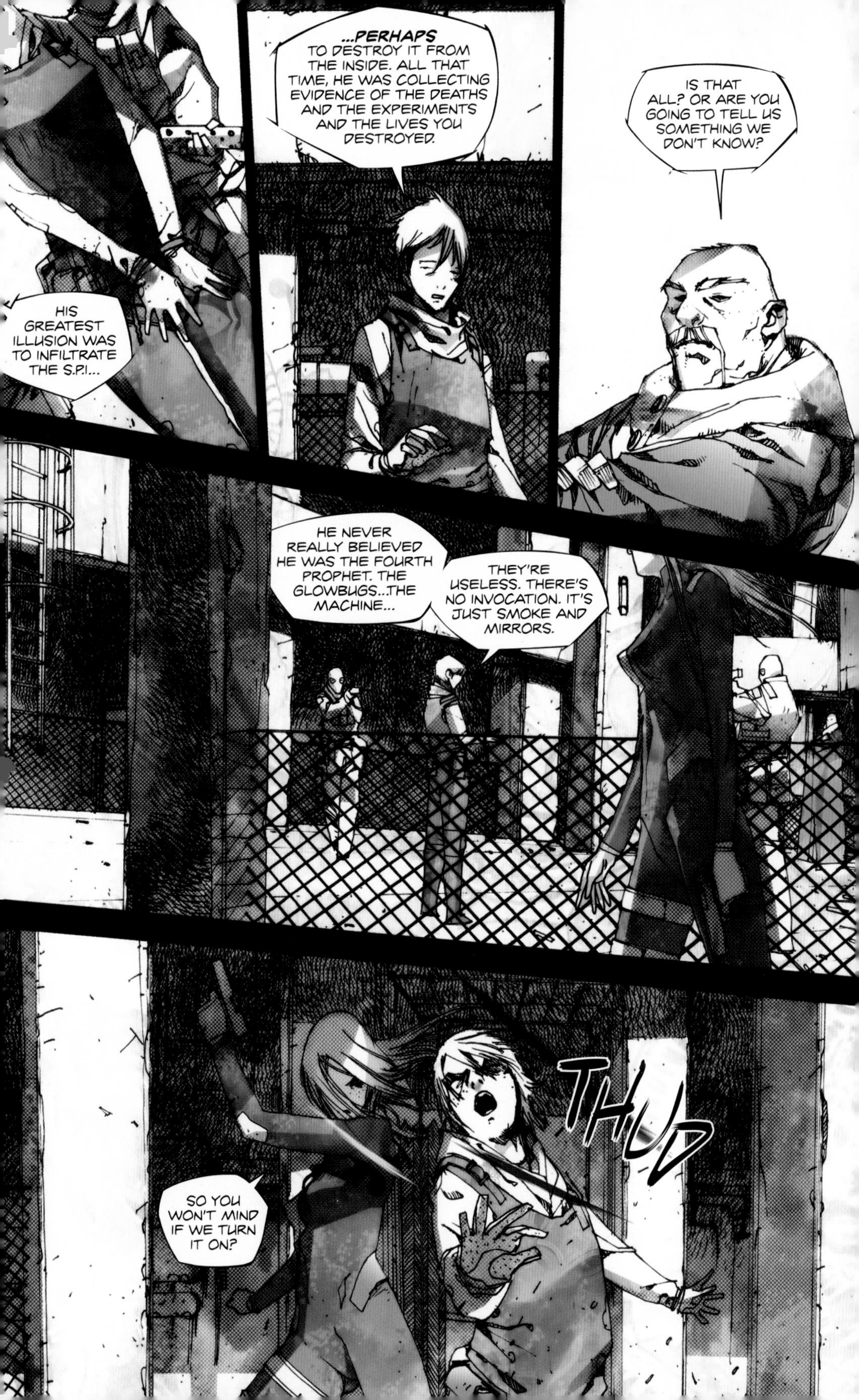
HIS GREATEST ILLUSION WAS TO INFILTRATE THE S.P.I...
...PERHAPS TO DESTROY IT FROM THE INSIDE. ALL THAT TIME, HE WAS COLLECTING EVIDENCE OF THE DEATHS AND THE EXPERIMENTS AND THE LIVES YOU DESTROYED.
IS THAT ALL? OR ARE YOU GOING TO TELL US SOMETHING WE DON'T KNOW?
HE NEVER REALLY BELIEVED HE WAS THE FOURTH PROPHET. THE GLOWBUGS...THE MACHINE...
THEY'RE USELESS. THERE'S NO INVOCATION. IT'S JUST SMOKE AND MIRRORS.
THUD
SO YOU WON'T MIND IF WE TURN IT ON?

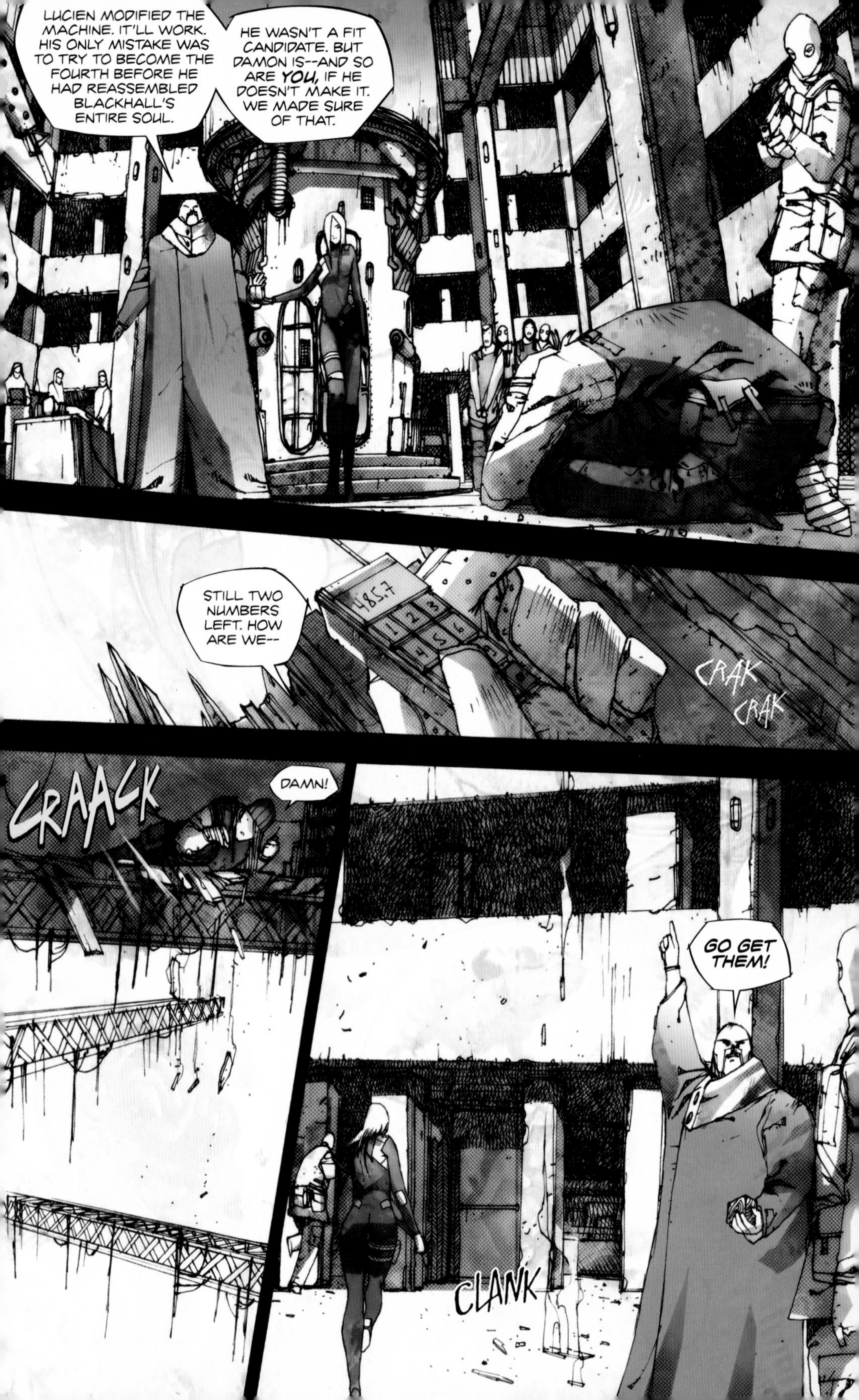
LUCIEN MODIFIED THE MACHINE. IT'LL WORK. HIS ONLY MISTAKE WAS TO TRY TO BECOME THE FOURTH BEFORE HE HAD REASSEMBLED BLACKHALL'S ENTIRE SOUL.
HE WASN'T A FIT CANDIDATE. BUT DAMON IS--AND SO ARE YOU, IF HE DOESN'T MAKE IT. WE MADE SURE OF THAT.
485.7
STILL TWO NUMBERS LEFT. HOW ARE WE--
CRAK
CRAK
CRAACK
DAMN!
GO GET THEM!
CLANK

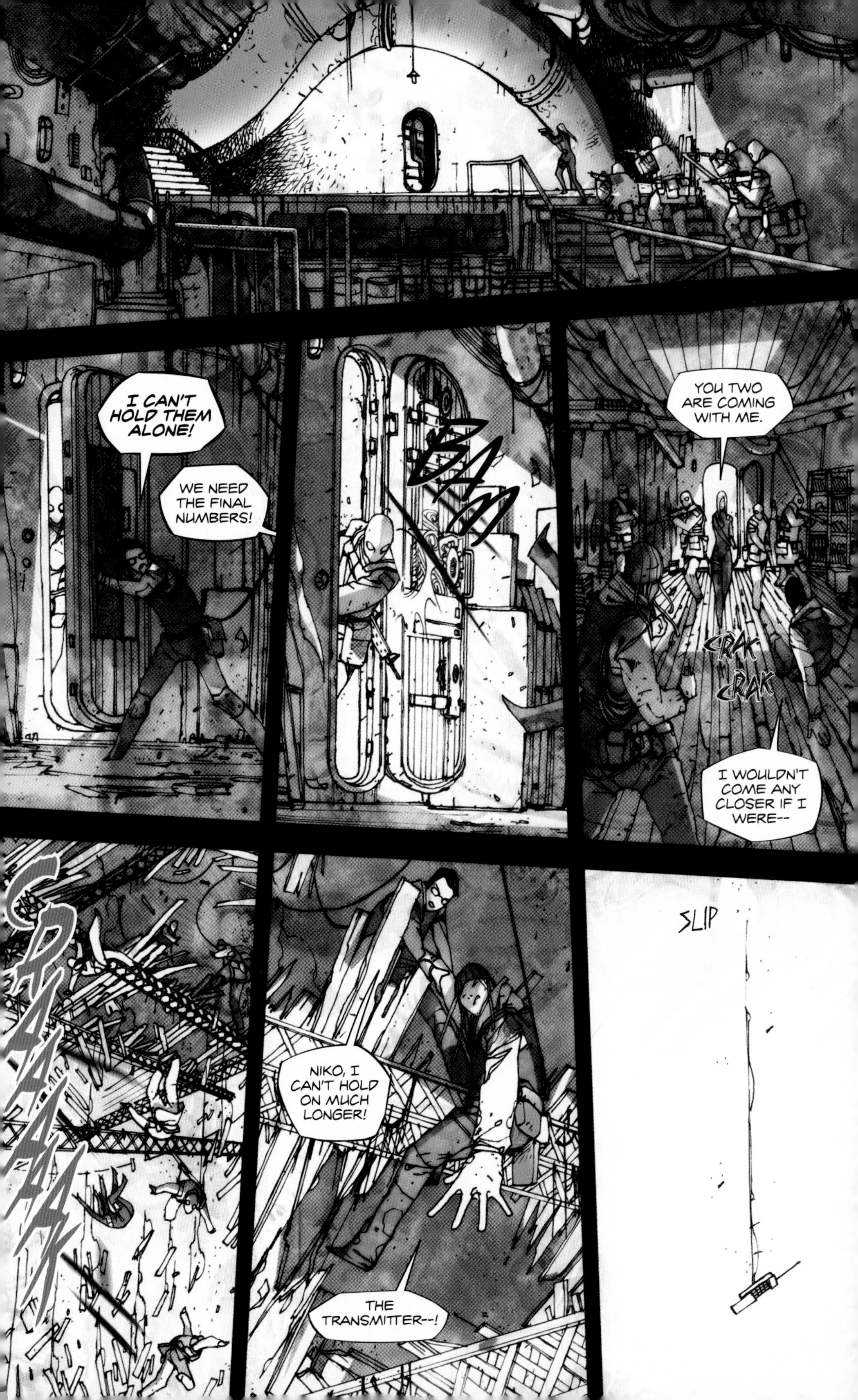
I CAN'T HOLD THEM ALONE!
WE NEED THE FINAL NUMBERS!
BAM
YOU TWO ARE COMING WITH ME.
CRAK
CRAK
I WOULDN'T COME ANY CLOSER IF I WERE--
NIKO, I CAN'T HOLD ON MUCH LONGER!
THE TRANSMITTER--!
SLIP

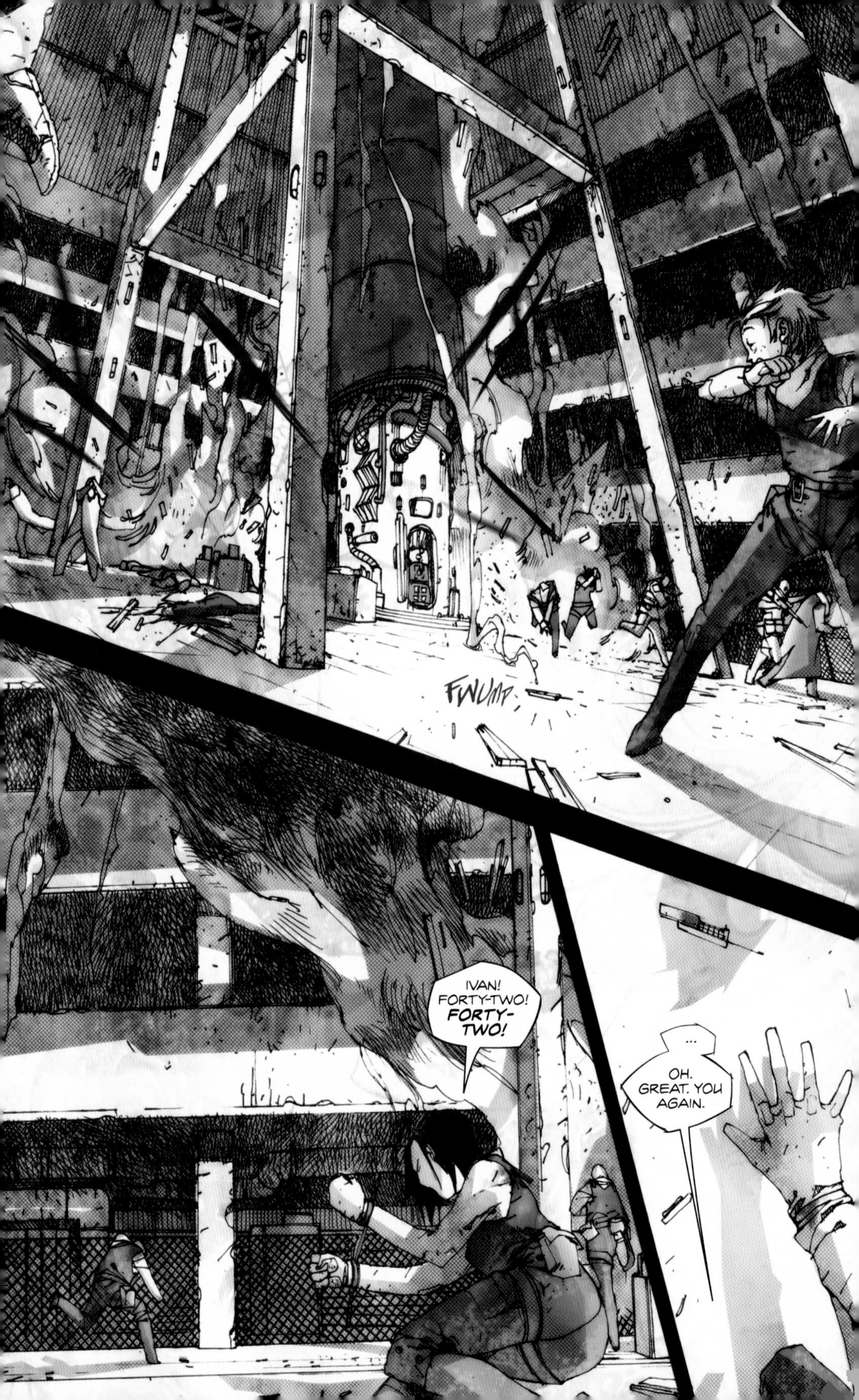
FWUMP
IVAN! FORTY-TWO! FORTY-TWO!
...
OH. GREAT. YOU AGAIN.

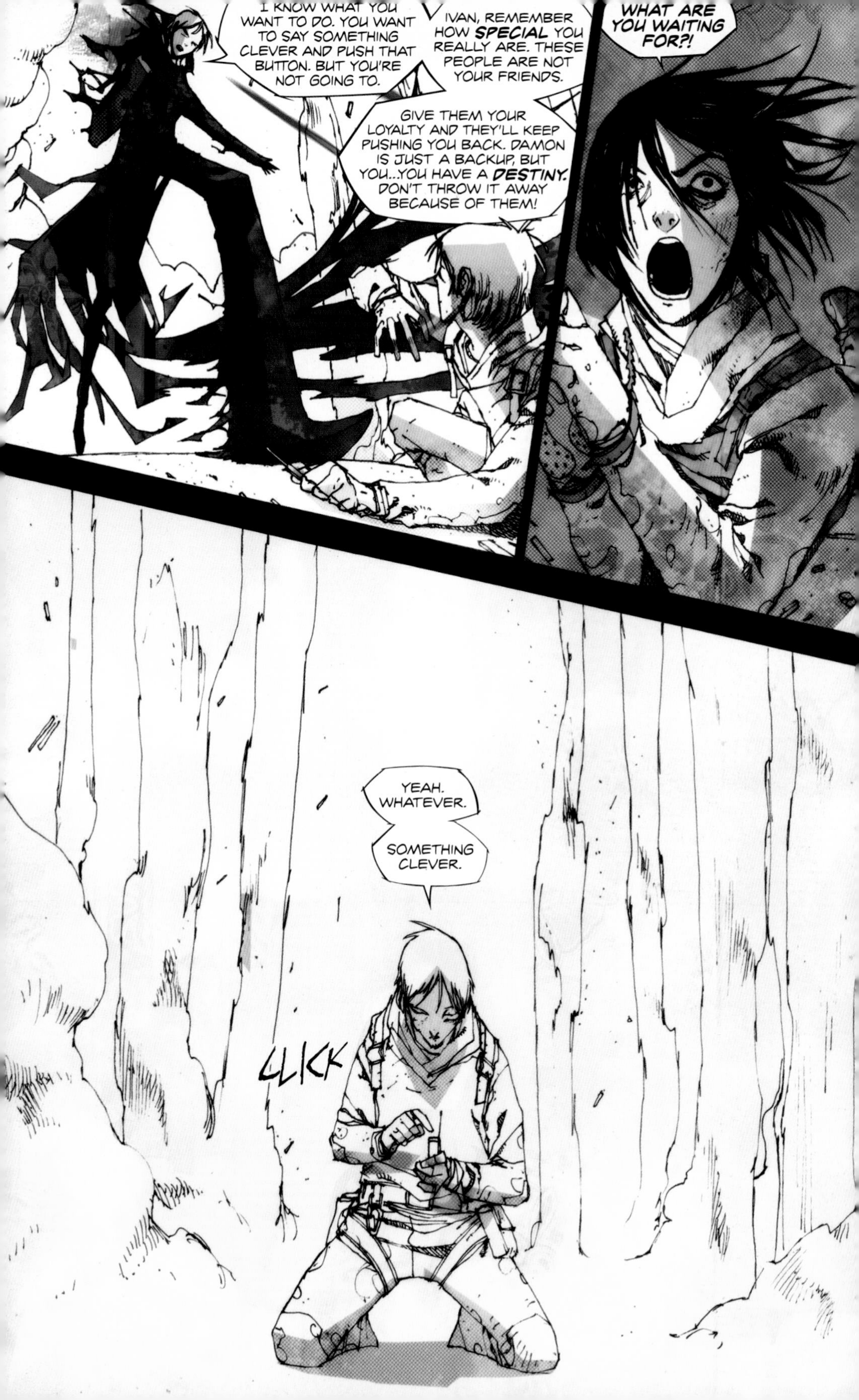
I KNOW WHAT YOU WANT TO DO. YOU WANT TO SAY SOMETHING CLEVER AND PUSH THAT BUTTON. BUT YOU'RE NOT GOING TO.
IVAN, REMEMBER HOW SPECIAL YOU REALLY ARE. THESE PEOPLE ARE NOT YOUR FRIENDS.
GIVE THEM YOUR LOYALTY AND THEY'LL KEEP PUSHING YOU BACK. DAMON IS JUST A BACKUP, BUT YOU...YOU HAVE A DESTINY. DON'T THROW IT AWAY BECAUSE OF THEM!
WHAT ARE YOU WAITING FOR?!
YEAH. WHATEVER.
SOMETHING CLEVER.
CLICK

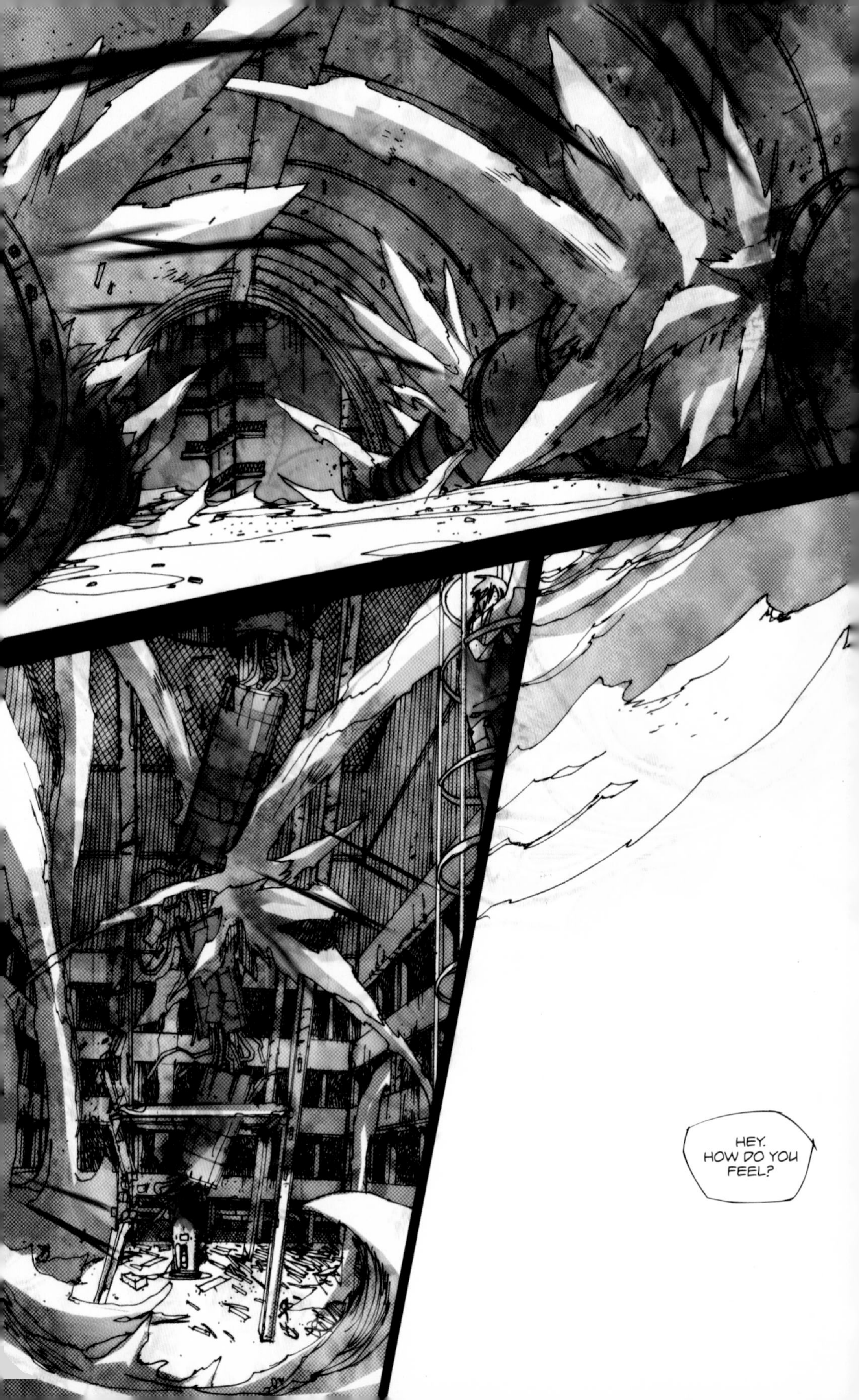
HEY.
HOW DO YOU
FEEL?

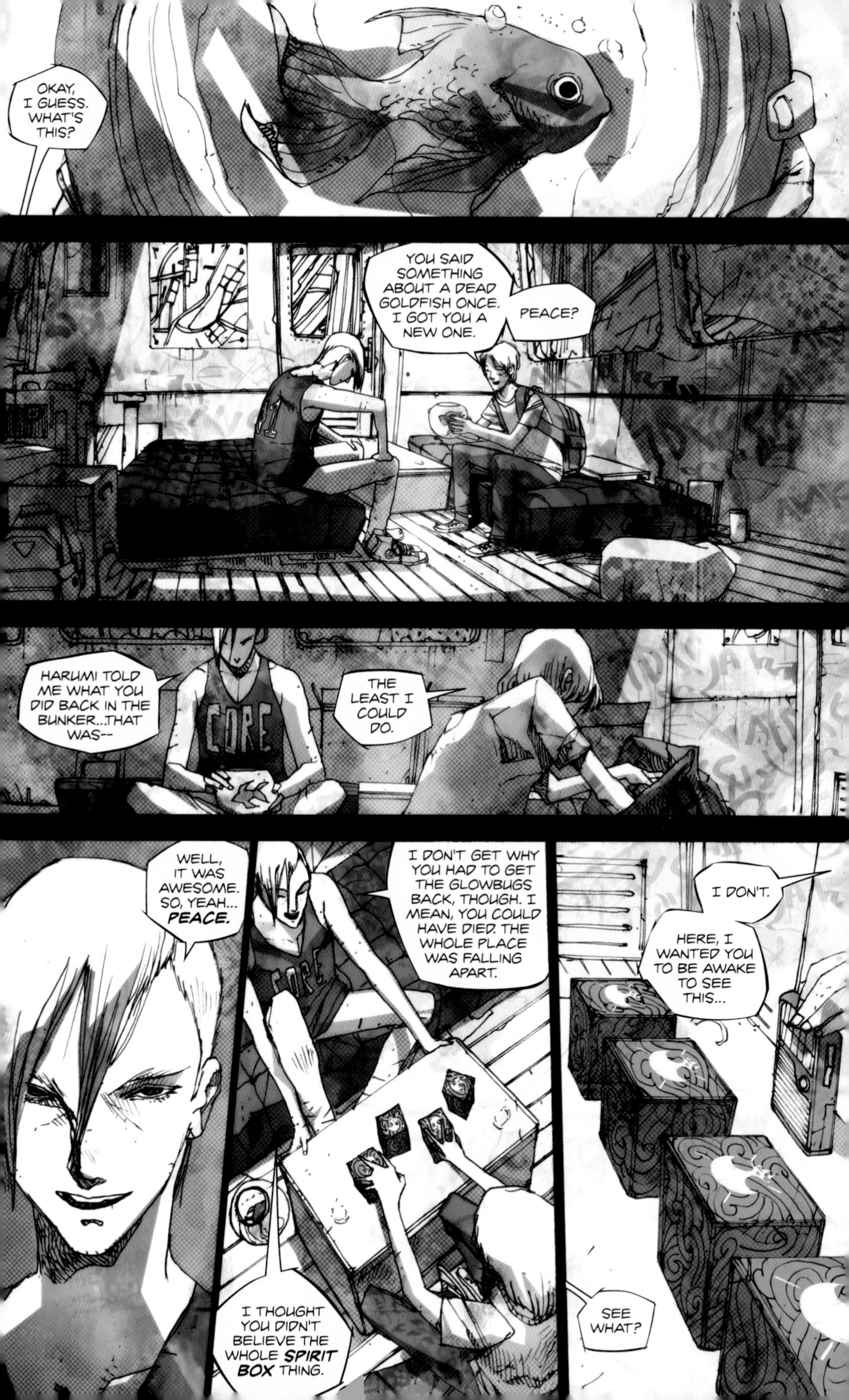
OKAY, I GUESS. WHAT'S THIS?
YOU SAID SOMETHING ABOUT A DEAD GOLDFISH ONCE. I GOT YOU A NEW ONE.
PEACE?
HARUMI TOLD ME WHAT YOU DID BACK IN THE BUNKER...THAT WAS--
THE LEAST I COULD DO.
CORE
WELL, IT WAS AWESOME. SO, YEAH... **PEACE.**
I DON'T GET WHY YOU HAD TO GET THE GLOWBUGS BACK, THOUGH. I MEAN, YOU COULD HAVE DIED. THE WHOLE PLACE WAS FALLING APART.
I DON'T.
HERE, I WANTED YOU TO BE AWAKE TO SEE THIS...
I THOUGHT YOU DIDN'T BELIEVE THE WHOLE **SPIRIT BOX** THING.
SEE WHAT?

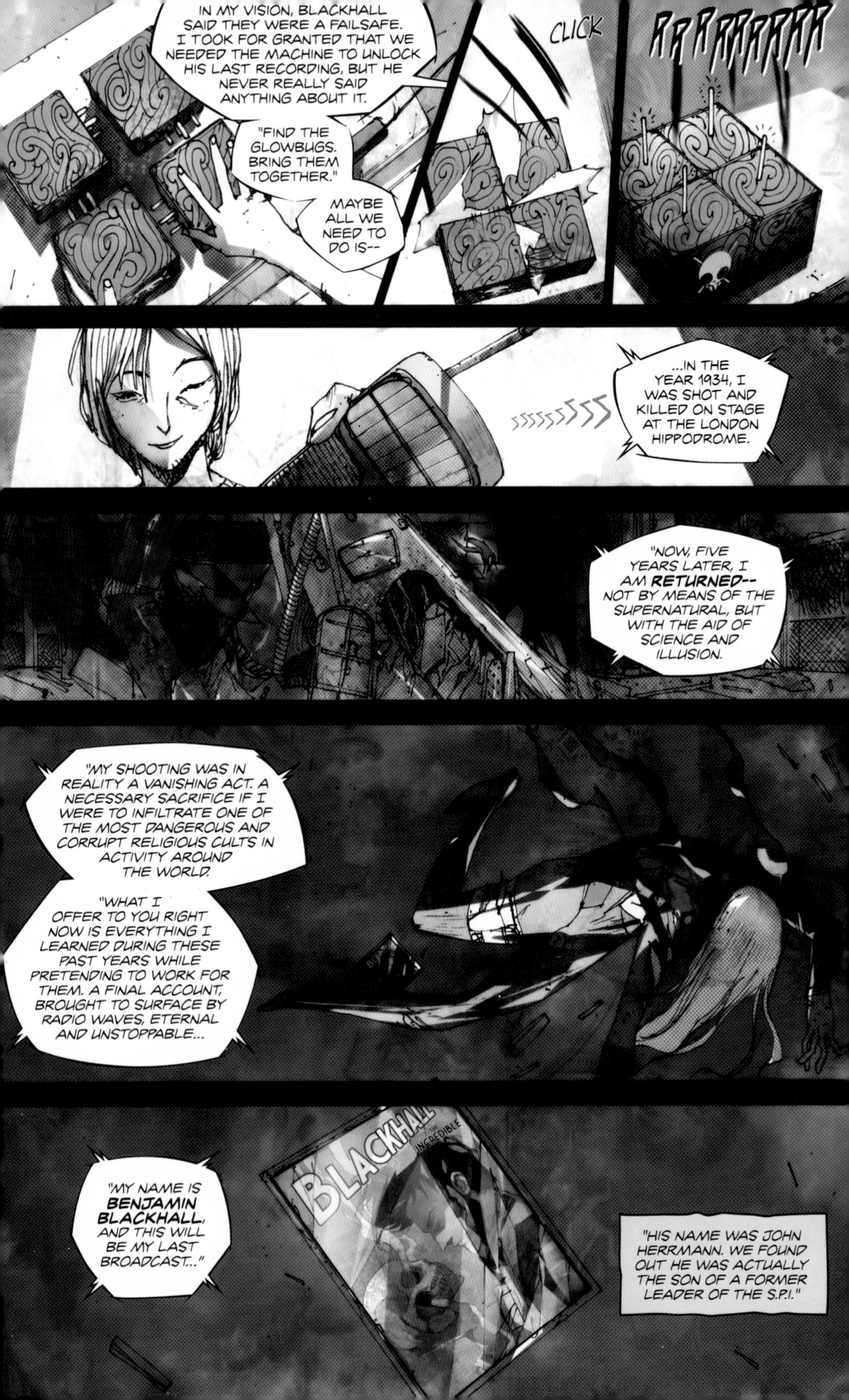
IN MY VISION, BLACKHALL SAID THEY WERE A FAILSAFE. I TOOK FOR GRANTED THAT WE NEEDED THE MACHINE TO UNLOCK HIS LAST RECORDING, BUT HE NEVER REALLY SAID ANYTHING ABOUT IT.
"FIND THE GLOWBUGS. BRING THEM TOGETHER."
MAYBE ALL WE NEED TO DO IS--
CLICK
RRRRRRRRR
SSSSSSSSS
...IN THE YEAR 1934, I WAS SHOT AND KILLED ON STAGE AT THE LONDON HIPPODROME.
"NOW, FIVE YEARS LATER, I AM **RETURNED**-- NOT BY MEANS OF THE SUPERNATURAL, BUT WITH THE AID OF SCIENCE AND ILLUSION.
"MY SHOOTING WAS IN REALITY A VANISHING ACT. A NECESSARY SACRIFICE IF I WERE TO INFILTRATE ONE OF THE MOST DANGEROUS AND CORRUPT RELIGIOUS CULTS IN ACTIVITY AROUND THE WORLD.
"WHAT I OFFER TO YOU RIGHT NOW IS EVERYTHING I LEARNED DURING THESE PAST YEARS WHILE PRETENDING TO WORK FOR THEM. A FINAL ACCOUNT, BROUGHT TO SURFACE BY RADIO WAVES, ETERNAL AND UNSTOPPABLE...
"MY NAME IS **BENJAMIN BLACKHALL**, AND THIS WILL BE MY LAST BROADCAST..."
BLACKHALL THE INCREDIBLE
"HIS NAME WAS JOHN HERRMANN. WE FOUND OUT HE WAS ACTUALLY THE SON OF A FORMER LEADER OF THE S.P.I."

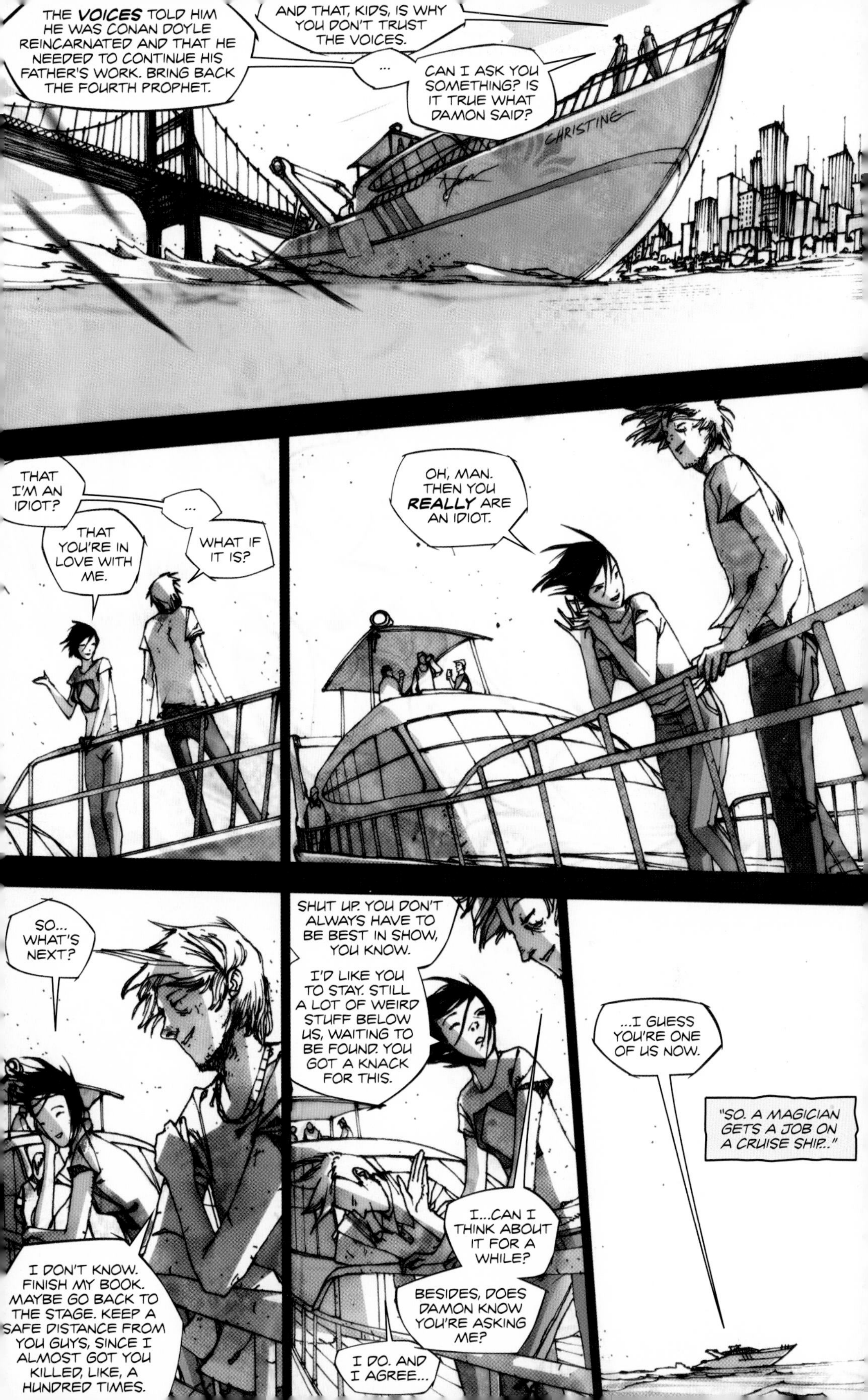
THE VOICES TOLD HIM HE WAS CONAN DOYLE REINCARNATED AND THAT HE NEEDED TO CONTINUE HIS FATHER'S WORK. BRING BACK THE FOURTH PROPHET.
AND THAT, KIDS, IS WHY YOU DON'T TRUST THE VOICES.
...
CAN I ASK YOU SOMETHING? IS IT TRUE WHAT DAMON SAID?
CHRISTINE
THAT I'M AN IDIOT?
...
THAT YOU'RE IN LOVE WITH ME.
WHAT IF IT IS?
OH, MAN. THEN YOU REALLY ARE AN IDIOT.
SO... WHAT'S NEXT?
I DON'T KNOW. FINISH MY BOOK. MAYBE GO BACK TO THE STAGE. KEEP A SAFE DISTANCE FROM YOU GUYS, SINCE I ALMOST GOT YOU KILLED, LIKE, A HUNDRED TIMES.
SHUT UP. YOU DON'T ALWAYS HAVE TO BE BEST IN SHOW, YOU KNOW.
I'D LIKE YOU TO STAY. STILL A LOT OF WEIRD STUFF BELOW US, WAITING TO BE FOUND. YOU GOT A KNACK FOR THIS.
I...CAN I THINK ABOUT IT FOR A WHILE?
BESIDES, DOES DAMON KNOW YOU'RE ASKING ME?
I DO. AND I AGREE...
...I GUESS YOU'RE ONE OF US NOW.
"SO. A MAGICIAN GETS A JOB ON A CRUISE SHIP..."

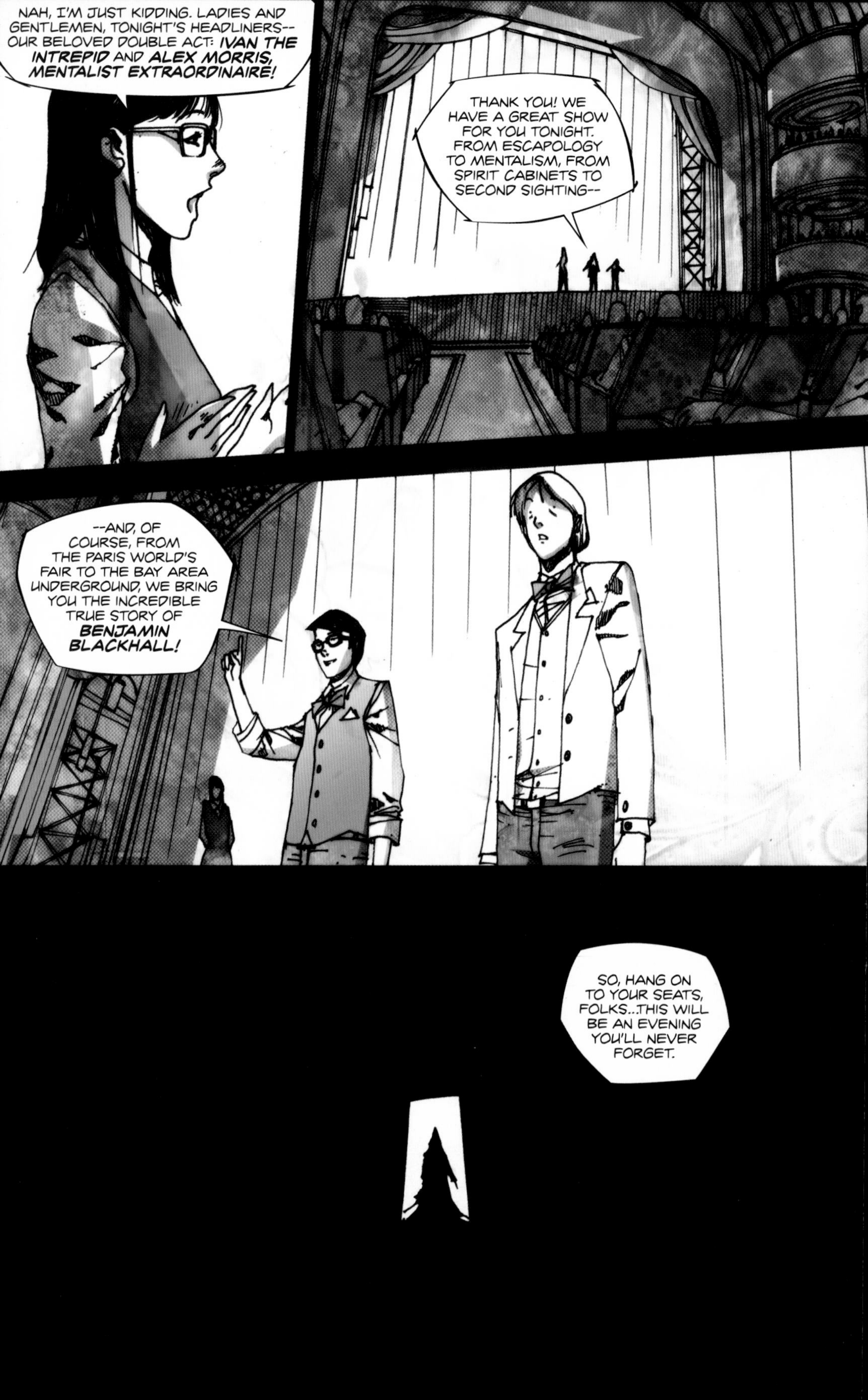
NAH, I'M JUST KIDDING. LADIES AND GENTLEMEN, TONIGHT'S HEADLINERS-- OUR BELOVED DOUBLE ACT: IVAN THE INTREPID AND ALEX MORRIS, MENTALIST EXTRAORDINAIRE!
THANK YOU! WE HAVE A GREAT SHOW FOR YOU TONIGHT. FROM ESCAPOLOGY TO MENTALISM, FROM SPIRIT CABINETS TO SECOND SIGHTING--
--AND, OF COURSE, FROM THE PARIS WORLD'S FAIR TO THE BAY AREA UNDERGROUND, WE BRING YOU THE INCREDIBLE TRUE STORY OF BENJAMIN BLACKHALL!
SO, HANG ON TO YOUR SEATS, FOLKS...THIS WILL BE AN EVENING YOU'LL NEVER FORGET.

ISSUE SEVEN COVER

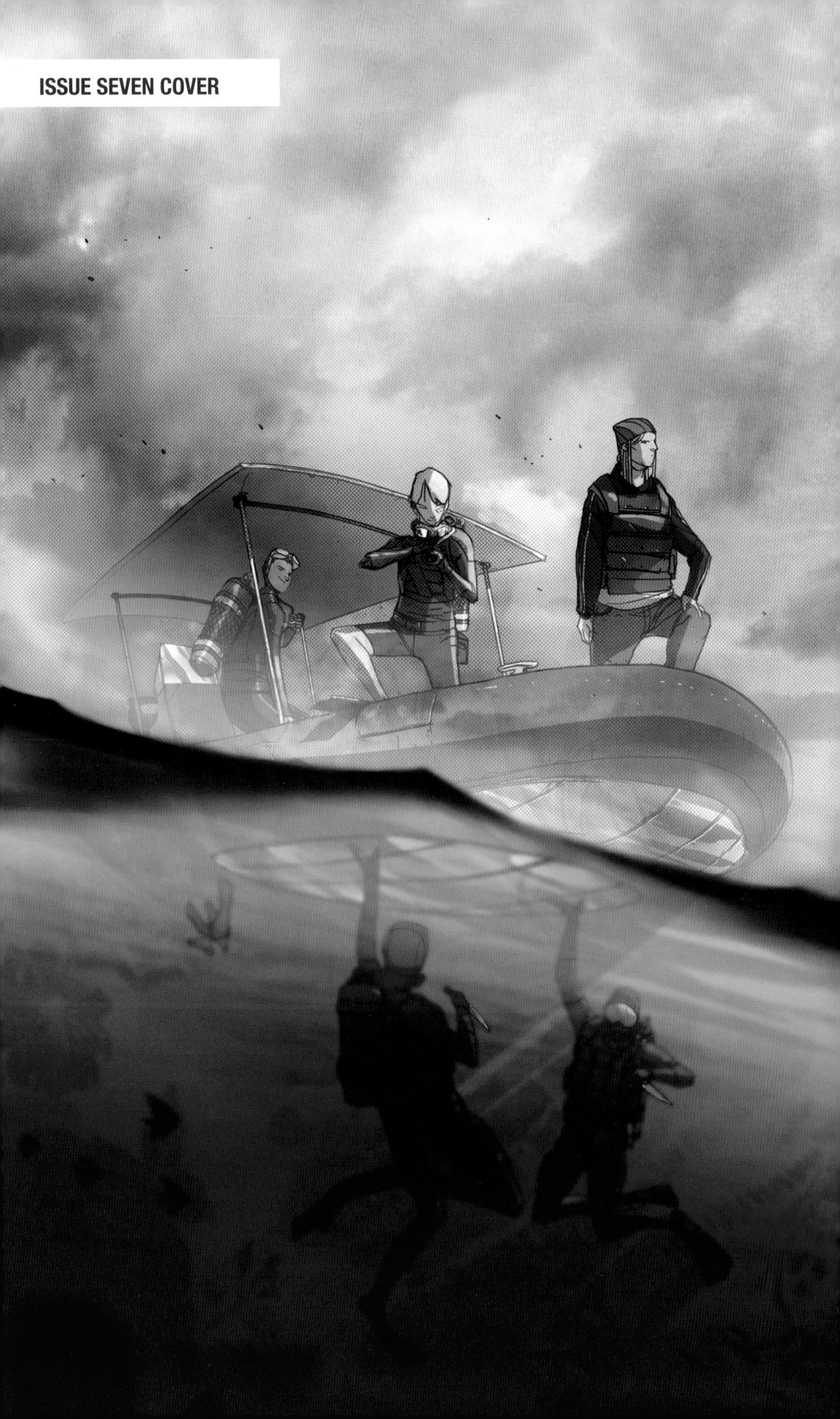

BLACKHALL RESEARCH

May 26, 1925

REAL MAGIC OR THE GREATEST TRICK IN THE WORLD?

BLACKHALL THE INCREDIBLE'S "PARIS TRANSMISSION" AT THE EXPOSITION INTERNATIONALE

One could think the very avant garde Paris World's Fair was the most improbable of places for a Victorian séance, but they would be wrong. With the "Paris Transmission" event, Benjamin Blackhall, also known as Blackhall The Incredible, has proved the mysteries of the spirit world never cease to amaze. After his performance, Mr. Blackhall has secured a place among the most skilled illusionists in the world.

Or has he? For a large portion of the audience, Blackhall's Spirit Boxes seemed to make the case not for illusion, but for legitimate otherworldly powers. Even though Blackhall, like Houdini and many others, is known for using his conjuring knowledge to debunk false mediums around the globe, some believe his powers of invocation to be *la vraie magie* disguised as stage folly.

April 8, 1934

HIPPODROME STAGE TRAGEDY

BLACKHALL SHOT DURING A TRICK

So the Master is dead! No more will Benjamin Blackhall mystify with his magic. As he lived, so he died -- a man of mystery, and the greatest mystery of all was the manner of his death... *(full article not found)*

June 19, 1934

DEATH BY MISADVENTURE

BLACKHALL SHOOTING DEEMED ACCIDENTAL

Benjamin Blackhall, the Great Magician, was killed by a single bullet, which passed through his right lung. The inquest on his death, however, proved much more difficult than expected. After all, how does one conduct an investigation on magic tricks previously kept secret to anyone but the dead himself?

Evidence, nonetheless, suggests that a real bullet inside the modified pistol--which was never intended to leave the barrel--was fired accidentally after bits of accumulated gunpowder exploded as the trigger was released. If only Mr. Blackhall had cleaned his "magic" weapon, his fate could have been a brighter one.

DISTANCE X MAGAZINE

ISSUE #3 - JUNE, 1999

"T. S. Eliot once wrote that 'Every writer owes something to [Sherlock] Holmes.' But even the poet, a dedicated fan, could not look away from Conan Doyle's painful decline--or, in Eliot's own words, 'mental decay'. How could Britain's greatest rationalist, father of literature's most famous and skeptical detective (...), become so entangled in the world of séances, sorcery and the occult? How could he so easily be fooled by 'evidence' of fairies, witches and poltergeists, some of them so clearly fraudulent that Holmes himself would waste but a second to dismiss?"

"The situation may, as it seems to me, be summed up in a simple alternative. The one supposition is that there has been an outbreak of lunacy extending over two generations of mankind, and two great

UT 7
UT 8
UT 9
UT 13
UT 14
UT 15
UT 19
UT 20
UT 21
UT7-1
UT7-2
UT7-3
UT7-7
UT7-8
UT7-9
UT7-12 (UT-13)
UT7-13 (UT-14)
UT7-14 (UT-15)
UT7-18 (UT-19)
UT7-19 (UT20)
UT7-20 (UT 21)

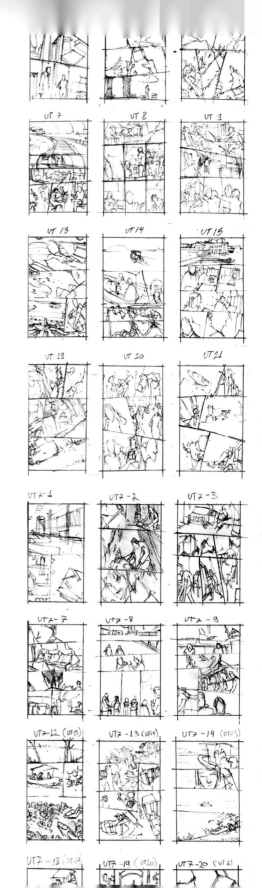

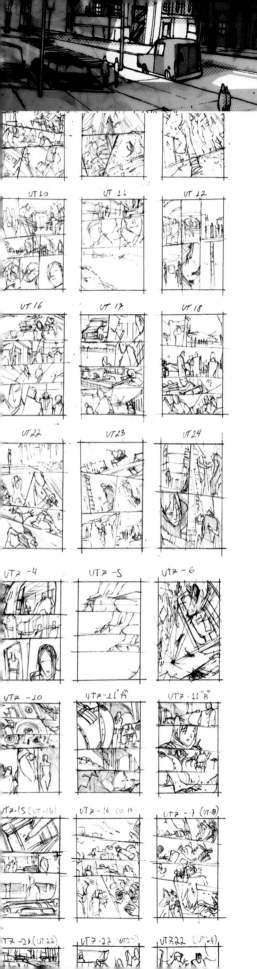

continents -- a lunacy which assails men or women who are otherwise eminently sane. The alternative supposition is that in recent years there has come to us from divine sources a new revelation which constitutes by far the greatest religious event since the death of Christ (...), a revelation which alters the whole aspect of death and the fate of man. Between these two suppositions there is no solid position. Theories of fraud or of delusion will not meet the evidence. It is absolute lunacy or it is a revolution in religious thought, a revolution which gives us as by-products an utter fearlessness of death, and an immense consolation when those who are dear to us pass behind the veil."

—ARTHUR CONAN DOYLE,
THE NEW REVELATION (1917)

July 15, 1930
CONAN DOYLE'S FINAL MESSAGE

A crowd of thousands gathered in the Royal Albert Hall for a chance to hear the final words of Sir Arthur Conan Doyle, who died of a heart attack in the past week.

The audience became witness to a séance conducted by medium Estelle Roberts, who claims to have the power to contact the dead. When she finally spoke, however, the organist hit such an enthusiastic note that her words could not be heard.

The famed author's final message was later convened privately to Lady Jean Conan Doyle and Sir Arthur's closest friends, including the medium Margery Crandon, American oil millionaire Clifford Herrmann and other members of the prestigious S.P.I. - Society for Psychic Investigation.

October 30, 1930
[...] Much has been speculated about the author's last words during last summer's séance, but it wasn't until now that witnesses have surfaced who claim to have heard a few of Estelle Roberts' words, even while the band was playing. These members of the audience were interviewed privately and separately, and, of all the words they recalled, only three were mentioned by each and every one of them. These words were: "Black," "Hall" and "Prophet".

December 20, 1937
RADIO EXPERIMENTS MAKE THE CASE
FOR EXTRA-SENSORY PERCEPTION

When Dr. Joseph Banks Rhine's theories on telepathy and "Extra-Sensory Perception" were first published, they became the talk of the town -- not just in Book of the Month clubs, but even among respected scholars and scientists. This fall, the Zenith Radio Corporation has sponsored an experiment that seems to prove that it is in fact possible to transfer thoughts via radio waves. This impressive study was conducted... *[full article not found]*

"My one aim in life is that this great truth, the return and communion of the dead, shall be brought home to a material world which needs it so badly."

-ARTHUR CONAN DOYLE

CREATING *THE LAST BROADCAST*

GABRIEL IUMAZARK: When I started mapping out the concept for The Last Broadcast, it was painful. I couldn't find the right angle for Ivan. Usually I do character studies in a crazy and random way, materializing my thoughts out on paper. It helps to get a broader view of where I want to go. When working on a design, I try to capture the most appealing traits for each character. I believe that charisma comes from imperfections and it's hard to find those sometimes. I did around 21 preliminary sketches to find the right style. I almost chose "S19", an ugly and annoying style with a big head, but later I thought it was a bit too much.

After mixing and matching, rinsing and repeating, I found the perfect style for Ivan. After that the other characters and the scenery just fell in place. Funny thing: I always loved drawing destroyed buildings and scarred people with bandages everywhere, and Sirangelo gave me a script full of these. I felt at home from the very beginning. Poor Ivan!

S1
S2
S3
S4
S5
S6
S7
S8
S9
S10
S11
S12
S13
S14
S15
S16
S17
S18
S19
S20
S21

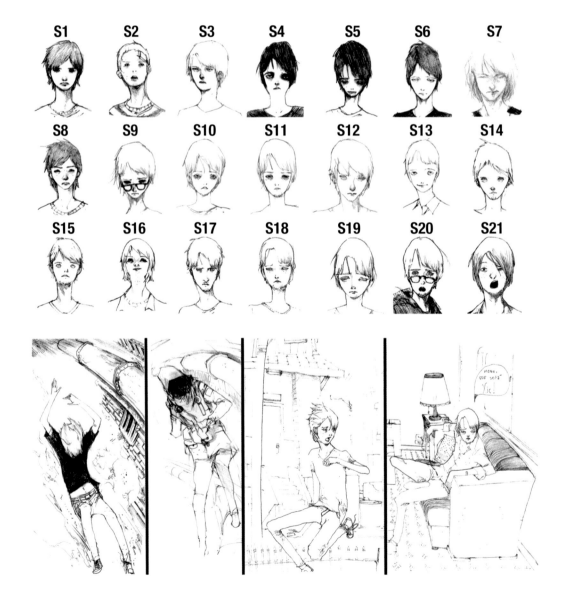

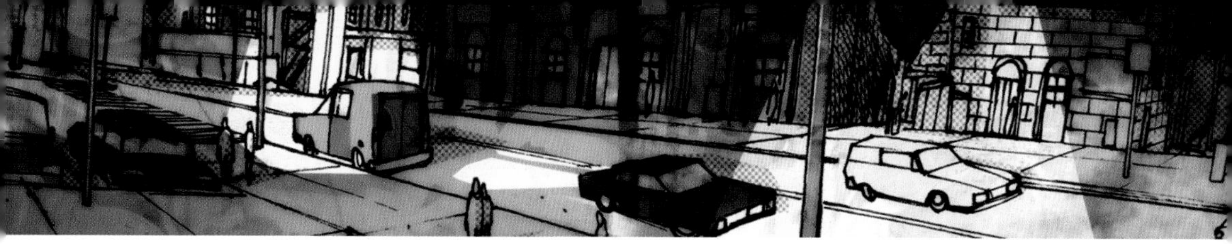

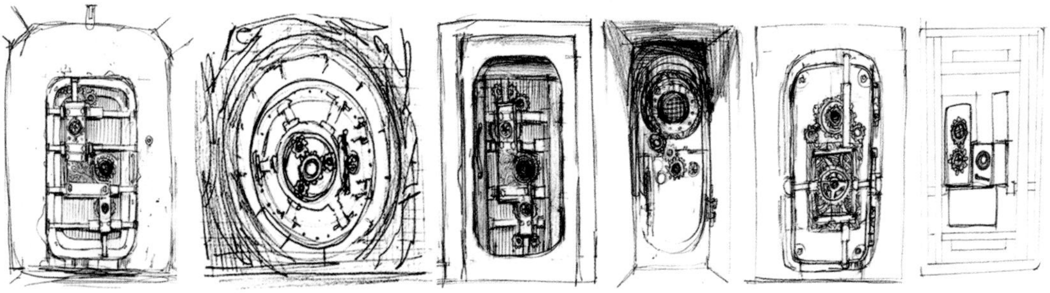

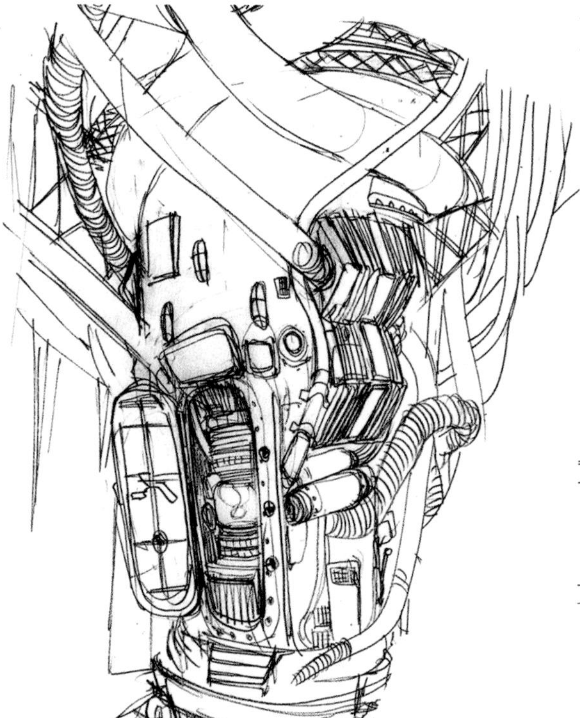

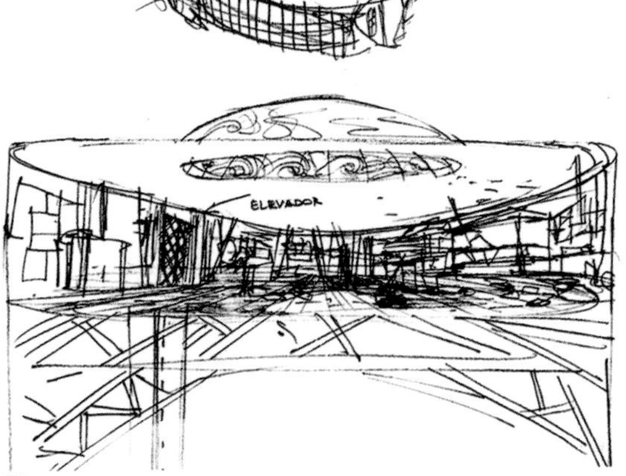
ELEVADOR

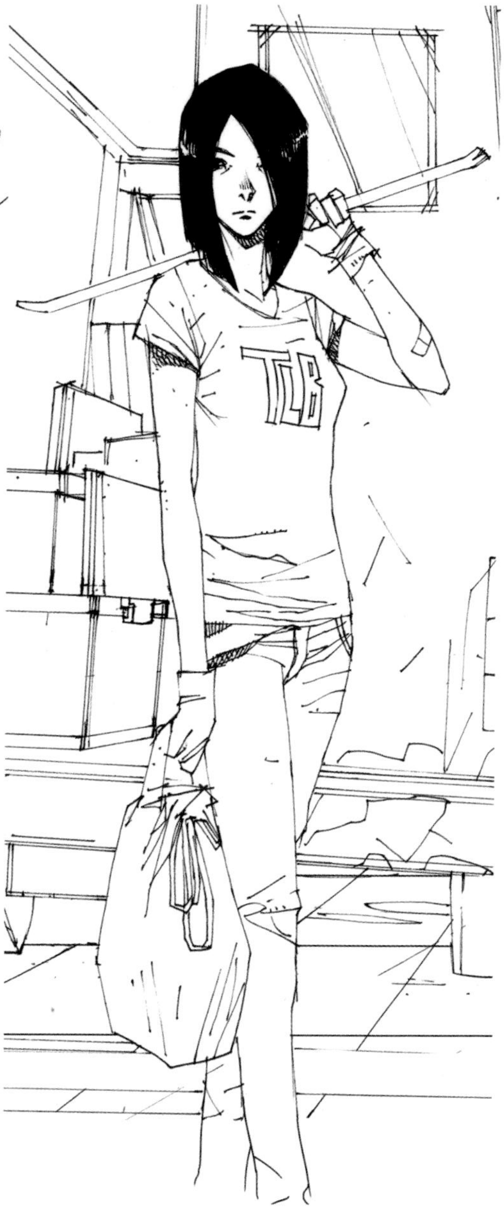
TLB

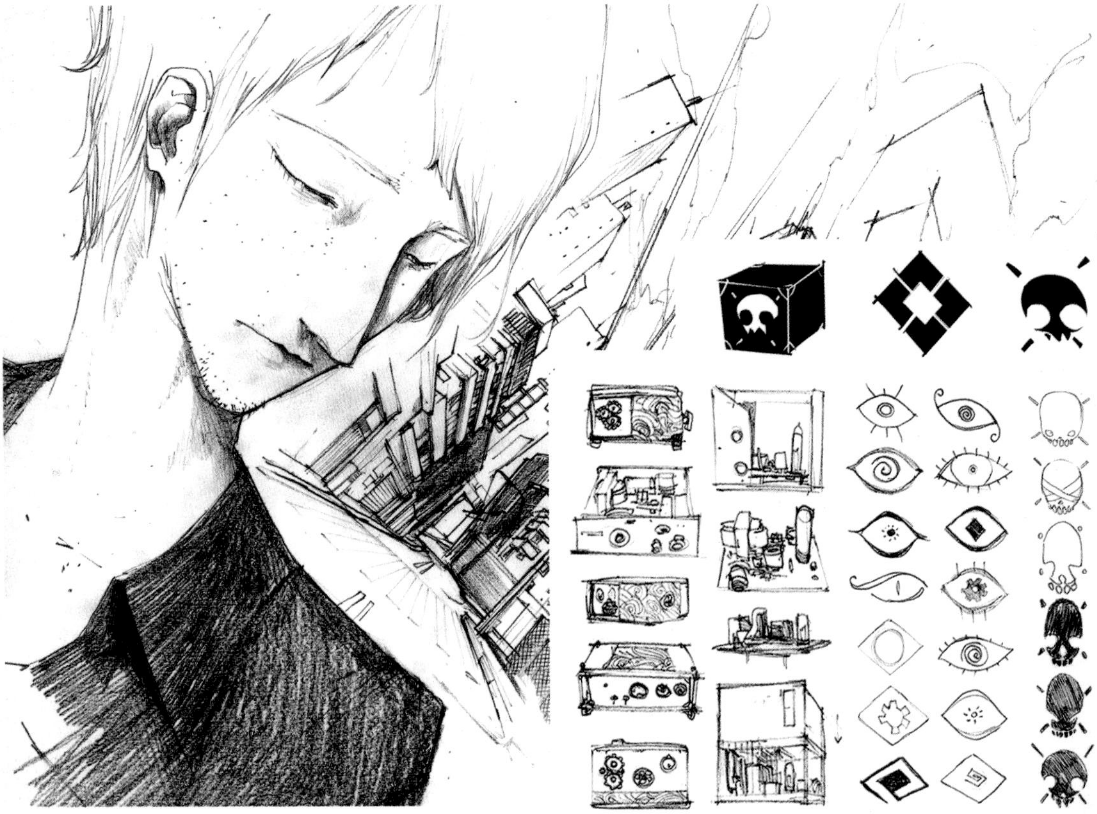

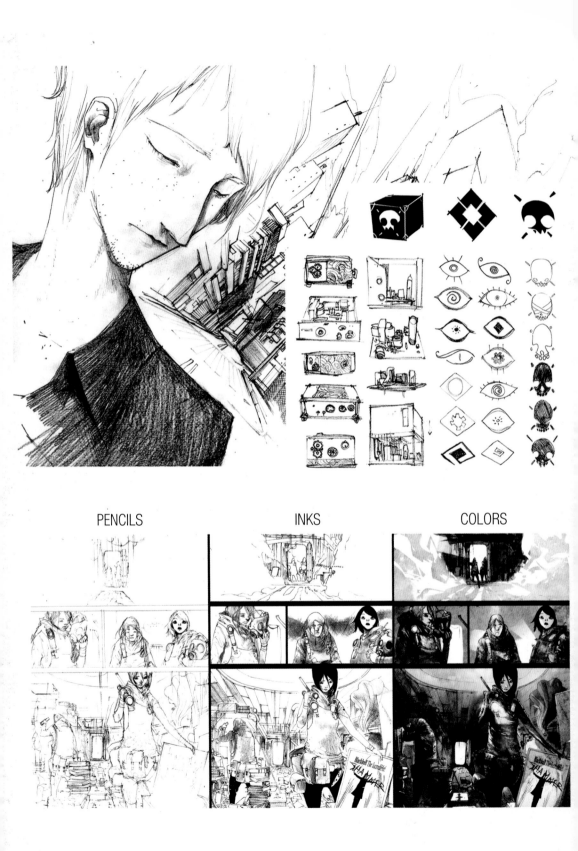

PENCILS

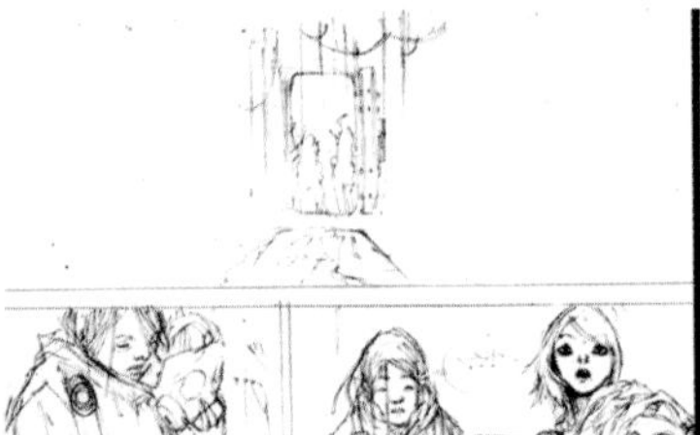

INKS

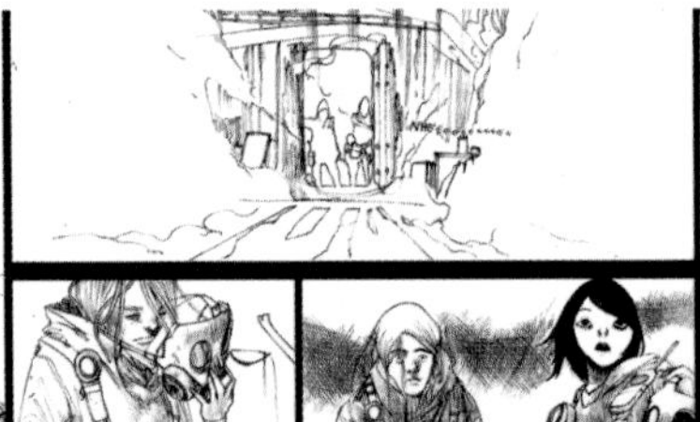

COLORS

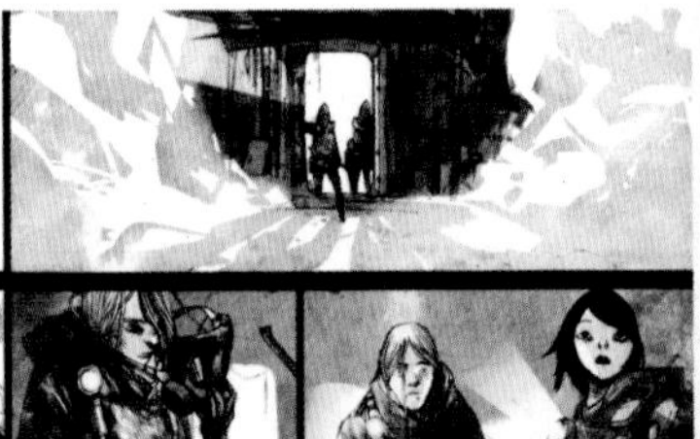